Public Policy in Britain

Edited by

Stephen P. Savage

Rob Atkinson

and

Lynton Robins

First published in Great Britain 1994 by
MACMILLAN PRESS LTD
Houndmills, Basingstoke, Hampshire RG21 2XS
and London
Companies and representatives
throughout the world

A catalogue record for this book is available
from the British Library.

ISBN 0–333–59596–3 hardcover
ISBN 0–333–59597–1 paperback

11 10   9   8   7   6   5   4   3   2
04 03 02 01 00 99 98 97 96 95

Printed in Great Britain by
Mackays of Chatham PLC, Chatham, Kent

First published in the United States of America 1994 by
Scholarly and Reference Division,
ST. MARTIN'S PRESS, INC.,
175 Fifth Avenue,
New York, N.Y. 10010

ISBN 0–312–12267–5

Library of Congress Cataloging-in-Publication Data
Public policy in Britain / edited by Stephen P. Savage, Rob Atkinson,
and Lynton Robins.
p.   cm.
Includes bibliographical references and index.
ISBN 0–312–12267–5
1. Great Britain—Social policy—1979-   2. Policy sciences.
I. Savage, Stephen P.   II. Atkinson, Rob.   III. Robins, L. J.
(Lynton J.)
HN390.P83   1994
361.6'1'0941—dc20
                                                94–24880
                                                CIP

To
NPS & JPS
Olive and Ken
SJR & MJR

Contents

List of Tables

Preface

Public policy in Britain is currently at something of a cross-roads. In virtually every area of policy, but most particularly those areas which come under the umbrella of 'social policy' – health, housing, education, social security, personal social services and law and order – radical reforms are either under way or are at least on the political agenda. Fundamental shifts in the role of the state, and the redrawing of the former boundaries between 'public' and 'private' provision, are the order of the day. In an earlier publication (Savage and Robins, (eds.) 1990) an attempt was made to assess the impact of 'Thatcherism' on each of the main policy areas. On balance the conclusion then made was that, at the very least, that impact, in terms of the development of radical, New Right, policy reforms, was uneven and in some respects hardly apparent. In the contemporary political environment, however, it would seem hard to deny that radical reform is very much on the agenda. If anything the influence of New Right thought and ideology has been more in evidence since the departure of Margaret Thatcher as Prime Minister than before, this despite the relatively low key nature of political rhetoric which has characterised post-Thatcher Conservative leadership. The central concern of this book, therefore, is to assess the current status of public policy in Britain, against the backcloth of the political agendas of the Conservative Party as they have emerged since 1979.

The book will be divided into two parts. Part I will set out the 'contexts' of policy. It will discuss the more general developments in politics and policy which have set much of the scene for policy reforms in specific policy fields. Chapter 1 will consider the broader political basis of contemporary Conservatism, and some of the key ideological influences underpinning the politics of post-1979 Conservatism. Chapters 2 and 3 will address issues of 'structures' and 'styles' of governance since 1979 respectively, and the relationship between them and the agenda for public policy which has developed under the Conservatives. Chapter 4 will assess the impact of policy made within the wider context of the European Union on the domestic political scene. Taken together these chapters should make apparent some of the common threads which have run throughout separate areas of public policy, and the origins of such common threads in fundamental political developments in the governance of Britain under the Conservatives.

Part II of the book will proceed to discuss in detail key issues and developments in each of the major areas of public policy, in the light of the contextual matters addressed in Part I. While each of these chapters can to an extent be treated as 'stand alone' discussions of discrete fields of policy, a fuller appreciation of each will be only possible when coupled with an awareness of the broader themes considered in Part I. Furthermore, the reader is advised to study the parallels and similarities between the various areas of policy, for example, between health reforms and educational policy, or between housing policy and reforms in the personal social services. In the Conclusion an attempt is made to draw together some of the general themes which have cut across public policy since 1979, and to place these in the context of the future of public policy in Britain.

A 'Guide to Further Reading' is provided toward the end of the book which indicates some of the key references within the literature in each area covered in the book.

STEPHEN P. SAVAGE
ROB ATKINSON
LYNTON ROBINS

Notes on the Contributors

Rob Atkinson is a Senior Lecturer in the School of Social and Historical Studies, University of Portsmouth. Urban policy and urban change along with public policy are his primary research areas. He has published articles and chapters in books on these areas and has recently published (with Graham Moon) *Urban Policy in Britain*.

Arthur Aughey lectures in politics at the University of Ulster at Jordanstown. His primary area of research concerns politics in Northern Ireland, on which he has published widely. He is author of *Under Siege*.

John Bradbeer is a Senior Lecturer in Geography, Department of Geography, University of Portsmouth. His interests are in environmental planning and policy, with particular emphasis on natural resources and the coastal zone, rural planning, and leisure and recreation. He has published a number of articles and chapters in books on these areas.

Fergus Carr is Head of the School of Social and Historical Studies, University of Portsmouth. His primary research interests are contemporary strategy and international politics in the Middle East. He has published a number of articles and chapters in books on these areas.

Stephen Cope is a Senior Lecturer in the School of Social and Historical Studies, University of Portsmouth. His primary areas of research are local government and public policy, on which he has published a number of articles. He is currently completing a doctorate on 'cutback management in local government'.

Mike Dunn is Head of the School of Economics, University of Portsmouth. He has published widely in the field of resource economics and has published (with S. Cunningham and D. Whitmarsh) *Fisheries Economics*.

Paul Durden is a Senior Lecturer in the School of Social and Historical Studies, University of Portsmouth. His primary areas of research are housing and educational policy; he has published mainly in the area of housing policy.

Neil Evans is a Principal Lecturer in Social Work in the School of Social and Historical Studies, University of Portsmouth. His current research interests include provision for the elderly.

David Farnham is Professor of Employment Relations at the University of Portsmouth. His publications include *Personnel in Context*, *The Corporate Environment*, *Employee Relations* (Institute of Personnel Management), *Understanding Industrial Relations* (with J. Pimlott) and *Public Administration in the UK* (with M. McVicar). He has also edited (with Sylvia Horton) *Managing the New Public Services*.

Michael Hill is Professor of Social Policy at the University of Newcastle upon Tyne. His primary areas of research are in social security policy and social policy, on which he has published widely. His publications include *Social Security Policy in Britain*, *The Welfare State in Britain* and (with Christopher Ham) *The Policy Process in the Capitalist State*.

Ian Kendall is Associate Head of School in the School of Social and Historical Studies, University of Portsmouth. His primary areas of research are social policy and health policy. He has published widely in both areas.

Carol Lupton is the Director of the Social Services Research and Information Unit (SSRIU) at the University of Portsmouth. She has published widely on the development of health and social care services and on unemployment and training policy. She has edited (with Terry Gillespie) *Working with Violence*.

Malcolm McVicar is Pro-Vice Chancellor of the University of Portsmouth. His primary area of research is education policy, and he has published a number of articles on this area. In addition he has published (with David Farnham) *Public Administration in the UK*.

Graham Moon is Principal Lecturer in Health Studies in the School of Social and Historical Studies, University of Portsmouth. He has researched and published widely in the field of health policy and geographical information systems. His publications include (with K. Jones) *Health, Disease and Society* and (with Rob Atkinson) *Urban Policy in Britain.*

Mike Nash is Senior Lecturer in Criminal Justice Studies, University of Portsmouth. He has worked previously at senior level in the probation service. His main research interests are in criminal justice policy, the probation service and offender 'seriousness', on which he has published a number of papers. He has also undertaken consultancy work with the Home Office.

Lynton Robins is Coordinator for Public Administration at De Montfort University. He is co-author of *Contemporary British Politics*, co-editor of *Two Decades in British Politics* and editor of the Politics Association's journal, *Talking Politics.*

Stephen P. Savage is Director of the Institute of Police and Criminological Studies, University of Portsmouth. His primary research interests are criminal justice and policing policy, on which area he has published widely. He is also the author of *The Theories of Talcott Parsons* and co-editor (with Lynton Robins) of *Public Policy under Thatcher*; he is also editor of the *International Journal of Sociology of Law.*

Sandy Smith is a Senior Lecturer in Economics at the University of Portsmouth, and has a particular interests in the economics of central planning and market socialism, on which he has published a number of papers and articles.

Part I

The Context of Policy

Part 1

The Context of Policy

1

The Conservatives and Public Policy

ROB ATKINSON and STEPHEN P. SAVAGE

The period since 1979 has in social and political terms been one of the most turbulent eras this century. Over the past fifteen years many of the key ideas which formed the basis for the post-war political system and the welfare state have been questioned, and agendas have emerged which have the potential to overturn many of the accepted principles of the state's role in society. Inevitably this has had major implications for public policy, both in terms of conception and practice. Specific policies will be discussed in the individual chapters of the book; this chapter will discuss the general thinking which has informed the post-1979 Conservative Governments' approach to public policy. However, before going on to consider 'public policy' specifically we will outline the key elements of New Right theory which have underpinned Conservative thinking, 'Thatcherism' and its subsequent modifications since Thatcher's demise.

The New Right

In talking about the 'New Right' there is a great danger of providing it with a coherence it does not possess. There are several distinct strands to the broad area of political thought which has come to be known by the label New Right. We will use the term as an 'umbrella category', covering both the individualist/market-oriented and social authoritarian ideas which have co-existed and at various times gained the political high-ground during post 1979 Conservative Governments.

4 *The Conservatives and Public Policy*

Many key thinkers associated with the New Right had been advocating their ideas for a number of years without attracting serious attention. In particular Hayek (1944; 1960) had argued for a free market and minimal state since the 1930s and his seminal book *The Road to Serfdom* was published in 1944. Other theorists, such as Friedman (1962), Buchanan and Tullock (1965), have been arguing for their particular brands of New Right theory since at least the early 1960s. It was, however, the economic, political and social 'crises' which beset Western societies from the late 1960s onwards that created conditions favourable to the emergence of the New Right as a major and influential social and political force (Bogdanor, 1983; Kavanagh, 1990 ch. 4). Its rise was intimately connected with its opposition to the social democratic consensus, Keynesian economics and the Welfare State (Boyson, 1970; Cowling, 1978; 1990; King, 1987; Offe, 1984 ch. 4; Bogdanor, 1983; Kavanagh, 1990 ch. 3).

The New Right can be separated into two broad strands: neo-liberalism and neo-conservativism. Both strands have influenced the policy areas covered in this book; we shall consider briefly the main elements of each.

Neo-Liberalism

Many of the themes, if not the substance, of neo-liberal thinking can be traced back to classical Liberalism, in particular Adam Smith's *Wealth of Nations* and John Locke's *Two Treatises of Government*. Neo-liberals place a great deal of emphasis on issues such as freedom, choice, the free market, a minimal or limited state and the primacy of the individual. Green (1987) has identified a number of distinct 'schools' of thought within neo-liberalism; however, we shall focus on the general ideas which have influenced policy development.

Hayek (1944; 1960), and the associated 'Austrian School', has been particularly concerned to identify and preserve the conditions conducive to the maximum amount of individual liberty and personal choice. In *The Road to Serfdom* Hayek argued that state intervention, collectivism and planning would produce a totalitarian society. Capitalism, with minimal state intervention and a free-market, was identified as the system most likely to create and encourage freedom – any situation in which a person has a choice, no matter how unpalatable the choice (Hayek, 1960; Robbins, 1977). Capitalism will be of benefit to everyone, not only in terms of freedom but also materially, if wealth creators are allowed to operate unhindered and reap the benefits of their industry (Hayek, 1960, ch. 1). Thus the perspective is anti-egalitarian. Furthermore, democracy is viewed with a degree of caution as it contains the ever present danger that majorities will oppress minorities and that politicians will interfere on behalf of special interests, i.e. the tyranny of majorities over minorities. Hayek therefore urged (constitutional) limits be placed on the power of governments suggesting that the market is the most appropriate mechanism for registering of consumer choice and supply of goods and services. This approach is sympathetic to 'supply-side economics' which aims to remove bottlenecks in the economy, such as restrictive practices in the capital and labour markets, to allow producers to respond more quickly to consumer demands (Thompson, 1986).

Milton Friedman, and the 'Chicago School', proposed the 'monetarist' policies championed by the Conservatives while in opposition and adopted during the early 1980s by the Conservative government in its Medium Term Financial Strategy (see Thompson, 1986). Crudely put monetarism argued that the money supply should expand in line with production. If it grows faster than production there will be 'too much money chasing too few goods' and the result will be inflation (Thompson, 1986). The Chicago School also emphasises the market as the primary provider of goods and services, perhaps more so than the Austrians. It is hostile to almost any state provision and has a preference for provision by the private sector with a residual state empowering those on low incomes via negative income tax and/or vouchers. It too is anti-egalitarian.

Finally there is the 'Virginia School of Public Choice', sometimes referred to as simply the Public Choice School. This approach is best represented by Tullock and Buchanan (see Buchanan, 1978; Tullock, 1975) who use neo-classical economic techniques to explain the behaviour of politicians and bureaucrats. In essence all individuals are assumed to behave as if they were 'rational utility maximisers' (Buchanan and Tullock, 1965; King, 1987). As a result state services are provided in the interests of their providers not their clients; politicians and bureaucrats aim to increase their power and security by expanding programmes and 'buying' votes to win elections. Thus, in competitive party democracies, there is an inherent tendency to expensive state 'overload' (Brittan, 1975; King, 1975). The answer is, once again, to return as much as possible to the market and, where this cannot be done, to introduce 'pseudo (or quasi)-market' disciplines and place constitutional limitations (e.g. balanced budget requirements) on the activities of politicians and bureaucrats. This School has been particularly influential *vis-à-vis* the reform of public service and its ideas have been strongly promoted in the UK by the Institute of Economic Affairs who, in tandem with the Adam Smith Institute, were able to exercise some influence over the development of policy during the Thatcher and Major administrations.

What should be clear from the above is that there are three notions which are crucial to neo-liberalism: freedom/liberty, a limited or minimal state and the free market – with the first being the most important of the three, the other two being seen as essential to the existence and defence of freedom. We will briefly discuss the three notions. Neo-liberal concepts of freedom are of the variety which Berlin (1990, pp. xxxviii, 118–72) has described as 'negative freedom'. For instance, the choice between either accepting a job which means working unsocial hours (e.g. Sundays) or being unemployed still constitutes freedom of choice. Freedom in this sense prioritorises the absence of coercion and means acting according to the dictates of one's own will. In contrast 'positive freedom' is more concerned with ensuring that everyone has the opportunity to exercise their freedom with the state playing a key role in assuring such opportunity. For neo-liberals such actions by the state would be a threat to freedom and should be avoided at all costs. According to Hayek (1960, p. 12): 'The task of a policy of freedom must . . . be to minimize coercion or its harmful effects, even if it cannot eliminate it completely.'

This leads us on to the notion of the minimal (or limited) state. The state is seen as essential to the creation of a general environment in which individuals can exercise their freedom, i.e. via the 'rule of law', but at the same time is also seen as the greatest threat to freedom. For writers such as Hayek (1944; 1960) the growth of collectivism threatens to undermine freedom and lead to 'serfdom' (or more correctly totalitarianism). Thus the role of the state must be limited and its actions strictly controlled and rendered compatible with a free market (Hayek, 1960, pp. 222–4; Friedman, 1962, ch. 2). This leads on to the final key neo-liberal notion – the free market. According to authors such as Hayek (1960) and Friedman (1962, ch. 1) the free market, and therefore capitalism, offers the best system for guaranteeing freedom because it is based upon individual choice, allows individuals to pursue their own self interest and provides a mechanism for co-ordinating the needs of the millions of free, self-interested, individuals who make up society (i.e. Adam Smith's 'invisible hand'). If the state interferes in this co-ordinating mechanism it risks not only encroaching upon individual freedom but also will undermine society's key means of production and growth.

Of course it could be argued that while these theories were influential amongst academics and elements of the chattering classes they had no real effects upon 'pragmatic' politicians such as Thatcher who were primarily concerned with achieving and retaining power. Whilst it would be foolish to deny the force of this argument there is evidence to suggest that Thatcher and her cohorts were strongly influenced by the ideas outlined above. For instance, shortly after she became leader of the party in 1975 Thatcher attended a seminar at the Conservative Research Department in Smith Square. One of the researchers presented a paper advocating that the party should pursue a policy largely in tune with the prevailing Social Democratic Consensus.

> Before he had finished speaking to his paper, the new Party leader reached into her briefcase and took out a book. It was Friedrich von Hayek's *The Constitution of Liberty*. Interrupting our pragmatist, she held the book up for us all to see. 'This', she said sternly, 'is what we believe', and banged Hayek down on the table. (Ranelagh, 1991, p. ix)

Neo-Conservatism

Neo-conservatives are an even more diverse and less organised 'body' than neo-liberals (Cowling, 1978; 1990; Scruton, 1980). However, again, there are certain general themes which they seem to have in common. In particular there is an emphasis upon authority, tradition, stability, order, the family and morality. Ironically they do not see the problems of post-war societies as stemming from a lack of freedom but from 'too much freedom' (Worsthorne, 1978). The permissiveness of the 1960s is frequently blamed for the break-down of law and order, decline of morality and the general disintegration which they see afflicting modern society. Unlike the neo-liberals they place a considerable emphasis upon collectivities and the responsibilities and duties of the individual towards the collectivity. These sentiments have been most vociferously and popularly expressed through organisations such as the Festival of Light and Mary Whitehouse's National Viewers and Listeners Association.

Perhaps the greatest influence of neo-conservatives on government policy has been in areas such as 'family' policy, on which a leading neo-conservative, Ferdinand Mount, was at one time adviser to Mrs Thatcher (see Mount, 1983). They have also been able to exercise some influence upon areas such as law and order and immigration control. Neo-conservatism draws upon themes which can be traced back to Edmund Burke's *Reflections on the Revolution in France*, ideas which have clearly been on display at many Conservative Party Conferences since the 1960s (Cowling, 1990).

It need hardly be said that there are considerable conflicts between neo-conservatives and neo-liberals, particularly over the issue of individual freedom and to a lesser extent over the role of the market and the state. However, they are united, in a general sense, by their anti-egalitarianism and opposition to the welfare state (good examples of how these notions have been translated into policies may be found in Chapters 9, 10, 11, 12 and 13). Indeed, many neo-conservatives accept that the state's role, and public expenditure, should be considerably reduced, that people should become more self-reliant, and that any state services should be selective (i.e. means-tested) rather than universal (Marsland, 1988; see also Chapter 13).

Moreover the issue of the family has provided an important element around which both neo-liberals and neo-conservatives have been able to unite. By the late 1980s/early 1990s neo-liberals were increasingly arguing that the state should take 'coercive' actions to preserve the family. David Green, of the Institute of Economic Affairs, even went to far as to argue with regard to the family that government:

> should attempt to undo some of the damage caused in recent years by changes in public policy . . . should introduce measures to encourage the traditional two-parent family. This would involve changes in divorce law, reform of the benefits and special advantages available to one-parent families, and revision of the tax treatment of traditional two-parent families. (Green 1992, p. 79)

Such views imply considerable (coercive) interventions by the state to influence personal choices and behaviour, and indeed many of these notions have subsequently been aired, and gained some high-level support, within the Conservative Party.

By 1993 key elements of the Party were utilising the notion of single-parent families, regardless of the evidence, to divert attention away from problems in other areas and to shift the blame for rising crime, rising welfare expenditures and what they saw as a 'dependency culture' on to this group. There was an attempt to 'demonise' or stigmatise single-parents, an approach tacitly supported by changes in social security payments (see Chapter 13) and by Major at the 1993 Party Conference when he advocated a return to traditional family values (see *Guardian* 9 October 1993), although whether this merely represented an attempt to create a sense of party unity or heralded the emergence of a 'pro-family' policy remains to be seen. Indeed, throughout both the Thatcher and Major years such issues frequently provided the basis of a series of temporary alliances within the Conservative Party, allowing it to paper over the fissures created by issues such as Europe.

Thatcher, Thatcherism and Major

Thatcherism clearly played a key role in setting the policy agenda from the mid-1970s onwards. Even after Mrs Thatcher's personal political demise, it continued to define the basic boundaries of political and social debate in Britain.

Thatcherism may be seen as the contradictory articulation of neo-liberalism and neo-conservatism presented in a populist manner, constrained by the exigencies of competitive party system, a liberal democracy and pre-existing institutions, organisations and social and political forces (i.e. issues of statecraft see Bulpitt (1986)). It was potentially riddled with contradictions (e.g. between freedom and authority), and inherently unstable, yet able, with its amorphous character, to shift ground quite effortlessly as the situation demanded and perhaps best encapsulated in the persona of Margaret Thatcher herself.

Whilst it achieved, and to an extent continues to exert, a degree of governmental and political dominance, Thatcherism should not automatically be assumed to have created a new and lasting consensus, indeed a number of authors have questioned whether Thatcherism was in any way an intentional development or a distinct ideology – or, even, sufficiently coherent to merit the status of an 'ism' (see Riddell, 1983; Keegan, 1984; Marsh and Rhodes, 1989). Here we will argue that the political agenda has been changed, perhaps decisively, but as yet events are too recent for any definitive judgements to be arrived at concerning the nature of Thatcherism.

Margaret Thatcher became the fulcrum around which the union of neo-liberalism and neo-conservatism against the forces of Social Democracy occurred. This process began when she became leader of the Conservative Party and evolved through her leadership style (Blake, 1985, ch. X; Ranelagh, 1991, ch. 7). She appealed to certain traditions which existed within the Conservative Party and to particular popular sentiments among sections of the electorate. Hall (1983) summarises this style as 'authoritarian populism'. She created what Bogdanor (1983, p. 17) has called a 'new electoral coalition' which challenged the existing establishment and set about attempting to radically restructure British society and internalised the contradictions between neo-liberalism and neo-conservatism. This entailed a constant battle between innovation and radicalism on the economic front and retrenchment and backward-looking glances on the social front. As a result whilst Thatcherism was frequently depicted as a radical departure from previous practice, there were also considerable elements of pragmatism in the practice of post-1979 Conservative administrations (cf Bulpitt, 1986).

Pragmatism

Margaret Thatcher was frequently characterised as a 'radical'. However, there was also a pragmatic side to her and, indeed, her Governments' character. As a result, the wilder urgings of her more radical supporters and advisers were often ignored and incremental approaches to reform favoured over root-and-branch revolution (Ranelagh, 1991, pp. 2–3). For instance, both industrial policy and regional policy should have, on strict free-market terms, been abandoned. For political reasons both were retained in diluted form. Further evidence of this pragmatism can be seen in that for much of the period up to 1987 the first two Thatcher administrations did not attempt to move forward on too many fronts at once, and it was only subsequently that issues such as the National Health Service and education emerged as major priorities (see Chapters 9 and 11). Also at certain times there was also a willingness to make a tactical retreat, as with the miners in 1981, in order to wait for more favourable conditions (the 1984/5 miners strike) to emerge.

Much of the achievement of Thatcherism required that the central state be strengthened. This would appear to contradict neo-liberal ideas on the state but posed no problems for neo-conservatives who saw it as essential to restore the authority of the state. Neo-liberals could argue, however, that the obduracy of existing entrenched interests (e.g. in local government) required that government, in the short term, took more powers in order to reduce government in the longer term. Elements of centralisation can also be justified in classic liberal terms by arguing that what few things the state does it should do with authority. As a result, in some areas the state was rolled back, but in other areas it was rolled forward. Thus, while privatisation (Steel and Heald, 1984; Young, 1987; Veljanovski, 1988, 1989, 1991; Marsh, 1991; Chapter 5) came to be seen as a centrepiece of the government's strategy of 'freeing up' the economy and reducing the role of the state, it required a considerable degree of centralisation for its objectives to be achieved.

Social Policy

This pragmatism can perhaps best be seen in relation to the welfare state. Here it can be seen that, despite constant urgings to dismantle the welfare state and replace it by a mixture of private insurance, friendly societies, charitable provision and workfare (Seldon, 1981; Green, 1982; Harris, 1988), Thatcherite social policy evolved rather cautiously. Thatcher was, for example, forced by political expediency to promise that the 'NHS was safe in her hands'. The sale of council housing represents perhaps the most striking attack upon the welfare state, yet the vast majority of council dwellings have not been sold (for an overview see Chapter 10). It was only towards the end of the 1980s, in the third term, that plans to reform the NHS, education and local government were put into practice (see Chapters 9, 11, 2 and 3). In an overall sense, Thatcherism therefore attempted to restructure rather than dismantle the welfare state (see McCarthy, 1989; Savage and Robins, 1990; Johnson, 1990 for assessments).

This restructuring sought essentially to shift the role of the state from that of provider to that of facilitator/enabler (Ridley, 1988), rather than a front-line provider of services (the NHS is perhaps the best example of this, see Chapter 9). One of the intended effects was to move individuals away from 'dependence' on the state to a position of independence and self-responsibility (see Chapter 13). The then Secretary of State at the Department of Health and Social Security, John Moore (1987, p. 5), argued:

> We [the Conservatives] believe that dependence in the long run decreases human happiness and reduces human freedom. We believe the well-being of individuals is best protected and promoted when they are helped to be independent, to use their talents to take care of themselves and their families, and to achieve things on their own, which is one of the greatest satisfactions life can offer.

Thus the emphasis is very much upon 'responsible individuals' and the family helping themselves, with the state only assisting those in real need and for as short a period of time as practicable in order to break the 'dependency culture' created by the welfare state (Baker [a former Cabinet Minister], 1990; for a sustained critique of 'dependency culture' see Dean and Taylor-Gooby, 1992). More recently these issues have coalesced around the family in general and single-parent families in particular. The late summer and autumn of 1993 saw a rash of television programmes and newspaper articles on the 'problems' of single-parenthood, culminating in an almost hysterical crescendo at the Conservative Party conference in October 1993 (see *Guardian*, 8 October 193, p. 7; *Independent on Sunday*, 10 October 1993, p. 3). In an attempt to launch a campaign around the notion of getting 'back to basic values', Major and his Cabinet colleagues chose to target single-parenthood as a source of social disorder and crime, and compared single-parents unfavourably with two-parent families. It was a populist campaign much cruder than anything delivered under Thatcher.

This leads us to consider the relationship between the political agenda set out by Thatcher and its impact on post-Thatcher Conservative policy. It is clearly difficult to offer any full assessment of the Thatcher years, as even central issues such as her Governments' economic record are subject to great controversy, although Middlemass (1991, pp. 259–77) provides an attempt at a balanced appraisal. What can be said with some certainty is that, although Thatcherism did not come to dominate British values – public opinion surveys have still shown a high degree of support for state provision of welfare, for example – it did undoubtedly dominate the political scene.

This is the legacy which was left to John Major and he appears to be continuing with and even intensifying key reforms initiated by Thatcher. For instance, Madsen Pirie has noted:

> In terms of the aims of Mrs Thatcher's governments, John Major is achieving those objectives no less well than she did. If Thatcherism denotes a set of principles translated into policies, John Major is arguably more

Thatcherite than she was. (Pirie, 1993, p. 14; see also *The Economist*, 31 July 1993:, p. 9)

In October 1993, Thatcher herself appeared to endorse Major's leadership when she argued:

Thatcherism is alive and well. I believe that was confirmed very much by the Prime Minister's speech at the party conference, which was back to fundamental principles. (*Guardian*, 18 October 1993)

However, at the same time Major has frequently been criticised, by Thatcher amongst others, for lacking a sense of vision and 'drifting with the intellectual tide', as *The Economist* (31 July 1993, p. 21) noted: 'The real trouble, according to colleagues, is that his skills are entirely short-term. He woefully lacks vision.' Thus we are presented with a contradictory view of Major which on the one hand suggests his adherence to a set of principles both in theory and practice, and on the other a pragmatist who has no ideas of his own and drifts with the prevailing political and intellectual tide.

While it is doubtful that such a thing as Majorism exists Major himself, in a speech to the Carlton Club, attempted to identify a coherent vision which inspired his government. He argued:

We have no repository of doctrine that we set on an altar above commonsense and instinct . . . But what we do have are four cardinal principles: the principles of choice, ownership, responsibility and opportunity for all. (Major, 1993, p. 14)

It was also in this speech that Major floated the idea of 'workfare' when he argued:

Increasingly, I wonder whether paying unemployment benefit, without offering or requiring any activity in return, serves unemployed people or society well.(Major, 1993, p. 34; see Chapter 13)

At the time of writing it would seem that this idea has dropped from view and it is the Citizen's Charter which best epitomises Major's attempt to carry the four principles over into policy and to stamp his personality on the government (see Major, 1993, pp. 26–8 and *passim*; see also Chapter 3).

It can certainly be argued that under Major there appears to have been some attempt to move away from the more contentious elements of the Thatcher legacy and establish an agenda which can be construed as more compassionate. Yet when developments are actually carefully observed it could be argued very little appears to have changed. Michael Heseltine may have promised, at the Conservative Party Conference in 1992, to help industry by intervening 'before breakfast, before lunch and before dinner. And I'll get up the next morning and I'll start over again' (*Guardian*, 15 October 1992). However, whilst business may have been created for caterers, little seems to have changed and the government appears no nearer to developing a proactive industrial policy than it did a decade ago. Events, such as the fiasco over the run-down of the coal industry and the abolition of the National Economic Development Council in June 1992, indicate that there will be no return to the type of relationships between government and interest groups which prevailed in the 1960s and 1970s. Nor is it likely that the welfare state will be safe from further restructuring; the Community Care initiatives are to proceed as are attempts to continue the break-up of council housing departments (see Chapter 10). Both of which, if successful, would mark a significant step in the direction of restructuring local government away from a service provider to a facilitative/enabling role (see Chapters 2 and 3). Major may be more willing to consult and listen than Thatcher but it is unlikely that he will be able to stray too far from the positions which she established. However, a more definitive assessment of the relationship between pre- and post-Thatcher Conservatism will have to wait until the Conclusion.

In this chapter we have identified the ideas which have inspired Conservative administrations since 1979; however, we have also suggested that those ideas have been modified by the practicalities of governing and the need to win elections. The reader can see, and judge, the extent to which modification has taken place by consulting the individual policy chapters in Part II of the book.

2

The Structures of Governance in Britain

STEPHEN COPE and ROB ATKINSON

Introduction

This chapter and the one following will discuss major changes in both the structures and processes of governance in Britain since 1979. Policy developments in each of the separate areas of public policy, as discussed in Part II of this book, have taken place within a broader context of political and policy change. Study across a range of policy fields reveals certain common threads in structure and organisation, which reflect a more fundamental series of processes which have affected the governance of Britain under the Conservatives. In order to address these wider, contextual questions, the current chapter will concentrate on the 'structures of governance', i.e. the institutional and organisational frameworks within which the processes of governance operate. In Chapter 3 we extend this discussion to consider the question of changing styles of governance. 'Styles' of governance refers to the ways in which those institutions and organisational frameworks are activated, the means by which the processes of government are carried through. Clearly there is no hard and fast distinction between structures and styles and in that sense the issues addressed in the current chapter will overlap with Chapter 3.

This chapter will first of all focus on government at the centre before turning to a consideration of the structures of sub-central government.

Government at the Centre

This section examines the cabinet system and government departments, and explores the major developments that have shaped the structure of central government.

Cabinet System

Writing in 1867 Bagehot exposed the myth of parliamentary government, and declared the cabinet was the 'efficient secret of the English constitution' (1963, p. 65). The cabinet comprises the prime minister and about 20 senior ministers, most of whom preside over major government departments, and meets once a week. In constitutional terms the position of the prime minister in cabinet is captured by the term *primus inter pares* (or 'first among equals'); as we shall see later in Chapter 3, this nostrum has been increasingly questioned by the notion of prime-ministerial government.

The role of the cabinet is regulated constitutionally by the convention of *collective cabinet responsibility*, which stipulates that ministers (both cabinet and junior ministers) are responsible for decisions made in government. Cabinet government implies that cabinet makes decisions collectively. In 1918 the Haldane Committee listed the following functions of cabinet:

(a) the final determination of the policy to be submitted to Parliament;
(b) the supreme control of the national executive in accordance with the policy prescribed by Parliament; and
(c) the continuous co-ordination and delimitation of the activities of the several Departments of state (Hennessy, 1989, p. 297).

Whilst these functions are still the constitutional preserve of the cabinet as a whole, in the post-war period, particularly since the 1970s, there has been a tendency on the part of prime-ministers to constitute what have been termed an 'inner cabinet' or in some cases a 'partial cabinet' (see Greenwood and Wilson, 1989, pp. 70–1) to facilitate decision making. However, none of these 'bodies' have any constitutional standing and, in theory at least, any decisions reached by such them are not binding on the cabinet.

However, as we suggest in Chapter 3 there have been serious challenges to this view, particularly in the post-war era and especially so since 1979. In effect the current debate is dominated by the argument that cabinet government has become prime ministerial government.

The cabinet as whole is supported and briefed by the Cabinet Office, Hennessy (1989, p. 388) defines its responsibilities as:

> Co-ordination of policy briefing for Cabinet and Cabinet committees, co-ordination of the security and intelligence services, preparation for economic summits, Civil Service security, top Whitehall and public appointments, honours, official histories.

Thus it provides secretarial support to the cabinet, but also contains bodies such as the Management and Personnel Office which have wider roles throughout the civil service, as well as being concerned with the secret services. This makes it difficult to clearly define the role of the Cabinet Office. However, there is no question that the Cabinet Secretary occupies a powerful position, simply because as Hennessy (1989, p. 390) notes: 'The Cabinet Office is *the* crucial junction box of the central government system' (see ibid., pp. 388–92, for more detail).

In addition the cabinet is surrounded by, and supported by, cabinet committees which are used extensively to make decisions in government. In 1992 the Government published a list of 16 cabinet committees and 10 cabinet sub-committees, e.g. Ministerial Committee on Economic and Domestic Policy (EDP) chaired by the prime minister (Cabinet Office, 1992b). This figure is a massive under-estimation of the number of cabinet committees in operation. There are many more committees in existence, including committees on which civil servants serve. In the mid-1980s there were at least 160 committees in existence (Hennessy, 1986b, p. 26).

It is the prime minister who decides whether to set up a cabinet committee, establishes its terms of reference and determines its membership. Whilst post-1979 governments were not the first to make use of cabinet committees, it does appear that under Thatcher their number increased as did the frequency with which they were used as decision-making centres (for an overview see James, 1992, pp. 59-69). In addition to this it has been argued that Thatcher also made greater use than previous prime ministers of *ad hoc* groups to make decisions (see James, 1992, pp. 109–10). The use and importance of committees is difficult to judge because they are hidden behind a veil of secrecy. Interestingly there is no real evidence that Major reversed the changes which Thatcher instituted, he largely continued to make use of the same means; what appeared to be different was his personal style of listening to his cabinet colleagues before taking a decision.

The prime minister is served by the Prime Minister's Office comprising the Private Office, Political Office, Press Office, and Policy Unit (see Hennessy, 1989, pp. 382–7 and Burnham and Jones, 1993 for more detail). The Policy Unit was first established in 1974, and was later strengthened by Thatcher after she disbanded the Central Policy Review Staff (CPRS), a 'think-tank' within the Cabinet Office serving the cabinet as whole. Unlike the CPRS the Policy Unit advises the prime minister only and for some this is a crucial factor in the prime ministerial government thesis. However, the significant point to make is that the prime minister only has a relatively small staff directly supporting him/her compared to the resources available to ministers.

Government Departments

The Whitehall departments (e.g. The Home Office, Department of the Environment, The Treasury, Department of Health) are in effect largely responsible for the governance, from the centre, of their own particular functional domains. The departmental structure of Whitehall is generally speaking stable, although in the last thirty years we have seen the Departments of Health and Social Security merged to form the DHSS and then later, in 1988, separated back into two departments. On the other hand the Departments of Trade and Industry were merged in 1983 to form the Department of Trade and Industry. This would seem to suggest that whilst there is a strong functional (and budgetary) element in establishing (and maintaining) departments other factors also play a part. Much seems to depend upon changing organisational fashion and the views of the party in power.

Somewhat surprisingly during the Thatcher years there were, on the whole, few changes, perhaps the most notable were those referred to in the preceding paragraph plus the abolition of the Civil Service Department and the spliting of its tasks and their absorption by other departments/bodies within Whitehall. Perhaps the greatest threat to the long-established departmental system has come in the shape of the Ibbs Report. It stated:

> The aim should be to establish a quite different way of conducting the business of government. The central Civil Service should consist of a

relatively small core engaged in the function of servicing Ministers and managing departments, who will be the 'sponsors' of particular government policies and services. Responding to these departments will be a range of agencies employing their own staff, who may or may not have the status of Crown servants, and concentrating on the delivery of their particular service, with clearly defined responsibilities between the Secretary of State and the Permanent Secretary on the one hand and the Chairmen or Chief Executives of the agencies on the other (Jenkins *et al.*, 1988, p. 15).

It recommended that agencies should be established to carry out much of the work previously done in government departments. It envisaged a civil service whereby a small number of senior civil servants would continue to advise ministers on policy matters, but the remaining civil servants would administer policy within agencies. The sponsoring government department would formulate policy which agencies administer. The Ibbs Report was very critical of the management of the civil service and placed a great deal of emphasis upon the need to improve civil servants' managerial skills. The report was welcomed by the Conservative Government, which planned a rolling programme of establishing agencies within central government. By August 1993 nearly 100 agencies had been established (e.g. Employment Service, and Social Security Benefits Agency). They employ roughly 350,000 civil servants, representing about 60 per cent of the civil service. The 'Next Steps' programme holds significant consequences for the convention of individual ministerial responsibility because ministers can be held responsible only for the framework agreement within which agencies operate.

Although the 'Next Steps' programme weakens the convention of individual ministerial responsibility it does not significantly diminish ministerial control. Ministers can still exert control over these agencies by setting their policy frameworks, determining their budgets and appointing their chief executives. In addition to civil servants ministers increasingly draw upon advice from political parties, political advisers, interest groups and 'think-tanks', thus weakening the monopoly of expertise previously held by civil servants.

Ministers are also using the market to undermine the position of the civil service. In 1993 the Government launched its market-testing programme (Prime Minister, 1991, p. 33). This programme was designed to open swathes of work traditionally carried out by civil servants to 'the cold winds of the market'. Market-testing is likely to lead to extensive contracting-out of work to the private sector, and to increased pressures facing civil servants to accept lower pay and conditions if they are to compete successfully against private contractors. However, the savings of market-testing may vanish if the European Community's Acquired Rights Directive applies.

Interestingly the full weight of the Ibbs Report was brought to bear upon the Whitehall departments by Major rather than Thatcher. Since Major became prime minister the 'Next Steps' programme appears to have been given a higher priority and the pace of change has noticeably quickened. If this rate of change continues by the end of the decade, whilst the existing overall departmental structure will still be recognisable, the size of departments will have been greatly reduced and the vast majority of 'departmental' administrative work relocated to agencies.

Whitehall does not lend itself easily to generalised caricature: government is complex, fragmented and interdependent. A significant trend in recent times has been the increasing division between the core executive and the rest of central government. The core executive includes 'all those organizations and structures which primarily serve to pull together and integrate central government policies, or act as final arbiters within the executive of conflicts between different elements of the government machine' (Dunleavy and Rhodes, 1990, p. 4). It comprises formal and informal structures and networks such as the prime minister, cabinet committees and the Treasury (see Dowding, 1993, pp. 178–83). Under the Thatcher and Major Governments its policy-making capacity has been enhanced, with the rest of central government transformed increasingly to execute policies made and co-ordinated by the core executive.

Government beyond the Centre

The study of British government 'is too often the study of Westminster and Whitehall' (Rhodes, 1988, p. 1). Rhodes argued:

> Central government may pass a law, provide money, inspect, and on occasion, directly provide a service but, for the most part, it needs the co-operation of other bodies in order to meet its electoral promises. Its influence lies in its ability to cajole, bully and persuade (but not command), and even this ability may not call forth the desired degree of compliance. . . . But if sub-central government . . . is the prime vehicle for delivering services, it does not do so in total isolation from the centre. (1988, p. 1)

There are many government agencies relatively autonomous from the command, though not the influence, of central government. Though it is not easy to draw a line where central government ends and sub-central government starts, this section examines government beyond the centre – the secret and security services, nationalised industries, local authorities, and quangos.

Secret and Security Services

The secret and security services have been long neglected in the study of public administration. The main agencies involved in this controversial area are MI5 (which counters domestic subversion including terrorism), MI6 (which collects and disseminates overseas intelligence), and GCHQ (which intercepts and decodes communications). Their operations 'are shrouded in complete secrecy and are not controlled via the normal Parliamentary process' (Dunleavy, 1990, p. 116). Parliament does not scrutinise the secret and security services. The Ministry of Defence, Foreign Office and Home Office exercise only minimal control over their operations; and the prime minister via the Cabinet Office is formally responsible for co-ordinating their activities. Recent events (such as the 'Spycatcher Affair') suggest that the secret and security services possess considerable autonomy and are not politically accountable. Ponting warned 'all Western democracies, apart from Britain, have some form of external control over intelligence activities' (1990, p. 27).

With the end of the Cold War and increasing pressures on public expenditure there are demands to make the secret and security services more accountable politically and financially to both Parliament and government. The Major Government responded to these demands by making them slightly more open and is holding out the prospect of further reforms.

Nationalised Industries

Despite recent waves of privatisation (see Chapter 5) there are still many public corporations running a variety of industries, e.g. British Broadcasting Corporation and Post Office. They are not managed by civil servants but a board appointed by their sponsoring government department; they exercise considerable managerial freedom within the general guidelines set by their sponsoring department; and they are self-financing unless their losses are underwritten by their sponsoring department (Greenwood and Wilson, 1989, pp. 226–43). Since 1979 the Conservative Government has forced nationalised industries to operate in a more commercial manner mainly to prepare them for privatisation. There were ideological, economic and political reasons behind government decisions to nationalise industries. As part of its drive to manage the economy the post-war Labour Government nationalised many strategic industries such as coal, steel, electricity, rail and gas. Conservative Governments, until the election of the Thatcher Government in 1979, accepted largely the post-war legacy of nationalisation.

The performance of nationalised industries has been widely criticised for being inefficient and losing large amounts of public money. Veljanovski argued their failure 'arose from three basic factors – monopoly, weak financial and managerial discipline, and political interference' (1990, p. 296). Governments have been criticised for interfering in the business of nationalised industries and failing to control them. Tivey wrote:

> There is a certain paradox about the whole government/nationalized industry relationship over the years, in that both sides have continually complained of weakness. While the industries have protested against excessive interference, changes of policy, or of absence of policy guidance, the departments have felt an inability to gain a firm hold on what was going on. (Tivey, 1982, p. 54)

The relationship between the Treasury and Bank of England illustrates this paradox. The Treasury has often complained that the Bank of England does not do what it wants, and the Bank of England has resented Treasury interference (see Grant, 1993, pp. 75–8; Healey, 1989, pp. 374–6; and Lawson, 1992, pp. 83–5).

Since 1979 many nationalised industries have been and are being privatised, e.g. British Telecom, British Gas and British Rail. There are three components in the privatisation programme of the Conservative Government. First, privatisation is an *ideological* strategy. Privatisation is a manifestation of New Right ideology which believes the market is superior to government in providing goods and services. Nigel Lawson said the Conservative Party 'has never believed that the business of Government is the government of business' (Steel and Heald, 1982, p. 333). Second, privatisation is a *financial* strategy. The Government's privatisation programme did not take off until its second term despite its ideological commitment to 'roll back the frontiers of the state'. From 1979 onwards the Government was committed to cutting income tax and hoped that public expenditure cuts would finance tax cuts. It failed to cut public expenditure, but by privatising 'profitable' nationalised industries it financed the tax cuts and kept an election promise. The privatisation of nationalised industries raised vast sums of money for the Government. For example, the sale of British Petroleum shares raised over £6 billion. Third, privatisation is a *political* strategy. The privatisation programme enhances the support of the Conservative Party from voters who have bought cheap shares and sold them quickly for profit, from the City which has made lots of money from handling the sales of nationalised industries, and from business which bought many industries cheaply. For example, British Aerospace received an illegal 'sweetener' of nearly £60 million from the Government for buying Rover.

The Conservative Government's privatisation programme has been accompanied by the formation of regulatory regimes within which privatised industries operate. Regulation 'is the new border between the state and industry' (Veljanovski, 1991, p. 4). The Government has established many regulatory bodies to watch over privatised companies, e.g. Office of Telecommunications (OFTEL), Office of Gas Supply (OFGAS) and Office of Electricity Regulation (OFFER). They 'have the power to monitor performance, prices and the quality of service, and to ensure that the consumer is afforded protection' (Veljanovski, 1990, p. 301).

Their record reflects the paradox facing nationalised industries before privatisation. They were privatised mainly to be freed from government control, yet regulation of these privatised industries represents government control in a different guise. Nicholas Ridley, as Secretary of State of Trade and Industry, claimed that the 'utilities we have privatised or intend to privatise are more easily controlled when they are in the private sector' (Ridley, 1989). Many privatised industries have complained the 'tightening corset of regulation' is impeding their performance (Veljanovski, 1991, p. 4). In contrast, others have claimed the regulatory agencies are too weak to check the 'monopoly power' of privatised industries and thus are unable to effectively 'protect the consumer from exploitation' (National Consumer Council, 1989, pp. 2–5). These criticisms reflect a fundamental tension between the Government's privatisation and regulation programmes.

Local Authorities

There are over 500 elected local authorities providing many services, e.g. education, housing and social services. Until recently the structure of local government was largely two-tiered with county councils (or regional councils in Scotland) providing certain services, and district councils providing other services. In 1986 the Greater London Council (GLC) and the six metropolitan county councils were abolished, and a single-tiered structure of local government exists in these conurbations. The Conservative Government is, at the time of writing, reviewing the structure of local government, and it seems likely that unitary local authorities will be imposed on the map of local government.

Local authorities are the only elected government bodies outside the House of Commons, though turnout at local elections is low. Elected councillors form party groups, which meet before local authority meetings to decide upon a party line. The majority party group dominates the decision-making process in a local authority, though there are many 'hung' local authorities where no party has control. The council is the formal decision-making body within a local authority but it delegates most decisions to committees.

The main role of councillors is to make decisions. Officers advise councillors before they make decisions, and implement their decisions. Officers are organised into departments. It is often claimed officers dominate decision making in local authorities far more than their counterparts in Whitehall, because councillors are generally part-time and officers are highly specialised professionals. However, councillors and officers are not in perpetual conflict, and depend upon each other. Councillors possess the statutory authority to make decisions but depend upon the expertise of officers to advise them and implement their decisions, and officers depend upon the support of councillors to implement their proposals. In making the annual budget most conflicts are not between councillors and officers but between committees and between departments fighting over money. There is interdependence between councillors and officers within broad policy areas.

The arena where there has been intense conflict is the relations between local authorities and central government. Since the mid-1970s central government has attempted increasingly to control local authorities. Stoker observed:

> Mrs Thatcher's legacy is not a transformed, renewed local government but rather a system that has been battered, abused and destabilised. . . . During

the Thatcher governments over 50 major acts were passed with significant implications for local government. (1991, p. 153)

Local government has become more centralised. On the financial front, central government has controlled increasingly spending of local authorities. In the mid-1970s the Labour Government cut grants given to local authorities. In 1979 the Thatcher Government continued to cut grants. In response many local authorities increased their rates to offset lost grant. In 1985 the Government retaliated by capping the spending of certain (mainly Labour controlled) local authorities. It also abolished the GLC and metropolitan county councils mainly because they were the largest 'overspenders' in local government.

In 1988 the Local Government Finance Act nationalised the business rates and replaced the domestic rates with the poll tax (called officially the community charge). The business rates were set by central government not local authorities, which meant that central government directly controlled about 75 per cent of local government finance. Local authorities were allowed only to raise monies by setting a poll tax; the rest of their monies was fixed by central government. The poll tax was an administrative nightmare for local authorities and a political nightmare for the Conservative Government. The Government argued the poll tax would increase the accountability of local authorities to their electors because more people would pay the poll tax and thus have a financial stake in their councils. However, just in case the voters did not make the 'right' choice the Government retained its capping powers limiting the spending of certain (again, mainly Labour controlled) local authorities. The poll tax was very unpopular because most people were paying more than they were paying under the rates. The unpopularity of the poll tax was translated into heavy local and parliamentary election defeats for the Conservative Party, and played a part in the downfall of Thatcher. The Major Government decided to replace the poll tax with the council tax before the general election of 1992.

On the policy front, the services provided by local authorities have been controlled increasingly by central government. Education is the largest function carried out by local authorities (see Chapter 11). Since 1979 city technology colleges funded directly by central government (with a little business money) have been established; the former polytechnics were removed from local authority control; the pay and conditions of teachers is now determined by central government; schools have been allowed to opt-out of local authority control; the

Inner London Education Authority (ILEA) was abolished; the national curriculum and tests for school children have been imposed; head teachers have more control over their school budgets; and further education colleges were removed from local authority control. Other functions of local authorities, such as housing and police, have been subject to similar central government interventions.

Local government has become increasingly privatised. Local authorities have been encouraged and forced to sell off many of their assets. The Housing Act 1980 paved the way for well over one million council homes to be bought by their tenants. Local authorities have been forced to compete with the private sector in providing services (see Chapter 10). The National Health Service and Community Care Act 1990 encourages the private sector and voluntary sector, as well as local authorities, to provide community care (see Chapters 9 and 12).

The Local Government, Planning and Land Act 1980 introduced compulsory competitive tendering into local government. The workforces of local authorities must compete with private contractors to carry out work on buildings and roads previously done in-house. The responses of local authorities were mixed, but were disappointing for the Conservative Government. Some local authorities (e.g. Wandsworth) were keen to contract-out work to the private sector. Many local authorities used the threat of contracting-out to restructure (and therefore cheapen) their operations to ensure their own workforces won the contract. Other local authorities (e.g. Manchester) were opposed ideologically to contracting-out and resisted all moves to contract-out services. Local authorities were not forced to accept the lowest bid; they were forced only to offer work to the private sector.

The Government passed the Local Government Act 1988 to push more local authorities to contract-out work to the private sector. It extended the services subject to compulsory competitive tendering to include refuse collection, cleaning of buildings and other 'blue-collar' services. It allowed only 'commercial considerations' to be used by local authorities in awarding contracts. About 80 per cent of work subject to compulsory competitive tendering has remained with the workforce of local authorities (Stoker, 1991, p. 221). The Local Government Act 1992 extended compulsory competitive tendering to 'white-collar' services such as library services and computing services. Compulsory competitive tendering reduced the costs of providing local authority services and attacked the position of trade unions in local government. Trade unions have seen the diminution of pay and conditions of their workers competing against private contractors. The main source of savings in contracting-out is the lower labour costs of private contractors, because they generally employ fewer workers on lower pay and conditions (though these savings may be threatened by the European Community's Acquired Rights Directive).

Since the mid-1970s, and especially since the early 1980s, local government has been increasingly centralised and privatised by central government. For many these trends confirm that local authorities are mere agents of central government. This observation is misleading because local authorities were not powerless in their battles with central government. Local authorities did not cut spending despite the financial controls of central government, and did not contract-out services on the scale that the Conservative Government had hoped. Stoker argued 'although central intervention has increased . . . it is far from clear that central control has been achieved in the sense of the centre achieving its objectives' (1991, p. 153). Nevertheless, there has been increasing centralisation and privatisation of local government.

Quangos

Quangos are quasi-governmental agencies which fall in the 'twilight zone' between the public sector and private sector, and between central government and local government. They include bodies like health authorities and urban development corporations. It is very difficult to generalise about quangos because 'their diversity in terms of finance, organization, objectives and accountability is enormous' (Greenwood and Wilson, 1989, p. 209).

Quangos are not elected and are therefore insulated from democratic control. Most quangos are appointed by central government. They have an 'arm's-length' relationship with ministers, and parliamentary control of these bodies is weak. In the 1970s the New Right was concerned about the growth of unaccountable and uncontrollable quangos. As a result the Thatcher Government pursued a policy of 'quangocide', and identified many quangos to be axed.

Within a few years into office the Government reversed this policy, and pursued a policy of veritable 'quangomania'. It realised quangos possessed certain advantages that were useful in achieving its political objectives. Its reforms of the health service have been pushed through largely because it placed a cadre of supporters and managers into key positions in health authorities to thwart the attempts to block the reforms by the medical profession and trade unions. Through its use of patronage powers the Government has appointed the 'right' people who could be trusted to do the 'right thing' (see Clarke and Newman, 1994). A government minister, Baroness Denton, responsible for over 800 appointments to quangos revealed that she 'can't remember knowingly appointing a Labour supporter' (Cohen *et al.*, 1993, p. 19). A survey found 'bosses of 40 per cent of the largest quangos had direct links with the Tories' (McGhie and Lewis, 1993, p. 11).

The Conservative Government has used quangos in its attack on local government. Many functions have been taken out of local authority control and placed into the hands of quangos, and functions which could have gone to local authorities have gone to quangos. Urban development corporations, housing associations, training and enterprise councils (TECs), grant-maintained schools, the Audit Commission, housing action trusts (HATs) and the Urban Regeneration Agency have been established to take over or deny functions from local government. This use of quangos is not new, but the Conservative ministers have made 'extensive use of such agencies as part of a wider attempt to by-pass local authorities unsympathetic to their aims' (Stoker, 1991, p. 61). The Conservative Government has also used quangos to restructure the operations of local authorities. The Audit Commission seeks to promote 'value-for-money' in local government. Other quangos, such as grant-maintained schools and housing action trusts, compete with local authorities. The Government has created a 'new magistracy' whereby 'a non-elected elite are assuming responsibility for a large part of local governance' (Stewart, 1992, p. 7). Quangos have become a significant feature of the landscape of governance in Britain. They are not elected but appointed, and can be controlled by the centre more than elected local authorities (Health and Education are perhaps the best examples; see Chapters 9 and 11).

Who Governs Beyond Whitehall?

Much government takes place beyond the corridors of Parliament and Whitehall. There are a plethora of government agencies that are not directly controlled by the centre. These bodies, excluding MI6, are statutory bodies, and must operate within the powers laid down by Parliament. However, they possess resources which allow them to exercise a degree of autonomy from the centre, though the centre does influence the way in which they operate. There are no lines that can clearly be drawn between government at the centre and government beyond the centre. They are interdependent arenas of government. The Conservative Government has presided over the gradual degradation of elected local authorities and the massive expansion of appointed quangos. Despite his roots in local government Major has not reversed this trend of governance beyond the centre.

Governing Britain

Britain is not governed from one place; it is governed from many places. The idea of parliamentary government does not explain how Britain is governed. Although Parliament still matters it largely scrutinises and legitimises decisions made elsewhere (see Judge, 1993). Even the present Parliament, where the Major Government has only a small majority in the House of Commons, has not been dominant in setting the policy agenda, and given the critical mass of 'Thatcherite' MPs it often reinforces the legacies of the Thatcher Government. Furthermore, the 'Next Steps' programme, privatisation programme and emergence of 'quangocracy', plus the growing influence of the European Community (see Chapter 4), have weakened parliamentary control of government. These structural changes have made the governance of Britain less democratic.

The system of government in Britain is complex and interdependent. There exists interests and networks cutting across government bodies that bind some bits together and divide other bits of government (see Marsh and Rhodes, 1992b). There are two dominant trends that have shaped and are shaping the structure of government since the late 1970s.

First, there is increasing centralisation of government. Central government has attempted to control the civil service. The 'Next Steps' programme allows ministers to control the budgets of agencies and lay down explicit policy guidelines. Central government has attempted to control local authorities. It has imposed financial and policy controls upon local authorities, and appointed quangos to attack local government. Second, there is increasing privatisation of government. The Conservative Government has privatised many nationalised industries, while retaining some regulatory control of newly privatised industries. It has attempted to privatise much of local government, especially by its policy of compulsory competitive tendering. The Government is privatising much of the civil service. Its market-testing programme is likely lead to contracting-out of much work in the civil service, and 'think-tanks' have to a certain extent privatised the supply of advice to ministers.

It is fashionable to argue that Thatcherism did not meet its ideological commitments. Marsh and Rhodes highlighted many 'implementation gaps' in which the goals of the Thatcher Government were not achieved, and concluded that the 'Thatcherite revolution is more a product of rhetoric than of the reality of policy impact' (Marsh and Rhodes, 1992a, p. 187; see also Savage and Robins, 1990). Their conclusion is undoubtedly true when the achievements are measured against the intentions of the Conservative Government's structural reforms of government since 1979. However, the structure of government has changed very significantly since the late 1970s, and though the changes may fall short of what the Government wanted they are largely manifestations of the politics and ideology of the New Right. Ironically it may now be argued that it was left to the Major administration to accelerate the rate of structural change in the direction of the goals aspired to by the Thatcher governments, prime examples of which lie in the 'Citizen's Charter' and the 'Next Steps' programme. These developments raise issues of government style which will be addressed in the following chapter.

3

Changing Styles of Governance since 1979

ROB ATKINSON and STEPHEN COPE

In Chapter 2 we considered the structural context of governance under the Conservatives as providing one set of constraints within which specific areas of policy have emerged. This chapter discusses the issue of 'styles' of governance as constituting a closely related set of processes which, together with structure, have further formed the context of public policy in Britain since 1979. 'Style' is an elusive notion, difficult to pin down and open to a variety of interpretations. In the world of politics 'style' is often used to refer to the general style of a government: its style of policy-making, style of management, the style of leadership of the prime minister, etc. All of these meanings convey the ways in which government seeks to govern and the image it presents to the public. Having discussed the structures of governance in Chapter 2, in this chapter we concentrate on the styles of governance that have characterised the period since 1979. We shall place particular emphasis on the debates surrounding the following dimensions of governance as they have functioned under the Conservatives since 1979:

(i)   the concentration of power within central government;
(ii) central-local government relations:
(iii) managerialism
(iv) the Citizen's Charter.

Changing Styles of Governance at the Centre

This section will discuss the issue of prime ministerial government, and the roles of ministers and Parliament, all of which raise crucial issues of style.

Prime Ministerial Government

For many it is the prime minister who sets the overall style of a particular government, thus a great deal of attention is focused on how the prime minister adapts to and alters the institutions within which s/he operates. We will concentrate on the role of the prime minister, cabinet, ministers and Parliament.

The view of collective cabinet government outlined in Chapter 2 has been challenged by both politicians and academics. Richard Crossman, a former Labour cabinet minister, believed the 'post-war epoch has seen the final transformation of Cabinet Government into Prime Ministerial Government' (1963, p. 51). Tony Benn, another former Labour cabinet minister, argued the power of the prime minister amounted to 'a system of personal rule in the very heart of our parliamentary democracy' (1980, p. 7). This argument gained favour when Thatcher was prime minister, and even retains some favour with Major as prime minister. In 1993 Foley argued 'the British prime minister has to all intents and purposes turned . . . into an authentically British president' (p. 283). Five arguments were used as evidence of 'prime ministerial government'.

First, the prime minister enjoys constitutional power. By convention the prime minister exercises Crown prerogative powers, such as the considerable array of patronage powers. The prime minister chooses the cabinet. It is argued the power to hire and fire ministers, and to promote and demote ministers, allows the prime minister to control the cabinet. A minister is dependent on the patronage of the prime minister, and is loyal to the prime minister. The cabinet is the prime minister's cabinet; and therefore cabinet government is prime ministerial government. However, the prime minister does not have a free hand in determining his or her cabinet. If a prominent faction within the ruling party is not represented in the cabinet the prime minister may have problems in securing the necessary support to get legislation through the House of Commons. For example, Major on becoming prime minister appointed both Douglas Hurd and Michael Heseltine as prominent members of his cabinet. Both received substantial support from Conservative MPs in their unsuccessful bids for leadership of the Conservative Party, and were too powerful to be left outside the cabinet.

Second, the prime minister is the chair of the cabinet. The prime minister decides how an item of business is to be handled in government. The cabinet discusses very little of the business of government. Most business is conducted formally by cabinet committees, and informally in meetings with ministers, civil servants and outside advisers.

Cabinet committees are used extensively to make decisions in government. It is argued they are used to strengthen prime ministerial control of government. The prime minister decides whether to set up a cabinet committee, establishes its terms of reference and determines its membership. A prime minister can create a cabinet committee which makes a decision that he or she supports. As prime minister, Thatcher kept any discussion of the economy off the cabinet agenda in the early 1980s because it was dominated by the 'wets', who were not trusted to make economic policy. These decisions were made by a carefully appointed cabinet committee on Economic Affairs (EA).

In addition the prime minister may decide not to establish a cabinet committee which would be serviced formally by the Cabinet Office, but may make decisions informally. Thatcher set up an informal group to resolve the conflict over the future of Westland Helicopters. But, as Hennessy noted, she had 'a tendency to stack the membership of such groups to secure the result she wants' (1986a, p. 425). The 'Westland Affair' demonstrates the power of the prime minister and the constraints surrounding the prime minister as chair of the cabinet. The prime minister opposed the European rescue package and preferred the American Sikorsky package recommended by Westland Helicopters. She attempted to steer the issue through the cabinet system by controlling the agenda of meetings and appointing trusted ministers on to various committees and groups deciding the fate of Westland Helicopters. The prime minister did not get her way. Although the European rescue package never materialised the prime minister lost two senior cabinet ministers, initially Michael Heseltine and later Leon Brittan over the leaking of a confidential letter. Her position as prime minister was seriously threatened.

Third, the prime minister is the leader of the ruling political party. He or she exercises considerable influence over the making of party policy. A prime minister can cultivate support within the party, thus strengthening his or her political standing in the cabinet. Thatcher, unlike Edward Heath, was very adept at rewarding her political friends. A party leader needs the support of the party. If the prime minister loses support his or her position is seriously weakened. Thatcher enjoyed considerable support within the Conservative Party over a prolonged period, although even her support evaporated when she was perceived to be a serious electoral liability. In November 1990 the Conservative Party abandoned her as leader, and elected John Major. However, after the 'honeymoon' period following the Gulf War and subsequently the General Election of 1992, he too had lost much party support, and there followed much speculation about his position as party leader (and therefore prime minister).

Fourth, the prime minister enjoys considerable media attention. He or she can build up popular support through the mass media, and can shape the political agenda by manipulating the media. In 1987 the prime minister, Thatcher, surprisingly announced in a television interview that there was going to be a fundamental review of the National Health Service. She forced the then Secretary of State of Health and Social Security, Kenneth Clarke, to support her decision despite one of his junior ministers claiming previously no review was to take place.

It is often argued the prime minister uses the media as a tool against his or her cabinet colleagues by controlling the lobby system (see Cockerell *et al.*, 1985). The lobby system is an arrangement where the government briefs journalists on a non-attributable basis – the government thus shapes how the news is reported, and the journalists get 'inside' information. Thatcher, through her Press Secretary Bernard Ingham, was very effective in manipulating the media to control her cabinet colleagues. For example, Bernard Ingham described John Biffen, a cabinet minister, as a 'semi-detached member of the Government' (Harris, 1990, p. 146). This non-attributable comment fuelled speculation that John Biffen was about to be sacked. On being sacked he realised that Bernard Ingham was only 'the sewer rather than the sewage' – the sewage clearly came from the prime minister (Harris, 1990, p. 148). Though the prime minister does have a privileged relationship with the media they are not pawns of the prime minister. Major found to his cost that the media can be as damning as they can be praising, particularly in his case in the aftermath of 'Black Wednesday' when Britain withdrew from the Exchange Rate Mechanism. The news media adopted from this point onwards a highly negative stance on Major's performance, contrasting sharply with the relationship enjoyed by Thatcher with much of the press.

Fifth, the prime minister exercises considerable influence over decision making in government. The prime minister is served by the Prime Minister's Office comprising the Private Office, Political Office, Press Office, and Policy Unit. It is argued the Policy Unit undermines cabinet government by providing advice that can be used by the prime minister against his or her cabinet colleagues. The prime minister also appoints special advisers who provide him/her with alternative perspectives to those emerging from departments. For instance, Alan Walters advised Thatcher on economic policy matters. He criticised the Chancellor of the Exchequer, Nigel Lawson, for allowing sterling to shadow the Deutschmark. Nigel Lawson believed his position had been undermined and eventually resigned partly because he felt the views of Alan Walters were really those of the prime minister in disguise. A year later, as a result of pressure from the Foreign Office and the Treasury, Thatcher allowed sterling to join the Exchange Rate Mechanism (ERM), accepting reluctantly that sterling should be pegged to other European currencies. This example demonstrates the limits of prime ministerial power by proxy. The prime minister's small number of advisers simply cannot compete with the army of civil servants at the disposal of other cabinet ministers.

These five arguments have been used to support the view of prime ministerial government. However, it fails to recognise that the prime minister is constrained by other actors, notably the cabinet, civil service, party, mass media and Parliament. The prime minister 'will remain only as strong as the colleagues let him or her be' (Jones, 1990, p. 6). The limits placed upon the power of the prime minister were very evident in the sudden departure of the prime minister, Thatcher, in November 1990. She resigned because she lost the support of the party, Conservative MPs and the cabinet. On taking over the premiership Major 'was determined to reunite both the government and the Conservative party, and he knew that one of the best means of accomplishing these linked objectives would be to be as collegial as Margaret Thatcher had been uncollegial' (King, 1993, p. 63).

The prime ministerial government thesis also fails to recognise the interdependence of the actors involved in the cabinet system. The prime minister and other cabinet ministers depend upon each other for political support. According to Middlemas, 'the cardinal axis of modern British government is that of British prime minister and

Chancellor' (Grant, 1993, p. 68). This axis explains why Major did not sack Norman Lamont until May 1993, eight months after 'Black Wednesday'. Dunleavy and Rhodes described government at the centre as 'a complex web of institutions, networks and practices surrounding the prime minister, cabinet, cabinet committees and their official counterparts, less formalized ministerial "clubs" or meetings, bilateral negotiations, and interdepartmental committees' (1990, p. 3). This core executive is fluid, fragmented and interdependent – neither the cabinet nor the prime minister governs alone.

The Issue of Prime Ministerial 'Style'
As should be clear from the preceding discussion the relative power of the prime minister depends upon the ability, and character, of the prime minister to mobilise the resources inherent in their position. As Jones (1985) and Mount (1992) have noted the constitutional situation is fluid and much depends upon the incumbent's temperament.

King (1987) has described basic prime ministerial policy styles: 'deliberative' and 'declarative'. Deliberative prime ministers discuss issues thoroughly within cabinet, decisions are only taken after extensive consultation and a consensus has emerged; such an approach represents the ideal of collective cabinet government. In the declarative case a prime minister simply declares policy, often publicly, in an 'off the cuff' manner, without consulting. As a result colleagues are committed to courses of action before they have had the opportunity to consider the issues, leaving ministers to honour the prime minister's commitment. In Thatcher's case this frequently occurred, but this perhaps reflects what Hennessy (1987, p. 66) referred to as her 'bias towards decision'. Another example of this type of behaviour was Thatcher's reported tendency to open cabinet discussions by stating her own views in such a manner as to defy other members to disagree. Such an approach conflicts with the usual assumption that the prime minister, rather like a chairperson, waits until everyone has spoken and then at the end of the meeting sums up, looking for common ground and attempting to create a consensus. In Thatcher's case she was clearly not temperamentally suited for this latter role and given the 'radicalism' of some of the her policies it was unlikely that any consensus would emerge.

Perhaps it is wrong to see the prime minister as someone striving to create a consensus. Mount (1992) for instance compares the role of the prime minister to that of a company chief executive who, whilst allowing discussion, has a duty to take decisions and give active leadership and direction to the ship of state. However the deliberative/declarative dichotomy is too simple, in the case of Thatcher in certain areas (e.g. reform of tax policy) she adopted a deliberative style (see King, 1987). Major on the other hand, partly out of temperament but also reflecting his position in the Party and Parliament, presented the style of a deliberative prime minister, allowing wide-ranging discussions within cabinet before announcing decisions. However, perhaps as a result of him following in the wake of Thatcher, Major has also been criticised in some quarters for his personal style of leadership, which is portrayed as being indecisive, weak and lacking in strategic vision.

Needless to say both declarative and deliberative forms are ideal types – every prime minister is to some extent a mixture of the two, with one tending to predominate. With reference to collective responsibility it would seem reasonable to suggest that Thatcher's style, coupled with her policy aims, predisposed her to bypass cabinet. Major's style, on the contrary, seems conducive to a greater degree of collegiality, although it should be remembered that while he has made less use of *ad hoc* groups than Thatcher did, the committee system created by his predecessor remains largely intact.

The Role of Ministers

Another key issue raised by the preceding discussion is the role of ministers. Senior ministers are members of cabinet and, in theory, play a crucial role in determining the overall strategy of the government. But perhaps most importantly they are responsible for their department – the notion of 'ministerial responsibility', which means that:

> Ministers are accountable to Parliament, in the sense that they have a duty to explain in Parliament the exercise of their powers and duties and to give an account to Parliament of what is done by them in their capacity as Ministers or by their Departments. (Cabinet Office, 1992a, para. 27)

The convention of ministerial responsibility holds that if something goes wrong either in a department or with the policies it is responsible for the Minister must answer to Parliament and if necessary resign. In the last thirty years few Ministers have resigned because of errors in their departments or policy failures. This partly reflects the fact that it is unreasonable to expect Ministers to take responsibility for everything that happens in their departments. However, a great deal depends upon the extent to which the Minister retains the support of the prime minister, cabinet colleagues the Party, and of course the mass media; these factors will, in reality, determine whether or not a Minister resigns.

In addition the 'declarative style' of Thatcher and her willingness to intervene in the policies and activities of departments appeared to suggest that the position of Ministers was being undermined. Whilst it would be wrong to deny that there were occasions when Thatcher appeared to pre-empt departmental roles the prime minister simply lacks the resources to do this on a regular basis (see Jones, 1985). Moreover, as Dunleavy (1990, p. 106) has argued:

> Even under Mrs Thatcher, Whitehall ... remained a federation of departments, each of which jealously guards its own position and administrative autonomy.

With the ascent of Major and his more 'deliberative style' there appears, notwithstanding Treasury demands for expenditure restraint, a willingness to allow ministers and their departments to operate according to their own dictates unless they appear likely to create political problems for the government.

The issue of ministerial responsibility has, however, received renewed impetus by the setting up of agencies (see Chapter 2), a process hesitantly initiated under Thatcher but considerably accelerated under Major's leadership. The 'Next Steps' programme is based upon the tacit assumption that policy-making can be separated from implementation (see Jones, 1989). The assumption here appears to be that once the 'framework agreement' has been negotiated and the agency set up there will be an 'arm's-length' relationship with the department, in other words the Minister will not interfere.

Jones (1989) suggests it is unlikely that Ministers will be able to refrain from interfering in the work of agencies when they are widely seen as responsible for their operation. Ministers, being political creatures, will be eager to accept the plaudits when things go well but unwilling to stand back when political considerations are at stake or to allow major blunders to come to light.

Overall it is perhaps fair to argue that the notion of 'ministerial responsibility', in the sense of resignation, is largely a fiction. What is more pertinent today is the extent to which ministers will attempt to manipulate agencies and whether Parliament can effectively hold ministers and agencies to account.

The Role of Parliament

It often been argued over the last thirty years that the role of Parliament has changed quite fundamentally from that of policy-maker to a 'rubber stamp' of policy emerging from the executive. The first question we must ask here is when did Parliament ever actually fulfil the role of policy maker. It is doubtful if Parliament has ever acted as a policy maker in other than the most marginal sense, and certainly in the twentieth century the scale of government and the lack of resources available to MPs have precluded Parliament from being a policy making body (see Lenman, 1992). What then is its role?

At best Parliament can function as a debating chamber, a scrutineer of legislation emerging from the executive and a means to hold government to account. The real issue is to what extent have even these limited roles been eroded since 1979, particularly when for thirteen years the Conservatives had majorities large enough to enable the most controversial of legislation to pass through Parliament largely unhindered (e.g. the Community Charge). Party discipline effectively means that where a governing party has a large majority it will get its own way, as Lord Hailsham put it almost twenty years ago, Parliament 'is now largely in the hands of the government machine, so that the government controls Parliament and not Parliament the government' (Hailsham, 1976, p. 496). In other words an 'elective dictatorship', or perhaps even a 'one-party' regime, has been created in which Parliament has been further marginalised.

Given the above and Thatcher's personal style one would have expected Parliament to have been virtually 'powerless'. However, on numerous occasions the Thatcher Governments were prepared to back down when confronted by opposition from significant numbers of backbenchers and/or when Thatcher perceived the threat of an electoral backlash from Conservative voters in the southern shires. Major on the other hand was first hamstrung by his lack of an electoral mandate and then by a small electoral majority; it should come as no real surprise that he has had a much more difficult time and that he has been forced to make concessions and/or engage in devious manoeuvres in order to get controversial legislation (e.g. the Maastricht Bill) through Parliament.

If there is a serious desire to give Parliament a greater role in policy making then one obvious solution is to give MPs and parliamentary committees more resources and greater investigative powers to expose government failings and hold it to account. However, so long as a disciplined party structure remains it is unlikely that MPs of the governing party will be willing to thwart their own government too often. The ability of Parliament to effectively carry out its roles of scrutiny, debate and accountability does seem to have declined during the last fifteen years, although here again it is more a case of accentuating an existing trend rather than creating something new.

Overall then it can be argued that during the Thatcher years there does appear to have been an increase in centralisation of power within a 'core executive'. In part this reflects a trend which has been operating throughout the twentieth century as power has increasingly been claimed by the executive. However, this tendency also reflected Thatcher's more activist and interventionist style. Yet at the same time Whitehall had managed to retain its structure of 'baronial fiefdoms', suggesting that the notion of centralisation does not fully capture the true complexity of the situation. Perhaps we should talk not only in terms of centralisation but also continued fragmentation at the centre.

The main change since November 1990 was that Major was more willing to discuss changes with ministers and, given the small parliamentary majority, listen sympathetically to MPs concerns rather than preempt discussions by public announcements. However, we doubt whether this really amounts to much in the way of real change. Indeed, Major seems to have maintained much of the 'decision making by committee style' of his predecessor. If there is a difference, and once again this largely goes back to the issue of personal style, it lies in Norman Lamont's (the former Chancellor) accusation that the government lacked any strategic vision and tended to make policy on an *ad hoc* and reactive basis – what he described as 'short termism'. As he said in the Commons:

There is something wrong with the way we make our decisions. The government listens too much to the pollsters and the party managers. . . . As a result there is too much short-termism, too much reacting to events, not enough shaping of events. (*Guardian*, 10 June 1993, p. 2)

Central–Local Government Relations

This section will focus on the relationships between central and local government within the context of structural and organisational changes outlined in the preceding chapter.

It has been argued that the style of central–local relations in the 1970s was characterised by compromise and bargaining and attempts to incorporate local government into Whitehall's decision-making process, most notably over public expenditure, whereas the 1980s was characterised by a confrontational style (Stoker, 1991). During the 1980s the centre adopted a much more 'top-down' approach in which policy was centrally determined and then handed down to local government with little or no consultation. This argument undoubtedly finds support in the widespread antagonism between centre and locality and the deluge of legislation which poured out from the centre, usually with the aim of restricting or bypassing the powers and decision-making capacities of local government (for an excellent overview see Stoker, 1991).

Yet as Rhodes (1988) has warned, it is unwise to simplistically assume that merely because the centre passes legislation and gives itself powers that both can actually be realised. In many cases the centre needs local government co-operation; centre and locality are interdependent and if the centre wishes to achieve its objectives it frequently needs to win the co-operation of local government by making concessions. It is the apparent predominance of compulsion and marginalisation which has raised so many questions and concerns over the last fifteen years.

Ironically, initially it appeared that the Thatcher Government was sympathetic to local government indicating a desire to give it more freedom from central direction. However, the centre's primary concern was the reduction of public expenditure, and as Thatcher already regarded local government, particularly Labour controlled authorities, as an 'overspender' the stage was set for a major confrontation which moved far beyond the initial issue of 'excessive local expenditure' (see Travers, 1989, for an overview of finance).

Many local authorities chose to obstruct and circumvent the centre's attempts to control local spending and to limit local government's room for manoeuvre. A torrent of legislation attempted to control and limit local expenditure. Other pieces of legislation set out to implement reforms which bypassed local decision-making powers, for instance

Urban Development Corporations were established, whilst in other instances troublesome authorities, such as the GLC and Metropolitan Counties, were actually abolished. Taken together these developments constituted a major restructuring of the system of local government and of central–local government relations, a situation which will be carried further by the reorganisation of local government (see Chapter 2).

Particularly during the period 1979–89 there appeared to be a clash between the power of the centre to implement a general programme of neo-liberal reforms and the desire of some localities to defend and extend a form of 'local socialism' (see Lansley *et al.*, 1989). It would be wrong, however, to simply see this as a clash between a determined Conservative Government and recalcitrant Labour authorities, many Conservative authorities and politicians were deeply disturbed by the actions of the Thatcher administrations. What took many people by surprise was the virulence of the relationship, local government appeared to be defined as 'the enemy within' and at times it appeared as if warfare had broken out between the two sides. It was in this context that the centre appeared determined to either dismantle or neutralise local government.

Yet by the late 1980s, and certainly after Major's succession to the position of prime minister, a *rapprochement* appeared to be underway and the word partnership began to reappear in discussions between centre and locality and once again it was possible to use the word 'bargaining' to describe the style of relations. However, by this stage the centre had effectively won the battle, although perhaps not as decisively as Thatcher would have liked, and local government was attempting to come to terms with a variety of pieces of legislation which were effectively 'privatising' key service areas for which it had previously been solely responsible (see Stoker, 1991, ch. 9). Increasingly the notion of local government as an *enabler or facilitator* (Ridley, 1988; Brooke, 1989; see Chapter 12 for a classic example) gained ground; henceforth the role of local government was to take a strategic overview of a localities' needs and to purchase services from the private and voluntary sectors wherever possible, acting only as a provider itself in the last resort. However, as Cochrane (1991, pp. 282–3) has noted: 'For some, the notion of an "enabling" authority is little more than a euphemism for the "end of local government".'

During the Thatcher years the centre adopted an inflexible and top-down style which eventually forced local government to rethink many of its basic assumptions and operating procedures. Major has been able to build upon these changes and as a result to adopt a more consultative and less top-down style of relations between centre and locality. This is perhaps best exemplified by the Government's willingness, under intense political pressure from its own supporters, to drop the Community Charge and replace it with the Council Tax, and the fact that it was willing to listen to the advice of the local authority associations.

Despite a *rapprochement* by the late 1980s the establishment of a large number of bodies responsible for 'local governance', but outside local government and local democratic accountability, appeared to have produced what Stewart (1992) has termed a 'new magistracy' (see also Stoker, 1991, ch. 3; developments in health and education are also examples of this tendency – see Chapters 9 and 11). He argued that:

> A new magistracy is being created in the sense that a non-elected elite are assuming responsibility for a large part of local governance . . . Accountability such as it is rests upon the accountability of these bodies to central government, although even that appears uncertain in the case of the governing bodies of, for example, hospital trusts and grant maintained schools. (Stewart, 1992, p. 7)

In part this reflects the creation of a wide range of new quangos during the 1980s designed to bypass local government, but also the clientelism of the centre which has increasingly appointed its own sympathisers to posts within its gift at the local level. Given the increased role of quangos at all levels of government, the implications are that this problem, of accountability only to and through ministers, is creating an accountability deficit which threatens to create a form of widespread clientelism in British government and undermine democratic forms of accountability (see *Financial Times*, 14 Jan. 1993, p. 9; *Independent on Sunday*, 28 Mar. 1993, p. 19; examples may also be found in Chapters 9, 10 and 11).

This would suggest that the return to a 'bargaining style' has been accompanied by a fragmentation of power at local level in which the powers of local government have been reduced. In some cases power has been centralised, in others power has been centralised only to be redistributed by the centre back to the locality, but put into 'safe hands' outside of the direct or in some cases even indirect influence of local government.

Whilst the confrontational style of relations characteristic of Thatcher's premiership appear to have abated since her downfall, under Major's premiership a new, less locally accountable, more fragmented and flexible style of local governance has begun to emerge. So while we can talk about 'bargaining' replacing conflict as the characteristic style of central–local relations it should be acknowledged that the two sides are far more unequal than they were in the 1970s.

Managerialism

One of the driving forces behind many of the reforms since 1979 has been a desire to both reduce the role of the state and to alter the managerial style of the residuum. Almost by definition public sector organisations are deemed to be overly bureaucratic and inherently inefficient and unresponsive to 'consumer' needs. A key constituent of this process, at all levels of government, has been the imposition of styles of management and operation which reflect an idealised notion of private sector management structures and methods – a new form of managerialism (see Pollitt, 1990; Stewart and Walsh, 1992 for excellent overviews).

There has been a determined attempt to restructure the internal administrative and organisational cultures of the British state by both importing private sector management techniques and artificially creating competitive market mechanisms within the state (the NHS is perhaps the best example, see Chapter 9). It is assumed that this will make state employees more aware of the costs and benefits of public service provision, give greater thought to how inputs might be best utilised and outputs directed to meet the needs of users/consumers. At the same time attempts have been made to make individual employees more aware of their duties and responsibilities via a clear definition of roles, the use of performance-related pay, regular performance assessments, better training, etc.

At central government level this has taken a variety of forms, such as the Rayner Scrutinies, the Financial Management Initiative (FMI) and Management Information Systems for Ministers (MINIS) (for excellent overviews see Fry, 1987; Jones, 1989). All of these examples sought to change civil service culture and make civil servants give greater attention to 'the task of managing their resources to achieve political objectives set for them by ministers' (Jones, 1989, p. 248) – thereby producing a more managerial style of government.

Reformers eventually realised that changes in administrative processes and culture could not be achieved in isolation from organisational change and the result was the 'Next Steps' programme (Jenkins *et al.*, 1988; see Flynn *et al.*, 1990, and Kemp, 1990 for commentaries). The aim was to separate policy-making functions from service delivery functions and to set up agencies to deliver services. As around 95 per cent of civil servants are engaged in delivery functions the opportunities for 'agencification' (Waldegrave, 1993a, p. 18) are considerable. It is hoped that agencies, once the framework agreements have been negotiated, will be released from the dead-hand of bureaucratism and given a free reign to employ management methods which make the best use of existing resources (i.e. produce more and better quality services) while developing new more imaginative styles of management to meet client needs.

More generally speaking there has also been an attempt within those services still provided by the state to create a split between 'purchaser' and 'provider', whereby a form of quasi-competition (or internal market) is established forcing state producer organisations to compete with one another over standards and cost thereby providing purchaser organisations with choice (e.g. reforms in the NHS, see Chapter 9 and in education, see Chapter 11). A form of 'choice by proxy' being established on the 'consumers' behalf. The 'competitive process' has become a key part of 'market-testing' (Waldegrave, 1993b), an on-going and rolling programme which by September 1993 aimed to cover £1.5bn worth of public service provision (*Hansard*, 25 Nov. 1992, col. 879).

Local government has also undergone, albeit somewhat more slowly and reluctantly, the same experiences. Similar pressures for greater economy, efficiency and effectiveness ('3 Es') have been felt here, partly brought about by a need to better utilise a declining resource base but also by legislative changes. This approach is based on the assumption that 'Competition is the best guarantee of quality and value for money' (Cmnd 1730, p. 1).

Overall then the public sector has undergone major changes in its management style. Today terms such as the '3Es', competition and value for money (VFM) have become part of the everyday vocabulary of public sector organisations, as has more recently the language of consumerism and citizens' charters (see below).

The implications of managerialism are open to interpretation. Government Ministers see it as part of a wider strategy to create a new style of government by 'reinventing government' and 'Bring the Government itself back towards its true role, steering, not rowing the boat' (Waldegrave, 1993b, p. 7, see also 1993a).Waldegrave has argued that this is part of a process which aims to transform:

> the way public services are run, moving away from the old command structures to more open, responsive management by clear and published contracts, which empower managers with the authority to run their organisation in the way that best suits the needs of those who actually use the service. (*Hansard*, 25 Nov. 1992, col. 870)

Managerialism, when allied with 'competition', will, it is argued, produce better quality services at lower cost.

For others managerialism is seen in a rather different light, its essence being defined as:

> A strong emphasis on the tighter control of . . . spending . . . [and] a growing emphasis on decentralizing management responsibilities once financial targets and other performance norms have been (centrally) fixed. (Pollitt, 1990, p. 55)

The pursuit of better management is seen as part of a wider political project, it offers the 'New Right' a means by which:

> private-sector disciplines can be introduced to the public services, political control can be strengthened, budgets trimmed, professional autonomy reduced, public service unions weakened and a quasi-competitive framework erected to flush out the 'natural' inefficiencies of bureaucracy. (Pollitt, 1992, p. 49)

For Pollitt managerialism represents 'the 'acceptable face' of new-right thinking concerning the state' (Pollitt, 1992, p. 49).

Other writers have been less hostile to these developments, arguing that they open up new, although potentially contradictory, opportunities for the public sector to make better use of its resources and to meet the needs of its clients more efficiently and effectively. Flexibility has become a crucial feature of public service provision, raising issues about how a service is provided, who provides it, how users are involved in assessing the quality of provision, etc. (see Huhne, 1993 for a useful summary of the issues). As a result of these developments terms such as 'contracts', 'decentralisation' (Hambleton, 1992) and 'empowerment' (Clarke and Stewart, 1992) have increasingly entered the lexicon of the public-sector. Such views suggest a style of public sector management which is more dynamic and responsive to citizens demands.

It should be pointed out that advocates of these latter views stress the differences between public and private sectors and the uniqueness of the 'public sector ethos'. And while these developments provide new opportunities for the public sector the issues are complex and that it is wrong to presume 'there is one approach to management applicable to public services based on an over-simplified model of the private sector' (Stewart and Walsh, 1992, p. 517).

Overall then the government at all levels has adopted a more managerial style of operation, a process which has been considerably accelerated since Major's rise to the premiership. Where Thatcher moved more slowly and incrementally over reforms the Major Government has accelerated change and pushed into new areas (e.g. prisons, the police).

The Citizen's Charter and Open Government

In 1991 Major launched the *Citizen's Charter* (Cmnd 1599, 1991) initiative as a centrepiece of his Government's strategy. Major claimed that it was the 'big idea' for the 1990s and this initiative, perhaps more than any other, represents a desire to present the Major administration as having a distinct open and responsive governmental style of its own. Moreover it also epitomises Major's attempt to stamp his own personal style upon government – an open and concerned style.

The prime minister claimed that the Charter would be 'at the centre of the Government's decision making throughout the 1990s' (Cmnd 2101, 1992, p. i; see also Major 1992a, b; Waldegrave, 1993a, b). It has become both a vehicle and justification for some of the managerial reforms referred to in the previous section. The Charter would thus appear to be central to the new style of governance adopted by the Major administration.

The Charter aims to 'empower' citizens and to give them greater choice and control in their lives, themes which would appear to be central to Major's personal 'philosophy' (see Major, 1993). Madsen

Pirie, of the Adam Smith Institute, has summed up the ideas underlying the Charter. He argued:

> The central idea behind it is that citizens, or consumers of state services, shall be equipped with rights which seek to provide substitutes for the rights which they would have in a private market. The Citizens' Charter, if it is to be effective, must imitate in some sense the rights which people have as consumers in a competitive market. (Pirie, 1991, p. 7; see also Mather, 1991)

As with other aspects of the Conservative's approach to service provision the Charter is premised upon the assumption that markets are the most efficient and effective providers of services because they entail competition and choice, the problem with the state sector being that it is both bureaucratic and a monopoly supplier, leading it to define user needs and how, and when, those needs are met. In most cases the user is at the mercy of the providing organisation being unable to go elsewhere. In order to counter this imbalance and empower citizens the Charter aims to redress the situation using, and building upon, existing programmes (see Cmnd 1599, 1991). Pirie has summarised how the Charter will function:

> The Citizen's Charter represents a radically new approach because it reinforces the idea of public service with the notion of a *contract* between those who pay for the service and those who provide it. Its assumptions are threefold. They are that the citizen is entitled to receive some level of service in return for the taxpayers funds used to finance it; that the citizen is entitled to know what level of service that is; and that he or she is entitled to some form of redress if that level is not attained. (Pirie, 1991, p. 8 emphasis added; see also Major, 1992a; Waldegrave, 1993a)

Mather (1991) has described this situation as *Governing by Contract*, thereby reproducing the contractual relations believed to be characteristic of the private sector within the public sector.

It is intended that the Charter should be applied to every area of government (see Cmnd 1599, 1991; Cmnd 1730, 1991). By November 1992 some 28 Charters had been published (e.g. the Council Tenants Charter, the Patients Charter, see Cmnd 2101, 1992, pp. 73–4 and Chapter 9 below), informing citizens of their rights, standards of service and means of redress. It is hoped that by doing this users will have both choice and redress and that these twin pressures will force providers to improve service provision. As Waldegrave (1992, para.20) has argued:

> The Charter is a way of making sure that the pressures which would be brought to bear to the user's advantage in competitively provided services are also brought to bear on public services where little or no competition is available.

The outcome of this process is hopefully that 'public services . . . are every bit as good as those that are offered by the private sector' (Major, 1992b, p. 2).

However, the Charter also 'involves a fundamental reappraisal of what the state should do and how it should do it' (Major, 1992b, p. 6), producing 'a smaller, less centralised and more customer-conscious public service' (Waldegrave, 1993a, p. 23). It appears that the Citizen's Charter is increasingly being used as a vehicle, and a justification, for a major restructuring of the state, i.e. what it does and how it does it. Waldegrave (1993a, p. 13) has argued 'The first step . . . should [be to] establish what the government really needs to do.' Citizenship in this context becomes part of a wider strategy for fundamentally reassessing the state, its forms, functions and relationship with the private sector. The initiative on Open Government (see below) should also be seen as part of this wider strategy.

As Waldegrave, the minister responsible for overseeing the implementation of the Charter, noted when summing up the first year's experience of the Charter;

> it is vital that public services be provided by the most competitive supplier – public or private – which offers the best quality of service and value for money for the user and the taxpayer. Wherever it is feasible and desirable, we will therefore continue to privatise services. (*Hansard*, 25 Nov. 1992, col. 870)

Thus the Charter appears to have a key role in determining the style, extent and nature of any future public sector (see Waldegrave, 1993a).

In July 1993 William Waldegrave, Chancellor of the Duchy of Lancaster, launched the government's new White Paper on *Open Government* (Cmnd 2290, 1993) which was presented as a component in the Government's expanding Charter initiative. The White Paper argues

> Open government is part of an effective democracy. Citizens must have
> adequate access to the information and analysis on which government
> business is based. Ministers and public servants have a duty to explain their
> policies, decisions and actions to the public. Governments need, however, to
> keep some secrets, and have a duty to protect the proper privacy of those
> with whom they deal. (Cmnd 2290, 1993, p. 1)

The aim is to create 'greater transparency in the aims, performance and
delivery of government services under the Citizen's Charter' (ibid.,
p. 1). Much of the information which will be released is intended to
facilitate the operation of the Charter and to increase financial and
managerial accountability. Whilst this is laudable one has to question
the extent to which the initiative is designed to open up the closed
world of government and provide more information about how policies
are actually made (e.g. the options considered and the advice offered to
Ministers).

Whilst we acknowledge the need to protect national security,
commercial and personal confidentiality (see Cmnd 2290, 1993, p. 2),
crucial areas of policy-making which do not fall under those headings
remain surrounded by a multitude of interdictions, leaving them largely
closed to outside scrutiny. The Government justifies this decision on
the grounds that it threatens 'a risk of loss of candour in discussions'
(Cmnd 2290, 1993, pp. 24–5) and the political neutrality of the civil
service. Publishing advice and discussions anonymously is pre-emp-
tively dismissed as inadequate. However, we suspect the real reason
behind this stance is that such publications would expose the options
considered (or not considered) and the advice offered (and rejected) by
government, which would provide outside observers with more
information with which to assess policy making, something no British
government seems to relish.

Overall, whilst the White Paper is a welcome first step it fails to
provide a *right* of access to information as would be the case with a
Freedom Of Information Act such as those to be found in the USA,
New Zealand and Australia. We are simply left to rely upon the
goodwill and discretion of ministers, qualities which the Matrix-
Churchill case (see Chapter 15) suggests are in short supply when
government feels events may expose it to charges of hypocrisy and
cover-ups. As a *Guardian* editorial noted:

> Detailed prohibitions arrive by the hundred. They are, let us be clear, a
> licence to allow government to obfuscate, delay and keep its secrets.
> (*Guardian*, 16 July 1993)

Conclusion

Although we have referred to 'style' in the title of this chapter it should
be apparent that the issues raised are complex and go far beyond mere
style and are of a more fundamental nature. Overall the Thatcher years
saw considerable changes, some traceable back to radical policy aims,
others to a style of governance which exhibited an ideological distrust
of the state and yet others to an acerbic prime minister impatient with
dissension. In many cases, however, change was in part the result of
government reacting to opposition, as in the case of local government,
which forced a temporary retreat, regrouping and the development of
new tactics. In other instances, such as the power of the prime minister,
change partly resulted from the personal style of the prime minister
(e.g. Thatcher's 'declarative' and 'activist' style), a development which
seems to have been attenuated since Major became premier. Elsewhere,
changes developed incrementally as a result of fifteen continuous years
of government by one party and a willingness to use patronage and
clientelism to achieve ends even if it meant reducing democratic forms
of accountability (e.g. the 'new magistracy' discussed above). Moreover
large majorities, at least until 1992, allowed the Government to do
virtually what it wanted; the small majority which Major had to endure
appears to have brought forth more concessions to his backbenchers,
but not necessarily any increase in Parliament's role or a reduction in
the use of patronage and clientelism. In this context the tendency
inherent in the British electoral system to produce 'elective dictator-
ships' has been accentuated under the Conservatives, almost to the
point of a degeneration into a 'one-party' regime, a tendency which
Major's premiership seems if anything to have continued. The irony is
that the vulnerability of the premier to dissent within his own party,
has meant that policy has been more inward-looking and one-party
oriented than might have been the case with a greater majority. In
other areas, such as 'managerialism', where change was relatively
incremental under Thatcher, the tempo of change appears in fact to
have increased since November 1990, being accentuated by policies,
such as the Citizen's Charter, which Major has claimed as his own. In
this instance it may be possible to identify a distinct style of governance
which Major has pursued more doggedly and vigorously than his
predecessor. Indeed, in this area Major may have been more radical
than his predecessor, pushing neo-liberal reforms further than she was
willing or placed to do.

Obviously there have been continuities and discontinuities between the style of the Thatcher and Major governments. However it is dangerous, at this point in time, to see the discontinuities that have appeared as being little more than reflections of the personal styles of the two prime ministers – Thatcher's conviction politics, her 'declarative' and, apparently, unyielding style, compared to Major's more deliberative, mild-mannered and, apparently, ambivalent style. Nor should one assume Major lacks resolve – as was demonstrated by his (eventual) 'sacking' of Norman Lamont as Chancellor, and his description of opponents within cabinet as 'bastards', a willingness to strike and hit back is apparent. Moreover, as has been stated, in some areas (e.g. managerial reform and the Citizen's Charter) the Major government can be seen to have been more radical than its predecessors. This suggests that attempts to categorise governmental styles in simple terms are, to say the least, hazardous.

When taken together with the developments outlined in the previous chapter, it seems to us that quite basic changes have occurred, and are continuing, in the scope and nature of British government. As a result, the wider context within which individual areas of policy have developed has undergone a significant transformation under the Conservatives. The precise impact of such contextual processes on specific policy fields is a matter the chapters presented in Part II will address.

4

Britain and Europe: From Community to Union

FERGUS CARR and STEPHEN COPE

Chapters 2 and 3 have focused on the internal mechanisms of governance in Britain; this chapter discusses the wider issues of governance and policy within the European Community/European Union and its impact upon Britain. It examines the themes of integration, interdependence and autonomy. The chapter is divided into three sections; the development of the European Community, policy-making in the European Community, and the future of the European Community.

The Development of the European Community

Origins

The origins of the European Community are complex. In terms of intellectual antecedents federalism has long been advocated as an alternative to the nation-state. During the Second World War the resistance movements called for a federal Europe. Whilst federalism was not adopted after 1945 a series of strategic and economic problems did challenge the nation-state. The Cold War divided Europe and led to American strategies to contain Soviet influence. America sought a united Western Europe that could withstand Soviet pressure. Washington granted economic aid but insisted it was administered by a multilateral organisation, the Organisation for European Economic

Cooperation (OEEC). The United States sought to create an integrated economic community in Western Europe.

America looked to Britain to play a leading role in the development of European unity. Churchill had given federalists hope with his call for Anglo-French union in 1940, and for a United States of Europe in his 1946 Zurich speech. Churchill, however, saw Britain as having a wider role than just Europe. He envisaged three sets of overlapping interests; Europe, North America and the Commonwealth. It was significant that in the Zurich speech Churchill saw Franco-German not Anglo-French rapprochement as the key to West European unity. Spinelli observed the 'poorly organized federalist movements . . . were completely deceived by Churchillian rhetoric' (1972, p. 59). In substance Churchill's position was similar to Bevin's, the Labour Foreign Secretary, who strove to cement the Anglo-American relationship as the basis for the retention of a global role. Bevin thus sought to be America's partner in Europe. He supported European unity calling for a Western union in 1948. Bevin's vision though was one of inter-governmentalism with consultation and co-operation between states, not federalism. The Labour Government accepted the OEEC and ensured the Council of Europe, established in 1949, would remain a consultative body. The establishment of the North Atlantic Treaty Organisation (NATO) in 1949 committing America to the defence of Western Europe was the crowning achievement of Bevin's policy.

The European Coal and Steel Community

Post-war French foreign policy was directed to the question of Germany. In May 1950 Robert Schuman, the French foreign minister, proposed that French and German coal and steel production be placed under a 'common High Authority in an organisation open to the participation of other countries of Europe'. The Schuman Plan for a European Steel and Coal Community (ECSC) provided for both economic integration and security against German rearmament. Jean Monnet, head of the French Planning Commission, was the prime mover of the ECSC. He saw the High Authority as a supranational body, and as the first step on the road to a federal Europe. Britain rejected the Plan believing it threatened national autonomy and sovereignty. West Germany, Italy, Belgium, the Netherlands, and Luxembourg agreed to join the ECSC with France.

In practice the ECSC was not a stepping stone to federalism. Its organisation did have a supranational element in the High Authority, but a Council of Ministers ensured national interests were represented.

The European Defence Community

France launched a second supranational initiative in 1950, the European Defence Community (EDC). It was designed to allow West German rearmament through a federal European army. The project was ill-fated; Churchill, who had returned to office in 1951, opposed it, and the French National Assembly refused to ratify the treaty in 1954. Defence proved too sensitive a subject for a federal solution. Britain proposed an alternative to EDC, inviting West Germany and Italy to join Britain, France and the Benelux countries in signing the Brussels Treaty that predated NATO. London proposed that the members signing the Treaty should form a Western European Union (WEU), which would control West German rearmament within NATO. The British proposal was successful and the WEU became subsumed within NATO.

The European Economic Community

At the Messina Conference of 1955, the six member states of the ECSC met to examine proposals on further economic integration and nuclear energy. A customs union leading to a common market was envisaged. An intergovernmental committee was charged with developing these proposals. British participation ceased when it became clear that the Spaak proposals involved more than a free trade association. Instead Britain founded the European Free Trade Association (EFTA) in 1960. In 1957 the Six signed in the two Treaties of Rome establishing the European Economic Community (EEC) and the European Atomic Energy Community (EURATOM).

The institutions were based on the ECSC with a Council of Ministers representing national governments and a Commission forming the supranational element. The EEC began effectively, and tariff barriers were removed on schedule to create a common market. Rapid economic growth amongst the Six facilitated these developments of the EEC.

The Community Crisis of 1965

Progress towards the supranational management of the European economies was not straightforward. In 1959 de Gaulle, the French President, proposed closer political co-operation amongst the Six but on an intergovernmental basis. Whilst the initiative failed it indicated the Gaullist stress upon nation-states, not federalism, as the basis for European unity; a position similar to Britain's. In 1965 French agricultural interests and opposition to supranationalism combined to produce a crisis in the EEC. France sought agreement for the development of the Common Agricultural Policy (CAP), and the Commission's response was to tie it to new budget arrangements for the Commission and enhanced powers for the European Parliament. In July 1965 France withdrew its representatives from the decision-making bodies of the EEC. The French protest was 'not so much about its inability to get its way on agricultural policy nor about the latter's incorporation into a package, but more about the political or supranational elements of the package' (Urwin, 1991, p. 111). The crisis was resolved in January 1966 when the Six agreed to the 'Accords de Luxembourg', which effectively granted member states a veto if their vital interests are threatened. From 1966 onwards the Council, not the Commission, determined the progress towards integration.

Summits and Enlargement

The Paris Summit of 1974 formalised intergovernmentalism as the process of decision-making. Summit meetings of heads of government and state were institutionalised as the European Council. It became the key decision making body of the European Community.

The enlargement of the European Community reinforced intergovernmentalism and the summit approach. Denmark, Ireland and Britain joined in 1973. Greece joined in 1981, and Spain and Portugal in 1986. Enlargement complicated decision making by making more complex the pattern of national interests represented in the European Community. The accession of Britain proved a different problem. Under the Labour Government in the 1970s the terms of accession were renegotiated and tested successfully in a referendum. Margaret Thatcher's policy towards the European Community was strident in presentation and defensive in character. She sought a change in the cost of Britain's membership and demanded 'our money back'. Her approach reinforced the image of Britain as the reluctant European.

The Single European Act

The Fontainebleau Summit in June 1984 established a committee to review possible ways to enhance integration. The Dooge Report recommended strengthening the Commission and European Parliament, reducing the need for unanimity in the Council of Ministers, and establishing an intergovernmental conference to plan these reforms. The conference was established in June 1985, and reported to the Luxembourg Summit in December 1985. The Summit agreed to several reforms and amended the Treaty of Rome by the Single European Act (SEA). It set the deadline of the end of 1992 to complete the single market, where trade barriers would be removed and 'the free movement of goods, persons, services and capital is ensured'. Voting in the Council of Ministers was amended to limit the requirement of unanimity to new policy proposals only. Margaret Thatcher welcomed the single market but remained wary of further integration. Britain also supported the formalisation of co-ordination procedures for foreign policy known as European Political Cooperation (EPC).

The Road to Maastricht

The SEA provided new impetus to integration and European union. At the heart of the new momentum was a Franco-German alignment of interests facilitated by favourable political and economic conditions. The Hannover Summit in June 1988 called on the President of the Commission, Jacques Delors, to report on the stages required for Economic and Monetary Union (EMU). The Delors Report envisaged that all member states would participate in the Exchange Rate Mechanism (ERM), establish a European central bank and adopt a single currency.

Margaret Thatcher's reaction was negative. In her Bruges speech she called for a Europe of States based on co-operation between 'independent sovereign states', and rejected the idea of a 'European conglomerate'. Within her Cabinet there was support for the ERM from the then Chancellor, Nigel Lawson, and the Foreign Secretary, Geoffrey Howe. At the Madrid Summit in June 1989 Margaret

Thatcher accepted sterling's participation in the ERM, though later attached conditions to its entry. This did not reassure the Chancellor who resigned in October 1989. Margaret Thatcher remained on the offensive and was the sole leader at the Rome Summit in 1990 not to endorse the rest of the Delors Report. She retorted:

> It seems like cloud cuckoo land. . . . If anyone is suggesting that I would go to Parliament and suggest the abolition of the pound sterling – no! . . . We have made it quite clear that we will not have a single currency imposed on us. (Watkins, 1991, p. 142)

In the House of Commons the Prime Minister continued her attack on the European Community precipitating Geoffrey Howe's resignation and her isolation.

At the Strasbourg Summit in December 1989 it was agreed to hold an intergovernmental conference on EMU. The Dublin Summit in April 1990 discussed Franco-German ideas for political union and established another intergovernmental conference on political union. The two conferences began in December 1990 and completed their work at the Maastricht Summit in December 1991. The Maastricht Summit reached agreement on EMU and political union.

Policy-making in the European Community

This section explores the roles of its main institutions – the European Commission, Council of Ministers, European Council, European Parliament and Court of Justice; and then examines their interplay in making policy.

European Commission

The European Commission, formerly the High Authority, employs about 16,000 staff mainly located in Brussels. It is headed by the College of Commissioners, consisting of 17 Commissioners appointed by the governments of member states. Each member state appoints at least one and the five largest member states (France, Germany, Italy, Spain and the United Kingdom) appoint two Commissioners. The Major Government recently renewed the appointments of Leon Brittan and Bruce Millan as the two British Commissioners.

Though obliged formally to be independent, Commissioners are 'national champions who defend national positions in the Commission' because they are appointed by and maintain close links with their national governments' (Ludlow, 1991, p. 90). Margaret Thatcher refused to renew the appointment of Lord Cockfield because he had 'gone native' in pushing for the completion of the single market. The President of the Commission, currently Jacques Delors, is appointed after informal discussions between member states and consultations with the European Parliament. He allocates policy portfolios between Commissioners, after considerable informal pressure from national governments and Commissioners. There are 23 'directorates-general' reporting to the responsible Commissioners, which constitute the bureaucracy of the European Community.

The role of the Commission is threefold; it initiates policy, oversees the implementation of policy, and acts as the guardian of the treaties establishing the European Community. As policy initiator, the Commission puts forward proposals to the Council of Ministers for decision. This formal power of policy initiation allows the Commission to control the policy-making agenda. The Council of Ministers can only amend a proposal with the agreement of the Commission, or if without its agreement, by acting unanimously. No decision can be made in the European Community without first being drafted by the Commission. However, the Council of Ministers can request the Commission to draw up proposals for its deliberation. Moreover, the European Commission does not generally put forward proposals if there is little chance of them being accepted by the Council of Ministers. Consequently, it consults very widely with national governments, interest groups and others before drafting proposals to ensure their political feasibility.

As overseer of policy implementation, the Commission does not implement many policies itself but supervises their implementation by national governments. It is very dependent upon member states for implementing policy, and as a result, there are often many 'implementation gaps' where national governments are unable or unwilling to implement policy. Britain has a better record at incorporating European Community law into national law than most other member states, though it has not fully implemented some directives mainly in the environment field. The Commission plays a greater role in implementing policy where it exercises delegated rule-making powers. It represents the European Community in its dealings with many international bodies and non-member states. It manages the external trade relations of the European Community, and plays a key role in the negotiations under the auspices of the General Agreement on Tariffs and Trade (GATT).

As legal guardian of the European Community, the Commission is responsible for ensuring that the laws of the European Community are observed. If laws are not respected, the Commission can refer matters to the European Court of Justice and impose fines in certain cases. It ruled that the Conservative Government's payment of a 'sweetener' to British Aerospace for taking over the Rover car company was illegal, and consequently British Aerospace have had to return nearly £60 million. The Commission is the watchdog of the European Community.

The Commission thus performs both bureaucratic and executive functions. It is more powerful than a traditional civil service because of its powers to initiate policy, and less powerful because of its lack of powers to implement policy.

Council of Ministers

The Council of Ministers is the main decision-making body within the European Community. It consists of one representative, usually a minister, from each member state. The Council is an intergovernmental body representing the interests of member states. Ministers serving on the Council are 'concerned about the impact of any decisions made in Brussels on the people back home and about the impact of those decisions on any upcoming elections' (Peters, 1992, p. 79).

Though there is only one Council of Ministers, its membership varies according to the policy area being discussed. Finance ministers attend meetings of the Council of Economics and Financial Questions (ECOFIN), and agriculture ministers attend those of the Agricultural Council. There are about 12 specialised Technical Councils, whose work is co-ordinated by the General Affairs Council consisting of foreign ministers. The Council has a rotating presidency, with each member state holding the presidency for a six-month period. The Presidency attempts to secure agreement between member states, and works closely with the Commission.

Below the Council of Ministers is a sub-structure of bodies servicing its proceedings. Each member state keeps a delegation of its civil servants in Brussels, known as its Permanent Representation. The Committee of Permanent Representatives (COREPER) is a committee of national civil servants that prepares the work of the Council. It acts as an intermediary between Brussels and the national capitals, and serves to safeguard 'national interests'. Similarly, the Special Committee on Agriculture (SCA) prepares the work of the Agricultural Council, and the Political Committee (PoCo) the work of the General Affairs Council within the EPC framework. About '80 percent of the Council's acts are decided on a professional bureaucratic level' (Wessels, 1991, p. 140).

The principal role of the Council is to legislate after receiving proposals from the Commission. Generally, the Commission proposes and the Council disposes. However, for a wide range of legislative matters the Council can only legislate after receiving opinions from the European Parliament and the Economic and Social Committee, though their opinions are not binding upon the Council. The Council refers proposals from the Commission for consideration to working parties, consisting of officials of the member states. COREPER, SCA and PoCo examine the recommendations of working parties, and attempt to resolve differences between member states before submitting their recommendations to the Council.

There are three different voting procedures in the Council. First, there is unanimity voting which is required when a new policy is being considered and when the Council wants to amend a proposal against the wishes of the Commission. The 'Accords de Luxembourg' of 1966 allows for a member state to exercise a veto if 'very important interests are at stake'. This veto has not been exercised frequently by member states. In 1982 the Thatcher Government vetoed a settlement of farm prices because of the dispute over its budgetary contributions to the European Community. Second, there is qualified majority voting which is required when a modification of an existing policy is being considered and when many matters relating to the single market programme are being discussed. Under this procedure the votes are weighted between member states, with the larger member states receiving more votes than the smaller ones. Third, there is simple majority voting which is required when procedural matters are being considered. The outcome of a vote depends to a large extent upon the procedure adopted. In 1993 the Council of Ministers, under qualified majority voting, agreed to limit the number of working hours of employees. The Major Government, which opposed the decision, is likely to appeal to the Court of Justice that this matter should have been decided unanimously. It could have, therefore, vetoed the proposal.

The Council is the legislature of the European Community. It is schizophrenic in the way it performs this role. Ministers are keenly aware to defend the 'national interest' in the Council but are also anxious to present their positions as serving the wider 'European interest'. The splintered structure of the Council of Ministers and its membership serving national governments 'have produced a policy environment which is both disaggregated and competitive' (Wallace, 1983, p. 65).

European Council

In 1974 member states agreed that heads of government and state should meet regularly as the European Council. They, accompanied by their foreign ministers and the President of the Commission, meet at least twice a year.

The agenda of these summit meetings is drawn up by the member state holding the Presidency of the European Community. Much of the preparatory work for these meetings is carried out by ministers, particularly foreign ministers. The Presidency 'plays an increasingly central role as a manager, initiator, and co-ordinator (consensus-broker) of EC affairs' (Kirchner, 1992, p. 87). For example, John Major embarked on 'a charm tour' of the national capitals in the run-up to the Edinburgh Summit of December 1992. The Presidency allows each member state to shape the agenda of the European Community. The European Council possesses no legal powers to make decisions. Its main roles are to resolve conflicts between member states and decide upon the future direction of the European Community.

The European Council attempts to resolve disputes that cannot be resolved in the Council of Ministers. It 'was quickly sucked into the political vacuum at the centre of the Community: to take decisions that the Council of ministers was unable to take' (Pinder, 1991, p. 28). Politically it is the final court of appeal. Given the fragmented and specialised structure of the Council of Ministers compromises that cut across policy areas were difficult to forge, until 'decision-making at the European Council level opened the way for participation of the top national decision-makers and for package deals which enlarged the EC decision-making capacities' (Kirchner, 1992, p. 6).

The European Council maps out the future of the European Community. It has addressed issues related to the enlargement of the European Community, the development of the European Community, and wider international problems such as the collapse of communism in Eastern Europe. The European Council has largely replaced the Commission as the main impetus behind the development of the European Community.

The European Council is an intergovernmental body. It sets the parameters within which the European Community develops, and resolves disputes between member states. The European Council makes 'no collective pretence at supranationalism' (Urwin, 1991, p. 175). Instead it concerns itself with forging compromises between competing interests of member states.

European Parliament

The European Parliament is located in three sites, with its plenary sessions being held in Strasbourg. Since 1979 it has been a directly elected body. There are 518 MEPs elected every five years, which will be increased to 567 MEPs after the 1994 Euro-election. In the Euro-election of 1989 there was nearly a 60 per cent turnout, though turnout was under 40 per cent in Britain. The number of MEPs that each member state elects reflects the population size of each country, with Germany sending the most and Luxembourg the least MEPs. Britain has 81 MEPs, and will elect 87 MEPs in the 1994 Euro-election.

Euro-elections are fought largely on national party lines. After the 1989 Euro-election the unpopularity of the Thatcher Government meant the Conservative Party won only 32 seats compared to the 45 seats won by the Labour Party, and the Green Party received a large 'protest' vote. Though the Green Party gained the largest share of votes of all 'green' parties in the European Community, it failed to return any MEPs because of the first-past-the-post electoral system operating in Britain. Once elected MEPs form transnational political groups. The largest groups are the Socialists, embracing the Labour MEPs, and the Christian Democrats, embracing the Conservative MEPs. In 1991 Conservative MEPs were allowed eventually to join the Christian Democrats, mainly because Margaret Thatcher had been replaced by John Major whose Government is less hostile towards the European Community. Though the political groups are organised on essentially ideological lines they are often divided on national lines over specific issues. They are not as disciplined as national parliamentary parties.

The European Parliament is not a legislature but an assembly. It is an advisory and supervisory body. As an advisory body, the European Parliament is obliged to issue opinions on draft legislation. The Council of Ministers must consider its opinions before legislating, but is not bound by them. The Council must consult with the European Parliament on most matters before making decisions, though sometimes it makes a decision pending an opinion of the European Parliament. This right of consultation gives the European Parliament some influence, particularly if it delays giving an opinion. The SEA supplemented the traditional consultation procedure with a new co-operation procedure. This procedure applies to certain matters only, particularly those relating to the single market programme, and makes it more difficult for the Council to ignore the opinions of the European Parliament. The European Parliament exercises more influence over setting the budget of the European Community and making of accession and association agreements with the European Community. As a supervisory body, the European Parliament attempts to scrutinise the work of the Commission and the Council of Ministers. It can table questions to them, debate the annual report and accounts of the Commission, inquire into their operations in its plenary and committee sessions, and sack the entire College of Commissioners. The European Parliament does not possess sufficient powers to control effectively what goes on in the European Community.

Although its powers have increased, the European Parliament 'has generally been regarded as a somewhat ineffective institution' (Nugent, 1991, p. 129). Many have argued for greater powers for the European Parliament to remedy the perceived 'democratic deficit' in the European Community.

Court of Justice

The Court of Justice, based in Luxembourg, consists of 13 judges, who are appointed by the governments of member states. Each member state appoints one judge, and one of the larger member states in turn appoints two judges. Because of the increasing workload of the Court of Justice, the SEA established the Court of First Instance to hear certain specified cases.

European Community law is binding upon member states, and takes precedence over national laws. National courts are obliged to uphold European Community law. The applicability of European Community law, however, is often contested. There is much dispute in Britain whether the Acquired Rights Directive, which protects the conditions of employment of workers affected in a transfer of undertaking, is applicable to undertakings transferred from the public to the private sector. The Major Government argues the directive does not apply to workers involved in contracting-out public services to private contractors. Generally when services have been contracted-out fewer workers have been employed and employed on worse pay and conditions by private contractors. For the Government contracting-out 'saves' money, but if the directive applies these 'savings' would largely disappear and the Government's contracting-out programme would be holed. There are several court cases, some of which are likely to go to the Court of Justice, to decide on the applicability of the directive.

The role of the Court of Justice is to enforce the law of the European Community. It interprets and applies the law when there are disputes. In 1986 the Court of Justice ruled that a woman employee had the right under European Community law to retire at the same time as a man, and consequently the British Government was forced to change the law to comply with its ruling. The Court of Justice is the final court of appeal in upholding European Community law. It is a quasi-constitutional court, which 'is frequently as much a maker as an interpreter of law' (Nugent, 1991, p. 191).

Governing the European Community

Decision-making in the European Community rests on the critical axis between the Council of Ministers and the European Commission. Their relations reflect a fundamental tension in the European Community. The structure of the European Community 'contains elements of supranationalism and elements of intergovernmentalism' (George, 1991, p. 16). The Council of Ministers and European Council are essentially intergovernmental structures, in which national governments strike intergovernmental bargains and veto proposals. The European Commission, European Parliament and Court of Justice are largely supranational structures, in which the accommodation of the competing and conflicting positions of national governments is mediated by relatively detached institutions to produce common policies. The tension between intergovernmentalism and supranationalism haunts the development of the European Community. The 'Accords de Luxembourg' of 1966, the emergence of the European Council, the introduction of majority voting in the Council of Ministers, and the passionate debates over sovereignty in the United Kingdom and other countries are all manifestations of this tension.

Policy-making in the European Community involves the interplay of many institutions, representing 'arenas of power' in which a myriad of actors defend their interests. These institutions are dissected by many political, bureaucratic and professional networks. Wallace argued that 'despite the attempts by governments to set up gatekeeping mechanisms, transnational networks of policy-making elites have emerged and become increasingly significant' (1983, p. 77). The idea of the single market programme emerged from a network of interests comprising the European Commission, European Parliament, multinational companies, and key member states. Policy networks have a profound effect on the policy development of the European Community. The process of 'engrenage' represents the growing bureaucratic interpenetration between the Commission and government officials of member states. This 'system of bureaucratic intermingling' transposes a network of interests over the formal structures of the European Community (Ludlow, 1991, p. 103). Policy-making in the European Community is competitive, fragmented and interdependent.

The Future of the European Community/Union

This concluding section looks at the future development of the European Community/Union. It focuses upon the Maastricht Treaty and the 'deepening and widening' processes of the European Community, and explores the tensions between the integration, interdependence and autonomy of member states shaping the development of the European Community.

Drafting the Maastricht Treaty

The Treaty on European Union was negotiated at the Maastricht Summit in December 1991, though formally signed on 7 February 1992. The Maastricht Treaty represents a significant milestone in the development of the European Community. It is an integrationist blueprint that envisages further deepening and widening of the European Community. Its supporters regard the Treaty as a significant landmark in forging 'an ever closer union' of Europe. Its opponents, such as Margaret Thatcher, regard it as 'a treaty too far' representing a fundamental attack on the sovereignty of independent nation-states. Other critics point to serious design faults in the Maastricht Treaty, especially its plans to achieve EMU, and claim to have been vindicated by subsequent events, most notably 'Black Wednesday'.

The Treaty is a compromise attempting to weld together the different interests of the twelve member states. Germany wanted to secure economic and political support for its unification project and its increasing role in Eastern Europe; France wanted to bind Germany even further into the European Community as a means of curbing her influence; Spain wanted extra monies from the European Community to compensate for the costs of integration and to modernise its economy; while Britain was clear only on what it did not want. The Major Government did not want a single currency, a commitment to enhance the rights of workers, a supranational element in the making of foreign and security policy, and a 'federal destiny'. As a result the Major Government secured opt-outs from the key stages of EMU and provisions of the Social Chapter, persuaded the other member states to exclude the European Commission from the making of foreign and other sensitive policies, and deleted any reference to the 'federal destiny' of the European Community from the Treaty. The Maastricht Treaty was widely recognised as a negotiating triumph for John Major, who proclaimed the Treaty as 'game, set and match' for Britain. At the time many believed that the Treaty would secure John Major's reputation as bringing Britain back into the heart of the European Community, and also keep the Conservative Party together by appeasing both its 'Eurosceptics' and 'Europhiles'. This view proved to be premature since the Franco-German axis remained dominant within the European Community, and the Conservative Party was torn apart in ratifying the Maastricht Treaty.

The Maastricht Treaty 'marks a new stage in the process of creating an ever closer union among the peoples of Europe, in which decisions are taken as closely as possible to the citizen'. It contains six key provisions affecting the development of the European Community and public policy in Britain.

First, the Treaty establishes the timetable towards EMU, which has long been on the agenda of the European Community. At the Hague Summit of 1969 the EEC committed itself to establishing EMU, and established a committee to make the necessary plans to achieve economic and monetary union by 1980. However, the Werner Report was never fully implemented because of French objections about loss of national sovereignty. In 1972 the Joint European Float, known as the 'snake-in-the-tunnel', was set up where currencies would be kept within certain bands. In anticipation of joining the EEC Britain joined the 'snake' but departed within a few weeks of sterling's entry because it had used most of its foreign exchange reserves in defending sterling against speculative pressure. The 'snake' collapsed later because of international monetary crises and speculative pressures against member currencies. Roy Jenkins as President of the European Commission, with Franco-German support, relaunched the idea of EMU. In 1978 the European Monetary System (EMS) was designed to achieve monetary stability. The ERM was the mechanism in which currency stability was to be achieved. Like the 'snake', it required governments to keep their currencies within certain bands; but unlike its predecessor, it encouraged them to realign their currencies if market pressures forced the currencies outside the bands and required them to support other currencies to keep within their specified bands. The EMS, with the ERM, did provide exchange rate stability throughout the 1980s. Following the Hannover Summit of 1988, the Delors Committee wanted to build on the perceived success of the EMS, and proposed the establishment of EMU. The Delors Report shaped the provisions of EMU contained in the Maastricht Treaty. There are three proposed stages in completing EMU. Stage One, which began in 1990, involves the participation of all currencies in the ERM, and the co-ordination of economic and monetary policies of member states; Stage Two, planned to begin in 1994, establishes the European Monetary Institute (EMI) to oversee the convergence of economic and monetary policies of member states; and Stage Three, beginning no later than 1999 for those member states who meet the convergence criteria, sets up a European System of Central Banks (ECSB) with a European Central Bank (ECB), and introduces a single currency. Britain opted out of the last stage, reflecting the Major Government's objections to a single currency, but may opt in later if Parliament agrees. In the run-up to the Maastricht Summit the British Government put forward an alternative plan based on the 'hard ecu', where the European Currency Unit

(Ecu) would become a trading currency along with other currencies. Market forces would decide whether there would be a single currency, and what currency it would be. This 'hard ecu' plan attracted no support with the rest of the European Community, still committed to the Franco-German dream of a single currency.

Second, the Maastricht Treaty contains a separate protocol outlining several social policy provisions, together known as the Social Chapter. They stem largely from the Social Charter adopted at the Strasbourg Summit in 1989. This Charter was signed by all member states except Britain. It is not binding upon member states; it is only a declaration, from which the European Commission will draw up proposals for decision by the Council of Ministers. Margaret Thatcher believed that the Social Charter would let in 'socialism through the back door', and opposed its adoption because it would have reversed her Government's attempts to deregulate the labour market. The Social Chapter provides legislative force to the Social Charter. It provides for a minimum level of working conditions throughout the European Community (e.g. dialogue between management and workers), though its provisions specifically exclude the setting of a minimum wage. It adds a social dimension to the single market programme. It aims to prevent 'social dumping' whereby companies move to member states with lower labour costs resulting from lower standards of working conditions, such as Hoover's decision to relocate one of its plants from France to Scotland. The Major Government opted out of the Social Chapter because it would have increased the costs of employing labour in Britain, making British companies less competitive and Britain less attractive for foreign investment.

Third, the Treaty enshrines the principle of subsidiarity, and states in areas outside its competence the European Community 'shall take action . . . only if and in so far as the objectives of the proposed action cannot be sufficiently achieved by the Member States and can therefore . . . be better achieved by the Community'. This legally binding principle was fleshed out further at the Birmingham Summit in 1992. The application of this test of subsidiarity, that the European Community should only act if member states are unable to act effectively, still remains vague. Indeed, Jacques Delors offered Ecu 200,000 to anyone who could define subsidiarity on one side of paper. The Major Government saw the principle of subsidiarity as a way of trimming the powers of the European Commission, and thus preserving national sovereignty. It is likely to use this principle to counter proposals from the Commission that it feels encroach in areas which should be left to national governments. Other member states, such as Germany, saw subsidiarity as embodying a commitment to federalism and decentralisation, a view not shared by the Major Government.

Fourth, the Maastricht Treaty grants new powers to the European Parliament that are designed to remedy the 'democratic deficit' of the European Community. The European Parliament is given greater decision-making powers in certain specified areas (e.g. many single market matters), whereby under the new co-decision making procedure the Council of Ministers and the European Parliament must adopt a common position before legislating. Also, it can request the European Commission to submit proposals for legislation, and veto the appointment of the European Commission. Britain, with France, were not keen to grant the European Parliament more powers preferring to retain an intergovernmental approach to decision-making that allows national governments to protect their interests in the European Community. The House of Commons is also fearful of an increasingly powerful European Parliament because it wants to protect what is left of parliamentary sovereignty.

Fifth, the Treaty on European Union sets up the Committee of the Regions. This body consists of representatives of regional and local authorities appointed by their national governments. The Committee of the Regions is consulted, wherever appropriate, by the European Commission and Council of Ministers, though its opinions are not binding upon them. Its establishment reflects the growing concern of the Lander in Germany that the European Community is increasingly encroaching upon their constitutional powers. The Major Government, deeply suspicious of local authorities, did not want to give them a mouthpiece in Brussels. It resisted unsuccessfully the creation of the Committee of the Regions, but insisted successfully that it appoints the representatives to serve on this body.

Sixth, the Treaty establishes the European Union, consisting of three pillars. The first pillar is the existing European Community which is run on intergovernmental and supranational lines. The European Community is given new responsibilities in several areas, e.g. education, public health, and environment. Furthermore, it is charged with promoting economic and social cohesion, involving providing financial assistance to its poorer regions, who stand to lose most in completing the single market and EMU. These cohesion funds consolidated the support of the poorer member states (e.g. Greece,

Spain and Portugal) for the Maastricht Treaty generally and EMU particularly.

The second pillar established by the Maastricht Treaty allows for intergovernmental co-operation in the field of justice and home affairs. This pillar includes co-operation on asylum, immigration, customs, judicial and policing matters. A European Police Office (Europol) will be set up to facilitate the exchange of information between police forces, especially information on terrorism, fraud and drug trafficking. The TREVI group of justice ministers had previously been involved in these areas despite the lack of provision in the Treaty of Rome. Furthermore, the Schengen Accord of 1985, signed by several member states of the European Community (but not Britain), provided for intergovernmental co-operation in many of these areas, though it has been bedevilled by problems of implementation. The TREVI group and the Schengen Accord provide the bases for the second pillar on justice and home affairs.

The third pillar of the European Union allows for intergovernmental co-operation in the field of foreign and security policy (see Chapter 15).

Seventh, the Maastricht Treaty states that citizens of member states are also citizens of the European Union, and thus enjoy certain additional rights. Citizens have the right to move freely within the European Community, to vote and stand as a candidate in local and Euro-elections wherever they reside, to diplomatic and consular representation by the embassies of any member state, and to petition an ombudsman about complaints of maladministration against any institution of the European Community.

Ratifying the Maastricht Treaty

The ratification of the Maastricht Treaty has proven a difficult process. The most significant opposition was found in Britain and Denmark. A referendum in Denmark in June 1992 rejected the Treaty, with 50.7 per cent of votes opposed. Following the Danish vote President Mitterrand announced France would hold a referendum. In the Irish referendum of June 1992 the debate centred on the implications of European Union for constitutional restrictions on abortion. The clear majority of Irish voters, none the less, supported the Treaty.

The Lisbon Summit in June 1992 decided to proceed with ratification despite the Danish rejection. The problem was that the Treaty of

Rome requires unanimous consent for constitutional revision. European Community leaders hoped Denmark would soon 'return to the fold', though confidence was eroded subsequently by the result of the French referendum in September 1992. French voters gave only marginal approval, with 51.05 per cent of votes cast in favour of the Maastricht Treaty. In light of the French vote, Danish rejection and mounting problems in the ERM, John Major, then holder of the Presidency, called a special summit in October 1992. The Birmingham Summit agreed to continue with ratification and rejected renegotiation of the Treaty.

In Britain the Bill to ratify the Treaty had been approved at its second reading in May but parliamentary consideration was suspended after the Danish referendum. The Prime Minister faced cabinet divisions, backbench opposition, Labour Party opposition to the exclusion of the Social Chapter, and pressure on sterling. Membership of the ERM required a high level of interest rates to maintain sterling's value against the Deutschmark which aggravated economic recession. The Chancellor of the Exchequer, Norman Lamont, claimed the Government was 'prepared to do whatever is necessary to maintain sterling's parity within the ERM'. He rejected leaving the ERM and cutting interest rates, which he called the 'cut and run option'. Yet the Government did 'cut and run' as pressure on sterling mounted in September. On 16 September 1992 substantial foreign reserves were used to support sterling and interest rates were put up to 15 per cent before defeat was acknowledged and membership of the ERM suspended. 'Black Wednesday' strengthened the Maastricht Treaty's critics, and the Conservative Party's conference in October revealed deep divisions over the Treaty. In November John Major secured only a three-vote majority to resume ratification and promptly announced Britain would await the outcome of the second Danish referendum.

In December 1992 the Edinburgh Summit overcame Danish objections to the Treaty by providing Denmark with opt-outs of citizenship of the European Union, a common defence policy, a single currency and co-operation in justice and home affairs. In May 1993 the Danes endorsed the Maastricht Treaty, with 56.8 per cent of votes cast in the second referendum supporting it. The Danish decision effectively left Britain amongst the twelve as the sole 'problem' member state.

The former Prime Minister, Margaret Thatcher, called for a referendum to determine Britain's decision. She described how 'we got our fingers burned' in negotiating the SEA which established the single market. She warned 'don't now go back to that same fire with a much bigger treaty with many more powers and get both your arms and perhaps your head burned as well'. The motion for a referendum was put and lost in the House of Lords. In the House of Commons the Bill to approve the Maastricht Treaty secured support at its third reading but the crucial parliamentary challenge came in July with Labour's attempt to secure inclusion of the Social Chapter. As John Major maintained his criticism of the Social Chapter as an 'unemployment charter', Conservative 'Euro-rebels' sided with the opposition. They reasoned the Prime Minister could not accept a treaty which included the Social Chapter. On 22 July 1993 the House of Commons voted against the Labour motion by just one vote, but also against John Major's motion noting the Government's policy on the Social Chapter by eight votes. John Major termed the 'Euro-rebels' 'cynical and unscrupulous', and turned to a vote of confidence on government policy, warning of a general election if defeated. This drastic measure completed the parliamentary process with the Government securing a majority of forty votes on 23 July 1993. The final impediments to ratification were court cases to decide the constitutional acceptability of the Treaty. In Britain Lord Rees-Mogg failed to secure a High Court ruling that the ratification process was unconstitutional. In Germany a Federal Constitutional Court ruling on the compatibility of Maastricht Treaty and the Basic Law is expected in October 1993.

Conclusion – Future Directions

The ratification of the Maastricht Treaty confirmed continuing British concerns regarding loss of autonomy to the European Community and opposition to federalism. It revealed also the gulf between decision makers and public opinion on European Union, not just in Britain but in Denmark and France too. The completion of the ratification process does not end the difficulties facing European Union. The probable widening of the European Community to new members challenges the congruence of interests necessary to sustain integration. Membership applications have been made by Austria, Sweden, Finland, Switzerland, Norway, Turkey, Morocco, Malta and Cyprus. Several Eastern and Central European countries have also announced their intention to apply for membership. The accession of the richer EFTA countries such as Austria, Sweden, Norway and Finland is likely to pose the least challenge to the balance of interests compared to the impact of membership of poorer Eastern and Southern European states (see Nugent, 1992). Of greater immediate significance to the fate of European Union was the virtual collapse of the ERM in early August 1993. The immediate cause of the crisis was a German decision not to cut interest rates. The effect in the ERM was to sustain recessionary pressures in other member states. The ERM was effectively abandoned when members decided that currencies (except the Dutch and German currencies) could float up to 15 per cent above or below their notional parities. The decision freed economic policies but questioned the attainment of a single currency. Amid European Community-wide attempts to rescue the EMU blueprint, John Major believed the timetable for EMU was 'totally unrealistic', and Kenneth Clarke, the Chancellor, claimed that 'exchange rate stability cannot be imposed from the centre – it can only come from convergence in economic policy objectives and outcomes'. Norman Lamont, the former Chancellor, went further and declared it 'dead, redundant and a bit of a fossil'. Whichever forecast proves correct, the process of deepening in the European Community is encountering a major obstacle which challenges the post-Maastricht dream of European Union.

Part II
Substantive Policy Areas

5

Economic Policy under the Conservatives

MIKE DUNN and SANDY SMITH

Introduction

Economics, if it is a science at all, is a science of fashions, in which differing theories hold sway over policy-makers for some time until they no longer seem so attractive. Sometimes the new fashions emerge slowly: at other times, the inadequacies of the old are ruthlessly exposed in public collapse. Unusually, during 1992–3 there were two such collapses: in the events of 'Black Wednesday' (16 September 1992) the UK government was forced ignominiously to withdraw the £ sterling from the European Exchange Rate Mechanism (ERM). Then in August 1993, the ERM itself effectively collapsed, throwing European economic policy into disarray. These momentous events signalled the end of a line of British economic policy that can be traced back to 1987, and set a challenging new context for economic policy in the 1990s. By mid-1993 it was far from clear that the government was rising to this challenge.

In this chapter we look at the longer run background to these events, and consider some of the main issues that will face policy-makers in Britain in the 1990s.

The Thatcher Revolution

The election of the Thatcher government in 1979 marked an important change in fashion in government economic policies. The main reason

77

was a growing disillusionment with the 'Keynesianism' approach on which economic policy in Britain since 1945 had been based. This approach emphasised the role of spending (aggregate demand for goods and services) in determining the level of economic activity. By regulating spending, governments controlled the level of unemployment and the rate of inflation; and by maintaining a steady increase in spending, the government stimulated increases in productivity and in standards of living. Furthermore, the theory suggested that, while the supply of money had some influence, the most effective way of regulating spending was by adjusting the relationship between government spending and government revenues – that is, by means of fiscal (budgetary) policy. Thus government spending, employment and rising standards of living were seen to be closely interconnected.

Although this Keynesian approach seemed to work tolerably well in the 1950s and 1960s, during the 1970s rising inflation, an increasing tax burden, and a growing perception that nationalised industries and the public sector generally were inefficient in terms of controlling costs, meeting public demand and in labour relations, led to an increasing disillusionment. From this arose a widespread acceptance of 'Monetarism', whose ideas were central to the economic policy of the Thatcher government from its election in 1979 through to 1985.

The three basic objectives of Government economic policy became: to bring inflation under control, to reduce the economic role of the government, and to curb the power of trade unions. These objectives were perceived to be complementary. The theoretical foundation of the new approach was that inflation was caused by excessive levels of spending, and that the level of spending depended on the amount of money in circulation (the money supply).

This approach gave rise to the Medium Term Financial Strategy (MTFS), which linked targets for the rate of growth of the money supply to targets for government borrowing which were consistent with these monetary targets. The criteria for determining government spending became not (as had been the case since the 1950s) 'what effect will the level of government spending have on output and employment?', but instead 'how can we finance a given level of government spending?' The government accepted that a short-run cost of reducing the rate of growth of the money supply by reducing the PSBR was that, as markets adjusted, there would be a transitional increase in unemployment. The quicker that people and markets adjusted to this, then the shorter this would last. Should trade unions resist the necessary adjustments and/or pursue unrealistic pay claims, the result would be persistently higher levels of unemployment. At its simplest, governments were responsible for inflation: trade unions caused unemployment.

Changing Emphasis

However, for the first four years the government, in fact, found itself quite unable to reduce either the rate of growth of the money supply (mainly because it proved in practice to be too difficult to define usefully, or to predict, or to stabilise), or indeed to control the overall level of government spending. Despite this the rate of inflation did fall dramatically, from 22 per cent p.a. in 1980 to 3.7 per cent p.a. in 1983. This cast doubt on the proposition that inflation was indeed caused by an excessive rate of growth of the money supply, and this led to a gradual reappraisal of the entire approach to economic policy.

Although failing to control the rate of growth of the money supply, the government's attempts so to do caused a large increase in interest rates, which in turn attracted funds from abroad. Consequently the exchange rate of the £ sterling rose, despite rapidly rising domestic costs and prices. This inflow of funds was reinforced by a rise in oil exports based on the North Sea oil boom, and by the fact that foreign investors were impressed by the government's policy approach and by its firm resolve to 'be tough' by sticking to its principles despite unemployment levels doubling. The rising exchange rate increased the price competitiveness of foreign imports into Britain, and reduced the competitiveness of British-produced exports in overseas markets.

The effect of all this on industry, particularly manufacturing, was devastating, coming as it did on top of a deep-rooted and long-run neglect of investment requirements for innovation in many sectors. The number of manufacturing jobs fell by almost a quarter between 1979 and 1983, and 'de-industrialisation' became a political as well as an economic issue.

A variation of 'pure' Monetarist theory was that if the government attempted to reduce the rate of growth of the money supply by restricting credit and raising interest rates, funds were attracted into the country from abroad through the foreign exchange market. This caused the exchange rate to rise. This in turn increased competition from imports (now becoming relatively cheaper) and made it more difficult to sell overseas through exports (relatively more expensive).

This increased competition forced domestic producers to reduce costs and hold back increases in prices, so that the rate of inflation was reduced. Thus, according to this view, it was the effects on the exchange rate of policies aimed at restricting the money supply that determined what happened to inflation, and the way to control inflation was to maintain the exchange rate.

This theory seemed to provide a more convincing explanation of what had happened between 1979 and 1983 than did the 'pure' Monetarist approach. By 1985 several influential policy makers, including the Chancellor Nigel Lawson, had come to regard attempts to control the growth of the money supply as not only impractical but misconceived. Controlling inflation was best achieved by using interest rates to maintain a strong exchange rate.

The logical extension of this position was that Britain should join the Exchange Rate Mechanism (ERM) of the European Community (EC), under which the exchange rates of the EC member countries were maintained at a (semi-) fixed rate against each other. By so linking British monetary policies to the policies of other EC countries (especially Germany), an effective anti-inflationary policy would be imposed and British competitiveness with other EC countries maintained. Moreover, a stable exchange rate against Britain's most important trading partners would stimulate trade and investment within the EC. Some also supported ERM entry because it represented a commitment by Britain to the future development and harmonisation of the EC.

Thatcher, however, remained committed to 'pure' Monetarism, and was also increasingly concerned about the direction of development of the EC. She therefore blocked this proposal. Nevertheless, Lawson steadily moved towards his objective, and in early 1987 as inflation began to accelerate Britain effectively 'joined' the ERM in order to control inflation by starting to shadow (maintain a constant sterling exchange rate value against) the German D-mark.

'Supply-side' Policies

Initially, as unemployment rose rapidly in the early 1980s, the rate at which money wages were rising fell by about a half, and the rate of increase fell significantly below the rate of increase of productivity, so that unit labour costs fell. However, as economic activity began to recover from 1982 onwards, the rate of increase of money wages stopped falling, even though unemployment continued to increase (albeit at a slower rate than during 1980–82). More significantly, money wages began to increase faster than productivity so that, by the mid-1980s, unit labour costs in British manufacturing industry were again rising. Unemployment remained at relatively high levels. As the government saw it, workers were 'pricing themselves out of jobs'. Their view was that the key to reducing unemployment was to change, by appropriate 'supply-side' policies, the response of individuals and firms to changing conditions in the market.

In particular, this approach emphasised the need to implement policies which, firstly, improved the way in which the labour market functioned by improving incentives to work, de-regulating, and reducing any 'distortions' which prevented labour working efficiently; and secondly, made markets for goods and services function more efficiently by encouraging greater enterprise on the part of suppliers and stimulating competition by giving people more choice. The overall supply-side strategy was summarised by Chancellor Lawson in 1989:

> Strong sustainable growth is achieved not through any artificial stimulus, but by allowing markets to work again and restoring the enterprise culture; by removing unnecessary restrictions and controls and rolling back the frontiers of the state; by reforming trade union law and promoting all forms of capital ownership; and by reforming and reducing taxation. (Budget Speech, 20 March 1989)

Privatisation

The aims of privatisation were never formulated in its early years, but evolved gradually, with changing emphases over time. Four principal aspects of the policy can be identified:

1. 'de-nationalisation', the sale of publicly owned assets and equity (shares) to the private sector, e.g. British Telecom, British Gas;
2. 'contracting out', subcontracting the provision of publicly financed goods and services to private contractors, e.g. hospital cleaning, refuse collection;
3. 'market testing', giving public agencies wide autonomy to spend budgets and respond to 'market' demand, e.g. hospital trusts, grant maintained schools;

4. 'deregulation', removing regulatory restrictions on enterprise and competition, e.g. the opticians' dispensing monopoly, coach transport regulations.

Privatisation had a number of aims that were not only economic but also political or ideological. To the intention of reducing government involvement in industry was added the wish to promote efficiency and increase 'value for money' by imposing the disciplines of the market-place on public sector organisations and workers. This complemented the desirability of reducing government spending and borrowing to relieve pressure on the PSBR. Encouraging enterprise, flexibility and imagination would also increase the diversity of provision and the exercise of 'choice' by users. In addition, and increasingly after 1985, the emphasis moved towards widening and deepening share ownership as part of 'popular capitalism', seen as desirable in itself as part of the new 'enterprise culture' and also as a political weapon to halt post-1945 'collectivism' in general and socialism in particular.

The government was impressed by various evidence that contrasted the relatively poor performance of the public sector industries with the private sector, particularly in terms of efficiency, meeting public demand, self-financing and labour relations. In fact, the evidence was and remains somewhat inconclusive; in particular, it is not clear that it is the *ownership* as such that matters, but rather the lack of *actual or potential competition* facing publicly owned firms. The government's view, however, was that the root causes lay in the ownership form itself, and the associated lack of incentives to managers to be efficient, 'thrusting' and competitive. To this was added the considerable opportunities for public sector unions to manipulate restrictive practices, seek high wage settlements and block technological innovations, safe in the knowledge that the consequences of this could be absorbed by higher subsidies, higher prices or poorer services to customers with no choice. Private ownership and the pressures from the goods and capital markets would stop this, and set managers free to manage.

In addition, there was the not inconsiderable financial benefit arising from privatisation. Public asset sales themselves raised substantial government revenue, totalling over £50 billion by 1992–3, and the floated-off firms would no longer require government financial support which added to the PSBR. Occasional accusations of 'selling off the family silver' were swamped by the sustained popularity of the process, arising partly from the profits that large numbers of small shareholders were able to make, as well as the income tax cuts made possible (in part) by the increased government revenue and reduced government spending.

Overall then, not only did privatisation fit well into the supply-side macroeconomic policy package, but it also met a number of other government objectives. The catch phrase became 'the business of government is not the government of business' (Nigel Lawson, 1985). By the early 1990s, over half of the public sector of 1979 had been transferred to the private sector. There can be little doubt that the *process* of privatisation was one of the success stories of the 1980s: whether the *performance* will be as successful remains unclear.

The Economics of Conservatism Reviewed

With its emphasis on controlling the money supply, reducing the power of trade unions, and 'rolling back the frontiers of the state', together with its willingness to replace the previous consensus with overt confrontation, Thatcherism appeared to mark a radical break with post-war Keynesian policies. How successful then was Thatcherism in its own time?

As we saw above, the initial effect was to push interest rates and the exchange rates to such high levels that many firms were forced out of business, causing output to fall sharply and unemployment to increase rapidly into the 1980–81 recession. Between 1981 and 1985 the economy slowly recovered. Output and productivity increased, but the rate of growth of output was below that of the rate of growth of productivity so that unemployment continued to increase, reaching a peak of 3.1m in July 1986. The rate of inflation, which had risen to 22 per cent in May 1980, fell rapidly, reaching a low of 2.4 per cent in July 1986. By the mid-1980s, many believed that it had 'created a world in which managers could manage and business could flourish', with British industry now 'leaner and fitter'. Given the importance of both perceptions and expectations in economics, this itself was a significant change.

As demand and output increased, government spending on income support and unemployment benefit fell, while revenue from taxes on income, profits and spending increased rapidly. These developments, together with increasing receipts from privatisation, meant that by

1987 the government's budget was in surplus. As part of the supply-side strategy, the government introduced a series of tax reforms which substantially reduced income and capital gains taxes. This contributed further to people's general sense of well-being. Between 1986 and 1988 demand increased rapidly. To prevent the economy from 'overheating', as we have seen, in 1987 the government adopted a *de facto* policy of maintaining the exchange rate of the £ against the West German DM.

The increase in demand was mainly due to higher spending by households. This was partly financed by higher incomes as the result of increased employment and higher wages. However, it was mainly financed by a substantial increase in borrowing and household indebtedness: the ratio of household debt to disposable income, which had remained steady at 40–45 per cent throughout the 1970s and early 1980s, rose from about 45 per cent in 1982, to just over 50 per cent in 1984, and then to *over 90* per cent in 1990. This was not caused (in any normal sense of the word 'caused') by lower interest rates. Contrary to the widely held popular belief, except for a brief period in 1988 real interest rates were higher throughout the 1980s than at any time since the early 1930s, and very much higher than during the 1970s when household debt in relation to income was significantly lower. The main 'causes' of the increase in household debt in 1986–8 were the effects of specific supply-side policies: the abandonment of direct government controls over lending by banks and building societies, the selling-off of local authority housing, the encouragement of home ownership through tax incentives, and the denationalisation of state industries.

As economic activity accelerated from 1985 onwards and households became more confident about the future the rate of growth of spending raced ahead of the capacity of the economy to meet the demand. Imports increased rapidly, causing a chronic balance-of-trade deficit, and the rate of increase in money wages and inflation accelerated. Rising inflation and the rapidly deteriorating balance of trade undermined confidence in foreign exchange markets that the government could maintain the exchange rate of sterling against the DM. Chancellor Lawson, however, was determined to maintain the exchange rate to control inflationary pressures. Hence, interest rates were increased progressively from June 1988 onwards so that, within just over a year, they had doubled.

At first the effects of this were offset by continuing increases in money wages and asset prices. But as monetary conditions continued to tighten, the full impact of higher interest rates on heavily-indebted households and firms and of rapidly rising labour costs under a 'fixed' exchange rate began to be felt. The rate of growth of household spending slowed down sharply and there was a sharp reduction in company profits. Firms responded by cutting output and laying-off workers. Household confidence began to evaporate, borrowing slowed down and asset prices (including houses) began to fall.

Lawson argued that, to prevent a prolonged recession, it was necessary to cut interest rates, but to ensure that inflation was brought under control (still a primary target), it was also necessary to maintain the exchange rate. This required that the government had to make unambiguously clear its intention to maintain the exchange rate, by entry into the ERM. Thatcher disagreed. As the recession deepened, unemployment rose, mortgage arrears mounted, bankruptcies increased, spending on income support and unemployment benefits increased while revenues from taxes fell, and the surplus in the government's budget was transformed into a budget deficit: eventually even Thatcher was forced to give way, and in October 1990 Britain joined the ERM.

It was the government's economic policies that caused Britain to move into the second recession under Thatcher, not joining the ERM. Indeed, joining was itself an attempt to prevent the economy from entering what turned out to be its most prolonged recession since the 1930s, and helped create the conditions under which Thatcher was eventually forced from office.

Conservatism and British Manufacturing

Despite its emphasis on supply-side policies, Thatcherism led to a serious weakening of Britain's 'manufacturing base', and this left the post-Thatcher era with two constraining legacies: a 'structural' deficit in government's budget and a 'structural' deficit in the balance of trade. Coping with these two legacies is likely to dominate British economic policy over the next decade.

In one very important respect, however, the performance of the manufacturing sector was impressive. In 1979–89 labour productivity in this sector rose by 4.75 per cent per year, compared to only 0.75 per cent per year in 1973-9 and 3.75 per cent per year in 1964–73. Only Japan, among the major industrialised countries, had a superior productivity performance in the 1980s, and the British manufacturing sector significantly narrowed the productivity gap between itself and its overseas competitors. As a result, the share of British manufacturing in total world exports of manufactured goods, which had fallen sharply during the 1970s, was maintained from 1982 on. Had this been achieved through increased investment, output and employment, it could indeed have been the Thatcher 'economic miracle': in fact, it was achieved in a way that significantly reduced the contribution that this important sector made to employment and the balance of trade, thereby creating serious 'structural' imbalances within the economy.

During the second half of the 1980s, like all the leading European economies and Japan, Britain experienced an investment boom. However, whereas elsewhere this boom was biased towards investment in plant and machinery, Britain was the only leading industrial economy to experience a lower rate of increase in investment in plant and machinery than in services and property. Thus, while business investment in Britain increased by 40 per cent over 1979–89, investment in manufacturing industry rose by only 10 per cent, and the share of investment in manufacturing in total business investment fell from 27 per cent in 1979 to 19 per cent in 1989. Whilst Europe and Japan strengthened their industrial base, Britain built shopping centres, houses, and office blocks (many now vacant). Moreover, much of the investment in the manufacturing sector was aimed at installing labour-saving technologies requiring greater job flexibility on the part of workers, a process which was assisted by changes in labour legislation and the weakening of trade union power. As a result, productivity in the manufacturing sector increased impressively but output and employment did not. It was only in 1987 that manufacturing output recovered to its 1979 level, and by 1989 (the peak of the 'Thatcher' boom) manufacturing output was only 12 per cent higher than in 1979. The productivity increase was largely achieved by shedding labour, not through increased investment and output. Why?

Part of the reason was that, despite its supply-side policies, Thatcherism failed to create the conditions that encourage the long-term investment in industry that was required. This requires a stable macroeconomic environment in which firms can plan for the future with a reasonable degree of confidence. But under Thatcher the British economy experienced its two most severe recessions since the 1930s and an unsustainable boom. Despite the high priority given to controlling inflation, the rate fluctuated from 22 per cent p.a. in 1980 to 3 per cent p.a. in 1986, back to 10 per cent p.a. by 1990, and then subsequently fell below 2 per cent p.a in 1993. Moreover, the exchange rate fluctuated as severely. This volatile and unpredictable economic environment of boom and bust, exacerbated by macroeconomic policy mistakes, did little to encourage sustained high levels of investment in industry.

This problem was compounded by the low rate of profit of British industry. The average rate of return on projects over 1980–91 in Britain was appreciably lower (maybe 50 per cent lower) than in our main international competitors, even though the real rates of interest internationally were fairly similar. Real wages in Britain rose by 28 per cent, more than double the increase in Japan, Germany and France (in the USA, real wages actually fell by 6.5 per cent over the period). Hence most of the increases in productivity were distributed as increases in real wages, so that profits remained relatively low (whilst the real net-of-tax living standards of workers rose rapidly at some 3 per cent p.a.). This relatively low rate of profit was undoubtedly one of the reasons why the rate of growth of business investment was significantly lower in Britain than in other industrialised countries.

Because of the unstable economic environment and this relatively low profitability, productivity increases in manufacturing industry were not achieved by increasing investment, output and employment, but by shedding labour. New jobs were created, especially between 1986-90, but many of these were part-time and relatively low paid. The share of part-time employment in total employment rose from 6.4 per cent in 1979 to 21.8 per cent (over one fifth of all jobs) in 1990. Almost 90 per cent of part-time jobs were filled by women (usually married women with children who typically earned less than 60 per cent of the hourly male wage). Consequently, whereas employment of women increased by about 1.2m over 1979–90, employment of men *fell* by 1.4m (although this was partly offset by an increase in the number of self-employed men). In 1990 unemployment among men under 25 and over 45 years was double the 1979 level. The increase in the number of relatively low paid part-time jobs for women in the service sector (and the increase in self-employment by men) was insufficient to offset the fall in the number of men employed in relatively well-paid jobs in the industrial sector.

This contributed to a significant increase in the underlying rate of unemployment. During the 1970s and the 1980s, unemployment reached its lowest points in successive economic cycles in 1973, 1979, and 1990. In 1973, 1.3 per cent of those available for work were unemployed, and in 1979 this had risen to 3.9 per cent: the Thatcher governments failed to reverse this upward trend, so that at the next low point in 1990, the rate fell only to 5.4 per cent.

Moreover, these figures understate the increase in the number 'out of work' because of changes in the way unemployment is defined. The rate of 'unemployment' includes only those who are 'actively seeking work': it does not include the 'economically inactive' i.e. those who have no job but are deemed to have given up 'actively' searching for work. The rate of 'non-employment' includes both the 'unemployed' and the 'economically inactive'. Whereas the rate of 'unemployment' halved over 1986–90, remarkably the rate of 'non-employment' fell by only 0.5 per cent. In other words, much of the fall in 'unemployment' in this period was not due to people finding work but due to the *reclassification* of people without work, particularly after 1986 when every 'unemployed' person was required to attend interviews to ensure (among other things) that they were 'actively seeking work'.

The increase in the number of people who were 'unemployed' and 'economically inactive' led to both a substantial increase in government spending on income support, unemployment and other social security benefits, and also a reduction in the potential revenue from taxes on income and spending. The answer to the oft-asked question 'whatever happened to the government's revenue from North Sea oil?' was that during the early 1980s it was used to finance this increase in social security spending. In the later 1980s this increase was then funded by increased tax revenues generated by the economic boom (despite substantial cuts in the rate of income tax), and by privatisation receipts.

However, both oil and privatisation sales constituted finite resources upon which to draw, and as receipts declined, the government was left with a large 'structural' budget deficit. This could only be controlled by increasing taxes, reducing government spending or by maintaining high levels of growth and employment in order to generate sufficient tax revenue to finance this expenditure.

The 'easiest' option would have been the latter: maintaining high rates of growth so as to generate additional tax revenue and to reduce spending on unemployment and social security benefits. But the government's ability to do this was severely constrained by the weakening of Britain's manufacturing base and its lack of capacity to meet domestic demand for manufactured goods. This left British manufacturing industry with a critical shortage of capacity to meet domestic demand in several important sectors. As demand increased from 1981 on, imports increased and by 1983, for the first time since the Industrial Revolution, imports of manufactured goods exceeded exports. As demand accelerated during the 1980s this deficit rose to £18.8 bn in 1989. The problem was that Britain was not able to export enough to support the increased demand for imports of manufactured goods. Between 1980 and 1989 exports of manufactured goods increased by 119 per cent, but imports increased by 205 per cent. Even when demand fell and the economy went into recession in 1990–91, the lack of capacity to produce import substitutes resulted in a substantial continuing deficit in trade in manufactured goods.

Thus while Thatcherism brought about significant increases in productivity in the manufacturing sector, too few firms were able to make enough profit to survive and invest in expanding the output of British designed and manufactured goods to meet demand and to create enough jobs to restore full employment. The consequences of this became apparent with the onset of the recession in 1990, when the government budget deficit rose rapidly to record levels and despite falling demand there was a chronic and persistent balance-of-trade deficit. Both of these tended to undermine confidence in the £ sterling on foreign exchange markets. To prevent a collapse of the exchange rate the government was compelled to keep interest rates relatively high. This again discouraged industrial investment and kept unemployment at high levels.

Conservatism and the 1990s

Since the mid-1960s the British economy has experienced four economic cycles, which peaked in 1964, 1973, 1979 and 1989. The 'Thatcher years' therefore broadly coincided with the 'peaks' of two cycles: between 1979 and 1989 real GDP in Britain (i.e. the actual quantity of goods and services produced in Britain) increased on average by 2.25 per cent p.a. This was significantly better than the 1.5 per cent p.a. achieved during the 1973–9 cycle, but not as good as the 3 per cent p.a. achieved in the 1964–73 cycle. The British growth performance over 1979–89 was marginally better than the average for Europe (excluding the former socialist countries) but not as good as that of Japan and the USA. Thus, economic policy in the 'Thatcher years' raised the growth performance of the British economy and brought it into line with that of other industrialised countries.

However, the legacy of Thatcherism set a testing agenda for subsequent administrations in the 1990s.

The positive legacies perhaps lay most in changed contexts and attitudes: the swing away from public provision and regulation towards private business, market forces and the importance of choice and competition will probably prove more durable than the swing of economic fashion from Keynesianism to Monetarism. Moreover, the balance of economic power in Britain has been changed, not least away from organised labour in trade unions and towards entrepreneurs. Despite this, the Thatcher years were excellent for the living standards of those in work. If the supply-side policies did not deliver the desired outcomes soon enough to avoid the débâcle of 1992, then it may be that these benefits will yet emerge in the longer run as increased flexibility, new technologies and greater efficiency have an impact. Inflation, the scourge of the 1970s, was beaten down by 1993 to levels much lower even than in Germany, an achievement that sometimes seemed impossible. Finally, perhaps the most lasting single legacy will be privatisation, the much copied policy stance in which Britain led the rest of the world in the 1980s.

Against these, however, must be set other less desirable legacies: low inflation was accompanied by a huge rise in unemployment to persistently high levels, with all its social and economic consequences. The depressed level of profits had insidious consequences for British manufacturing industry, leaving the economy emerging into the mid-1990s with a narrower productive base and major structural weaknesses. The success of privatisation left the challenge of regulation, in which any failure to control effectively the huge private utilities that have been created could have serious consequences for individual households and industry throughout the decade. Deregulation and the reliance on market forces leaves private enterprise doing only what is profitable, whilst the government seems willing only to do as little as possible, opening up potential 'gaps' in provision (e.g. transport, medical services). The quantity and quality of public services, and indeed the Welfare State itself, have all been under assault and have an uncertain future.

There were two further legacies: first, the real level of government spending had not been reduced, despite the rhetoric, and second the real level of taxation had not declined and at best remained level; indeed in the early months of 1994 the Treasury was forced to admit that the *overall* level of taxation was higher under the Conservatives than during the last year of the 1974–9 Labour Government. Between 1979 and 1989, the supposedly anti-spending Thatcher government increased the tax burden from less than 35 per cent to more than 37 per cent of GDP. Whilst this then declined back to 35 per cent by 1993, nearly all of this was due to the recession. Although there was a significant switch from direct taxes (income) to national insurance and indirect taxes (VAT, etc.), nevertheless the marginal rate for most taxpayers in 1993 was still above 50 per cent. However, *income* taxes were substantially reduced, and this contributed to one of the least attractive features of Thatcherism, the enormous increase in income inequalities: the percentage share of post-tax income earned by the poorest fifth of households declined from 9.5 per cent in 1979 to 6.3 per cent in 1990, whilst that of the highest fifth increased from 37 per cent to 45 per cent. Ironically, this exacerbated the government's other problems. Higher income groups import relatively more, which affects the balance of trade, whilst welfare benefits and income support to the poorer sector have grown, and the government provides an increasing share of the income of the working poor, all burdening public expenditure: by mid-1993, the social security budget was costing the equivalent of £13/day for every working person in Britain.

Overall, 'Thatcherism' never had a fully coherent package of economic (or political) policies, but rather a few basic tenets and what *The Economist* called ' an instinctive list of friends and enemies'. Whilst in some ways it achieved its broad objectives, the inadequacies of the underlying real achievements were ruthlessly exposed as Britain entered the 1990s.

From Thatcher to Major: The ERM Experiment

The decision to join the ERM in 1990 was just as important in its way as the move from Keynesianism to Monetarism. Keynesianism based economic policy on an internal economic target, essentially that of avoiding unemployment. Joining the ERM represented adopting an external target, which subsumed all other policy objectives to that of maintaining the exchange rate. More significantly, the 'pure' Monetarist position *also* was against joining: it too had an internal rather than an external target, in this case, the money supply. The principal economic advantage cited was that, by joining, the UK would acquire some of the economic credibility of the German Bundesbank, which would enable the government to achieve low inflation and low interest rates (making possible rapid growth and lower unemployment).

The impact of joining was, predictably enough, a fall in inflation and a rise in unemployment, but with both taking place at surprising speed. Some argued that this was because Britain had joined at too high a fixed exchange rate, others that any fixed rate quickly becomes inappropriate anyway. More important, British economic policy now ceased to target domestic problems but concentrated explicitly on maintaining the exchange rate. Thus in 1992–3 Chancellor Lamont could not reduce domestic interest rates, which had become far too high in absolute terms for comfort (e.g. for encouraging investment), because the foreign exchange markets distrusted Britain's commitment to accept the constraints imposed by membership of the ERM. Conversely, the German Bundesbank wanted British interest rates increased to support sterling, but Lamont could not possibly respond for domestic reasons. An unstable impasse developed, with Britain experiencing the 'burden' of membership (an 'overvalued' £ sterling) without the advantage (lower interest rates).

However, at least the battle against increasing inflation, which Thatcherism had shown signs of losing in the late 1980s, was won, if temporarily, as inflation rates fell rapidly. Meanwhile, however, membership of the ERM exposed the full impact of the Thatcher years in terms of the structural deficits in the government's budget and the balance of trade. Faced with this, the foreign exchange markets became increasingly unsure how the government would react to problems. Accordingly, the sterling exchange rate within the ERM gradually became vulnerable to even minor daily shocks within an increasingly turbulent Mechanism. Eventually, in September 1992 speculation in the £ sterling moved out of control, despite last minute spending of huge sterling reserves and rises in UK interest rates (the base rate rose briefly from 10 per cent to 15 per cent in one day). The government was forced to suspend sterling's membership of the ERM on 'Black Wednesday', 16 September, the victim of an economic fiasco which left it without any obvious alternative economic policy. The ensuing effective massive devaluation of over 20 per cent in sterling was in direct contradiction to the government's previous policy, and subsequent claims of its success in helping to increase exports of the cheaper British goods and services had a somewhat hollow ring.

In so far as any coherent policy then emerged during 1992–3, it was to seek economic recovery and growth by having a 'clear and predictable framework for policy'. The new MTFS was based on three principles, elucidated by Chancellor Lamont in various speeches after 'Black Wednesday':

1. growth is generated by private sector initiative: the role of government is to establish the right climate;
2. the essential condition for growth is low inflation;
3. the supply-side performance of the economy must be improved, competitive pressures increased, and efficiency maximised.

In essence this was a return to the policies of the period 1983–5, but without any coherent analysis of why such policies would not lead to a repetition of subsequent events, except an explicit commitment to maintain inflation within a (more stable) band of 1–4 per cent . These policies remained at the heart of Conservative economic strategy even after Lamont was 'sacked' in 1993 and replaced by Kenneth Clarke; the only difference between Clarke and his predecessor being Clarke's ability to handle the media with greater panache. The other 'innova-tion' introduced was a commitment to a greater degree of 'openness' in economic policy, which effectively meant the wider publication of information and of the reasoning behind economic policies, together with the appointment of the Council of Economic Advisers (the so-called 'Seven Wise Men'), to debate issues and advise the government. Predictably, the traditional propensity of economists to disagree quickly emerged, with contradictory advice and no small element of acrimony within the Council. As a basis for the sought-after stability to assist internal and external activities, it is difficult to see a less convincing structure, and the contrast to the monolithic and austerely silent Bundesbank in Germany could not be more marked.

Prognosis

Overall, it is not easy to conclude that Conservative governments since 1979 have put the British economy firmly on the path towards sustained non-inflationary growth. Certainly, by June 1993 the govern-ment had achieved the remarkable feat of reducing inflation to 1.2 per cent p.a., the lowest level for thirty years. But there is substantial evidence that very low inflation is not a sufficient condition for sustainable economic growth, and may not even be a necessary condition (although opinions differ). What *is* required is a degree of predictability to encourage investment for growth: wide-ranging *fluctuations* in the rate of inflation create unpredictability and acute uncertainty, and in this respect Thatcherism did not provide any answers.

The post-Thatcher government of John Major threw in its lot with firmly supporting the ERM as the means of achieving a low and stable level of inflation. When this failed spectacularly in autumn 1992, the economic policy cupboard seemed to be bare. The effective collapse of the unstable ERM itself in mid-1993 then threw serious doubts on whether this was a viable policy under any circumstances in a world where economic policy making is dominated by the massive and rapid movement of funds across international exchanges.

Moreover, despite the change in contexts and attitudes brought about by supply-side policies, in 1993 the country and the government still faced high levels of 'unemployment' (some 3 million) and even higher levels of 'non-employment'. This has led to high levels of spending on social security (and a reduced capacity to raise revenue through taxes on income and spending), resulting in a huge and unsustainable PSBR (£37 billion in 1992–4, and estimated at perhaps £50 billion in 1993–4). In policy terms, something must give, for the freedom of governments to do what they would ideally want is severely constrained: if an expanding budgetary deficit cannot be funded by tax generated from high growth and employment, then there *must* be increases in tax income *or* government expenditure cuts, *or* both. The likelihood seems that, by the end of 1994, both will have been employed. The extent to which the latter might involve dismantling elements of the 'Welfare State' remains unclear. And over all this lies the shadow that any misjudgement could send an economy still struggling to emerge from recession into growth straight back into recession again.

One strong possibility would be to reconsider the tax base itself. The PSBR before privatisation proceeds was some 3.3 per cent of GDP in 1982–3, and will be some 8 per cent in 1993–4. The problem is not only increased government spending but also the shrinkage of the tax base: commercial (legal) tax avoidance is widespread, and personal tax receipts have been much affected by the increasing proportion of those working who are in relatively low-paid and/or part-time jobs. Add to this the running-out of tax revenues from North Sea oil, particularly after the 1986 oil price fall (less was collected in 1992–3 than in 1979–80), and the inevitable drying-up of privatisation receipts, and the case can be made that the problem is as much one of income as of expenditure. But no government ever likes to raise taxes, particularly one that had recently won an election by accusing the Opposition of planning to do just this. Signs of a political furore to match the Poll Tax were indeed apparent during 1993 in the move to apply VAT to domestic fuels (to raise £3 billion), and a wider use of indirect taxation would no doubt be politically dangerous.

Whether or not 'dismantling' the Welfare State to reduce expenditure and/or substantially increasing indirect or direct taxes is socially or politically sustainable is open to question. During the 1970s 'conventional wisdom' held that it was impossible to tolerate sustained unemployment over 1 million, but the Thatcher governments proved otherwise. Nevertheless, during the 1990s the British government must again confront the basic problem of the 1960s and 1970s that Thatcherism exacerbated: the relative decline of manufacturing industry, and its lack of appropriate capacity to lead any recovery towards growth. Thatcherism, Monetarism and supply-side policies did not solve this, nor did the brief formal flirtation with the ERM, but rather they have created a different and no less difficult context in which the Major government and its successors will address the problem, with whatever may prove to be the next fashion in economic policy.

6

Employment Relations and Training Policy

DAVID FARNHAM and CAROL LUPTON

Introduction

The election of a new, radical Conservative government in 1979 saw the end of the Keynesian demand-management approach of previous governments and its replacement with a 'free-market conservatism' emphasising financial and supply-side management (see Chapter 5). In contrast to what was felt to be the excessive interventionism of previous governments the general approach of industrial policy through 1980s was essentially negative: largely concerned with removing the barriers to the unimpeded operation of the market. By means of a range of 'supply-side' measures such as tax reform, privatisation, market deregulation and control of the trade unions, the aim was to establish a strong free-market framework within which British industry could operate more efficiently and effectively. Legitimation was given to these central policy shifts by the concept of the new 'enterprise culture'. This was characterised by the virtues of individualism, independence, self-help and above all by the end of the collectivism and corporatism that was seen as a major cause of Britain's industrial decline.

Central to the success of the new enterprise culture was seen to be a greater ability on the part of individual firms to respond flexibly to changing national and international conditions. In particular, in the face of increasingly competitive markets and sophisticated technological advances, firms were to be enabled to develop more flexible labour and employment strategies. Industry needed greater freedom, it was felt, not only to adjust the volume of labour employed (numerical flexibility) and the rates and levels of pay (pay flexibility), but also to achieve an enhanced 'functional flexibility'. This is defined as '. . . a firm's ability to adjust and deploy the skills of its employees to match the tasks required by its changing workload, production methods and/ or technology' (NEDO, 1986, p. 4).

In the diagnosis of Britain's economic ill health two particular, and related, 'supply-side' factors were increasingly identified as barriers to greater functional flexibility. The first was what Cutler (1992) has termed 'The British Labour Problem'. This identified the trade unions as the cause of continued rigidities in labour and employment patterns. The unions were held responsible for the low productivity and relatively high cost of labour as a result of trade disputes, restrictive working practices and a general resistance to technological changes (Cutler, 1992). Paralleling an emphasis on the regenerative role of small business, much political acclaim was increasingly given to the 'small firms model of industrial relations' characterised by a minimum of state intervention, the absence of trade unions and the shared interest of worker and employer in the success of the business.

The second central barrier to industrial regeneration was seen to be a continued shortage of key skills, politically reconstituted as 'The British Training Problem' (Cutler, 1992). Many studies emerged over the 1980s revealing a significant 'skills gap' between the UK and its major industrial competitors. In particular it was argued that the shortfall in middle-ranking or supervisory skills meant that British firms made less efficient use of their labour and were restricted to the employment of simpler technologies. Importantly it was not just functional skills that were felt to be required but increasingly those that were transferable: '. . . skills as a general polyvalent resource that can be put to many different and, most importantly, as yet unknown future uses' (Streeck, 1989, p. 97). This chapter examines the nature and impact of successive Conservative governments' response to both the 'British Labour Problem' and the 'British Training Problem' in the context of the wider attempt to stimulate an 'enterprise revolution' in Britain in the late 1980s and early 1990s.

The British Labour Problem: Employment Relations Policy since 1979

Employment relations policy is the means by which the state seeks to influence relations between employers and employees, employers and trade unions, and unions and their members. The state has a number of roles in this policy area including: as an actor in the labour market and in the determination of wages and employment; as a regulator of industrial conflict; as a law maker and law enforcer and as an employer.

From 1945 until 1979, apart from the period 1971 to 1974, there was in effect a consensus on employment relations policy in Britain. This consensus emphasised: state intervention in the labour market to promote full employment, state support for collectivist employment relations, using the law as a 'prop' to promote collective bargaining, and excluding the courts and the judges from intervening in the internal affairs of unions and the regulation of industrial conflict (Farnham, 1993b).

Since 1979, however, successive governments have rejected Keynesian economic theory and Beveridge social welfare principles. This has had considerable implications for employment relations policy. There has been a shift from voluntary collective bargaining in conditions of full employment and strong trade unions – with attempts at bargained corporatism through 'social contracts' – to a policy of neo-*laissez-faire*. It is a policy rooted in market liberal economic principles and weak trade unions (Crouch, 1979). As a result, British trade unions collectively, through the Trades Union Congress (TUC), and individually, have looked more towards European Community institutions and the European Trade Union Confederation to achieve their industrial relations and social policy goals. To what extent this strategy will pay off is too early to say.

The strategic basis of employment relations since 1979 has been neo-*laissez-faire*. This emphasises: deregulating the labour market; individualising employee relations, with the legal props to collective bargaining being loosened or removed and legal restrictions on trade unions being enacted; and depoliticising the unions. The policy instruments used include: legislation, economic measures, government example and the creation of the Commissioner for the Rights of Trade Union Members (Farnham, 1990).

The theoretical and moral underpinnings of employment relations policy since 1979 have been rooted in market economics and liberal individualism. Market economics assumes that supply and demand, acting through the price mechanism, are preferable to political interventions by politicians in deciding overall employment targets and wages policies. Liberal individualism pinpoints the individual, rather than interest groups, as the prime decision-making authority in employment relations, with the freedoms and natural rights of the individual, being held as inalienable. Free labour markets, free product markets and free capital markets, it is argued, lead to economic efficiency, whilst entrepreneurs and those seeking employment, in doing what is best for themselves, maximise economic welfare generally.

The market economic model makes three assumptions about the relationship of the market to the individual. First, individuals act rationally in pursuing their own self-interest in the market place. Second, the free play of impersonal, decentralised market forces is the best way of increasing the prosperity and welfare of the individual and the community. Third, the individual is sovereign in the market because of freedom of choice and market competition amongst buyers and sellers. For market liberals, because individuals are central to economic decision making, the role of government is limited to providing an economic and constitutional framework for individuals to pursue their own self-interest. The state only intervenes to protect the individual's rights to property, liberty and access to markets. Market liberal employment relations policy, in short, aims to optimise labour market efficiency, minimise government intervention in private employment affairs and protect individual rights against vested interests.

Deregulating the Labour Market

Market liberal macro-economists emphasise the contexts of the general labour market, whilst market liberal micro-economists try to explain how rational agents in disaggregated labour markets produce different responses to changes in wage levels and unemployment. The macro-economists focus on how factors independent of the labour market – such as inflation, the exchange rate and mortgage tax relief – are likely to influence wages and unemployment; the micro-economists try to evaluate the influence of institutional factors within the labour market.

The Micro-Issues

Labour market deregulation has been a central plank of government policy since 1979. Given that labour services are commodities which are bought and sold by rational actors in the market, market liberals argue that wages and employment are determined by supply and demand. In a free labour market, the quantity of labour supplied equals the quantity demanded at the market wage. Unemployment is symptomatic of labour market rigidity, meaning that the price of labour is too high so that wages need to fall if the market is to clear. Where there are barriers to a free labour market, it is necessary to deregulate it to make it more competitive.

One cause of unemployment and labour market rigidity identified by market liberal economists is institutional. Where employers have to compensate for unfair dismissal, they are deterred, it is claimed, from increasing demand for new employees. Extending employment protection rights thus has the overall effect of increasing unemployment.

Second, fiscal factors, such as changes in taxation and social security, are also claimed to increase unemployment, because higher taxes reduce labour supply, whilst higher social security payments result in people being unemployed longer, with more time being spent in job searches.

A third cause of unemployment is seen by market liberals to be collective action by organised workers. Unionised workers are viewed as restricting labour supply and limiting access to jobs for non-union workers who are likely to drive wage rates down. A rise in demand for unionised labour results in higher wages but not in higher employment, because the supply of labour is fixed in the short term. Indeed, trade unions contribute to higher unemployment because they restrict labour supply, whilst union wage rates do not reflect changes in labour supply or labour demand. Also the unionised sector is the benchmark by setting wage norms for other workers to follow. In the non-unionised sector, labour supply is seen as being responsive to changes in wage rates. An increase in labour demand there is reflected in higher wages and higher employment.

The Policy Prescriptions

For market liberals, government can reform and deregulate the labour market by improving the supply side of the market in four ways. First, it can reduce the time spent by the unemployed in job searches, by reducing the rates of social security payments. Second, government can increase labour supply by reducing personal taxation to increase incentives to work, so that more people join the labour market. A third measure is removing minimum wages legislation, since this is likely to increase the price of labour thus resulting in a fall in labour demand. The fourth way is by reforming trade union immunities and making it more difficult for unions to take lawful industrial action, without incurring severe financial costs. All these measures were, to varying degrees, adopted by Conservative governments during the 1980s and 1990s.

Individualising Employment Relations

The necessary conditions for promoting collectivist employment relations are: freedom of association for workers to join unions; 'free' trade unions independent of employers and the state; employer recognition of unions; and bargaining in good faith. Since 1979 one plank of public policy has aimed at encouraging employers to use individualist methods of determining and implementing the wage–work bargain. This policy has seen government attempting to weaken union organisation, strengthen the right to manage and discourage union militancy.

Weakening Union Organisation

Whilst freedom of association and independent trade unions continue to exist in Britain, union organisation has been weakened dramatically since 1979. First, union density, normally the percentage of the potential workforce in union membership, has fallen dramatically, especially in the private sector. This is largely as a result of the structural reorganisation of the economy and high levels of unemployment during the 1980s and 1990s (Daniel and Millward, 1983; Millward and Stevens, 1986; Millward *et al.*, 1992). Smaller employment units and the reduction in size of the manufacturing sector have adversely affected union organisation. High unemployment weakens union bargaining power, makes the retention of union members more problematic and makes the recruitment of new members a more difficult.

Second, as a result of changes in employment law, closed shop agreements, or union membership agreements (UMAs) between employers and trade unions are unlawful. A UMA is any arrangement by which employees are required to be members of a union as a condition of employment. Pre-entry closed shops are where jobs are restricted to individuals already members of the union, whilst post-entry closed shops require employees to join a union, within a set period of starting work. Where individuals claim that their legal right not to belong to a union is infringed, they have a right to make an application to an industrial tribunal. UMAs covered around one quarter of the employed workforce in the late 1970s but it is estimated that only some 300,000–400,000 employees are now covered by them.

Third, other legal measures, now embodied on the Trade Union and Labour Relations (Consolidation) Act (TULRCA) 1992, provide rights for union members to elect by postal ballot, at least once every five years, union executive committees and union leaders. These legislative changes in union election procedures stemmed from the government's desire to ensure that trade union leaders are truly representative of their memberships. Because the unions had not reformed themselves, the government claimed that it 'had reluctantly come to the conclusion that some legislative intervention is necessary' (Department of Employment, 1983, p. 16). Another interpretation of these provisions is that they are a further means of weakening trade unions and links between members and their unions, thus loosening union solidarity.

Strengthening the Right to Manage

The right to manage is that area of decision making which management considers to be its alone and is unconstrained by collective bargaining or the law. The boundaries of the right to manage are the interface between unilateral management control and the ability of employees, individually or collectively, to influence decisions affecting their working lives. Given government commitment to the enterprise culture and the free market since 1979, one policy goal has been to strengthen the right to manage. Its rationale is to provide managers with more autonomy in decision making and to restrict union activity and collective action (Farnham and Horton, 1993). It is aimed at enabling employers to react more swiftly to changing product markets, to obtain greater flexibility from their human resources and to have more control over worker productivity. Employing organisations should then become more efficient, effective and competitive thus boosting economic growth and employment.

The pressures for employers to recognise unions for collective bargaining purposes have been considerably weakened since 1979. One of the first measures in 1980 was to repeal, in the Employment Act (EA) 1980, the Section 11 procedures embodied in the Employment Protection Act (EPA) 1975. This means that the Advisory Conciliation and Arbitration Service (ACAS) no longer has a statutory duty to investigate and make recommendations on union recognition.

The powers of wages councils to set wage rates for those aged under 21 and other conditions were abolished by the Wages Act 1986, which limited wages councils to setting minimum adult hourly and overtime rates. Subsequently, the Trade Union Reform and Employment Rights Act (TURERA) 1993 abolished wages councils completely. Fair Wages Resolutions have been rescinded and the comparable terms and conditions procedure – Schedule 11 of the EPA 1975 – has been repealed. Where 10–99 employees are to be made redundant, the minimum period for trade union consultation has been reduced. Further, 'union only' or 'union recognition' clauses in commercial contracts are now void in law. It is also unlawful to discriminate against or victimise public contractors on these grounds.

Discouraging Union Militancy

Changes in employment law since the 1980s have aimed at reducing union ability to take part in lawful trade disputes. Legal immunities, the legal definition of a trade dispute and industrial action ballots are at the root of the issue. Where employees take industrial action, they are normally in breach of their contracts of employment. Under common law it is unlawful to induce people to break a contract, to interfere with the performance of a contract or to threaten to do so. Without legal immunities, unions and their officers could face legal action for inducing breaches of contract when organising industrial action. Legal immunities provide protection for unions and individuals so that they cannot be sued for inducing breaches of contract when furthering industrial action. The EA 1980, and that of 1982, withdrew immunities from certain types of action, opening up the possibility of unions and individuals having injunctions issued against them where their actions are unlawful. These legal provisions are now incorporated in the TULRCA 1992.

The law also provides that those organising industrial action are only protected when acting 'in contemplation or furtherance of a trade dispute'. To remain within the law, those calling industrial action must be able to show that there is a dispute and that the action is in support of it. Lawful disputes are those between workers and their own employers and must be concerned with matters 'wholly or mainly' connected with terms and conditions, negotiating machinery and so on. The following types of disputes are now unlawful: interunion disputes; 'political' disputes; disputes relating to matters occurring overseas; disputes with employers not recognising unions or employing non-union labour; and 'secondary' or 'sympathy' disputes between workers and employers other than their own. Where unions act unlawfully, they lose their legal immunity.

Unions are also required to ballot union members before a dispute. The action is only lawful where a majority of those voting support it. The EA 1988 went further by providing union members with the right to apply to the courts for an order restraining their union from inducing them to take industrial action without a properly conducted ballot. The TURERA 1993 requires unions to give seven days' notice to the employer of their intention to hold a ballot, which must normally be a full postal one, independently scrutinised. Where an unlawful act is authorised by a union official, or by a union committee, the union is liable unless it disowns the act in writing.

The effect of removing legal immunities from certain industrial action is to provide those damaged by the action, such as employers or union members, with the right to take civil proceedings against the union, or in some cases the individual, responsible. The remedies are to seek an injunction to prevent the action or to claim damages from the union for behaving unlawfully.

Under the TULRCA 1992 and the TURERA 1993 union members have the right not to be unjustifiably disciplined by their union. It specifies the actions counting as discipline and the conduct for which discipline is justifiable. Unjustifiable discipline for union members includes: refusing to take part in balloted industrial action; crossing a picket line; refusing to pay a levy for supporting a strike or other industrial action; working or proposing to work with members of another union or with non-union members; and working or proposing to work for an employer who employs non-union members.

Depoliticising Trade Unions

Union political activity has always been a sensitive and ambivalent issue for the Conservative party. The underlying assumption of recent public policy in seeking to depoliticise the trade unions is that the economic and political roles of unions can be dissociated. This accepts the unions' economic role as legitimate but asserts that their political role needs to be circumscribed, by law. This is on the grounds that it makes politicians democratically accountable to their constituents, not to special interest groups such as trade unions, and that the unions can concentrate on the more legitimate role of protecting their members' employment interests. Depoliticising the unions could also facilitate an ideological change on the part of the unions and their members, enabling them to identify more closely with the goals of a dynamic enterprise capitalism.

Political Strikes

The TULRCA 1992 now requires disputes to 'relate wholly or mainly to' the subjects listed. This raises doubts about the lawfulness of disputes having political elements. This change in the legal definition of a trade dispute effectively restricts some types of actions aimed at defending or improving terms and conditions of employment.

Political Fund Review Ballots

The TULRCA 1992 requires unions with 'political objects' and political funds, which are normally used to support the Labour party and to conduct political campaigns, to ballot their members at least once every ten years on whether they wish their union to continue to spend money on political matters. Ballots must be postal and subject to independent scrutiny. The scrutineer has access to a union's membership register and must inspect the register where appropriate. The distribution, counting and storage of voting papers must be undertaken by independent scrutiny. If ballots are not held, the authority to spend money on political objects lapses.

Privatisation

Privatising substantial parts of the public sector, and contracting out public services, has transferred large numbers of workers out of public employment. This means that the government is no longer their employer. These businesses cannot call upon government to increase public spending to finance their wage settlements and are now required to have regard to market considerations when responding to terms and conditions claims. This takes wage determination out of politics, thus in effect depoliticising the wage bargaining process.

Settling Trade Disputes

Since 1979 successive governments have publicly rejected any role in industrial peacekeeping. Government ministers have abstained from directly intervening, by conciliating or mediating, in intractable trade disputes, even in the public sector, no matter how bitter the disputes. This assumes that dispute resolution must be left to the employers and unions to settle themselves. The outcomes can then be determined by strong employers relying on market forces to generate financially prudent wage settlements and a sense of economic reality amongst the workforce and their union leaders.

Rejecting Corporatism

Public policy since 1979 has resulted in governments excluding the Trades Union Congress (TUC) from industrial policy making. Successive governments refused to consult directly with the TUC on policy decisions and they have abandoned top level meetings with TUC officials. A series of government Green Papers on trade union law reform, for example, was not used for consultative purposes but in effect as draft legislation which was subsequently enacted in virtually the form in which it had been presented. The only remaining corporatist body, the National Economic Development Council, was formally wound up in 1991. After the general election of 1992, tentative attempts were made by the TUC to renew political contacts with government but with little success to date.

Another dimension of employment policy, and one which has undergone substantial changes in policy and practice under the Conservatives, has been employment training. We shall now move on to consider this area in detail.

The British Training Problem

It is clear that throughout the 1980s there were significant changes in the nature and organisation of work in most post-industrialised countries. Many identify a central shift away from the 'deskilling' inherent in mass production (Taylorist or Fordist methods) to 'post-Taylorist' forms of production involving more flexible working methods and a multi-skilled workforce (Streeck,1989). Although we can question the extent to which such a shift has taken place equally across all sectors of the economy, the object of increased managerial flexibility has nevertheless been a central feature of evolving labour strategies in the 1980s. Central to this flexibility is the creation of the multi-skilled 'transferable' worker. If the political assault on the trade unions over the 1980s and 1990s lessened the possibility of their resistance to the new skill requirements of the 'flexible firm', the continued lack of appropriate available skills, even in a context of high unemployment, remained a major barrier to industrial recovery. If the 'British Labour Problem' had its political moment in the 1980s, Cutler argues, the 'British Training Problem . . . politically promises to be a creature of the 1990s' (1992, p. 163).

Training Policy Pre-1979

Until the mid-1960s the dominant approach to training in Britain was characterised by the 'pragmatic tradition of voluntarism' (Sheldrake and Vickerstaff, 1987): the assumption that individual firms should bear the primary responsibility for skilling their own workers. The pursuit of technological modernisation begun in the mid-1960s, however, revealed an acute shortage of key skills, especially in engineering and construction trades. In response, the 1964 *Industrial Training Act* established 30 tripartite Industrial Training Boards (ITBs) to improve the quality and quantity of skills training. While reasonably effective in their own sectors, however, the ITBs were less effective in meeting the economy's more general training needs, or in dealing with regional variations in labour markets. In the face of continued shortages of key skills the 1973 *Employment and Training Act* established the Manpower Services Commission (MSC) whose role was to promote training in areas not covered by the Boards but of key importance to the national economy. With the establishment of MSC the British state developed for the first time the ability to develop an active labour market policy (Finegold and Sockice, 1988).

Under the 1974–9 Labour government the Commission expanded in both size and ambition, attempting to establish itself as the centre of a comprehensive national manpower policy, linked to and underpinning the government's wider industrial strategy. On the assumption that the economy was facing a temporary economic downswing, the Commission was to identify in each industrial sector the skills needed to facilitate economic take-off. In particular it was to prevent the emergence of the 'manpower bottlenecks' that had resulted from the previous 'stop-go attitude' to training (MSC, 1977, p. 7).

As the 1970s progressed, however, there was little evidence of the recession 'bottoming out'. Unemployment levels continued to rise dramatically, and the MSC was pressured by the government to develop a series of 'special employment measures' or 'make work' schemes to deal with what was perceived to be a temporary situation. It soon became clear, however, that these 'special measures' were not to be a temporary feature of the Commission's work but a permanent and increasingly central one. By the end of the 1970s the Special Programmes Division of the MSC, which administered the special measures, accounted for just under half of the Commission's total expenditure. The overall policy emphasis was thus tipped away from development of longer-term strategic planning towards the administration of short-term 'fire-fighting' responses to rising unemployment.

Training Policy After 1979

The election of the Conservatives in 1979 marked the beginning of the end for the strategic ambitions of the Commission and for corporatist interventionist approaches more generally. Alongside the concern to combat trade union power in the workplace grew the desire to reduce their involvement in the development of training and employment policy. The tripartite nature of the ITBs and the MSC was seen to inhibit the creation of a more flexible, multi-skilled workforce and neither escaped political attention. After a series of cuts to their funding and reviews of their operation the 1981 *Employment and Training Act* abolished the majority of the ITBs. Responsibility for funding those remaining was returned to their respective industries and union involvement in the Boards was considerably reduced (Finn, 1987, p. 135).

While the political usefulness of its special measures meant that the Conservatives stopped short of abolishing the MSC altogether, they nevertheless made clear their dislike of its corporatist nature and its relative autonomy from central political control. The early 1980s saw a growing tension between the Commission and the government over plans to cut the funding of MSC programmes. There was evidence too that the government was prepared to circumvent the Commission if faced with any resistance to its proposals (*Guardian*, 20 Mar. 1982). In 1982, for example, the government announced a new scheme for long-term unemployed people (the Community Programme), without consulting the Commission (Lupton, 1989). In the face of this and other attempts to increase the degree of central political control over the Commission the tensions between it and the government grew. These culminated in the Conservatives' 1987 election manifesto proposal to change the role and composition of the Commission. Its scope would be reduced, with the responsibility for employment services being returned to the Department of Employment, and the number of employer representatives would be increased at the expense of the trade unions.

The New Training 'Promises'

As high levels of unemployment continued through the 1980s successive Conservative governments unveiled a series of more and more ambitious training initiatives. These were initially focused on the political problem of young unemployed people, particularly school-leavers. The *New Training Initiative* (NTI) in 1981 extended the existing Youth Opportunities Programme (YOP) into a new and more comprehensive *Youth Training Scheme* (YTS) guaranteeing everyone leaving school at the minimum age a full year's vocational preparation and training. The 1988 White Paper *Training for Employment* (Cmnd 316) extended this approach to adult unemployed people. As with the YTS this initiative combined all existing adult training schemes into one unified vocational programme. Launched in 1988, 'Employment Training' (ET) was presented as the 'largest and most ambitious training programme ever undertaken . . . anywhere in the world' (Norman Fowler, Secretary of State for Employment, *Guardian*, 6 Sept. 1988). It aimed to transform the training of adult unemployed people, ensuring a better fit between the supply of and the demand for skills.

Although these schemes could be seen to represent a considerable extension of the state involvement in training many argue that they actually involve just the opposite. Rather than an extension of state responsibility they should more appropriately be seen as part of a general attempt to return that responsibility to individual employers: a 'radical reformulation' of the voluntarist tradition (Lee, 1991, p. 160). Although subsidised by the state, employers provide the bulk of the work placements and, as managing agents, assist in the organisation and delivery of training programmes. As the schemes has expanded, moreover, the element of state subsidy has been gradually reduced. The dominance of employers in the design of programmes and the tailoring of work placements to employers' needs has, it is argued, effectively subjugated the scope and content of training to the operation of market forces. Peck refers to this as the 'enforced marketisation' of training provision (1991, p. 16). Lee (1989) argues that by the end of the 1980s over three quarters of training places were privatised in this way.

Many also question the extent to which the objective of such schemes is actually the provision of training as opposed to the social management of those without work. Evidence indicates that the quality of training provided is often poor, involving broadly-based 'introduction to work' programmes or fairly low level skill training (Finn, 1987). The government has stated explicitly that the function of such schemes is to retain the motivation to work, particularly on the part of young and long-term unemployed people. In his 1985 'Budget for Jobs' speech, for example, the then Chancellor argued that the programmes would create a workforce '. . . that is adaptable, reliable, motivated and is prepared to work at wages that employers can afford to pay' (Finn, 1987, p. 165). Increasingly the focus of such schemes is on the short-term labour needs of local employers rather than on the training needs of individual participants.

The expansion of these high profile 'training' schemes over the 1980s moreover was accompanied by a decline in government support for other forms of training. The early 1980s saw the widespread collapse of the apprenticeship system: over the Conservatives' first term the number of engineering and technician trainees was cut by nearly half (Finegold and Sockice, 1988). There was a general rationalisation of other initiatives such as the Training Opportunities Programme (TOPs) that did provide reasonably high quality training in transferable skills. Twenty Skillcentres were closed in 1980 and plans were announced for the privatisation of others (*Guardian*, 11 Jan. 1983). The government made clear that the remaining TOPs schemes were not there to provide 'training on tap' for unemployed individuals, but were to be geared to identified areas of business demand (MSC, 1983, p. 198).

As the special training initiatives proliferated they caused increased political concern about the quality of training, the lack of statutory protection and the impact on local wage rates. Evidence was growing about employers' use of 'trainees' to substitute for fully-paid workers. In particular there was unease about the extent to which the closer alignment of schemes such as ET and YT with the benefit system represented an extension of US style 'workfarism' (the requirement that unemployed people are made to work in some way for the benefits they receive). Although the Trades Union Congress (TUC) had previously given the government's training initiatives its grudging support, the active hostility of some constituent unions, most notably the TGWU and UCATT, was growing. In 1988 the TUC voted by a narrow margin not to co-operate with the ET scheme. The government's response was decisive: it would abolish the Commission and thus the role of the trade unions in implementing the programmes at a national level. It was simply not possible, it argued, for the Commission to administer a scheme to which a significant minority of its membership was actively opposed. Although the TUC subsequently reconsidered its decision and agreed to co-operate with the scheme on a selective basis, the damage was done: the Secretary of State took back the Commission's functions and transferred the responsibility for training programmes back to the Department of Employment. Given its long-standing dislike of the corporatist MSC, it is clear that the confrontation over ET merely served to hasten the government down a route it was already preparing to take.

The Training and Enterprise Councils

The government's commitment to the privatisation of training services was made most explicit in its subsequent White Paper *Employment for the 1990s* (Cmnd 540). This set out its alternative to the corporatist and interventionist MSC/Training Commission. A national network of Training and Enterprise Councils (TECs) would be established. These would be independent companies which entered into commercial contracts with the Secretary of State to develop 'enterprise training' within their local areas. The TECs would not themselves provide training but would sub-contract to a range of existing local training providers on a competitive basis. In April 1990 the first ten TECs signed contracts and the remainder (82 in all for England and Wales) came on stream in April 1991, each with a budget of between £20–50 million. Two-thirds of the members of the TEC Boards were to be private sector chief executives, with the balance of membership left for those executives to decide, but with the expectation that they would be recruited from the local authority, trade unions and the voluntary sector.

The TECs were given three main tasks: to run existing training schemes and meet the government's political guarantees; to analyse local markets and identify areas for future skill requirements and to act as a forum for co-ordinating community action on economic development. They were to tailor existing programmes to meet local needs and to achieve better value for money. Centrally the TECs were to reflect the values and aspirations of the new 'enterprise culture': they were to be given a 'broad charter' to tackle the barriers to enterprise development and create the skill-base necessary to underpin it; to represent: '. . . a passport to a more enterprising and better skilled workforce' (Training Agency, 1989, p. 19).

The establishment of TECs thus reflects the culmination of the privatisation process that characterised the development of industrial training in Britain throughout the 1980s. The explicit intention of the TEC initiative is to limit the extent of state responsibility for workforce training; to transfer the '. . . prime responsibility for investment in the skills and knowledge of our people to employers' (Norman Fowler, Introduction to the TEC Prospectus Training Agencies, 1989). The Councils are to encourage employers to invest voluntarily in their own training without recourse to statutory control: '. . . to shift the cost of training to employers without reverting to anything akin to the failed levy and grant processes of the Industrial Training Board system' (Bartlett, 1990, p. 77). In particular they are expected to pursue the objective of 'additionality' (Meager, 1991): to 'lever in' additional expenditure from individual companies either to the TECs themselves or into greater investment in training within their own companies. In their Business Plans TECs are expected to demonstrate detailed plans to attract additional resources, including the possibility of charging for services (TEC Operating Manual, para. 1.14).

The establishment of the TECs must also be seen as a continuation of the attempt to move away from a supply-led to a demand-driven approach to training: to link the provision of skills to the particular requirements of individual firms at a local level rather than to the training/employment needs of those without work. From the government's perspective, training initiatives were limited in so far as they were designed to respond to the central political problem of unemployment rather than to the specific skill needs of local labour markets. Thus the Head of the TEC's Project Team explained the rationale of the Councils: '. . . the Government's training and enterprise programmes are largely geared to high unemployment; they are centralised, they are not local and they do not recognise the changes that are taking place in different parts of the country's labour market' (quoted in Bennett, 1990, p. 71).

In addition to re-privatising training, the role of TECs is to ensure the decentralisation or localisation of training policy: '. . . a key aspect of TECs (is) that they give flexibility to local areas. Together with private leadership, this is the most important innovation that TECs involve' (Bennett, 1990, p. 69). Individual TECs are to have a wider community development role, acting as '. . . total stakeholders in the development of training and enterprise in their areas' (ibid.). By facilitating the creation of local networks of local employers and other key agencies (Chambers of Commerce and Trade, small business clubs as well as the local enterprise networks (LENs), rural development commission, inner-city task forces, etc.), the TECs are expected to harness existing local knowledge and expertise to create a collective response to local labour market need.

This emphasis on the local organisation and delivery of training, however, does not involve a reduction of central political control over this key policy area. Despite the explicit aim of the TECs to hand over the ownership of the training and enterprise system to local employers it is clear that the operation of the contract mechanism in effect subjects the workings of the TECs to fairly detailed political scrutiny. In particular, payments to TECs will be linked to centrally established 'output' targets, such as the number of trainees entering work or gaining relevant qualifications (Peck, 1991). The government has been quite explicit about its intention to use output-related funding (ORF) as a means of monitoring and controlling the expenditure of the TECs (*Hansard*, col. 533, 17:5, 1990). As the 1990s progress there is evidence that the autonomy of the TECs is a growing area of potential tension with many TEC Boards beginning to press for a greater degree of local control. As one commentator closely involved has argued: 'A view has emerged from some quarters that (the TECs) are being asked to take responsibility for directing what will be no more than localised units of the Civil Service, without sufficient authority to alter them significantly' (Bartlett, 1990, p. 78). As far as the TECs themselves are concerned therefore their ability to respond flexibly to local labour market requirements will depend in no small part on the resolution of this central issue of their 'right to manage'.

Conclusion

The 1980s and the 1990s saw major changes in the development of employment relations and training policy in Britain. The current solution to the 'British Labour Problem', to a large extent, involves the 'rebirth' of traditional, deregulatory labour market policies, with a shift away from corporatist, collectivist and interventionist approaches. Governments have taken direct policy initiatives to decollectivise employment relations between employers and unions and to weaken the unions' ability to undertake lawful industrial action. They have also sought to exclude the unions from national economic and social policy making. What government is seeking to encourage is market-centred, employer-driven and individualist employment and personnel policies at the level of the firm, and within firms, and the reassertion of the right to manage. The ideal 'model' of employment relations, and the preferred method of determining the wage-work bargain, is direct negotiation between employers and their individual employees, with unions having a marginal and peripheral role in the workplace. Where trade unions continue to be recognised by employers, they are to be constrained from disrupting employment relations by a restrictive and potentially punitive set of legal rules, embodied in the TULRCA 1992 and the TURERA 1993. Remarkably, the trade unions have survived, with membership at the levels they were during the early 1960s, in spite of government policies. In consequence, the unions are beginning to look externally to the European Community for legal and political support to further their institutional goals and objectives.

The current solution to the 'British Training Problem' similarly involves a rejection of the corporatist and interventionist approach of the past and its replacement with one based on the twin principles of privatisation and decentralisation. This general shift has been effected with and legitimised by the wider political discourse of the new 'enterprise culture'. Particular efforts were made over the 1980s to diminish the role of trade unions in the development of training programmes and to encourage greater involvement on the part of employers. The 'enterprise solution' to Britain's training problem has enabled the government to place greater responsibility for the day to day administration and management of training initiatives on employers at a local level, whilst maintaining and strengthening the degree of its overall political control. Thus the development of training policy mirrors the wider process of 'franchising the welfare state' (Wallace and Chandler,1989) that has characterised changes in the organisation and delivery of education, housing, health and social services over the 1980s and 1990s. In this process the state operates as a 'holding company' which sub-contracts key parts of its operation to a range of localised units such as school governing bodies or health care trusts. Although having the appearance of independence and autonomy these units may actually have relatively little room to manoeuvre, being subject to centrally imposed measures of performance or output. As Randall has argued, despite all the rhetoric about local flexibility and control, the TECs in reality '. . . have the sort of freedom which business people gain through franchising from a Pizza Hut multinational' (1992, p. 4, quoted in Ainley, 1993, p. 126).

7

Environmental Policy: Past and Future Agendas

JOHN BRADBEER

Introduction

It is unlikely that any review of British politics and policy in the 1960s, 1970s or early 1980s would have devoted much attention to the environment. However, as the 1980s progressed it became apparent that the environment had emerged as a substantive part of the British political agenda, and by the General Election of 1992, the environment appeared in some form in all of the major party manifestos – although in the event environment issues played a very small part in the campaign. This chapter examines the status of environmental policy through the 1980s, and assesses the current agenda for environmental policy.

One of the difficulties in discussing the environment as an area of public policy is that environmental issues cut across the established structures of Whitehall. Although there is a Department of the Environment (DoE), its main work since its creation in 1970 has been to oversee housing and local government, two issues which have had special prominence in the 1980s. Perhaps only a tenth of the DoE's work concerns the environment in its wider and more usually accepted sense. Equally important in formulating environmental policy are the Ministry of Agriculture, Fisheries and Food (MAFF), the Department of Transport (DoT) and until its abolition in 1992, the Department of Energy (DoEn). The Treasury has also been a significant force in shaping the environmental debate in Whitehall and, of course, in Scotland and Wales, the Scottish and Welsh Offices respectively have overseen environmental policy.

The rise to prominence of the environment as a political issue can be attributed to a combination of factors, including growing public concern, greater media interest, environmental disasters and the influence of European Community (EC) legislation. However, more specifically, what seems to have legitimated environmental issues as a part of the political agenda was the fairly abrupt change of stance of Mrs Thatcher on the question of the environment. Indeed, it is not an exaggeration to talk of the 'greening' of Mrs Thatcher during 1988. Until then she had virtually ignored the environment, and most famously said as the Falklands War neared its climax in May 1982, 'When you've spent half your political life dealing with humdrum issues like the environment, it's exciting to have a real crisis on your hands.' After her speech to the Royal Society in September 1988, environmental issues were secure on the political agenda. It is perhaps true that this was as much an international issue as a domestic matter, and that it was one more of rhetoric than of substance. Nevertheless, the stage had been set.

Environmental policy since 1979 has been a mixture of piecemeal evolution with a strong emphasis on continuity, and of more extensive change provoked by external pressures or by opportunist intentions, as well as calculated policy innovation. In these ways, the 1980s were not greatly different from previous decades, and there is no reason to assume that Conservative governments in the 1990s will produce any major departures from this. What has apparently altered is public concern for the environment, which has grown appreciably and which has been reflected in increased media attention. Furthermore, the EC has now become a very significant influence on United Kingdom environmental policy. The future of environmental policy is likely to reflect such mixtures of continuity and change but with pressures for change from growing public awareness and from EC legislation gradually leading to change.

This chapter commences with a brief review of some of the salient features of environmental policy in the 1980s. It then reviews contemporary environmental policy, taking the 1990 Environmental Protection Act and the White Paper *This Common Inheritance* as key statements. The chapter concludes by examining the main issues in contemporary and future environmental policy and the challenges they pose both to Conservative governments and to other established ideas and principles.

Environmental Policy in the 1980s

As we have seen, it is likely that the 1980s will be regarded as the decade in which the environment established its place on the United Kingdom's political agenda. There is a broad agreement that environmental policy in the 1980s fell into two unequal periods, with the speech made by Mrs Thatcher to the Royal Society in September 1988 as the dividing point. This section outlines these themes and takes as particular exemplars the fields of *land-use planning* and *pollution control* (more detail on these and on other wider environmental policy issues can be found in Blowers (1987), Bradbeer (1990), Lowe and Flynn (1989), McCormick (1991) and O'Riordan (1991)).

Environmental policy in the 1980s, as in many other policy areas, saw a mixture of continuity and change; of piecemeal evolution and of new departures in policy; of premeditated and of opportunist decisions. The main forces promoting continuity and piecemeal evolution were those of the government machine, while pressures for change came from the six Secretaries of State to be at DoE, the ideological agenda of the Conservative party, public opinion, the environmental movement and the EC.

In the early and mid-1980s, the environment did not feature prominently in either government thinking or in public opinion. Economic problems and the intensification of the Cold War had very much dominated the agenda. Throughout these years, the general tenor of government to the environment was one of indifference. In particular, the idea that environmental policy required substantial and continuous government intervention and regulation was often vigorously challenged. EC Directives on environmental policy were dismissed as being typical and silly pieces of unnecessary bureaucracy dreamed up in Brussels. Similarly, the main emphases of domestic legislation in the environmental field were those of deregulation and of voluntarism. None the less, in the field of pollution control administration, new structures foreshadowed in the 1970s were finally implemented, underlining how the themes of continuity and change are linked in environmental policy.

In her speech to the Royal Society in September 1988, Mrs Thatcher acknowledged the importance of environmental issues to human existence. Various explanations have been given offered for this quite abrupt volte-face. Significantly she emphasised global environmental issues such as global warming and climatic change, and the depletion of the ozone layer rather than domestic issues such as habitat destruction or pollution. It is said that the scientific arguments struck a chord with this graduate in chemistry, but equally important could have been growing public concern for the environment as revealed in private opinion polls carried out for the Conservative party. Another possibility suggested by McCormick (1991) is that Mrs Thatcher found the global environment a suitable vehicle for her ambitions to play a leading role on the international stage. Whatever the reasons, Mrs Thatcher's speech and her subsequent pronouncements firmly placed the environment on the political agenda and ensured that a green gloss, albeit often a very thin one, had to be given to government policy. One significant casualty of this 'greening' of government policy was Nicholas Ridley, who was felt to be too unsympathetic to the environment, and who was replaced as Secretary of State at DoE by Chris Patten.

Main Influences on Environmental Policy in the 1980s

Five main influences on British environmental policy in the 1980s can be identified:

1. Conservative party policy and especially its recent ideological agenda.
2. Public opinion.
3. The environmental movement.
4. The European Community.
5. Administrative incrementalism in Whitehall.

Conservative party policy has emphasised the need for economic growth to be a priority and argued that a deregulated economy and reduction in state activity are key elements in achieving this goal. Environmental regulation has thus been doubly suspect, as an impediment to economic growth and as a classic example of unnecessary bureaucracy. Conservative rhetoric has also stressed individual initiative and criticised collective and especially state action. A further strand in recent Conservative ideology has been a renewed emphasis on national sovereignty, especially against what has been portrayed as an unelected bureaucracy in Brussels. In these senses there has been to an extent an inherent opposition to policies which take the environment as a priority. However, the other influences on UK environmental policy referred to above have acted as a brake on and influenced a re-direction of the 'natural' inclinations of Conservative ideology.

Public interest in environmental affairs grew from a relatively low level in the early 1980s to considerable significance in the latter years of the decade. This was partly in response to some major domestic and international environmental incidents, especially the Chernobyl nuclear accident in 1986 and in 1988 the voyage of the toxic waste ship, *Karin B*, which attempted to land its cargo in Britain, and the mysterious deaths of thousands of seals in the North Sea. As some measure of growing public interest, it is significant to note that by the late 1980s the media all had environment correspondents and more extensive news coverage of environmental issues reflected and stimulated public concern. The environmental movement in Britain went from strength to strength in the 1980s. It enjoyed a vastly increased membership, a wider range of activities, and in particular, a far more professional approach. The movement now has the resources to commission its own research and is able with some skill to handle and to generate media interest.

While some interest groups have always had a good relationship with the Whitehall machine, environmental groups as relative newcomers on the scene had not enjoyed such access. Much of this too had changed in the 1980s. For many environmental pressure groups, the controversies over the 1981 Wildlife and Countryside Act were a significant learning experience. While the environmental movement won almost all of the intellectual arguments, it had virtually no influence on the final content of the legislation. Now with access to the media and a recognition of the importance of the EC as a policy forum, the environmental movement has become a significant force.

The EC has steadily grown in importance in British environmental policy. The Treaty of Rome made no explicit mention of environmental policy and not until 1973 did the EC adopt its first Environmental Action Plan. Since then an increasing number of Directives on environmental policy has followed. Boehmer-Christiansen (1989) has characterised the UK's relationship with the EC on environmental policy as falling into three periods:

1. 1973–*c*1979: a defensive and rather passive phase in which the United Kingdom protested the strengths of its policy, institutions and traditions and learned to its surprise how different these were from those elsewhere in Europe;
2. *c*1979–1988: a more aggressively hostile phase in which the United Kingdom actively resisted EC Directives, partly as an element in a wider campaign against the EC;
3. Since 1988: when the United Kingdom has become more accommodating but not necessarily more enthusiastic about EC environmental policy. A certain embarrassment about the tag 'the dirty man of Europe' and at being linked with Greece, Spain, Portugal and Ireland as the environmentally blighted fringe of Europe was clearly felt by some ministers and considerably eased the process.

The Whitehall administrative machine has always proceeded by steady evolution. It has worked particularly through informal consultation with interest groups and has usually sought consensus before proposing policy. Although the rhetoric of Mrs Thatcher frequently decried consensus, in practice both the government and the Civil Service continued to consult approved interest groups. At the beginning of the decade the environmental movement had relatively poor links with Whitehall, but the gradual 'greening' of government gave greater opportunities for involvement in later years. This same limited 'greening' of government provided scope for a number of evolutionary developments in pollution control to be brought forward and to contribute to the government's attempted counter-attack on environmental issues.

Continuity in Environmental Policy in the 1980s

In many areas of environmental policy, the decade was one of continuity, or perhaps rather one of slow evolutionary progress. The area of pollution control is one of the clearest examples of this. Although EC Directives played some part in this process, the major initiative came as a result of domestic developments which can be traced back to the 1970s.

The institutional structure of pollution control in the United Kingdom has evolved by piecemeal change and extension since the 1960s. By the early 1980s, powers had been concentrated in the hands of four main bodies, the Industrial Air Pollution Inspectorate, the Hazardous

Waste Inspectorate, the Radiochemicals Inspectorate and the Water Quality Inspectorate. As long ago as 1976, the Royal Commission on Environmental Pollution had called for the creation of a unified pollution inspectorate. The Royal Commission saw great advantages in considering pollution as a whole, as all too frequently existing pollution control policy simply displaced pollution from one medium to another. It hoped that a unified inspectorate would lead to multi-disciplinary teams of experts considering industrial processes, wastes and the environment as a whole and the proposals were thus more than simply administrative rationalisation and reform. Successive governments ignored the Royal Commission's recommendations, but gradually arguments that such a system could be more cost-effective and would appear to be less bureaucratic gained favour. In 1987, the government dropped its opposition and announced the creation of a unified pollution control inspectorate (Her Majesty's Inspectorate of Pollution, HMIP).

The Royal Commission had advocated administrative reform to produce policy change, in particular a more integrated view of production and waste management and a shift of pollution control from 'end of the pipe' back into the production process. However, the new HMIP was staffed by members of the formerly distinct inspectorates and working practices within HMIP have not greatly altered. British pollution control remains essentially pragmatic, consultative, secretive and to operate on a case by case basis. In all of these ways it differs from the much more formalised approaches advocated by the EC. Furthermore, the impact of the unified inspectorate has been reduced as it has received few extra resources to undertake its responsibilities.

Change in Environmental Policy in the 1980s

One area of environmental policy which has seen considerable change in the decade is land use planning. This became an early target of the government's zeal for deregulation and reliance upon market forces. As the Secretary of State is also the final arbiter in planning appeals, a fragmentation or loosening up of the system can be achieved without recourse to legislation. However even in planning, the pressures for change were not overwhelming and what has emerged is less a radical change than a splintering of the planning system into three distinct regimes, one of which exhibits very clear continuity with practice of the

1970s. These three regimes also broadly correspond with government preceptions that there are three different planning problems, each spatially distinct. In inner cities, planning is held to represent the dead hand of bureaucracy and to have been a major cause of economic decline. In scenically attractive areas, development is felt to be a threat to the national heritage and planning is accused of failing to offer sufficient protection. In the rest of the country, the planning system is regarded as being too insensitive to the needs of development and should be relaxed, without being totally abolished.

In the 1980 Local Government, Planning and Land Act, Enterprise Zones (EZs) were created. This was taken further with the Simplified Planning Zones (SPZs) introduced by the 1986 Housing and Planning Act. In both cases, zones were to be created in cities which would have minimal planning controls and which lay beyond the local authority planning system. Almost all EZs and SPZs were in inner cities which had seen major job losses and economic decline. The evidence so far is that they have attracted some new employment, frequently from other parts of the city not so designated.

In the protected parts of England and Wales, particularly in Areas of Outstanding Natural Beauty (AONB) and in National Parks, planning policy if anything had hardened against development. New AONBs have been created and after a gap of three decades, the eleventh National Park in England and Wales was established in the Norfolk Broads and plans are being prepared to confer quasi-National Park status on the New Forest and the South Downs. However, suggestions in the late 1980s that National Parks be created in Scotland met with government hostility and uniquely in Britain, Scotland still lacks National Parks.

Contemporary Environmental Policy

Although the environment has a place on the contemporary political agenda, it is not an especially prominent one. The broad structure of current environmental policy was laid down by the 1990 Environmental Protection Act and more especially by the White Paper, *This Common Inheritance*. Many of the proposals and initiatives of these statements show continuity with policy from the late 1980s. This is hardly surprising as both were products of the 'green offensive' which followed Mrs Thatcher's new interest in the environment after 1988. Debate continues about the appropriate way in which to enforce environmental policy. Increasingly the accepted wisdom of relying upon state regulation and direct enforcement is being challenged by alternatives. These involve harnessing market forces, either by fiscal policy to make the polluter pay or through more novel methods such as tradeable pollution permits. Environmental policy is also an area where the EC plays an important part in setting and forcing the agenda. A relatively new element in environmental policy is the international dimension. While pollution has long been recognised as transcending national boundaries, only in the last few years have environmental issues been placed on the international political agenda. At present this remains more a symbolic presence but the importance of environmental issues is attested by the Earth Summit, held in Rio de Janeiro in June 1992.

The 1990 Environmental Protection Act was the first-fruit of Mrs Thatcher's conviction that environmental issues were too important to be ignored. It was also the first large piece of purely environmental legislation for a decade. Some sections of the bill had become necessary to enact into British law a number of new EC Directives on genetically modified organisms and on toxic chemicals and wastes. To these were added a number of new clauses which introduced, among other things, stiffer penalties on litter, new obligations on local authorities to keep public places free of litter, new powers for local authorities to control noise and a ban on the practice of burning stubble from arable crops. These measures could be seen as a continuation of a tradition of civic amenities and the abatement of nuisance.

Other measures in the Act reflected continuity with the past, opportunist actions and some more directly ideologically motivated decisions. The Act formally recognised the concept of integrated pollution control, to which end HMIP had been formed in 1987. Belatedly, the Act also contained powers to restrict dumping of wastes in British territorial waters and could be presented as a response to public concern at this practice. For non-toxic wastes on land, the Act compelled local authorities to separate their operations to collect waste from their operations as statutory regulators of waste disposal sites. The aim here was not just to avoid conflicts of interest within a local authority but also to make possible the contracting out, or even the privatisation of the former while retaining public regulation of the latter. Perhaps the most controversial and most obviously politically motivated measure was that to reorganise the Nature Conservancy Council (NCC). This has been the government's primary nature conservation arm, acting as both adviser and as a management body for Britain's National Nature Reserves. Unusually for such advisory bodies, it operated throughout Great Britain. By the mid-1980s it was clear that the NCC had incurred the hostility of land-owning interests in Scotland and Wales and these interests persuaded the government to break up the NCC. The Act formally merged the Scottish and Welsh operations of NCC with those of the Countryside Commissions of Scotland and Wales, but left a rump, now called English Nature to operate independently of the Countryside Commission in England. While many commentators have argued that the distinction between nature and landscape conservation, which has been a feature of United Kingdom policy since the late 1940s is artificial, the 1990 decision had nothing to do with rationalisation but everything to do with satisfying a vociferous lobby.

Chris Patten replaced the unpopular and distinctly un-green Nicholas Ridley as Secretary of State for the Environment. Patten's first opportunity to establish a new environmental agenda came with the White Paper. This was an unusual White Paper in that no consultative Green Paper had preceded it but it was the first overview of the environment ever undertaken in Britain. All commentators commended its comprehensiveness but much criticism was levelled at its proposals for action. There were relatively few statements of new policy but many promises for government to consider, to study or to review possibilities for later action. Where action was suggested, this was usually left to individuals and voluntarism was emphasised. Proposals to deal with carbon dioxide emisions illustrate these points. Carbon dioxide is the single most important gas in contributing to global warming and is an inevitable consequence of the burning of fossil fuels. The White Paper promised renewed support for the Energy Efficiency Office, after years of severely reduced funding. Enhanced energy conservation is clearly a vital element in reducing carbon dioxide emissions and reliance on market forces and self-interest which had been advocated by government had failed to bring this about. On transport, the source of about a quarter of carbon dioxide emissions, there were statements of encouragement for cleaner and more efficient cars and for improvements to public transport. Signally missing were comparable statements to discourage car use and to commit finance to modernise public transport.

The White Paper received a generally muted reception. It was welcomed as a first tentative step and the promise of annual reviews has ensured that environmental issues remain on the agenda. Some commentators saw clear signs of intervention by the Treasury and the DoT to blunt any more radical intentions Chris Patten may have had. The White Paper emphasised the desirability and the feasibility of 'green' economic growth but stopped short of advocating fiscal and other measures which would promote this and most significantly, it contained no estimates of government spending on the environment.

Foreshadowed in the White Paper was the promise of a new body, the Environmental Protection Agency, to oversee environmental regulation. While this would further consolidate powers over the environment, coming so soon after the creation of HMIP, it smacks of structural reform as a substitute for real action and radical innovation in policy. It is unlikely that the new EPA will have much impact without significant new powers and resources to enforce them.

A continuing feature of debate in contemporary environmental policy is the way in which pollution control should be effected. Traditionally, this has been by regulation, with some standards set by legislation and then enforced by statutory agencies, either through the consultative processes of HMIP or by licence fees for pollution discharges, such as those administered by the National Rivers Authority. These methods do ensure that the polluter pays but new ways of achieving this have been advocated. Environmental economists have long argued for measures to ensure the optimum level of pollution which will balance the costs of pollution control and the benefits of pollution abatement. During his period at DoE, Chris Patten commissioned a report from David Pearce, a leading environmental economist. Pearce recommended as policy options fiscal measures such as a carbon tax, and tradeable permits in pollution. These options form the basis of the current debate about alternatives to statutory regulation of pollution discharges.

The attraction of fiscal measures is that they leave decisions on behaviour to individual polluters, whether companies or citizens. The oft-quoted example is that of the carbon tax which would be levied on the carbon content of fuels. By raising the price of fossil fuels, energy conservation would be encouraged and emissions of carbon dioxide would fall. Individuals would buy more economical cars, drive more slowly, even make journeys by public transport or face the consequences of making the polluter pay. The problems with such taxes are that they are regressive and hit the poor hardest. The poor spend disproportionately more of their incomes on fuel than do the wealthy and the poor also often live in the least energy efficient part of the housing stock. A widely voiced fear of the impact of a carbon tax is that it will raise transport costs on all goods and will be passed on directly to consumers.

The more novel approach is that of tradeable pollution permits. Once an acceptable level of waste discharge to a specific environment has been established, this is divided up among the existing waste generators. Each will receive an entitlement to discharge a given amount of waste and can chose whether to invest in pollution control technology and sell surplus permits or to seek to buy permits from others to make up any shortfall. It is argued that the firms best able to invest in new technology will do so and that a given level of reduction in pollution will be more efficiently attained than by imposing a uniform and statutory standard. There are only a few examples, mainly in the USA, of such systems at work and many environmentalists are hostile as the permits seem to legitimate pollution. There are also other fears that the system may be hard to police. The White Paper has ruled out neither tradeable permits nor fiscal measures.

Although the United Kingdom has become less hostile to the EC, the relationship with Brussels on environmental matters is still a difficult one. Considerable differences between British and European environmental policy remain. This is well illustrated by approaches to pollution control. The United Kingdom has historically preferred to consider the environment into which wastes are discharged. If this environment is in pristine condition and the volume of waste to be discharged is not excessive, the discharger would not be required to treat the waste. However, a similar volume of waste being discharged to an already partly polluted environment would be required to be treated. EC policy is to require a uniform quality standard for all wastes to be met before discharge, irrespective of location. This is justified on several grounds. First, such uniformity treats all polluters equally, irrespective of their location. This has become an important issue with the advent of the Single Market, for it ensures that pollution control measures bear equally heavily across the entire community. Secondly, this can be made into a technology forcing measure, for as standards are progressively raised, companies have to invest in new technology either in production or in pollution control. A further attraction of the uniform emission standard is that it more effectively embodies the precautionary principle – that is when in doubt err on the side of caution and reduce pollution rather than wait for proof of damage.

The precautionary principle emphasises the differences between United Kingdom and EC pollution control practice. For a century or more, the United Kingdom has espoused an approach called best practicable means. This has meant that standards have been set at levels which an average plant with typical pollution control equipment could be reasonably expected to meet. Further, this has been enforced in a consultative manner and on a case by case basis. By contrast, the EC has followed North American practice and adopted the best available technology approach, which sets standards at levels attainable by the latest plants and technology. The best available technology approach can easily be extended as a regulatory instrument to encompass the precautionary principle. The precautionary principle with its emphasis on action on the basis of doubt or uncertainty rather than awaiting proof of causal links between wastes and environmental damage partly reflects the Roman Law traditions of Europe and there are few obvious parallels in English Common Law.

The United Kingdom has made some recent changes in its pollution control and these have led to some convergence with EC practice. These are summed up in the new approach of best practicable environmental option (BPEO) which was advocated by RCEP as long ago as 1974. BPEO was made the basis of pollution control by the 1990 Environmental Protection Act and seeks to avoid pollution displacement from one medium to another and to raise environmental quality. However, consultation and discretion on a case by case basis remain the method of enforcement.

Subsidiarity is likely to add a new dimension to the debate about environmental policy. When Secretary of State, Michael Howard said that he saw environmental policy as an obvious area for the application of subsidiarity. He envisaged a handful of broad guiding principles being established by the EC Commission and the detailed application of these and choice of policy instruments being left to national governments. Environmentalists have been quick to criticise this view of subsidiarity. They argue that environmental problems are no respecters of national boundaries and that many require co-ordinated and consistent action at a continental, if not global scale. Others have suggested that subsidiarity does not stop at national government level, but should involve devolution to regional and local level. In the case of

environmental policy, this could mean the revival of the local government role which until the 1960s was the primary locus. Certainly such a
division of responsibilities between Brussels and town halls would be
closer to the environmentalist rallying call to think globally and to act
locally.

The Earth Summit, Rio de Janeiro

Environmental issues have been growing in importance on the
international agenda and this was underlined by the United Nations
Conference on Environment and Development (popularly called the
Earth Summit) held at Rio in June 1992. The Summit was intended to
see the signing of a number of new accords and agreements on the
environment. Four such documents formed the final agenda – the Rio
Declaration, Agenda 21, a World Climate Convention and a Biodiversity Convention. Much work had been done before the Rio Summit
but in the process differences between the G7, the wealthy Western
nations and the G77, a grouping of poorer countries, had become
polarised and some differences with the G7 also emerged.

The Rio Declaration replaced a more ambitious Earth Charter which
was to have been an international agreement on a set of global
environmental ethics. Instead, the Declaration was a set of broad
principles and acted as a preamble to Agenda 21. This document is a
lengthy action plan which seeks to apply the principles of the
Declaration. However the key issues of funding for programmes,
transfer of technologies, setting of timetables and specific targets and
of devising sanctions against non-compliance were not addressed. The
two international conventions on world climate and biodiversity had
resulted from a growing scientific consensus in the 1980s on the
urgency of the problems and appropriate policy actions.

In the pre-Summit meetings, Britain had adopted a largely conciliatory position. However, anxieties expressed by the United States
about many of the proposed accords became greater and President
Bush threatened to boycott the Summit. The United Kingdom moved
closer to the American position and supported its calls for fewer and
less far-ranging commitments. However at Rio itself, the United
Kingdom did sign all the accords and was at pains to maintain some
distance between its position and that of the USA. One major initiative
announced at Rio by John Major was the Darwin Programme on
biodiversity. It later transpired that this was to have virtually no new

funding and that its aims partly conflicted with existing international priorities and guidelines. The Rio Summit perhaps showed how superficial the 'greening' of government policy has been, but at the same time it illustrates how important a green gloss has now become.

Environmental Policy: Outcomes and Issues

Environmental policy is a particularly challenging issue as the twentieth century draws to a close. The development and application of environmental policy cross so many other established fields and challenge many widely held values and beliefs. Environmental policy also poses problems to governments, not just in the practical realm but also at an ideological and structural level. This brief review focuses first on some of the particular challenges faced by Conservative governments in Britain and then goes on to examine wider issues which affect all liberal democracies.

Environmental Problems and Conservative Governments

Conservative governments since 1979 have strongly emphasised the importance of market forces in all areas of social and economic life. They have also stressed the importance of consumer choice and of individual freedom and have endeavoured to sustain a maximum of national sovereignty. Environmental issues challenge all of these tenets of contemporary Conservativism.

Markets
For some environmental resources there are no markets and it is extremely hard to see how there ever could be. Clean air, attractive scenery, rare plants and animals fall into this category. Market forces will not ensure their protection, and as they have no market prices, market forces elsewhere in the economy could lead to their destruction. Traditionally regulation has been the way to protect such resources. The environment stands as a reminder to the limitations of market forces. Many environmental economists have been ready to offer indirect monetary valuations of non-market environmental resources and sophisticated methodologies exist to do this. However, environmentalists remain unconvinced and many reject the use of money as the

sole arbiter of environmental value. Pollution is classically described by economists as an externality – a cost imposed on others by individual consumers or producers. Pollution too is evidence of the absence or of the ineffectiveness of markets in environmental affairs. Again, regulation and direct government intervention have been the most favoured ways of dealing with pollution. It is now more widely accepted that fiscal policy, which changes prices of goods and activities in the market, can be exploited to deliver environmental policy. None the less, this requires deliberate government intervention and continued monitoring and is a reminder that free market forces are defective.

Further problems are raised by the use of fiscal measures to implement environmental policy. First, it is by no means obvious that Conservative governments committed to reducing the burden of taxation would be amenable to new forms of taxation. Secondly, there is the problem of whether environmental taxes will replace or supplement existing taxation. As noted above, environmental taxes are in effect indirect taxation and thus are regressive, bearing more heavily on the poor. If the yields from environmental taxes were to be redistributed in the form of grants and subsidies to improve resource use efficiency or used to fund higher benefits in the social security system, then some of the disadvantages could be mitigated. Whether the Treasury would be happy to see tax yields being redistributed in this way is another matter. There thus remain significant issues in efficiency but also in equity in the use of market signals to implement environmental policy.

Voluntarism and Individualism
Conservative governments since 1979 have encouraged individual action and generally been reluctant to introduce compulsory measures. The environment is particularly vulnerable to careless, irresponsible or deliberately malicious behaviour by individuals. It is not readily protected by the unco-ordinated voluntary efforts of individuals, even if they form a majority.

Garret Hardin (1968) has described these features of the environment as the *Tragedy of the Commons*. He sees many environmental resources as commons – things which are not owned by individuals but which are open to use by all. Acts of personal altruism entail considerable personal sacrifice but collectively, society does not gain from such sacrifices. Equally, if only a handful of individuals abuse their common rights, these more selfish individuals gain but society as a whole suffers. Hardin argues that environmental commons are always abused and become degraded. He advocates individual private owner-ship, in effect a monopoly control, but as effective would be collective regulation and sanctions against recalitrant individuals. Whichever response is chosen, the Tragedy of the Commons argument shows the real limits of individualism and voluntarism in environmental policy.

Commodification of the Environment
Placing monetary values on environmental resources encourages the idea that they are commodities like any others. While the aim of such attempts to value the environment is to ensure that the costs of environmental degradation are considered, monetary values can also encourage the over-consumption of environmental resources. Once a commodity has a price in a market it can be purchased by any individual with sufficient money. Such a view of the environment is problematic in several ways. Markets work on the assumption that commodities can continue to be produced and delivered to it and thus one purchase hardly precludes subsequent purchases. Many environ-mental resources are finite and their consumption when it leads to pollution or to degradation is a once and for ever action. Furthermore, some environmental resources such as clear water and air and uncontaminated food are vital to survival and making their acquisi-tion and consumption solely dependent on wealth raises a host of moral and ethical issues.

Government and Sovereignty
Contemporary environmental problems are no respecters of national boundaries and some of the most challenging are truly global in extent, most notably depletion of the ozone layer and global warming. The culprits in both cases are predominantly the industrialised nations of the North but all the earth's peoples suffer the consequences. Interna-tional agreement has been reached to curb emissions of CFCs, the gases which destroy the ozone layer, but national self-interest has prevented comparable progress in dealing with global warming. In the former case, there were substitute products available and further opportunities for profitable investment but there are no simple and easy substitutes for the fossil fuels whose consumption produces global warming. On issues like these, the problems of markets, voluntarism and individualism are again encountered but this time also at the

governmental level. International collective and co-ordinated action is necessary, with a concomitant reduction in national sovereign rights.

The Challenge to Liberal Democracies

The problems discussed above pose a particular challenge to the ideology of contemporary Conservative governments. There are also problems which challenge more widely the ideologies, values and assumptions of the liberal democracies. Three of these problems are:

1. Social and cultural views of nature.
2. The relationship between science and policy.
3. Sustainable development.

(a) *Social and cultural views of nature.* Environmental policy has proved to be a particularly vexatious area, for hidden beneath apparently technical debates are deeper but conflicting views about nature. Conflicts about the need for policy action or over appropriate policy instruments are not about the 'facts' but rather are symptomatic of divergent but deeply held beliefs about what nature is and how it behaves. A stimulating account of the different social and cultural views of nature is that by Schwarz and Thompson (1990).

They recognise four *myths of nature* and link these to four *forms of social relationship*, each with their own rationality. Nature may be seen as:

- *capricious*: nature is random, unpredictable and unknowable;
- *benign*: nature is tolerant and forgiving and quickly returns to an equlibrium which sustains human life;
- *perverse/tolerant*: nature is forgiving of most but not all human action. Some actions will tip nature into a new and unpredictable state;
- *ephemeral*: nature is very delicate and fragile and even the slightest action may lead to catastrophic change.

People in their social relationships may be seen as:

- *fatalists*: those who see themselves as having no control over their lives and whose strategies of coping are to enjoy or to endure but never to aspire nor to achieve;
- *hierarchists*: who see themselves as a part of bounded social groups in orderly but ranked relationships to others and whose rationality

is one of sustaining hierarchies rather than of controlling outcomes;

- *individualists*: who emphasise their personal autonomy and independence and whose rationality is a satisfactory outcome for themselves;
- *egalitarians*: who emphasise the collective but voluntary basis of actions and are critical of the social relationships of non-egalitarians. Survival of the group in an unchanged form is the primary rationality.

Schwarz and Thompson link the views of nature and social relationships thus:

- fatalists see nature as capricious
- individualists see nature as benign
- hierarchists see nature as perverse/tolerant
- egalitarians see nature as ephemeral.

Fatalists, by definition, exclude themselves from debates about any policy. The other three positions are well represented in the debates on environmental policy. O'Riordan (1981) has independently recognised similar positions and called them business as usual, managerialist and deep ecologist respectively. The present debate in government circles is between the individualist/business as usual positions and the hierarchist/managerialist positions, with both sets of positions arguing that egalitarians/deep ecologists are both too radical and too idealistic. Perhaps there is an element in the mainstream debate which wishes that nature were benign but secretly fears that it is perverse/tolerant. The exasperation and hostility of deep ecologist opinion, which sees nature as ephemeral, to government and institutions which do not share this view is reflected in the intensity and bitterness of the exchanges between the two. For if environmental science provides evidence to sustain the cultural view of nature as ephemeral, then really radical changes in society, economy and policy will be necessary.

(b)   *The relationship between science and policy.* The established view of the relationship between science and policy in Western society is that science supplies the facts and politics the values to be combined in an unproblematic way in policy. In part this also reflects popular and professional conceptions of what science is. As environmental problems have been identified and investigated, these views of science and especially of its relationship to politics have been challenged.

Environmental processes are complex and dynamic. Indeed, the environment is most unlike the laboratory in which 'classic' science can be carried out under controlled experimental conditions. It is most unusual to be able to close off a part of the environment for a classic laboratory experiment and so knowledge of environmental processes has to be gained by field observation and can only be complemented by laboratory or computer simulation. There is a contrast between 'classic' science of closed systems and the incomplete knowledge of the environment gained from working in open systems. Such work as often as not yields as many new questions as answers and partial rather than complete knowledge. Environmental scientists when asked for facts by politicians tend to offer at best qualified statements and at worst have to admit that they have little idea of the processes at work. Also, for every environmental scientist speculating that one particular process is at work, another can be found who will claim that another process is really crucial. Politicians and the public are not used to such divergence of opinion and of such uncertainty among scientists.

For politicians wanting to act on environmental problems and keen to meet public anxieties, such a situation is perplexing. By contrast, politicians seeking reasons to avoid making new policy which would prove to be politically unpopular, uncertainty and ambiguity in science is a welcome excuse. In the face of the uncertainty of scientific knowledge about the environment, social and cultural views of nature come to the fore. Environmental problems in Britain have seen both types of political response. Disposal of nuclear waste has caused great public alarm and the government has sought scientific advice upon which to act. This has not been as clear cut as was hoped and some feel that policy has been over cautious. By contrast, the uncertainties of the complex chemistry of the global carbon cycle have been used to justify inaction on curbing emissions of carbon dioxide.

(c) *Sustainable development.* This has become one of the key phrases in discussion of environmental issues since the mid-1980s. It is a suitably ambiguous phrase, which accounts for its popularity. The main problems arise from which aspects of sustainable development are intended. There are geographical, economic, ecological and ethical dimensions to sustainability and what is sustainable in one dimension and at one geographical scale may not be sustainable in others.

At present the richest third of the world's population consumes over two-thirds of the earth's resources. This poses ecological problems, most notably of pollution, but has been economically sustained for most of this century. Whether this is ethically sustainable is quite another problem. The complexity of the issues and of the choices to be faced is illustrated simply by the question of foodstuffs. With typical contemporary Western diets, the world could perhaps support some 2 billion of its 5 billion people. With a change of diet to that typical of the West about a century ago with far less animal protein being consumed, the world could support about 10 billion people.

The Earth Summit at Rio saw much polarised debate about sustainable development. The Northern nations saw population growth in the poorer South as threatening the environment. Southern governments and many environmentalists countered by claiming that the poor tread lightest upon the earth and consume disproportionately less of its resources. Poverty rather than population pressure is the cause of environmental degradation. Southern governments called for sustained economic growth for their countries and the transfer of resources and technology to allow it to happen. At a time of economic recession, Northern governments, including Britain's have been slow to act. Of course the recession itself could be regarded as evidence of the non-sustainability of Northern development.

Thus environmental problems and the policies necessary to address them pose very deep questions and challenge the ways in which we think about ourselves and our home on the planet Earth. The debates about appropriate policy are more than technical disputes and to be resolved they will need far-reaching social and economic changes. For if the 1980s have seen the advent of an environmental policy debate, the 1990s will start to show the extent of the challenges which will have to be faced for human survival in the twenty-first century.

8

A Criminal Record? Law, Order and Conservative Policy

MIKE NASH and STEPHEN P. SAVAGE

Introduction

> The demand in the country will be for two things: less tax and more law and order. (Margaret Thatcher, 28 March 1979)

There is no denying the central role played by the 'law and order ticket' as the Conservative agenda for Britain emerged in the late 1970s. The Conservatives, of course, had for many years previous to that been regarded as the 'party of law and order', but Thatcher's campaign lifted that banner to new heights as the 1979 General Election approached. An image was painted of a Britain which was increasingly lawless, with rising crime rates, industrial unrest and political protest presented as related indicators of a deep malaise affecting the country. As the above statement makes clear, new strategies for law and order were placed alongside fundamental changes in the state's relationship with economy as the two main pillars of the General Election campaign.

The aim of this chapter is to discuss the policies and legal reforms which have arisen under the Thatcher and post-Thatcher governments in the areas of policing, criminal justice and the penal system. It will assess the 'radicalism' of the Conservatives law and order policies, consider the extent to which those policies form some sort of ideologically coherent whole, and discuss the overall impact of law and order policy on crime in Britain. It will also discuss likely future reforms of the current system of policing and criminal justice, in the light of a number of inquiries into the workings of the law and order system. The overall conclusion will be that the Conservative record on law and order since 1979 has been an often inconsistent blend of ideologically driven strategy, 'progressivist' policy influenced by rationalism at the Home Office, and 'event-led' reforms, in some cases dictated by the pursuit of immediate political advantage. The result has been a curious mixture of policies which reflect both classically right-wing philosophies (such as 'just desserts') and more liberal strategies, along lines approved of by the other political parties, such as 'diversion' from custody and 'community' approaches to crime reduction. As a consequence, it will be argued that what has characterised Conservative 'law and order' agendas are policies and reforms which have undergone often dramatic policy shifts, some of which have involved nothing less than U-turns in strategy.

The Thatcher Years – From 'Post-War Permissiveness' to a Law and Order Society?

While the Conservative party have been long regarded as the 'party of law and order', prior to 1979 there was very much a bipartisan approach to major issues of policing and criminal justice. Despite differences over areas such as capital punishment, it is fair to say that the post-war period was characterised by a broad consensus between the parties over fundamental aspects of the law enforcement and the penal system, even if within that there was room for political contention (Ryan, 1983). Indeed, over questions relating to policing, there appeared to be little evidence of any substantial disagreements along party political lines on issues such as police powers, or even police accountability. One of Thatcher's achievements was to disrupt this broad consensus with a number of controversial measures, which were to render law and order very much a site of party political division.

Criminal justice and penal policy for much of the post-war era had been dominated by what is referred to as a 'welfarist' approach (Hudson 1993). Both of the major political parties lent their support, in differing degrees admittedly, to strategies which, at least officially, focused on the 'welfare' rather than the punishment of the offender.

Programmes of 'treatment' for offenders, particularly young offenders, were established, which rested on the principle of 'individualised justice'. Increasingly, more discretion was given to social workers and other caring professions to determine or influence the decision on what to do with convicted offenders. Disposals more tailored to the identified needs of the individual offender, who was often seen as the victim of social deprivation, emerged during the 1960s and 1970s, and attempts were made to divert young offenders and potential offenders from the formal systems of criminal justice where possible. It seemed, at least in part, that in following such strategies governments were taking on board the views of liberal social science, which had long argued, on grounds of both morality and effectiveness, against penal and punitive measures for offenders.

Not only did the Thatcher leadership seek to undermine the welfarist and consensus approaches to crime by previous governments, it actually blamed such approaches for contributing to rising crime during the post-war period. The 'permissiveness' of welfare strategies, and their apparent failure to really address the problem of crime, was attacked, and a case was made that 'liberal' social science and social work were actually encouraging crime amongst the young. By 'protecting' offenders from the consequences of their actions through treatment programmes, and by neglecting to send out the message that 'crime does not pay', welfarist approaches were seen as part of the problem, rather than the solution to the problem of crime and disorder. In the run-up to the 1979 General Election, the Conservative Party responded by pledging to 'get tough' with offenders, by, on the one hand, strengthening the police service, and on the other by introducing new and more punitive sentences for the courts. The seeds were sown for the abandonment of the post-war consensus on policing and criminal justice. We shall provide a broad overview of these developments, and then proceed to consider the current agenda for law and order policy. The discussion will be developed under two headings, the police service on the one hand, and the criminal justice system and penal system on the other.

The Police Service

Margaret Thatcher, on taking office, lost little time in making clear her intentions regarding the police service. The earliest step was to honour a pre-Election pledge by implementing in full the recommendations of the Edward Davies Committee, set up under Labour to review police pay, which led to substantial increases in salaries for all ranks. The pay status of the police service was maintained at favourable levels throughout the 1980s. In addition, funds were made available for increases in police establishments and improved equipment, particularly for public order policing (policing demonstrations, etc.).

It has been argued (Scraton, 1985) that the early 'favouritism' meted out to the police service, in comparison with the treatment of other public sector professions, was part of a deliberate strategy not just to strengthen the forces of law and order through financial support, but more particularly to 'win over' the police in preparation for what was to come. One of the things to come was the National Union of Mineworkers strike of 1984–5. In one of the most controversial periods in the history of the British police (Green, 1990), thousands of police officers from all over the country were deployed to the coalfields involved in the dispute. The primary target of police operations was the mass picket, and the eventual defeat of the NUM in their campaign – and the overall weakening of trade union power with which this could be associated – could be put down in part to the role of the police, using a range of contentious tactics (ibid.), in reducing the effectiveness of the picket. Controversy, however, dogged policing in the 1980s in other respects. To some extent these were only indirectly the result of government policy on law and order (but arguably directly the result of government economic and social policy). In the early 1980s there were major disturbances in Britain's inner-cities (Brixton, St Paul's in Bristol, Toxteth in Liverpool), involving clashes between the police and, typically but not exclusively, young black people. Similar events took place in Handsworth, Birmingham, in 1985. Although the Government denied that these incidents could in any sense be attributed to its own policies – Giles Shaw, a Home Office Minister, dismissed such sentiments by saying after the 1985 disturbances 'it is no use trying to find excuses for criminal behaviour' – they did nevertheless place pressure on the Home Office to introduce reforms, particularly of the police. The Scarman Report on the Brixton disorders (1981), criticised police methods and their approach to policing ethnic minority communities, and recommended a range of reforms of the police service, most of which were hardly in line with the Government's own 'get tough' line on law and order. Many of these recommendations have since been implemented, including new training methods and a longer period of training, more 'community policing', and forums for police–community consultation, all seemingly 'liberal' reforms.

Other controversial features of policing during the 1980s however, were linked directly to Conservative law and order policy. At centre stage in this respect was the introduction of the Police and Criminal Evidence Act 1984 (PACE). PACE involved the wholesale reform of police powers – including stop and search, arrest, detention of suspects, interrogation, search of premises – measures which were highly contentious in the eyes of critics of the Act (see Benyon and Bourn, 1986). Civil liberties groups expressed the view that PACE involved a massive extension of police powers and the loss of basic liberties for the individual citizen. Police commentators, on the contrary, considered the Act, with its attending Codes of Practice (which set out requirements for the police in such areas as record keeping, cautioning of suspects, and care for people detained at police stations), as just the opposite – as restricting the police in going about their duties (ibid.). Since implementation of the Act, research seems to have shown that PACE in practice is somewhere between both views. It has improved the lot of individuals suspected by the police on the one hand, in terms of increasing access to solicitors and the general treatment of suspects in police stations, but on the other hand has failed to come fully to terms with some pre-PACE practices (see Reiner, 1992, pp. 228–32).

In general, it is dangerous to view PACE as a part of a right-wing 'law and order' strategy to extend the powers of the police (Brake and Hale, 1992). Its origins in fact lie in the recommendations of the Royal Commission on Criminal Procedure (1981), which was set up under the Labour Government in 1978, and which would most certainly have been influential whatever party was in office. Furthermore, accompanying PACE was the Prosecution of Offences Act 1985, also based on the Royal Commission recommendations. This established the Crown Prosecution Service, which took responsibility for the decision to prosecute suspects out of police hands. Both PACE and the Prosecution of Offences Act have, to an extent, had the effect of *reducing* the discretion of the police to decide on action rather than increase it.

Other developments since the early 1980s have made it even more difficult to live with an image of the police as 'Thatcher's boys in blue', or the 'Conservative Party in uniform', as some radical commentators would have it. Despite the commitment to funding levels for the police and other law-enforcement agencies ('never, ever, have you heard me say we will economize on law and order' – Thatcher, 10 August 1985), the Conservatives as early as 1983 were applying the strictures of the Financial Management Initiative (see Chapter 3) to the police service. Circular 114/1983, issued from the Home Office to all police forces, made it quite clear that spending on the police was not some sort of bottomless pit, and that the Inspectorate of Constabulary, the Home Office watchdog over policing, would be looking closely to ensure that expenditure on the police would be subject to the famous '3 E's' – Economy, Efficiency and Economy. Pressures were imposed on police forces to extend 'civilianisation' to reduce costs, and to pursue other means of pushing the police service towards a more 'business'-like approach to management (Leishman and Savage, 1993a). These were early signs of what was later to become very apparent: the police could not rely indefinitely on any 'special case' status in the eyes of the Conservatives. Other signs to this effect which emerged towards the end of the 1980s were also apparent. Thatcher herself was beginning to make critical noises about the 'quality' of top police managers, and noises were being made about introducing an 'officer elite', including former members of the armed services freed up by the 'peace dividend' (Leishman and Savage, 1993b), into senior positions within the police. Many in the police service, having experienced the relatively comfortable days of the early 1980s, were by the end of the decade feeling that perhaps they, as with other public services, were about to feel the full weight of Thatcher's 'handbag'.

Criminal Justice and the Penal System

As with the police, the status of the criminal justice system and the penal system in the early years of the Thatcher Government bore very much the marks of the 'law and order' lobby. After pre-Election commitments to reverse the 'softly softly' approach of previous governments to young offenders, the 1980 White Paper *Young Offenders* (Cmnd 8045) set out proposals, which were eventually embodied in the Criminal Justice Act 1982, to strengthen the deterrent and punitive aspects of the justice system. The Act established new sentences for the courts of between 21 days and 4 months in newly 'militarised' detention centres – the 'short sharp shock' so popular in Tory Conference parlance. The Act also reduced the power of social workers and strengthened that of magistrates to determine the disposal of young offenders, again, very much in line with the right-wing attack on 'welfarism'. The first Thatcher Government in addition embarked on a major programme of prison-building, work on which continued into the 1990s, with the aim of providing the places the sentencers would need in the 'war on crime'. Subsequent policies in the 1980s could be seen similarly consistent with right-wing ideology. The 1988 Criminal Justice Act, for example, introduced a right for the prosecution to appeal against 'over-lenient' sentences passed by the courts; prior to that, appeal could only apply to excessively severe sentences (see Morton, 1988). It also abolished the defence right to challenge, and therefore replace, members of a jury without cause (the 'peremptory' challenge), and reclassified a range of offences as summary offences, so that they could no longer be tried by a jury, but had to be dealt with by magistrates' courts. These steps were seen as supporting the interests of the prosecution over those of the defence (ibid.).

Despite the rhetorical appeal of such policies to the law and order lobby, however, the full picture was much more complicated. Alongside these measures were less publicised regulations to *reduce* the use of custody, particularly for young people. For example, the 1982 Act sought to limit the powers of the courts to sentence young offenders to custody, by introducing conditions under which the custody could be chosen as a sentence. This was reinforced by the 1988 Act with the establishment of 'custodial criteria', without which a custodial sentence could not be passed, and obligations on the courts to pursue non-custodial, 'community-based' sentences as far as possible.

This 'twin-track' approach to criminal justice and the penal system – tough on the outside, softer on the inside, extending custody in some areas, reducing it in others – tended to give Conservative policy in the early 1980s something of a Jekyll and Hyde image. Policies which were perfectly consistent with the rhetoric of the law and order lobby, had to live hand-in-hand with policies which seemed more at home with liberal strategies of the 1970s – diversion from custody, community-based disposals, and so on. One reason for apparent contradiction would seem to be that the Government was faced with a tension between its ideological commitments and the political agenda on the one hand (as the 'party of law and order), and the 'rationalist' case being made by researchers and permanent staff working within the Home Office on the other. The latter were inclined to the view that custody was an ineffective and expensive means of disposal of offenders, a view of course well established in academic criminology (Bottomley and Pease, 1986).

From the mid-1980s however, signs of an ideological solution to this dilemma began to emerge. In place of the traditional couplings of custody with punishment and deterrence, and alternatives to custody with 'welfare', a theme emerged based upon the notion of *punishment in the community*. This began with the 1988 Green Paper *Punishment, Custody and the Community*, which argued the case that community-based sentences, such as community service orders, can be as much a punitive measure as prison. This was continued with the 1990 White Paper, *Crime, Justice and Protecting the Public*, which went even further and argued that prison was potentially *less* punitive than community penalties because prisoners were not, while in custody, required to be self-reliant; they were, rather, forced into the 'culture of dependency' of the prison! Non-custodial measures were in this way offered as more suited than prison to deliver offenders their 'just desserts'. A rather clever ideological about-face was presented in an attempt to reconcile a growing preference for non-custodial penalties with traditionally right-wing principles of retribution and punishment.

The White Paper set the tone for criminal justice legislation at the commencement of the 1990s. Together with the emergent changes in policing referred to above, the law and order agenda at the end the Thatcher era appeared very different from that which was on offer in 1979. We shall now move on to consider the contemporary status of policy on policing, criminal justice and the penal system.

Law and Order: Contemporary Agendas

There was, of course, no clean break between the policy agendas of the Thatcher and Major Governments (see Chapters 2 and 3). In the case of law and order policy much of the drift of the contemporary agenda was very much apparent from the mid- to late 1980s. A central platform of that shifting agenda was that of *community*. Despite being a term employed traditionally by left and liberal approaches to crime, the Conservatives had managed to integrate the principle of community-based approaches to crime within their own ideological framework. As we have seen, the community has been advanced as the ideal basis for punishment. Another sense in which the 'community' approach began to hold centre stage was in relation to *crime prevention.* Alongside the encouragement of 'community policing' schemes in the mid-1980s, came a massive campaign to mobilise the community in the direction of crime prevention. 'Neighbourhood-watch' schemes began to proliferate throughout Britain, with the support of government and the assistance of the police service. In 1987 a Ministerial Group on Crime Prevention, which brought together no less than 11 government departments, set up 'Crime Concern', a movement which, in alliance with businesses and the statutory and voluntary agencies, sought to extend preventative strategies for crime control – better security against crime, better design of buildings and estates to reduce opportunities for crime, and so on. What was interesting was the way in which this movement was presented as quite consistent with traditional right-wing values. John Patten, then Minister of State at the Home Office, linked crime prevention and community-based strategies for crime reduction to the virtues of individualism:

> Individual responsibility for one's own property and responsibility towards the wider community are both important in reducing the opportunities for crime. (*Guardian*, 9 April 1988)

What had happened as the end of the 1980s approached was that the focus of crime control had shifted from being almost exclusively targeted at the *offender*, to one increasingly focused on reducing *opportunities* for crime (although, as we shall see later, this was reversed to an extent, yet again, in 1994). This strategy, it needs to be emphasised, was one long advocated by the Home office research staff as being the most cost-effective approach to crime reduction. Again, the 'rationalist' case was being pursued under the ideological clothes of right-wing rhetoric. What then lay in store for the agencies more traditionally charged with law and order?

The Police Service

We have seen that the police service had ended the decade somewhat less favoured by the Conservatives than in the early years of the Thatcher Governments. It could be argued that it was only a matter of time until the pressures previously placed on other areas of the public sector, in terms of financial constraints, organisational restructuring, performance measurement, and so on, were to be felt by the police service. The logic of the Conservatives strategy for the public sector would dictate this. However, other factors were at work which accelerated the pressures for change within the police service into the 1990s. One the one hand, the Government was increasingly embarrassed by the relentless rise in the crime rate (see later). The label of the 'party of law and order' was looking distinctly frayed after more than a decade of government, and the police were placed in the firing line as having to take some responsibility for that, given their preferential treatment in the past. On the other hand, there was evidence, possibly convenient for the Government, that the police were losing public support. Evidence from opinion polls indicated that public support for the police had declined significantly from the late 1980s, although such support remains comparatively high (Reiner, 1992, pp. 262–3). This must have reflected in part the damage done to the image of the British police by the now famous roll-call of miscarriages of justice which were revealed from that point onwards – the Guildford Four, the Birmingham Six, the Maguire Seven, the Tottenham Three and the Cardiff Three. The police were, of course, not the only agency involved in these cases – the role of the judiciary, not least, was at issue – and the events in question took place in most cases many years before PACE (although not in others). Nevertheless, some fall-out from these cases undoubtedly has occurred.

These factors were used to add urgency to longer standing pressures for change in the police service (the service itself was also, in some quarters at least, anxious to reform certain aspects of its approach, in areas such as equal opportunities and training). One source for such change has come from what may be been seen as an increasing control of the Home Office, through the Inspectorate of Constabulary, over the way individual police forces go about their business (Reiner, 1992, pp. 241–4). Police forces have had little choice but to implement policy changes deemed desirable by central government – in such areas as the civilianisation of certain posts formerly held by police officers, equal opportunities, the formation of 'policing charters', decision-making processes and training. This is not to say that such reforms are not worthy; on the contrary. It is nevertheless the case that central Government has sought to increase its influence, if not control, over what has traditionally been a locally-based service. This longer term strategy, however, pales in significance in comparison with two major initiatives launched by the Home Office in 1992.

The then Home Secretary, Kenneth Clarke, announced in that year that two reviews would be undertaken in relation to the police service. One would be targeted at the 'governance' of the police – the relationship between the police and local and central government. The other would be focused on police management, pay and conditions. The outcome of these reviews was two documents published within a week of one another in the summer of 1993 – the White Paper *Police Reform: A Police Service for the Twentieth-Century*, and the Report of the Sheehy Committee *Inquiry into Police Responsibilities and Rewards*. Both, and particularly the latter, were to send shock waves through the service. Ironically, they were released within days of the publication of the recommendations of the Royal Commission on Criminal Justice (see later), which also impinges on the future of the police service.

The 1993 White Paper – Police Reform
The 1993 White Paper proposed the first major changes to the relationship between the police and central and local government since the Police Act of 1964. It was clearly influenced by earlier Government initiatives in the area of the health authorities (see Chapter 9). It also dealt with a range of aspects of the police service. The main proposals put forward in the White Paper were as follows:

- Police forces to have their performance measured in terms of the Government's stated objectives for the police, and they will be placed on 'league tables' to allow comparison with other forces.
- Chief constables to be given greater freedom in deciding how to allocate resources, but they will also be made more accountable for the performance of their forces.
- Local police authorities to be reformed. They would be made smaller, and the ratio of elected councillors to other members would be reduced from two-thirds to one-half, with a fixed number of 16 members for each authority. Chairs of the new authorities to be appointed by the Home Secretary, and local business people would be encouraged to become members.
- Opportunities to be created for small police forces to be amalgamated with other local forces at the discretion of the Home Secretary.
- Changes to be made to the procedures for dealing with misconduct by officers, including making it easier for police managers to discipline officers and to dismiss officers where necessary.

The White Paper was criticised on a number of grounds, both from within and outside of the police service. The major concern of critics was the reduction of local or democratic accountability of police forces and the increased powers the Home Secretary would enjoy in influencing the membership of the new police authorities. While at one end of the spectrum police forces are encouraged to decentralise decision-making to 'basic command units' – equivalent to the size of a sub-division under an inspector – at the other end central government, beyond doubt, was to accumulate more power to influence decisions on the direction of policing.

The Sheehy Inquiry

The Sheehy Inquiry was commissioned to consider issues of rank structure, pay and conditions of employment of police officers. Its main recommendations were:

- To abolish three tiers/ranks of police management – deputy chief constable, chief superintendent, and chief inspector. The concern was the police service had 'too many chiefs and not enough indians'.
- To introduce performance related pay for police officers – skilled officers would be paid extra, under-performing officers would receive no pay rises.
- Officers should lose their 'job for life' status – eventually all police officers would be placed on fixed-term contracts, and officers could be denied renewal of contract if their performance was below standard.
- A variety of bonuses, special payments, overtime, and early retirement would be phased out.

In December of 1993 the Government published the first *Police and Magistrates' Courts Bill*, which set out for statute most of the recommendations of the White Paper and a number of those from Sheehy. The major initial climb-down by the Home Secretary was over fixed term contracts for officers – this would apply only to superintendents and above. Clearly the concerted opposition to Sheehy across the police service had met with some success. Nevertheless, the first Bill did contain a number of dramatic reforms to the policing of Britain. Alongside the strengthening of central government referred to earlier, dangers lurked in the push for business-like 'performance measures'. The constant pressure to meet performance targets (e.g.

arrests, stop and searches, checking of motor vehicles, and so on) threatened to actually put the service back a decade or two, in the sense that it could have led to the more 'reactive' approach to policing which was so heavily criticised in the 1970s and early 1980s. Another concern was that, with the greater controls exerted from central government, the 'local' flavour of the British police may become a thing of the past. However, immediately after the publication of the first Bill, a combined force of senior police officers, shire Tories, and several former Home Secretaries (including Lord Whitelaw) began a campaign, which quickly succeeded, to force Michael Howard to back down on key elements of the White Paper proposals, including the plans for the Home Secretary to appoint chairpersons of the new police authorities, and the reduction in the size of those authorities. As with Sheehy, the police had proven to be a powerful lobby group, able to force major concessions from the government in defence of its perceived interests. Nevertheless, the drift towards the increasing centralisation of policing policy was to be enhanced with the new legislation.

Criminal Justice and the Penal System

The contemporary agenda for the criminal justice and penal systems can only be described as one in disarray. No sooner had the central piece of legislation, reflecting the drift of Home Office thinking the previous four-to-five years, been enacted – the Criminal Justice Act 1991 – than major reversals of that same policy were being considered. We shall consider the 1991 Act in depth and then outline the extent to which the Government took steps to distance itself from it.

The Criminal Justice Act 1991
The 1991 Criminal Justice Act was brought into force on 1 October 1992, enacting the following provisions:

Principles
- the sentence should reflect the seriousness of the offence, not the offender's previous record;
- custody should be reserved for the most serious offenders, a sharper distinction should be drawn between offences against the person and against property;
- community sentences should stand in their own right, young people should be dealt with in ways which reflects their maturity;

- the intention of the court should be properly reflected in the way the sentence is served;
- the whole criminal justice process should be administered efficiently and without discrimination.

These principles epitomise most of the legislative change covering the areas of sentences and release from prison.

Sentencing. Four sentencing bands were created by the Act, discharges, fines, community penalties and custody. The test for entry into each category is that of offence seriousness, with a reduction in the court's use of offender mitigation. In determining sentence, particularly for community penalties and above, courts were likely to consider a probation officer's Pre-Sentence Report, replacing the Social Inquiry Report.

Fines. Fines were to be based on the offender's ability to pay, based on a calculation involving disposable income, levels of fine and units. The aim simply was the rich would pay more than the poor but the penalty would be proportionate and felt equally. This piece of legislation met with enormous criticism, for example the media protest over a defendant being fined £1000 for dropping a crisp packet. It was revised in the summer of 1993 by reverting to the previous system of imposing fines.

Community penalties. These included Probation Orders with or without extra requirements, Community Service Orders, Curfew Orders (not yet enacted), Supervision Orders with or without requirements (in the Youth Court which replaced the Juvenile Court), Attendance Centre Orders and Combination Orders (this last being a combination of probation supervision and community service work).

Seriousness would again be one of the deciding factors in which sentence to impose as well as suitability for the offender. As part of the new rhetoric of punishment sentences would be a *restriction of liberty*, dependent upon offence seriousness. People placed on probation would become known as *offenders* rather than *probationers*, another example of rhetoric dictating practice.

Custodial sentences. In future all custodial sentences will require justification (building on earlier legislation), the criteria being that the offence is *so serious* that *only* custody will do, the offence is of a violent or sexual nature and custody is needed to protect the public or that the offender has refused a community sentence. Partly suspended sentences were abolished by the Act.

Early release. Prisoners would serve longer under the Act, remission was to be abolished and parole to all but disappear. The following arrangements were introduced:

1. *Prisoners serving less than 12 months.* These prisoners to be unconditionally released after one half of sentence but liable to recall if convicted of a further imprisonable offence during the balance.
2. *Prisoners serving 12 months to less than 4 years.* Conditionally released after one half of sentence but supervised by a probation officer for the following quarter of the sentence. As with the group above liable to recall from day of release to end of sentence.
3. *Prisoners serving 4 years or more.* Possibility of discretionary conditional release between one half and two thirds of sentence (parole). If not granted then released at two thirds stage and supervised to three quarters point with conditions as above.

Another Agenda for Change

The unfortunate abduction and killing of James Bulger in Liverpool in February 1993 triggered a moral panic on the subject of youth crime and in its wake was included the 1991 Criminal Justice Act. The age of the alleged offenders was 10 and there followed a 'moral crisis' over offending by children, producing an apparent party political consensus in the direction of more punishment, for example the Labour Party's Home Affairs spokesman saying that 'we must be tough on crime and tough on the causes of crime' (*Guardian*, 23 February 1993). Although this concern was directed at what to do with the problem of serious and persistent young offenders, other clauses of the Act were included in the criticism, most notably the use, or non-use of previous convictions in the sentencing process. We therefore apparently have two major policy shifts, one in the direction of increasing punishments for juvenile or youth offenders, and one which attempts to roll back what was viewed as an 'enlightened piece of legislation' – the 1991 Act – on the other (*The Times*, 21 August 1992).

Ironically, the 1991 Criminal Justice Act was to have been the 'finishing touch' to the successful 'justice model' of juvenile justice in the late 1980s (Hudson, 1987). The 1982 Criminal Justice Act had begun the process of attempting to limit the use of custody by the courts by creating a framework for sentencing decisions, notably in the area of custodial sentences. When allied to a practitioner policy of 'minimum intervention', a massive expansion of cautioning and indications of a falling juvenile crime rate, the success of the 'systems approach' (see, for example, Cavadino and Dignan, 1992), at least as justified by the official statistics (Barclay and Turner, 1991), appears to have been guaranteed. The figures were an apparent illustration of success. For example the use of custodial sentencing fell from 7900 in 1981 to 1800 in 1990. This fall was replicated elsewhere with supervision orders also falling from 10,400 in 1981 to 3900 in 1990. Both sets of figures can be set alongside a fall of 37 per cent overall in cautions and convictions for indictable crimes 1980 to 1990 (source, *NAPO News*, February 1993).

In the light of this apparent success why then were there calls to reform the legislation? It appears that the Bulger case referred to above acted as a catalyst for those who were unhappy with the provisions not only of the Criminal Justice Act 1991, but also the general drift of juvenile justice policy throughout the 1980s. Was it the case, they alluded, that the police were so demoralised by the failure of the criminal justice system to punish offenders that they were not inclined to proceed with the processing of suspected offenders? A Home Affairs Select Committee sitting in 1993 heard evidence from a Police Inspector that, 'Juveniles are coming in and continually laughing at you' and Hampshire's Chief Constable saying, 'We have a small hard core who have absolutely no fear of the criminal justice system' (*Independent on Sunday*, 14 February 1993).

No doubt these sentiments had been expressed by practitioners before 1993, yet why did one incident apparently help roll back a tide which had appeared to be all engulfing and unstoppable? The link between 'law and order' policy and the fortunes of the Conservative government must surely explain the about turn.

As the original Criminal Justice Bill passed through both Houses there was not a uniform acceptance of its provisions. An Act which expressed a clear intention to reduce the prison population was never going to receive uncritical support from the party of government. Criticism was also widespread in legal and criminal justice circles, notably around the intention to completely eliminate the use of previous convictions in the sentencing process. Despite opposition from groups of its traditional supporters, the government only slightly amended its proposals to ultimately allow for previous convictions to be considered as aggravating features in the establishment of 'seriousness'. Within seven months of the Act coming into force on 1 October 1992, the then Home Secretary Kenneth Clarke had announced that he was finding Parliamentary time to introduce legislation which would reverse key provisions of the Act. The government indicated that they were listening to the voices of sentencers, but the timing of the announcement, following on from a humiliating by-election defeat at Newbury in May 1993, may just perhaps be coincidental!

The 1991 Criminal Justice Act had therefore witnessed perhaps the zenith of the process described as bifurcation (Bottoms, 1980) and dubbed as 'punitive bifurcation' (Cavadino and Dignan, 1992). The provisions for increasing sentences on violent and sexual offenders, and re-introducing a form of protective sentence (Nash, 1992) enabled an Act committed to *reducing* the use of imprisonment to pass through a Conservative dominated Commons. The *Criminal Justice and Public Order Bill* (1993) began to unpick key features of that Act. Before outlining the 1993 Bill, however, and having already discussed the status of the police service, we need to comment on the impact of Conservative policy on other sectors of the criminal justice system.

The Probation Service
The 1991 Criminal Justice Act should not be seen in isolation from policy changes elsewhere in the penal and criminal justice system. The probation service was to take centre stage in the process of administering 'punishment in the community', and to do so was subjected to a substantial realignment of its objectives and the imposition of 'national standards' covering almost every aspect of its work. A process building on the Statement of National Objectives and Priorities (1984), the Audit Commission (1989), the FMI (1982) and the green, white and blue papers (1988,1990 and 1991) all sought to tightly define the work of the service to bring it in line with government policies. Cash limiting would also ensure that parts of the local service budget would be reserved for government preferred schemes such as probation centres. Those areas that failed to provide would receive less money. Central government would no longer slavishly follow the budget set by the local authority and increasingly began to push funds in the direction of the independent sector working in collaboration with the probation service.

Privatisation of some of its functions remains a suspended threat and clearly the probation service faces a breaking up along the lines of court and prison services. If the Service continues to struggle with the more punitive and controlling role ascribed to it then the government has indicated that others may be recruited to do so. Knock-on effects may be the changing nature of probation training away from its traditional social work base and the recruitment of a non-probation officer grade, for example the possibility of non-commissioned officers from the armed forces. The private security industry would no doubt be able and willing to take on the running of bail hostels and possibly the running of more 'demanding' probation programmes.

It could be said that in challenging the basic assumptions inherent in the work of the probation service the government is setting it up to fail. In the UK 'alternatives to custody' have never really secured the longer-term reduction in the use of imprisonment intended, and despite the change of language of punishment introduced by the 1991 Criminal Justice Act (abolishing the term 'alternatives' and introducing 'community penalties'), the service is still expected to deliver to meet the confidence and expectations of the court. Failure to do so could well accelerate the move to dismemberment highlighted above.

The probation service is therefore to be as subject to the influence of the 'market' and the new 'managerialism' (see Chapter 3) as much as the police service. Increasingly objectives for the work of the service will be centrally determined, backed by powers inherent in cash limiting, policed by a strengthened Inspectorate.

The Prison Service

The process of devolving budgets within the organisation but placing ever stronger external constraints on where the money is spent, was also a process identifiable in the prison service, following the 'Fresh Start' review in 1987. It is perhaps not without coincidence that the Sheehy Committee referred to above contained a member who was also involved in the Fresh Start review. Aspects of the prison service role have increasingly become ripe for privatisation, beginning with court escort services and leading not only to the private running of the Wolds remand prison but the open tendering for the running of the refurbished Strangeways prison in Manchester. Despite the very public criticism of Group 4 services in April and May 1993, culminating in the death of a prisoner in the back of an escort van, the government appears determined to press ahead with the privatisation programme (a further nine establishments were mentioned in September, 1993); this is despite there being no mention of privatisation in the Report of the Committee of Inquiry into prison disturbances led by Lord Justice Woolf, which was to set out central reforms of the prison service. The Woolf Report contained twelve major recommendations, most of which were tentatively accepted by the government. However, the financial cost of many of the recommendations would be very considerable, hence the desire to hive off part of the cost to the private sector.

The Woolf Inquiry, established following the virtual demolition of parts of Strangeways prison, an event televised daily to the world, perhaps went much further than the government ever intended (Shaw, 1992). The vision contained in the Woolf Report must be greatly commended, as it identified not only basic living problems, such as a lack of sanitation, underemployment, censorship and visits, but also a lack of coherence and integration within the criminal justice process. The Report also identified a lack of visible leadership by the prison department and the familiar difficulties of delegating authority. The government's response to the recommendations has been indicative of the general direction of law and order policy under the Conservatives. The initial guarded welcome for the Report resulted in a certain amount of hasty promises by the government – in particular the recommendation to end the degrading process of 'slopping out' by 1996 was brought forward to the end of 1994. Commendable though this promise was it does have consequences and ramifications elsewhere in the prison system. In particular the building work necessary, often resulting in three cells being converted into two, has led to further pressure on available space and continued the use of police cells for prisoners. Clearly the provision of internal sanitation arrangements, along with increased visiting and time out of cells, imply a resource cost to the prison service which a government committed to reducing public expenditure is unlikely to meet. Hence one can again see the attraction of private tendering. By inserting basic minimum requirements in the tender document the government can be seen to be keeping to the spirit of Woolf whilst avoiding the cost. For example, the tender document for Manchester prison speaks of minimum standards which include prisoners spending at least 12 hours a day out of cells, 7 days a week, one hour out of doors, bathing and clothes changing daily, six hours education and six hours physical education weekly, etc. All of these expectations have a considerable financial implication and it is interesting that the government is resisting the establishment of minimum standards in its own prisons. It is also of great significance that the government rejected the recommendation to establish a prison rule which would prohibit prisons from exceeding the certified normal accommodation (CNA).

Perhaps though the most significant change to the prison service is its move to become an executive agency under the 'Next Steps' programme. In launching the agency the Home Secretary spoke of a 'unique opportunity to change its management culture, to respond to the challenge of competition and to achieve its own vision . . .' The post of Director-General disappeared to be replaced by a Chief Executive in the form of Derek Lewis, chairman of UK Gold, a television company. The replacement of 'in-house' leadership by outside business leaders is a process not confined to prisons, but when added to the privatisation of detention services it raises very considerable questions over the moral efficacy of a profit imperative determining the custody of an offender punished and held on behalf of the state.

Courts and Legal Services
Those parts of the criminal justice process traditionally most resistant to change have themselves been unable to resist the tide of government policy initiatives. The all-embracing Royal Commission on Criminal Justice (see below) may well have a significant impact upon the delivery of justice. Already, however, the process of central control has increased as it has elsewhere. Attempts to reduce the discretion of sentencers and hence the disparity of sentencing decisions has fallen short of the creation of a sentencing council or a framework as tight as that used in many American states (Christie, 1993). However 'sentencing guidelines', produced by the Magistrates Association and also issued by the Court of Appeal attempt to introduce greater coherence to the sentencing process. Increasing use is being made of the Attorney-General's right to send cases to the Court of Appeal if the original sentence was felt to be too lenient.

Courts have also been subjected to the type of three E's scrutiny that other public sector organisations have faced. As a result points are accumulated (and funding obtained) by indicators such as throughput, waiting times and fine repayment periods. Cash limited budgets may result in the closure of many smaller courts, hastening the move away from justice delivered by local people in the community (much as it has with the regionalisation of prosecution services). A speedier disposition of cases is also envisaged with the reduction in payments to solicitors in Magistrates Courts. Payments will be on a fixed fee basis rather than the number of appearances. This may well reduce the occasions on which a case is adjourned, but it does raise the prospect of defence cases which are not sufficiently well prepared, and hence poses questions of justice.

In the wake of such changes in the probation, prison and court services the Report of the Royal Commission on Criminal Justice was published in 1993, with wide-ranging recommendations for reform of the criminal justice system.

The Royal Commission on Criminal Justice

The Runciman Commission Report (6 July 1993) represents the culmination of a massive inquiry into the effectiveness and indeed purpose of the criminal justice process. The role of Royal Commissions had very much declined in the Thatcher years, and the announcement of the Commission in 1991 came as a refreshing surprise to those concerned with criminal justice. To a great extent, however, the decision to set up a Royal Commission was 'event-led'. A series of successful High Court Appeals, extensively reported in the media and the subject of high profile public campaigns, led to widespread anxiety over the extent of miscarriages of justice and what seemed to be a decline in public confidence in the police and criminal justice system. At issue were areas such as the police conduct of investigations, the right to silence, the nature of the adversarial system, forensic evidence, pre-trial disclosure, pre-trial review and corroboration of confession evidence, among others. Evidence and research reports were submitted by numerous groups involved in the administration of justice, police organisations, legal bodies, academics and penal reform groups.

The Final report contained over 350 recommendations. The evidence submitted to the Royal Commission tended to polarise around issues concerning the right of the defendant to a fair trial and of the prosecution to secure a conviction. In simple terms it rested on the question of how to devise a system which ensures both the acquittal of the innocent and the conviction of the guilty. As it was put by the Home Secretary in his response to the Report:

> What I want to see is a system that will minimise miscarriages of justice. It is a miscarriage of justice if an innocent person is convicted, but also a miscarriage if a guilty person is acquitted. (*Guardian*, 7 July 1993)

It is evident that a fundamental restructuring of the criminal justice process has not been recommended. The adversarial system was not to be replaced with a more inquisitorial system, although support was given for more pre-trial reviews and a more formal and open system of plea bargaining. The Commission did not come out in favour of changing the suspect's right to silence. Equally the Commission did not see the need to introduce a recommendation that all confessions should be corroborated, despite very heavy lobbying from penal reform groups. However, it was recommended that defendants disclose the substance of their case before the crown court trial or risk adverse judicial comment.

The recommendation which perhaps excited most comment was that concerning jury trial. The Commission proposed that the decision to elect trial should be removed from the defendant and placed in the hands of magistrates, a change which could have affected some 35,000 cases per year. Although the opposition was vocal, notably from penal reformers and legal groups, it failed to note that jury trial had actually been under attack throughout the 1980s, through the mechanism of re-classifying offences from 'triable either way' to summary offences. Jury trial has always been and was becoming increasingly a very limited option for defendants.

A most significant recommendation, and one which met with broad support, is that the power of the Home Secretary to decide upon referral to the Court of Appeal in cases of alleged miscarriage of justice, should be removed. The proposal was for a Criminal Cases Review Authority which would not be led by a Judge. However, the Home Secretary, Michael Howard, indicated that implementation of this proposal would be delayed for some time.

The Royal Commission Report was published in the midst of a highly charged environment for law and order policy. While such a Commission would traditionally have carried much weight in determining forthcoming policy, it was released at a time when political considerations would dominate proceedings. Four sources of pressure confronted the Home Secretary: firstly, a media and public panic about crime, particularly juvenile crime; secondly a small Parliamentary majority in the House and a right-wing of the Party, ever anxious about crime, holding key votes and demanding to be heard; thirdly, a Labour party which seemed to be gaining ground on the law and order issue at the Conservative's expense; fourthly a police service, itself feeling threatened by Government plans, with its own demands for reforms of criminal justice, and in the game of some form of 'trade-off'. With these political considerations to juggle with, the recommendations of the Royal Commission were only one set of factors for the Home Secretary to consider as planning was under way for new justice legislation. Arguably, the *Criminal Justice Bill 1993* reflected more the mood and appetite of the Conservative Party Conference, at which he announced a '27-point plan to fight crime' (see Chapter 16), than rational thinking on criminal justice – red meat for the blue rinse!

The Criminal Justice Bill 1993
It has already been said that 1993 Bill reversed key elements of the earlier legislation. It also flatly overturned some important recommendations of the Royal Commission. Central measures were:

● Changes to the right of silence (opposed by the Commission) to allow juries to infer guilt if a defendant refuses to give evidence;
● New powers for the police to take DNA samples from suspects without consent;
● New custodial centres for 12–14-year-olds (which could be run by private operators) and extended custodial sentences for young offenders;
● Reduction in the right to bail, and prohibition of those on bail serving on a jury;
● New laws prohibiting 'rave' parties and limiting the activities of hunt-saboteurs.

The Bill was notable not just for its particular clauses but also for the rhetoric with which it was presented. At the 1993 Conservative Conference the Home Secretary made clear his commitment to the *increased* use of custody. Referring to the fact that his measures would lead to more people going to prison, Howard said:

> I do not flinch from that. We shall no longer judge the success of our system of justice by a fall in our prison population. . . . Let us be clear. Prison works . . . it makes many who are tempted to commit crime think twice.

What is remarkable is that this very claim had been openly rejected in the Government's own 1990 White Paper (discussed earlier), where the effectiveness of deterrence and imprisonment was denied. By any standards, it was a U-turn of baffling proportions. Nevertheless, a law and order agenda for the mid-1990s was by these means established.

Conclusion

It was almost with a sense of despair that many of those working within the system of criminal justice, and many commentators and experts on criminal justice, greeted the Conservative's latest stance on law and order. Although the 1993 Bill was welcomed by the police service, its commitment to measures which promised to extend the use of custody was criticised by those well versed in the effectiveness, or lack of effectiveness, of the custodial approach to crime reduction. More generally, its potential effect on the destabilisation of a criminal justice system recently geared to a strategy of reducing the use of custody was very much in evidence. It could be argued that the Conservatives record on criminal justice policy has now entailed no less than *three* different and conflicting phases. The first phase, which ran from 1979 until roughly 1985, was based on a traditional 'law and order' platform, with a heavy emphasis on deterrent sentencing and an expansion of prison places; its political strategy appeared to be one of establishing the Conservatives as *the* 'party of law and order'. The second phase, which we might label the 'age of reason', and which ran from the mid-1980s until 1993, seemed to accept a more rational and realistic approach to criminal justice, with an emphasis on non-custodial penalties, diversion from custody and other 'liberal' strategies; financial considerations of the costs of imprisonment were undoubtedly a factor in this respect. The third phase, that introduced at the 1993 Conservative Party Conference and which might well set the tone of policy for some time to come, involves a reassertion of deterrence and custody and a return to the rhetoric of the early 1980s; underpinning it has been a political strategy of 'winning back the high ground' on law and order, in the face of acute political pressures within and without of the Conservative Party.

The overall effect of yet another major shift in policy and philosophy on criminal justice must be to further destabilise a system already in flux with the pursuit of 'value-for-money' and the new managerialism. What those policy shifts have certainly not done is have any significant effect on the extent of crime. Despite the range of policies tried out since 1979, and despite substantial increases in expenditure – law and order expenditure rose as a percentage of general public expenditure from 4 per cent in 1981 to 6 per cent in 1991 (HMSO, 1993, p. 177) – crime rates have continued to rise. The number of recorded crimes rose by 96 per cent between 1981 and 1991 (HMSO, 1994). An intelligent observation of these figures would be that law and order and criminal justice policies themselves can only ever have a marginal impact on crime – social and environmental factors such as unemployment are far more significant. The paradox is that it has been the Conservatives above all who have dismissed such factors as accounting for crime. In the light of the evidence of increasing crime, the Conservatives have rejected their only viable defence.

9

Health Policy and the Conservatives

IAN KENDALL and GRAHAM MOON

> We are in a situation where the management of key health care resources is in the hands of a network of relatively small, seemingly autonomous and undemocratic management units; there is little semblance of national and regional planning and where health services are 'subject . . . to miserly penny pinching'; at times cost containment seems to be the only priority.

The above may strike some observers as a reasonable description of the National Health Service (NHS) after twelve years of 'Thatcherism' and a longer period of Conservative government. In fact, it is a description of the NHS hospital services in the 1950s – another lengthy period of Conservative government, but not one so associated with radical rhetoric and policy agendas about the 'welfare state' (see Eckstein, 1958, pp. 259–60, and Kendall and Moon, 1990, pp. 103–4).

It is important to retain this broader historical perspective in analysing recent and current government policies for the National Health Service. Some of these policies are less novel and radical than the rhetoric of their supporters and opponents might imply. Yet, in certain important respects, aspects of the finance and management of health care in Britain are changing. In particular, the post-1979 governments seem to have embraced the concept of 'welfare pluralism': at its most basic, a situation where welfare (including health care) is provided by a plurality of state and non-state institutions. More specifically, post-1979 welfare pluralism was associated with arguments that the relationship between state and non-state providers should be recast to increase the role of the latter.

162

In contrast to the radical right, most advocates of welfare pluralism envisaged no significant diminution in public expenditure on welfare; the state was seen as retaining a key role as a guarantor of welfare rights, a regulator of standards and a provider of resources. However, welfare pluralists shared with the radical right, misgivings about the role of conventional state welfare bureaucracies in service delivery; they were characterised as remote, rigid, unresponsive institutions. It is for this reason that elements of the day-to-day provision of services were to be shifted to non-state service providers – most obviously to voluntary and not-for-profit private institutions. The welfare pluralist tradition was well-represented in health and social care provision in other European countries, but was a major break with tradition for the NHS.

This chapter explores the growing impact of welfare pluralism on the previously monolithic NHS. The main concern of the chapter is with the period since the Conservatives reforms of the NHS in 1989. However, the events of the 1980s paved the way for the shift to welfare pluralism and, consequently, consideration will also be given to the considerable changes which took place before 1989. The chapter will conclude with a brief assessment of current policy themes: the *Patient's Charter* (DoH, 1991a) and *The Health of the Nation* (DoH, 1992).

Health Care in the 1980s

The election of the first Thatcher government in 1979 introduced a government whose ideological position on the 'welfare state' seemed to be more attuned to the radical right than that of the welfare pluralists. In particular there was a commitment to reduce public expenditure on welfare. A still officially unpublished 1981 review of the NHS was intended to reduce the extent to which health services were financed by the taxpayer and involved examining a number of alternatives including an almost total switch to private spending. However, political expediency dictated a recognition of the considerable popular support enjoyed by the NHS.

Rather than some dramatic retreat from state involvement in health care, the government sought to encourage and emphasise the virtues of non-state alternatives. Steps were taken to reduce significantly the role of the NHS in the provision of ophthalmic services. Previous attempts by Labour governments to limit pay beds in NHS hospitals and control private hospital development were both abandoned. Supportive comments were made regarding private hospitals and nursing homes as alternatives to the NHS and the latter received dramatically increased indirect support via the social security budget. A White Paper on services for elderly people contained an unequivocal statement that the advancement of community care would rely less on public provision and more on the community itself (DHSS, 1981) and the voluntary sector found itself drawn back into mainstream provision in areas such as day care.

The burden on the taxpayer was diminished by increasing the burden on the service user and by greater efforts at controlling and reducing budgets. The 1980s saw the introduction of new charges (eye tests) and significant increases in dental and prescription charges. They also saw the more rigorous application of cash limits: health authorities were required to produce efficiency savings, there were cash-limited drug budgets and generic prescribing and resource management were introduced. However, the major developments in the NHS during the 1980s concerned administrative and managerial changes.

Administrative Change

Following in the well-worn footsteps of its predecessors, the first post-1979 Conservative Government undertook a relatively conventional exercise of administrative restructuring. This was unsurprising given the considerable body of criticism that had been directed at the 1974 reorganisation. The Conservatives abandoned the attempt to maintain a geographical relationship between local government and health authorities and adopted a simple structure based on districts and regions.

The new administrative structure came into effect in 1982. Subsequently it was confirmed that the Family Practitioner Committees (FPCs) would be reconstituted as separate health authorities in their own right which, with separate local authority Social Services Departments, meant that there was a tripartite organisational structure responsible for health and social care. It was a strange conclusion to a process of administrative restructuring that had begun in the early 1960s and which, at one point in time, had aspired to unify health and social care services in a unitary system of local government.

The exacerbation of the administrative, budgetary and professional divisions between health and social care on policies for community care was to be the subject of a series of critical reports in the 1980s. This, and the burgeoning social security budget for private sector nursing and residential care, were key factors in drawing the government into a set of community care reforms that paralleled the changes introduced in the NHS (see below and Chapter 12).

General Management

The presumed relative merits of private sector management over public sector administration were introduced into the NHS by a system of contracting-out of ancillary services such as catering. Competitive tendering between profit-seeking private sector firms was clearly seen as a way of effectively containing costs and bringing the virtues of private sector management into a large public sector organisation. However, this approach had its limitations. How could the virtues of private sector management be brought to those parts of the NHS that contracting out could not reach? The answer lay in a more fundamental reform of management arrangements within the Service.

Prior to the 1980s the NHS had embodied a range of management traditions. The self-employed general practitioners were virtually beyond management in any formal sense, although they had maintained a strong professional consensus and were often extremely effective at managing their own workload and what amounted to their own small businesses. Community and public health services were, until the 1974 NHS reorganisation, managed in a manner similar to other profession-based departments in local government. Within the hospital sector there had emerged a form of shared management by doctors, nurses and administrators based on a perceived need and demand for considerable professional autonomy – especially for the hospital consultants. This was most obviously and formally recognised in the 1970–74 Conservative Government's White Paper on NHS reorganisation (see DHSS, 1972, p. 57). At regional, area and district levels, the NHS was to be managed by consensus-forming management teams including doctors, nurses and administrators.

The 1982 proposals for administrative restructuring indicated that the government was additionally interested in managerial reform within the Service (DHSS, 1979). However, it also restated the commitment to the appointment of consensus-forming teams of equals to co-ordinate activities in the new district health authorities (DHAs); the DHAs were required to organise their hospital and other services in consensus management units. But at a time when the new management units were still coping with the impact of this most recent reorganisation and some DHAs were still in the process of appointing staff to their new unit management teams, the Secretary of State announced the establishment of an independent NHS management inquiry headed by Roy Griffiths.

The inquiry team's key observation was that there was a 'lack of a clearly defined general management function throughout the NHS' (DHSS, 1983, p. 11). To remedy this situation they recommended the introduction of a single general manager acting as a chief executive and final decision-taker to replace the consensus management teams. This commitment to general management was to be extended above and below the level of health authorities. As a well as a District General Manager for each DHA, there would be a general manager for every unit of management within the DHA. Each Regional Health Authority (RHA) would have a Regional General Manager and there would be a small management board at the centre, the Chair of which would have the general management function at a national level.

Furthermore, the new general managers were to be appointed regardless of discipline. This involved a significant move away from the previously stated position that some NHS professionals should be exempted from managerial hierarchies and others should be managed by their fellow professionals. It instigated the notion of health care as a business in which managers should manage efficiently using management skills which might be applied with equal effectiveness in other public or private sector organisations.

The new managerial culture was introduced relatively quickly into the NHS with an emphasis on objective setting, performance measurement and business planning. On to a tradition of public services were grafted private sector concepts whereby efficiency savings were exhaustively sought in all elements of the operation of the service. Managers were also encouraged to develop local measures and participate in national initiatives to combat issues such as waiting lists and to look to the private sector when buying services. Some also sold NHS services to the developing private hospital sector.

The government went into the 1987 General Election seemingly confident that the reforms it had put in place, culminating in the introduction of general management, had provided the basis for a more efficient NHS and that no new major reforms were required. Unfortunately for the government the period immediately after the General

Election seemed to see the view gaining ground that cash limits were leading to 'real cuts' in services. The mounting public concerned in the latter half of 1987 led to the establishment of a major review of the NHS.

The NHS Review

The initial presumption was that the Review would be a root-and-branch reorientation of the NHS in accordance with the more radical tenets of Thatcherism (Timmins and Cash, 1988). But the creation of the Department of Health from the old Department of Health and Social Security (DHSS) and the change of responsibility for the NHS from John Moore to Kenneth Clarke, was taken to indicate a move away from this radicalism towards the assurance of political acceptability. The NHS Review was published as the White Paper, *Working for Patients* (DoH, 1989a) on 31 January 1989 and was billed by the Prime Minister as the most far-reaching reform of the NHS in its forty-year history.

The key recommendations of the White Paper concerned the development of internal markets. This involved the separation of purchasing and providing functions within the NHS. The unitary health service, in which a health authority both planned care and provided it through hospital or community services, was seen as inappropriate. Cartels could too easily flourish in which inefficient hospitals would be sustained by captive markets unable to use any other service. The solution was the functional separation of purchasing – buying health services to satisfy local need – from providing – the day-to-day business of delivering that care. Purchasing agencies, holding a budget to ensure the health of a defined population, identifying health needs, planning ways to satisfy them and ensuring the quality of the service, were to develop contracts with the providers who would, in turn, invoice the purchaser for care.

The purchaser/provider split would be most clearly established through the creation of NHS Hospital Trusts to run the larger hospitals. General practitioner services were to be brought into the internal market through direct allocation of budgets on a voluntary basis to larger general practices to enable the buying of certain hospital services. The operation of the market was recognised to be heavily dependent upon information provision and, accordingly, it was additionally indicated that there would be an enhancement of computerisation and resource management initiatives.

In organisational terms the Review recommended the replacement of the existing resource allocation system with one based on population weighted for age and the relative cost of providing services. It also proposed local governance of the NHS through management boards with no local authority representation and a restructuring of the DoH into a NHS Policy Board and a NHS Management Executive taking, respectively, strategic and day-to-day decisions. The separate Family Practitioner Authorities would become more managerially oriented and be subject to overall control by Regional Health Authorities.

The House of Commons Social Services Committee noted the generally hostile reception given to the White Paper, both inside and outside of the NHS (Social Services Committee, 1992, p. vi). The BMA warned of the dangers of fragmenting the NHS; claimed that concerns with costs might override the need for treatment; rejected moves to involve managers in appointing consultants; and condemned GP budgets and hospital trusts. The Association of Community Health Councils deplored the disappearance of local authority representation from the smaller, management-orientated health authorities, criticising the change as a distancing of the service from the service-users.

Doubts about the wisdom of either the basic principles of the White Paper and/or the manner of its implementation were compounded and confused by its coincidence with negotiations over a new contract for GPs which followed on the publication of an earlier White Paper on primary care. This included measures to introduce more competition among GPs, tougher monitoring of their work, more preventive and health promotion, and more information and consumer choice for patients (see DHSS, 1987).

Thatcherism and the NHS

The relationship between the Conservative governments of the 1980s and the National Health Service is an interesting one. There is some evidence to support the contention that the government soon discovered that blanket condemnations of the 'welfare state', of the sort favoured by its supporters from the radical right, did not strike a uniform chord amongst the general public. A disinclination to vote for restrictions on private health care was not the same as a vote for abandoning the National Health Service. Reservations about public expenditure in support of unemployed people in times of fuller employment, were not necessarily associated with similar reservations about public expenditure on sick children in hospital. The White Paper which introduced the internal market was prefaced with a personal statement unequivocal in its support for a tax-funded universalist health service.

Whilst the government may have abandoned any notion of significantly diminishing a major social policy programme of public expenditure on health care, it did appear to have a growing commitment to displacing the traditional modes of public service administration and professionalism by a form of private sector managerialism. Whilst the emphasis of efficiency was far from new, it did seem to be taking a particular form. The traditional ideal of 'rational' coherent planning to meet needs, seemed to be displaced by a new idea of 'strong' managerial control to remain within cash limits. However, in its impact on the NHS, this retreat from 'rational planning' was more rhetorical than real.

The political background to the NHS Review would seem to be fairly represented as an exercise in crisis management. Its establishment was announced within eight weeks of a general election in which the Conservative Party's manifesto had contained no indication that such a review would take place and within a fortnight of John Moore (Secretary of State for Social Services) dismissing rumours that any such action was intended. Government action – setting up the Review – was a response to public disquiet over ward closures and a perceived resource crisis in the NHS.

Contemporary Health Policy Issues

Attention now turns to the development of the internal market in health care. The pressures and themes which emerged in the years following the implementation of the NHS Review proposals in 1991 will be examined. Coverage will also be given to the development of the first health strategy for England, *The Health of the Nation* (DoH, 1992), the growing interest in consumerism manifested through *The Patient's Charter* (DoH, 1991a), and the nature of the barrier between health and social care.

The Internal Market

Following the introduction of the internal market, there was an initial period of 'steady-state' during which purchasing largely followed traditional patterns (Ham, 1991). Local provider units contracted with their 'parent' district health authority through block contracts in which the scope for close equation between activity and cost was relatively limited. Creative contracting was eschewed in favour of the status quo. The basis for this approach was the need for NHS management and professional groups to undergo a period of adjustment in which the purportedly new market disciplines were recognised and the necessary cultural adjustments made.

Steady state was an acceptable compromise which did much to aid the introduction of the internal market. It was in operation at the time of the run-in to the 1992 general election and had undoubted elements of political expediency. It also bought time from key professional groups, notably from the doctors whose trenchant opposition to the internal market was considerably mollified over the period. It was not, however, a long-term option. Crucially, it acted as a brake on the fuller development of managed competition within the NHS. This fuller development manifested itself in five interlinked forms: the emergence of NHS Trusts as the dominant form of provider unit, the development of the purchaser role, the growth of GP fundholding, continued debates over the structure of the service, and the impact of the operation of the internal market itself.

The first wave of NHS Trusts contained a very few hospitals, community units and ambulance services. These were not experiments, such was not the Conservative style, rather they were flagship ventures on which was focused considerable attention. Some, such as Guy's Hospital, were particularly noteworthy for the strength of the support which managers and a few clinicians gave to the concepts of the internal market. The source of this support is unsurprising. A form of the internal market was operating in the NHS before the NHS Review. For example, as early as April 1987 it was reported that some teaching hospitals were refusing to accept patients from outside their boundaries without some form of payment from the patient's health authority (see *Independent*, 30 April 1987). Indeed, the concept of NHS Hospital Trusts as set out in the White Paper did seem to have been constructed with Guy's Hospital and the other teaching hospitals in mind.

Initially, most provider units remained directly managed by a district health authority, but by the third wave of trust creations in April 1992 the situation had changed radically. Trusts became the norm and the disappearance of the directly managed unit was becoming a possibility, particularly in the acute sector. Trust creation had become a political imperative; a symbol of the internal market and an outward sign of the progress of the reforms.

Trusts did not, however, particularly in the first two years of the reformed NHS, emerge with ease. They were often the subject of considerable opposition from professional and support staff. Their creation was generally, although not always, prefaced by processes of local consultation and debate, frequently of a somewhat symbolic nature. Business plans were written and much was promised; financial safeguards and stability were underlined. Independence and autonomy were stressed and, at the same time, promises of continuity of service were made. Ultimately the emergence of the Trusts can perhaps be traced to the proselytising actions and hard work of groups of managers, to the political will of central government and local appointees on health authorities, and to a growing degree of acquiescence by the medical profession perhaps reflecting a perception of autonomy and the guaranteed medical representation on Trust boards.

While Trusts, particularly in their hospital guise, offered a clear public image of a changing service, the same could not be said for the second pressure area: purchasing. This was, arguably appropriately, the more covert side of the internal market. Indeed, being relatively distant from patient care, purchasing faced considerable problems in gaining legitimacy as a valid element in the NHS. This difficulty was heightened by the fact that the internal market was not a panacea for the pre-existing problems of access, standards and service availability; resource crises persisted and purchasing increasingly began to address questions of rationing in the guise of priority-setting. This development clearly conflicted with historic perceptions of the NHS as a total service although, in reality, it merely brought into the open debates and difficulties which had been evident for many years.

Purchasing remained relatively uncontentious while the reformed NHS was in 'steady-state'. However, this situation did not allow the perceived benefits of the internal market to be realised; purchasers held back from chasing out lower contract prices and existing purchaser–provider alliances were maintained, not necessarily to the benefit of cost-efficient care. The end of 'steady-state' was politically inevitable for the development of the internal market and it was accomplished by unfettering the purchasers.

By 1993 therefore, purchaser development had become another key area for achievement in the development of the internal market. Purchasers sought to move away from historic patterns of contracting where they could not be justified through clearly articulated criteria of quality and cost-effectiveness. They also endeavoured to put in place more sophisticated contracts linking costs to activity levels, setting performance indicators, and acting on prioritisation decisions. Contracts were scrutinised and negotiated in a generally more purposeful way as the key instrument for the management of scarce resources. This process was assisted by the growth in the numbers of Trusts; the disappearance of the directly managed unit enabled the health authorities to concentrate on purchasing.

This focus on the purchasing function revealed limitations in the existing jurisdictional partitioning of the NHS. Effective purchasing could often only be achieved when health care was being bought for populations rather larger than the average health authority area. Simultaneously, a consumer-aware purchaser often wished to purchase services which fitted with the needs of population groups living in local communities of much smaller size than a health authority. Two potentially contradictory tendencies resulted. First, several health authorities merged or found ways of working very closely together. Second, attempts were made to preserve or create some degree of localism. Locality purchasing took a variety of forms. In some cases it was a genuine attempt to devolve budgets to objectively identified communities, in others it consisted of initiatives focused on 'hearing the local voice', in some newly merged authorities it merely recreated the former authorities as local outstations of the new body (NHSME, 1992).

The enhanced status for purchasing also led to questions about functional elements of the jurisdictional partitioning of the NHS. The continued separation of the family practitioner services from the hospital and community services had been one of the enduring features of the NHS. After the reforms, the FHSAs were increasingly recognised as purchasers, buying services from independent providers – general medical and dental practitioners, ophthalmic opticians and community pharmacists (NHSME, 1991). It was inevitable that a unified vision of purchasing would emerge. FHSAs and DHAs increasingly began to work together as health care purchasing commissions covering both primary and secondary care across considerable areas. This development signalled a long-overdue integration of primary care into the mainstream of the NHS.

The family practitioner services were now incorporated into the mainstream of the NHS under the control of Family Health Service Authorities (FHSAs) with general managers. The reactive approach of the earlier Family Practitioner Committees was abandoned. As with the adoption of general management for the rest of the NHS, the new managers were appointed largely from the ranks of former administrators. In addition, the FHSAs sought to present themselves as purchasers of primary health care from independent contractor family doctors and dentists, pharmacists and opticians.

The development of the purchasing side of the internal market included larger general practices becoming fundholders and appointing practice business managers exercising their right to purchase some care directly from providers rather than via a DHA purchasing agency. These GP fundholders were originally termed GP budgetholders. Since budgets are usually limited and can run out, the new terminology may have been intended to convey something less akin to the harsh realities of the market place! The original guidelines about the size of GP practices eligible for fundholding were also amended. The lower limit of list size fell first to 9000 and then to 7000 (Glennerster *et al.*, 1992). A variety of other tactics also emerged. Practices generally began to work much more closely with health care purchasers, sometimes effectively operating as quasi-purchasing agencies in discrete localities. Some practices also began to work together forming fundholder consortia in order to access the advantages of fundholding.

The consequence of these developments was an explosion of fundholding which paralleled that of Trusts. Some 300 practices made up the first wave of fundholders. Latterly, although there remained exceptions, relatively large areas of the country became dominated by fundholding. This had advantages and disadvantages. For the doctors there were undoubted benefits in terms of the ability to negotiate locally-specific contracts; this was one of the grounds on which the BMA ultimately come to drop its outright opposition to fundholding despite the considerable administrative and management overheads. For the customer, the contract could also prove beneficial but problems might arise for people considered high cost cases; in such situations the DHA Purchaser theoretically acted as the guarantor of care. For the DHA Purchaser, the emergence of an effective partnership with the fundholders was a threat to their status as sole purchasing agency. Although fundholding remained limited in terms of both what it covered and the cost of what it could cover, it reduced the scope of DHA purchasing.

Collaboration between the two types of purchaser increasingly became necessary. In part, such collaboration was politically encouraged in order to challenge allegations that fundholding promoted a two-tier service where fundholder patients were advantaged. In the event, aggressive marketing and contracting by some fundholders meant that fundholding patients did sometimes find themselves in an advantageous position. For the critics this was proof that a two-tier service was being introduced. For advocates, it provided additional pressure to drive down contract prices.

The reform of the NHS recast district health authorities as purchasers. Hospitals and community units became providers. Purchasing strategies took a strategic overview of the provision necessary to satisfy the health needs of a given population. Central direction of these strategies came from the newly created NHS Management Executive (NHSME). The strategic nature of purchasing, the growth of purchasing agencies through merger, and the role of the NHSME and the general desire to limit expenditure, placed considerable questions over the continuing relevance of regional health authorities (Ham, 1992).

These questions were emphasised by three factors. First, when they were Health Secretaries, both Clarke and Waldegrave were thought to be opposed to the continuation of the regional role. Second, through 1992 and into 1993, there were continued revelations about the financial affairs of the West Midlands Region and the awarding of a regional computer contract by Wessex Region; these did nothing for regional reputations for fiscal probity and control. Third, throughout the post-reform period, the NHSME grew substantially notwithstanding its decentralisation to Leeds. It also set up outposts to decentralise some of its own work.

Despite these pressures, regions were retained. As Health Secretary, Virginia Bottomley was more kindly disposed towards them, possibly because, despite the parallel activities of the NHSME outposts, they provided a protective screen between the grand designs of central politics and the everyday operation of the internal market. The retained regions were, however, subject to review, to the stringent attentions of the Audit Commission, and to a staffing cap of 200 employees. The possibility of later abolition remained.

An idealistic view of the internal market would be that it was intended to drive down costs through managed competition while, at the same time encouraging quality. This ideal was far from the reality of the operational impact of the purchaser provider split. While quality control and quality assurance certainly moved on to the NHS agenda in a way which had previously been absent, the extent to which the commitment was real as opposed to rhetorical remained open to doubt. Only when purchasing began to develop did the means to really focus on quality become available, through more sophisticated and better monitored contracts. On a broader level, two particular operational problems emerged as the internal market began to settle down.

First, despite the best-laid business plans and the attractions of semi-autonomy within the NHS, the financial stability of several trusts was questionable. Financial projections and plans were revealed to be over-optimistic largely as a consequence of being based largely on data derived from the period before the introduction of the internal market. With the advent of more strategic purchasing, traditional purchaser-provider alliances were challenged and long-present markets evaporated. Nowhere was this truer than in London where the level of secondary and tertiary referral to London hospitals from the provinces shrank dramatically as non-metropolitan providers sought to develop more local provision. This development coincided with pressure to develop primary health care and resulted in the Tomlinson Review of London's hospital provision – the establishment of which was an interesting indication that the Government was certainly not prepared for this problem to be resolved by the operation of an internal market (Tomlinson, 1992). By 1993, parallel pressures were emerging in Glasgow, Liverpool and Leeds.

The Tomlinson review, along with an earlier King's Fund review on the same topic (King's Fund, 1992), recommended radical reductions in the extent of hospital provision in London. Subsequent reports recommended similarly radical surgery to the distribution of specialties such as renal and cardiac medicine. Not surprisingly, these recommendations were poorly received. The medical and scientific community argued that London, although historically over-provided with hospital beds had high need by virtue of its high daytime population; the provision was also justified because London was represented as an international centre of excellence in medical research. Opponents of the internal market saw the possible changes in London's hospital care as further evidence that the market was simply a prelude to cuts in the

NHS. More positive interpretations saw the changes as a long-needed prelude to a reorientation of the NHS resource away from the locus of the medical establishment towards the consumers of health care. These debates were not easily concluded and ensured that the process of implementing the proposals was lengthy.

The second operational problem which emerged with the internal market concerned the central role of information/computing in the reformed service. From the outset, both had been recognised as crucial to the operation of the internal market. Yet both were, despite much comment, markedly inadequate for requirements. Good information was required on health needs, on the costs of care, on the economics of care and on care outcomes, but fully integrated computer systems capable of delivering timely and accurate data remained rare. This became particularly so when the internal market began to develop and fractured the formerly close relationships between purchasers and local provider units. Information on contract activity which may have been hard to extract from a local provider with whom computer links might exist became even harder to extract as contracts were struck with more distant providers. The progressive integration of primary care and closer relationships with social care agencies made matters worse. Nor was the situation helped by an increasingly commercial attitude to 'business' information and the difficulty of convincing an ever-more pressed nursing and medical workforce of the relevance of information collection. It would certainly be true to say that deficiencies regarding information hampered the emergence of genuinely informed purchasing; they also limited the scope of evaluations of the operation of the internal market.

The publication of the White Paper *Working for Patients* provoked a number of concerns about the operation of the internal market. Would hospital trusts specialise in areas of greatest 'economic gain' and would the market ensure that these were appropriate to the needs of local communities? Might hospital trusts tend to discharge patients to the community before it would otherwise be appropriate? Would budget-holding GPs have an incentive to get their patients admitted to hospitals as emergencies rather than straightforward referrals? Would people with costly problems of ill-health find themselves being treated by reference to the size of a general practitioner's budget and the accessibility of specialist hospital care, rather than by reference to their real care needs? These remain questions to be satisfactorily answered. Any definitive evaluation of the internal market, NHS trusts and GP fundholders remains difficult in view of the Government's predilection for encouraging, rather than requiring, the adoption of trust and fundholder status. The first trusts and fundholders constituted a distinctly biased sample. Furthermore, some of the identified benefits – especially of fundholding – may not be sustained if the status is more widely adopted. Whatever its political or other merits, this approach to organisational change does not lend itself to systematic or swift policy evaluation.

Linking Health and Health Care

The internal market clearly provides a key theme in contemporary health policy. It is concerned with the effective operation of a health care system, the NHS. This goal requires targets. Some of these may be simply economic, providing care within a limited budget. Others are more normative and concern the levels of health to which health care provision should aim to contribute. Health targets, focused on major areas of morbidity, mortality and under-use of preventive services, provide goals which, within the context of the internal market, purchasers should work towards through performance-oriented contracts, intelligence about effective medical and non-medical interventions and a general concern to optimise the health status of their client population.

Health gain as an operational and strategic target for health services is not new. The Black Report and *The Health Divide* (Townsend *et al.*, 1992) both noted the marked and continuing inequalities in health within the British population. Both also gave an indication of the scope for improving health. The World Health Organisation's targets for health for all by the year 2000 (WHO, 1981) identified more specific quantitative targets. The latter were used relatively extensively within public health and more particularly so when, after the Acheson Report (DHSS, 1988), directors of public health were required to produce annual reports on the public health of their health district. Yet, despite this background material, there was no clear health policy in England until 1992 (the situation in Scotland and Wales was rather better). Arguably, it was the introduction of the internal market and purchasers' requirements for health needs assessments which enabled the incorporation of health into health services policy.

The health policy for England was first produced as a consultative paper in 1991. It focused on major causes of morbidity and mortality, health-related behaviours, areas of ill-health where there was clear scope for improvement, and areas of potential harm to health. These broad subject areas were subsequently reduced in the final White Paper, *The Health of the Nation* (DoH, 1992), towards a focus mainly on causes of substantial mortality and morbidity along with relevant health-related behaviours. Targets were chosen as the key instrument by which the strategy was to be achieved. The targets were all quantitative and calibrated to be achievable within a measured time-scale; tricky and politically unacceptable issues such as health inequalities were avoided.

The operationalisation of *The Health of the Nation* approach entailed major effort by the NHSME and the RHAs and a subsequent focusing of purchasing activity in general, and public health activity in particular. Local targets were derived when, through local circumstances, the national targets were felt to be too easy or too difficult; the emphasis was on setting realistic goals for population health improvement. On the positive side, the initiative provided a clear health gain focus to purchaser and provider activity. Activity alone was no longer the sole criterion for comparative judgement; outcome in terms of movement towards the targets became equally important. Less positive was a tendency for health gain to be related to health of the nation target areas at the exclusion of other topics and for the somewhat artificial nature of some of the health of the nation categories to blur the care needs in related areas – mental health, for example, was an accepted key area. The sheer scope of the label tended to encourage a focus on to relatively easily measured issues – suicide in the case of mental health.

Consumerism

A second area of growing attention after the reform of the NHS was the theme of consumerism. Like the linkage of health to health care, consumerism had been relatively neglected in the pre-reform service despite considerable lip-service. It was also, similarly, an issue which the growth of the internal market did much to encourage. Arguably, the impact of consumerist notions on the NHS owed more to the internal market than to Prime Minister Major's advocacy of charters for different consumer groups.

The reformed NHS was remarkable for the absence of formal consumerism. The limited democratic accountability which had been present on the old health authorities was abandoned in favour of appointed boards of executive and non-executive directors. The community health councils, set up as the 'patient's voice' in 1974, were often excluded from meetings. Yet consumerism became important. First, providers needed positive consumer feedback in order to improve and market their services in a competitive environment. Second, purchasers needed grass roots information about health need in order to purchase wisely. The result was a flood of patient/client satisfaction surveys, community health needs studies, and other attempts to get the views of consumers. The Patient's Charter (DoH, 1991a) certainly assisted this process, but much of the impetus was already in place for business reasons associated with the internal market.

By late 1993, consumerism was rampant within the NHS. Yet much of the activity was arguably of limited effectiveness. While hospitals were offered the choice of going self-governing and general practitioners were offered the choice of becoming fund-holders, it was unclear whether consumer choices were increased in any real sense. Genuine involvement of consumers remained rare. Real consumer inputs to decision-making were limited and often aimed to legitimate existing decisions rather than promote a person-centred service. In part this shortfall was an inevitable consequence of the realities of managing a complex service; few consumers possessed the necessary information, knowledge and even inclination to contribute effectively to debate. In part it was undoubtedly a legacy of the relatively non-participatory style of management which had evolved in the NHS through the 1980s. In part it may be a more substantial legacy of the relatively non-democratic traditions of the NHS. Only historians recall the period when local government regulated all state financed hospital and community health care and three-fifths of the membership of the equivalent of FHSAs were patients. This remains an area where much has to be done for the reality to match the rhetoric.

Boundaries and Barriers

Successive reorganisations of health and social care between 1971 and 1985 made limited contributions to creating a framework which would encourage rather than hinder effective co-operation and co-ordination between health and social care agencies and professionals. Basic organisational and budgetary divisions were compounded by differences in professional and managerial cultures. Formally, neither the

NHS nor the related community care reforms, made a significant contribution to the enduring dilemma of establishing a seamless web between hospital care and community health and social care.

This unsatisfactory division is perpetuated through the identification of health authorities as purchasers of health care and local government as the lead agency for social care. However, the purchaser/provider split may provide the basis for the emergence of multi-professional and service-user focused providers of health and social care. There are indications that primary health care providers (GPs) are beginning to develop much closer working relationships with other community health services and exploring the potential for more effectively integrated care management systems.

As local authority social services departments develop their lead agency role and take on the characteristics of purchasers, there may be increasing potential for closer co-operation between them, FHSA managers and DHA purchasing agencies, laying the base for comprehensive health and social care purchasing. The concept of the internal market may facilitate the emergence of a co-ordinated approach to health and social care delivery. Agencies with traditionally very different working methods, may come together to manage jointly the purchase and provision of services. It is possible that the working of the internal market may lead to a set of organisational arrangements for health and social care that have eluded the more conventional forms of restructuring previously undertaken.

Cost-Containment

Perhaps the most pressing policy issue is the least contemporary one. The first few months of the operation of the NHS were sufficient to indicate the limitations of a widely held assumption – mentioned in the Beveridge Report – that an improved health service would diminish the need for health care (and associated health and social security costs) by producing a healthier population. Demographic trends, medical advances and the provision of accessible and acceptable health services increase the potential volume of treatable illness in all industrial societies.

The resulting cost-containment problem seems universal and might be presumed to be particularly difficult in the UK, since the finances of the British NHS continue to rely more significantly on general taxation than do those systems operating elsewhere in the European Community. The result is a system largely free at the point of use. Conventional economic analyses suggests that this a recipe for abuse and waste by consumers. In the event the UK spends significantly less of its resources on health care than a number of other countries leading to the paradoxical conclusion that a universal, open access, free service making little or no use of conventional market mechanisms is much better at containing costs than more market-oriented systems. Whether the introduction of an internal market will detract from this cost-containment success story remains to be seen. At least part of this success may be attributable to a modest degree of planning, the NHS's traditional role as a monopsonist with regard to health care personnel and the absence of complex systems for charging and billing individuals or organisations – all of which are subject to at least some change in the new system of management and finance.

Conclusion

In so far as the radical organisational changes associated with general management and 'internal markets' have moved the NHS in the direction of a form of 'welfare pluralism', they have also moved it closer to organisational models long employed for health and social care in other European Community countries. The idea that these changes herald the end of the 'welfare state' will seem perversely ethnocentric to social policy analysts in other European countries which would claim equal right to the label of 'welfare state'.

For the moment the form of 'welfare pluralism' adopted by the NHS affords only a limited place for resources other than public sector expenditure or agencies other than locally managed public-sector organisations. In addition there seems to be continuing commitment to a universalist service whose limited reliance on direct service-user charges remains amongst its more distinctive characteristics. Ninety per cent of reported illness and a significant proportion of non-reported illness is now dealt with by personnel whose mode of operation is akin to that of small businesses and shops. But then the self-employed independent contractor general medical practitioner and the local chemists shop were always integral parts of the British NHS.

10

Housing Policy since 1979: Developments and Prospects

ROB ATKINSON and PAUL DURDEN

Introduction

Housing is crucial to peoples' well-being and whilst it may appear that Britain is a well housed nation significant numbers of its citizens find themselves living in inadequate conditions or homeless. One might ask why, as we approach the twenty-first century, should significant numbers of people find themselves in this situation? Instinctively many people turn to government to solve these problems, however, increasingly government has been unwilling to take upon itself the role of housing provider and has emphasised the role of the private sector and individual responsibility.

These issues will be examined in the context of a discussion of the development of housing policy since 1979. First we outline the situation during the 1980s, then discuss recent developments and future prospects before finally moving on to focus on two key issues currently dominating the housing field: homelessness and the 'crisis of owner-occupation'.

Developments Pre-1979

The post-war years saw considerable progress in tackling the housing problems of the UK with major programmes of council house building, slum clearance and improvement being undertaken by Labour and Conservative governments (see Atkinson and Durden, 1990). These developments must be placed in the context of a wider set of assumptions by governments of all parties; from about the mid-1960s both Labour and Conservative parties agreed upon the superiority of owner-occupation as a housing tenure and favoured a residual role for council housing, i.e. it should be a safety net available only to those unable to provide for themselves in the owner-occupied sector. Other major developments in the period prior to 1979 included the *Homeless Persons Act 1977*, which broadened the definition of 'homelessness'. The other key development of the 1970s was the increased role, post 1974, given to the housing association movement.

By the time the Thatcher government came to power in 1979 a major restructuring of the housing system was already under way.

Housing Policy 1979–93

This section outlines the general stance of the Thatcher government on housing in 1979, the immediate problems it faced and how it attempted to restructure social housing and revive the private rented sector.

The Thatcher governments housing policy had four basic objectives (see Cmnd 214 for more details): (1) to encourage owner occupation; (2) to minimise local authority housing provision; (3) to revitalise the private rented sector; (4) to target resources more accurately on the most acute problems, thus alleviating the most pressing housing problems and obtaining better value for money (Atkinson and Durden, 1990, pp. 119–20). This strategy saw housing as basically a consumer good which the market should provide, the public sector's role being that of enabling or facilitating people's participation in the market.

Social Housing

The term social housing has been used during the 1980s to refer to the activities of both local authorities and housing associations, denoting a continued major role for the state sector but at the same time a restructuring of roles within the state sector with housing associations increasing the scale and range of their operations.

Local Authority Housing

Thatcherites believed that council housing was financially 'feather-bedded' and that it played a major role in creating a 'dependency culture' – it was viewed as a problem. Government thus decided to fundamentally reduce and restructure the council sector. This was pursued by a variety of means, most notably through a series of Acts. The key points are summarised in Table 10.1.

TABLE 10.1   *Main points of key housing legislation*

Housing Act, 1980
- gave local authority tenants security of tenure
- gave local authority tenants the right to buy their dwellings at a discounted price
- encouraged more 'sensible' management
- effectively abolished long term security of tenure for new private tenants
- easier for landlords to regain possession of their properties
- created two new types of private tenancy – assured and shorthold – with rents largely determined by the market

Housing and Planning Act, 1986
- allowed councils to transfer their stock to other landlords (e.g. housing associations, private landlords)

Housing Act, 1988
- offered council tenants the 'Tenants Choice', tenants could initiate the transfer process (to housing associations, tenants co-operatives or to commercial landlords)
- allowed housing associations to draw upon private finance
- Housing Action Trusts established
- further deregulation of the private rented sector

Perhaps the most obvious and dramatic evidence of this hostility during the 1980s was the reduction in council house building, as Table 10.2 clearly shows.

TABLE 10.2   *Local authority dwellings completed in the UK, 1981–91*

1981	45 948	1987	15 625
1982	28 486	1988	15 764
1983	28 471	1989	14 043
1984	27 302	1990	13 956
1985	22 513	1991	8073
1986	18 813		

Source: *Housing and Construction Statistics*, 1981–91, Table 6.1.

Councils also faced considerable pressures to reduce expenditure on housing and this added to and intensified the already serious problem of disrepair facing the council sector in 1979 (see AMA, 1979; Inquiry into British Housing, 1985). Along with the continued favourable treatment of owner–occupation this produced a major restructuring of overall housing expenditure. Public expenditure on social housing fell from £4.5 bn in 1980/81 to £1.4 bn in 1991/92 whilst 'expenditure' on mortgage interest tax relief (via MIRAS) rose from £2.19 bn in 1980/81 to £7.8 bn in 1990/91 (Inquiry into British Housing, 1991; Raynsford, 1989).

As Table 10.3 demonstrates large numbers of council houses were sold. However, sales have tapered off somewhat in the late 1980s and early 1990s; moreover the vast majority of sales were in England.

TABLE 10.3   *Sales of dwellings owned by local authorities and new towns in Great Britain, 1981–91*

	Local authorities	Housing associations	New towns	Total
1981	109 652	7 263	5 598	122 513
1982	212 949	17 431	6 601	236 981
1983	151 119	16 464	7 044	174 627
1984	115 044	12 565	6 069	133 678
1985	103 257	9 520	4 596	117 346
1986	98 452	10 500	4 016	112 968
1987	112 582	7 946	5 215	125 743
1988	169 816	8 570	7 204	185 590
1989	189 959	7 114	8 411	205 914
1990	132 492	6 024	4 351	142 867
1991	76 993	5 086	2 725	84 804

Source: *Housing and Construction Statistics*, 1981–91, Table 9.6.

Scottish tenants, however, were much less eager to purchase their dwellings, reflecting the historical difference in housing tenure and policy between England and Scotland. Indeed, in Scotland sales took off much more slowly, starting from a low point of 8731 in 1981 rising to a peak of 33,196 in 1989 and declining to 20,420 in 1992.

Moreover, at least up until the mid-1980s, most sales occurred in the south-east and adjacent regions (Dunn *et al.*, 1987) suggesting that there were major regional differences in sales which accentuated already existing variations in tenure patterns between regions. The main point made by critics of the 1980 Act was that council dwellings should be retained for those in greatest need and that sales reduced the availability of dwellings for the homeless and thus increased housing stress.

The 1987 White Paper (Cmnd 214) signalled the intention of the government to proceed down the transfer road and thus to end local governments' role as a provider of housing. The White Paper acknowledged that while local authorities would continue to play a major role in meeting local housing needs:

> there will no longer be the same presumption that the local authority itself should take direct action to meet new or increasing demands. The future role of local authorities will essentially be a strategic one identifying housing needs and demands . . . maximising the use of private finance, and encouraging the new interest in the revival of the independent rented sector. (Cmnd 214, p. 14)

In essence the local authority would become an enabler (see Malpass 1992 for a rather different view).

The 1986 and 1988 Acts suggest that government believed many local authority tenants, who could not afford or did not wish to buy their homes, were eager to move out of the public sector. All that was required was for government to provide the opportunity. Yet this ignored a serious question – 'who will take them on?'. The obvious answer was the housing associations. However it is doubtful if they could absorb, even if willing, large numbers of dwellings. The actual transfers which have occurred have frequently involved councils coming to some 'agreement' with an established housing association or establishing 'satellite' associations to which they could transfer stock and housing department staff *in toto*. In both cases councils have retained significant nomination rights over the stock thereby preserving some form of 'council housing'. By May 1991 only 80,000 units had been transferred out of council control (Inquiry into British Housing, 1991, p. 67).

Throughout the 1980s one of the key weapons in the Conservatives' strategy to encourage council tenants to buy was to increase rents so that they approached 'market levels'. It was assumed this would have the effect of encouraging those not reliant upon state benefits to purchase either their council dwelling or one already in the owner-occupied sector. The 1989 Act included a number of provisions which increased central governments' control over local authority housing finance (see Malpass, 1992 for more detail). The intention was to force local authorities to charge 'market rents' thereby encouraging people to move out of the council sector.

These developments accentuated an established trend towards the residualisation of the council sector, i.e. the concentration of those whose rents were paid by the state in this sector (see Forrest and Murie, 1983, 1986). As a result during the 1980s council housing increasingly became the tenure of the poor, a fact indicated by the constant increase in housing benefit throughout the 1980s, by 1990/91 it had reached £5.3 bn per annum (Inquiry into British Housing, 1991, p. 20).

Housing Associations

The other major arm of social housing is the housing association movement (for overviews see Cope, 1990; Langstaff, 1992). Traditionally housing associations have provided both new build and refurbished accommodation for rent by low-income households; refurbished dwellings providing the bulk of their accommodation. However, during the 1980s as council building declined dramatically housing association building fared somewhat better. For instance in 1980 in England councils built four times as many dwellings as housing associations, by 1991 housing associations were building more dwellings than local authorities (see Tables 10.2 and 10.5; Inquiry into British Housing, 1991, p. 11, Figure 2). Although, as Table 10.4 shows, housing associations did not have an entirely untroubled decade as regards building, they did fare a great deal better than local authorities. Langstaff (1992) puts this down to a case of 'benign neglect' on the part of the government which left housing associations with a relatively favourable subsidy structure that encouraged their continued expansion.

TABLE 10.4   *Housing association dwellings built in the UK 1981–91*

1981	16 823	1987	10 909
1982	11 176	1988	10 774
1983	14 336	1989	10 604
1984	13 944	1990	13 695
1985	11 368	1991	15 169
1986	10 521		

Source: *Housing and Construction Statistics*, 1981–91, Table 6.1.

The Acts of 1988 and 1989 had major financial implications for housing associations, forcing them to turn to private sector finance in order to proceed with their housing programme. The involvement of private sector finance means that serious consideration must be given to rates of return to private investors. The outcome of this has been major increases in the rents charged which runs the risk of excluding those low-income households the sector has traditionally aimed to house (see Langstaff, 1992).

Government also saw housing associations playing a major role in the reduction of the council sector and the provision of 'choice' within the public sector. Government hoped that the 1988 Act would encourage local authority tenants to transfer to housing association control. According to the government they had more sensitive and more efficient housing management practices than their local authority counterparts (see Kearns, 1991 for a somewhat different view). A few housing associations began to take on larger estates, which in some cases, in the early 1990s, builders had initially intended for owner-occupation but were unable to sell (Page, 1993). It appears that some of these estates, along with other new properties, are being used to house the homeless and those on low incomes; as Page has pointed out associations now house a much greater proportion of the poor (Page, 1993, ch. 7). Associations now face the problem of running large estates with large numbers of low income residents. However, as Page (1993, p. 5) has noted '. . . there is no intrinsic reason to assume that housing associations are better managers than local authorities'. Associations now run the risk of becoming the landlords of 'stigmatised' estates like their local authority predecessors.

Thus during the 1980s the housing association sector also experienced a major shake-up, the full extent of which is unlikely to be clear for several years. Indeed, Page (1993) has gone so far as to argue that the 1988 Act:

> heralded a new role for housing associations. They were to become the 'main providers' of social housing in place of local authorities. (p. 3)

This in turn raises issues about the accountability of housing associations which have been criticised as 'self-perpetuating oligarchies' (Kearns, 1991, pp. 28–9).

What conclusions can we draw from the above? Clearly council housing had been under considerable pressure during the 1980s and there have been major transfers of stock from the council to the owner-occupied sector. Yet despite this the vast majority of stock owned by councils in 1979 still remains under their control today. Government attempts, via the 1986 and 1988 Acts, to pressurise tenants into transferring to other landlords (most notably housing associations) is an implicit recognition of a failure to fundamentally dismember the council sector. At the same time as the council sector has been contracting the housing associations have been expanding their role. This expansion appears to have been partly a result of design and partly a result of 'benign neglect'. However, by the late 1980s/early 1990s it would seem that this sector too was undergoing a restructuring, most notably through the influx, albeit limited to date, of former council dwellings, an increase in the number of its tenants living in poverty and a restructuring of its financial system. The use of private capital, which threatens to increase rents, and the increasing number of low income tenants creates a potential contradiction which may cause serious problems as housing associations attempt to reconcile the demands of the two groups. Taken together these developments posed major dilemmas for the future development of housing associations.

The Privately Rented Sector

As we have already indicated the government wished to revive the private rented sector, it having declined from around 50 per cent of the housing stock in 1939 to between 11–12 per cent in 1980. One of the government's first moves in this direction was contained in the 1980 Act which reduced security of tenure on new lettings, making it easier for landlords to regain possession of their properties, and assured and shorthold tenancies were created (see Atkinson and Durden, 1990,

p. 124, for more detail). Government hoped these developments would produce an environment which would provide landlords with a good return on their properties thereby persuading more owners to offer their properties for rent and lead to an influx of capital investment into new building for rent, thus reviving the private rented market.

Ironically, there was (and is) no guarantee that the rents people could afford to pay, even with the help of housing benefit, would be sufficient to make investment in rental property an attractive investment except at the top end of the market and in dwellings for multiple occupation. What is required is a major restructuring of the taxation system if new investment is to be attracted into private renting; the reduction of security of tenure on its own will have little effect as many landlords, particularly in London, prior to the 1980 Act managed to avoid giving tenants security of tenure (see Crook, 1992; Coleman, 1992). In fact, the 1980 Act seems to have had only a marginal effect on the privately rented market and this led to further attempts to revitalise this tenure via the Housing Act 1988 (see also Cmnd 214).

In an attempt to remove the stigma surrounding this sector (e.g. 'Rachmanism', i.e. the harassment of low-income tenants to vacate properties in favour of higher paying ones or transfer of the property to owner-occupation) government attempted to lump the housing associations and the privately rented sector together into what they referred to as the 'Independent Rented Sector', but this was strongly resisted by the associations. The use of this term would suggest that government recognised any revival of the sector, numerically speaking, also necessitated its ideological and political 'rehabilitation' in order to detach it from the long established associations with poor housing conditions, 'greedy' landlords, etc. Success in this sector has been limited as the 1987 White Paper was forced to acknowledge. The White Paper noted that despite six years of attempts to revive the sector:

> there is now very little private investment in providing new rented housing. And when landlords obtain vacant possession of dwellings at the end of tenancies they often prefer to sell outright into owner occupation rather relet. Owners who do not want to sell their property sometimes keep their houses vacant rather than let to a tenant because of the inadequate returns, and the difficulty of regaining possession when they need it. Many of the remaining private landlords also have difficulty in finding sufficient resources to keep their property in good repair. (Cmnd 214, p. 9)

In recent years some new private investment has come into the sector through the Business Expansion Scheme (BES), but it is unlikely that this has provided much new housing for low-income families, and the likelihood is that this investment will be withdrawn after the minimum investment period of five years as investors attempt to realise their investment by selling the properties on (see Crook, 1992; Coleman, 1992 for more detail). Moreover, with the slump in the owner-occupied sector since 1989 there is some evidence that a minor revival has taken place in this sector as owners unable to sell their properties have rented them out. However, this source of rented properties is likely to last only as long as the slump in the housing market and as soon as owners can sell their properties at a reasonable price they will be withdrawn from renting.

In fact, as Coleman (1992; see also Minford *et al.*, 1987) argues, any revival of the private rented sector will require a more fundamental and radical series of policies, affecting the whole housing system, than those so far attempted by Conservative administrations. Such reforms would involve the end of the favourable financial treatment accorded to home-owners and the creation of a subsidy system along the lines of a 'needs-related housing allowance' as advocated by the Inquiry into British Housing (1991). Whilst most commentators recognise the need for such reforms it seems unlikely that any government, in the foreseeable future, will dare to risk the political fall-out from them. Thus the best that seems likely is that the decline of the private rented sector can be halted and possibly undergo some modest expansion. However, any expansion will do little to assist the growing numbers of homeless people as it is likely to be directed at those able to pay rents high enough to guarantee rates of return comparable to those achievable elsewhere in the economy. The full scale of the government's failure to revive this sector is revealed by the fact that from 1980 to 1990 the privately rented sector declined from 11.6 per cent to 7.7 per cent of the total stock in England and Wales (Page, 1993, p. 26).

Overall then it can be argued that housing, particularly council housing, has experienced major changes since 1979. In fact, a case can be made that council housing has experienced the most radical change of any part of the welfare state. There is little doubt that attempts have been made to break up council housing and to commodify significant sections of it. Yet despite this some five million dwellings still remain under council control. Housing associations remain firmly within the public sector, although the full extent and implications of changes in their role and recent financial reforms to encourage financial partnerships with the private sector remains unclear. As regards the private rented sector attempts have been made to tinker with it but government has not been prepared to embark upon the sort of radical policies pro-market commentators believe are necessary. Thus whilst advocating free-market style reforms and praising private sector provision Conservative governments have consistently failed, largely due to political factors, to address the fundamental problems of the housing system (most notably MIRAS) and have been forced, by public opinion, to turn their attention, at least symbolically, to issues such as homelessness (see Kemp, 1992, for a useful overview). As we shall see in the following two sections the problems of homelessness are considerable and owner-occupation is under a shadow the like of which has not been seen in the post-war era.

Homelessness

During the 1980s the issue of homelessness took on a much higher profile particularly as the streets of Britain's major cities increasingly become the sleeping places of Britain's homeless. This increasingly visible problem, and the public sympathy it aroused, forced the government to react and to take measures to counter it. This section will consider homelessness and the initiatives developed to counter it.

The statutory definition is given in Part III of the *Housing Act 1985*, which consolidates the provisions of the *Homeless Persons Act 1977*; this places upon local authorities the duty to secure permanent accommodation for people without satisfactory accommodation and/or in imminent danger of losing it (within 28 days), who are not intentionally homeless and who are in 'priority need'. Priority need is defined as: families with dependent children; pregnant women; people who are vulnerable because of old age, physical disability, mental illness or handicap; special reasons including young people 'at risk' and victims of domestic violence; people made homeless by an emergency (Burrows and Walentowicz, 1992).

In Great Britain in 1991 over 170,000 households (nearly 500,000 people) were accepted as homeless by local authorities, approximately half of the number who applied. Another 7000 were found to be intentionally homeless, but placed in temporary accommodation. However, Shelter is of the opinion that these figures must be treated with caution because local authorities interpret the legislation in different ways and may not submit their returns promptly. There is no appeals procedure readily accessible to rejected applicants and although the legislation does provide for judicial review few applicants have recourse to such action.

Any reasonable definition of homelessness must include not only those registered by local authorities, the 'official homeless', but also the far more numerous *unofficial homeless*. These include the great majority of single people and couples without children who are without satisfactory housing, but are not considered to be in priority need, although they may well be 'roofless' or their accommodation temporary or insecure.

In the absence of an agreed definition of homelessness there is no single measure of the incidence of the problem. The narrower definitions focus on 'rooflessness', the total lack of anywhere to live, while broader definitions include judgements about the quality of accommodation and about its social functions. The broader definitions of homelessness encompasses a variety of groups, e.g. long-term residents of institutions who have nowhere else to live, people living in hostels or bed and breakfast accommodation. Table 10.5 gives some indication of the numbers of people 'homeless' but not recognised as such by government. The sheer magnitude of these numbers explains the unwillingness of the government to accept these broader definitions.

As the figures in Table 10.5 show, most of the 'unofficial homeless' are 'hidden', sharing a home with relatives or friends, but in need of a place of their own. Without wanting to deny the significance of this

TABLE 10.5 *Estimate of 'unofficial homeless': actual and potential, 1990s, England only*

Description	Estimate of numbers
People sleeping rough	Up to 8000 (Shelter estimate)
Unauthorised tenants/squatters	Up to 50 000 (Shelter estimate)
Single people in hostels	Up to 60 000 (1991, DoE)
Single people in lodgings	Up to 77 000 (1989, DSS)
Insecure private tenants	Up to 317 000 (1992, OPCS)
'Hidden homeless' people	Up to 1 200 000 (Shelter estimate)
Total 1 712 000 +	

Source: L. Burrows and L. Walentowicz, *Homes Cost Less than Homelessness* (London: Shelter, 1992), p. 8.

group, the problems of the other 'unofficial homeless' are perhaps more immediately pressing. It is difficult to estimate accurately the number of people sleeping rough, squatting and unauthorised tenants, although the Shelter figures are generally accepted as likely to present a fair picture.

There can be no doubt as to the seriousness of the problem; official homelessness has tripled since 1978 and in the past ten years over 1.25 m households have been registered as homeless, giving a total of more than three million people, of whom half are children (Burrows and Walentowicz, 1992). Moreover, some 70 per cent of households registered as homeless are headed by women (London Housing Unit, 1989).

Although homelessness is unevenly distributed through out the country, being most common in London (in 1992 11 per cent of the population of Great Britain, but 28 per cent of the homeless) and a few other major urban areas and certain resorts, the problem is found even in small country towns. The focus on those areas where homelessness is most evident, especially on the public tragedy of the 'roofless', has tended to distract attention from the economic roots of the problem: the economic decline and subsequent lack of jobs which cause many people to leave home and the housing stress of the areas to which some of them migrate.

The Causes of Homelessness

The reasons for homelessness fall into two broad categories, supply and demand causes.

Supply Causes

While it may be the case that there is not an overall shortage of dwellings nationally there is a shortage of low rental dwellings in certain areas. The continued decline in the private rental market has deep causal roots and despite government attempts this sector has continued to decline since 1979. These developments have been exacerbated by the contraction in the supply of social housing caused by the sale of council houses into owner occupation and by the savage cutback in the construction of new council dwellings, a situation intensified by the growing number of council dwellings standing empty because they are in need of repairs which local authorities cannot afford to do. Furthermore, other aspects of government economic and social policy have contributed to the growth of homelessness, in the words of Harrison (1992, p. 43):

> The closure of DHSS Reception Centres and the discharge of patients from mental hospitals into 'community care' has in practice resulted in increased homelessness because the replacement facilities for such changes were not adequately planned to meet the needs of those formerly housed within these institutions.

The reductions in local authority housing provision have only partly been offset by the expansion of housing association activities. The financial regime under which the latter now operate makes it increasingly difficult for many to provide accommodation that low income families can afford.

Demand Causes
The main demand reason for homelessness is the proliferation of households, particularly of poor households. Although the overall population is likely to remain stable into the next century the total number of households is likely to increase by 10 per cent between 1990 and 2001 and the number of single person households by 34 per cent (Thornton, 1990). The household formation rate is driven by several factors, perhaps the most important being the break up of existing households.

Burrows and Walentowicz (1992) found that about 43 per cent of registered homeless households became so because parents, other relatives or friends were no longer able or willing to accommodate them. The break up of a marriage or settled relationship accounts for about 16 per cent of those registered; about 15 per cent were private sector tenants commonly becoming homeless through termination of a shorthold tenancy, others being evicted because of rent arrears. In the first six months of 1992 about 10 per cent were homeless because of mortgage arrears and subsequent repossession; only 2 per cent were registered as homeless because of eviction from council dwellings (Burrows and Walentowitz, 1992, p. 11). A particularly disturbing aspect of homelessness, especially in London, is the over-representation of ethnic minorities; there are no definitive statistics on this, but the London Housing Forum enquiry (1988) found that although the Black (Afro-Caribbean and African) population of London was only 10 per cent of the total they accounted for 30–40 per cent of households accepted as homeless by London boroughs.

When one turns to the 'unofficial homeless' the break up of former relationships, whether due to disagreements with partners or parents, accounts for the majority in this group. In the case of many young homeless people Randall (1988) suggests that the consequences of family breakdown (e.g. children who have been in care) may have a link with later homelessness (see Killeen, 1988; Watson, 1988 for other dimensions of the situation). While one can argue that personal factors play a role in causing homelessness they are less important than the economic plight (i.e. low incomes or unemployment) of those likely to be without suitable accommodation.

Furthermore, failure to increase transfer/social security payments in line with wages and imposition of additional restrictions on access to such payments can only serve to aggravate the position of those already most vulnerable to homelessness. The plight of young persons in the UK over 18 years of age but under 25 is an example of this; under the Social Security Act 1988, they receive only 80 per cent of the Income Support paid to persons over the age of 25, the assumption being that they need less support because they can live at home with their parents. Young people aged 16 to 18 have no entitlement to Income Support save in quite exceptional circumstances (for more detail see Donnison, 1993), thus forcing them to either stay in the parental home or leave and risk the very real possibility of becoming homeless.

Some Solutions?

Some local authorities (particularly in the London area) lease unoccupied private dwellings and let them to high priority applicants, often registered homeless. In 1991 the Department of the Environment estimated that only 26,000 dwellings were leased and let in this way and so there is ample room for expansion in this direction. Access to the private sector can also be facilitated by rent deposit schemes whereby some agency, either a local authority or voluntary body, pays rent in advance (later recouped from Housing Benefit payments) or guarantees payment for low income people taking on a private sector tenancy. A number of local authorities, encouraged by the DoE, have launched similar initiatives (*Roof*, Sept/Oct 1992, p. 9). The recent introduction into the UK of 'foyer' for young people, modelled on those of France, is also a development of considerable interest (*Guardian*, 23 July 1993). A French 'foyer' provides low rental hostel accommodation for young people in need and a range of recreational facilities and counselling services for residents and young people in the wider community. The 'foyer' might be seen as a secular YMCA, possibly serving a less advantaged stratum of the population than does the YMCA.

It is possible that in some areas, for example, those with high student populations, hybrid BES housing association schemes will improve the supply of accommodation available to single persons. However, these are roundabout and costly measures in terms of the tax incentives necessary to get them going and not likely to be as effective as a construction programme targeted directly on those in greatest need of adequate housing. More worthwhile is the *Cash Incentive Scheme* funded by the central government under which local authorities are enabled to make grants of up to £12,000 to council tenants for purchase of private sector dwellings. The Government's 'Single Homelessness Initiative' of 1990 and the 'national homeless advice centres' (run in conjunction with the Citizens' Advice Bureaux) are welcome developments, but, as Greve (1990) has pointed out, the former is concentrated in London and there are many homeless people elsewhere and, although many homeless people do need advice, advice does not necessarily put a roof over one's head. These measures are at best palliatives.

Overall then while the numbers of homeless people and the attention accorded them has increased considerably during the 1980s there has, in terms commensurate with the size of the problem, been a less than wholehearted response. This situation is unlikely to improve over the new few years as government focuses its attention on reducing public expenditure.

The 'Crisis' of Owner-Occupation

As we have already noted during the 1980s owner-occupation expanded rapidly; between 1981 and 1991, in England and Wales, it grew by almost 3.5m dwellings expanding from almost 58 per cent to just under 70 per cent of the housing stock (*Housing and Construction Statistics*, 1981–1991, Table 9.3). About half of this expansion was caused by the 'right to buy scheme' and sales of private rented dwellings, the remainder coming from new building (see Page, 1993, p. 26). Even in Scotland, between 1981–91 owner occupation expanded from 35.6 per cent to 52.8 per cent of the housing stock (*Housing and*

Construction Statistics, 1981–1991, Table 9.3). Government viewed this growth as an unequivocal success story demonstrating that owner-occupation could provide accommodation for almost everyone. Yet this situation disguised major problems.

During the first half of the 1980s research indicated that owner-occupation had its problem; not every owner benefited from it. Most notably it was shown that there were major socio-economic and spatial variations in the distribution of benefits, particularly between those living in inner city areas and elsewhere. The work of Karn *et al.* (1985) clearly demonstrated that low-income owner-occupiers in inner city areas faced considerable difficulties. In essence the problem was that the type of dwellings low-income purchasers could afford to buy were often those in the worst condition and in the most run-down areas. This had two basic effects, particularly when compared with their middle-class suburban counterparts: firstly they had higher payments and maintenance outlays relative to their incomes and second, they did not experience the same level of house price inflation. The outcome being that the 'benefits' of the boom in owner-occupation were unevenly distributed with some locations and their inhabitants being by-passed. Doling *et al.* (1985) argued that the problems faced by low-income owner-occupiers generated a potential instability at the lower end of the market. However, this attracted little governmental, or public, attention at the time as the problem was largely confined to discrete locations and had little or no effect on the vast majority of Conservative voting owner-occupiers, particularly as rapid house price inflation provided enormous additional purchasing power for those people and also fuelled economic growth.

With the onset of a savage and lengthy recession in the late 1980s the house price inflation bubble burst and the 'chickens came home to roost' in a quite devastating fashion. Conservative voting middle-class owner-occupiers suddenly found themselves suffering from unemployment and reeling under the effects of apparently ever increasing interest rates as the government attempted to maintain its membership of the Exchange Rate Mechanism (ERM). The result was that most dreaded of outcomes: repossession. A dramatic increase in mortgage repossession occurred between 1980 and 1990 when numbers increased from 3400 to 43,890, while over the same period mortgages in arrears between 6–12 months increased from 15,530 to 123,110 (Inquiry into British Housing, 1991, pp. 16–17). Yet this only tells part of the story as the figures in Table 10.6 indicate.

TABLE 10.6 *Mortgage possession action statistics, 1988–93 (first quarter)
(local authority and private)*

	Actions entered	Orders made*
1988	72 655	47 769
1989	91 309	53 066
1990	14 5350	103 508
1991	18 6649	142 905
1992	14 2162	126 907
1993	11 6181	105 283

Source: *Lord Chancellors Department*, 1993, Table 1.

*Includes suspended orders.

Table 10.6 requires a few words of explanation. The first column, *Actions entered*, simply indicates the number of lenders who began court action for possession, while the second column, *Orders made*, refers to the number of possession orders granted by the courts. This latter figure also includes suspended orders where the court has granted possession but suspends it provided the 'owner' meets certain conditions (e.g. meets a schedule of payments to the lender).

What should be clear from Table 10.6 is that an explosion in possession actions occurred between 1988 and 1992 and even though we can detect a clear decrease in 1992/93 actions were still running at very high levels. The Lord Chancellor's Department figures also show that the problem is at its worst in those areas which experienced the most rapid house price inflation in the second half of the 1980s, most notably Greater London and the South East and adjacent areas such as the South West (Lord Chancellor's Department, 1993, Table 2).

It should be noted with regard to possession orders that suspended orders are likely to be greater than the numbers of dwellings actually repossessed, this means there is a hidden threat for many owner-occupiers. As we noted above rising unemployment and increases in interest rates have brought about this problem, and while it now appears the economy is slowly emerging from recession it still seems likely that unemployment will continue to increase and that disposable incomes will not grow significantly over the next year or two. The result of this will be many people still struggling to meet payments attached to suspended orders which can be activated as soon as the borrower fails to meet the payments attached to the order. While the majority of orders are taken out by banks and building societies there is some evidence that a significant number of the orders have been obtained by what are termed 'secondary lenders' (e.g. where a dwelling has been used as security for a loan and/or improvements to the dwelling such as double glazing) and they may choose to activate orders as soon as owners fall behind with their payments. So although it seems that the problem is easing the potential for instability remains. Ironically, the government's decision to withdraw from the ERM, whilst it caused them considerable problems on other fronts, was a source of relief to borrowers. Had the interest rates stayed at the level to which they were temporarily increased (i.e. 15 per cent), for a few hours, on 'Black Wednesday' in September 1992, one shudders to think of the effect that might have had on already hard-pressed borrowers.

Repossession is not the only problem which owner-occupiers face. Many who entered the market in the halcyon days of 1988 and 1989 have found themselves with dwellings worth less than they paid for them, a problem known as *negative equity*. Whilst the exact extent of this problem is difficult to specify precisely UBS estimated the problem reached a peak in May 1993 when some 1.9 m owners were in this position (*Independent*, 1 May 1993), by September 1993 the number was estimated to be 1.4 m (*Guardian*, 4 Sept. 1993). This means that many owners will, should they either wish or need to sell, find themselves unable to realise even what they paid for the dwelling several years ago. The result is that many, particularly in Greater London and the South East, will find themselves essentially 'trapped' in their current property for some years to come. The full extent of the problem is shown by the fact that between 1989 and 1992 house prices in the south-east, outside of London, fell by 19 per cent whilst those in Scotland rose by 26 per cent (*Regional Trends*, 1993).

Whilst the worst appears to be over it is likely that the problems created between 1988 and 1992 will continue to haunt the home ownership market for some years to come, not only will many owners have suspended possession notices hanging over them but many will find themselves unable to move because of the negative equity trap. All in all the developments of the last few years seem to have brought into question many of the apparent benefits of owner-occupation, suggesting that it is not necessarily the best tenure for everyone.

In addition there is still, as we mentioned earlier, the issue of MIRAS (Mortgage Interest Tax Relief At Source) which effectively distorts the whole housing system giving preferential treatment to one tenure – owner-occupation – over all others. While the experiences of the late

1980s/early 1990s may have reduced the appeal of owner-occupation, at least in the short term, the problem still remains of how to develop a housing subsidy system which is equitable and directs support where it is most needed. As the Inquiry into British Housing (1991, p. 32) noted with regard to MIRAS:

> the system is unfair because it is of greater benefit to the rich than the poor; and it is also inefficient because much of the tax relief goes to people who would have housed themselves satisfactorily without it.

This has been one area which the Thatcherite commitment to free-markets never penetrated; Mrs Thatcher, despite all her rhetoric about not bucking markets, was never prepared to create a genuine free market in housing for fear of the electoral backlash from 'feather-bedded' owner-occupiers. Despite the fact that almost every commentator, including the Treasury, acknowledges the problems of the system it seems unlikely that the system of subsidies will be abolished in the foreseeable future. The government's strategy appears to be one of 'death by a thousand cuts' as demonstrated by the 1993 Budget in which it was announced that the rate of mortgage tax relief will fall from 25 per cent to 20 per cent in April 1994 and then to 15 per cent from April 1995. Thus owner-occupation in its present form acts as an obstacle to the creation of a more equitable and efficient 'needs-related housing allowance', as advocated by the Inquiry into British Housing (1991, pp. 42–5).

Conclusion

In the preceding pages we have provided an overview of developments during the 1980s and early 1990s. We have suggested that considerable changes occurred during this period, most notably the continued growth in owner-occupation and also, though perhaps less dramatically, the declining role of local authorities as housing providers. The decline of local authorities has only been partially offset by the development, in the later 1980s/early 1990s, of a much wider role for housing associations. At the time of writing the exact form which this new role, or whether housing associations can or will take it on, remains debatable. The evidence is contradictory, some housing associations appear willing to take on the role of a mass provider of social housing, others are less sure. This situation is complicated by a financial system that demands some input of private capital which will require an adequate rate of return suggesting that any accommodation provided through such joint public–private partnerships will be beyond the reach of people on low incomes, the only solution being to increase housing benefit limits, something which looks unlikely in the present climate. We have also pointed to the problems of homelessness which is growing ever greater despite various government backed initiatives.

Whilst it would be foolhardy to suggest that one change would create the momentum for a major reform of the housing system there is little doubt that the abolition of MIRAS along with the reform of the housing benefit system and their replacement by a 'needs-related housing allowance' could, potentially, open up the possibility of a much more efficient and equitable housing subsidy system. However, until the log-jam surrounding MIRAS is tackled the best that can be hoped for is tinkering around the edges.

Even if the reforms we advocate were initiated they would not immediately solve the problems outlined above. The issue of council, and perhaps increasingly housing association, house maintenance has reached such a level that it will take a major influx of capital to remedy it, and whilst the revitalised HATS and Estates Action Programme may help to deal with the problem it is still on too small a scale to provide anything other than relief to a few in even the medium term.

Overall then the problems of the housing system have in some ways grown, they have certainly changed and are likely to continue to change, but until some overarching crisis forces government to take radical action it seems unlikely that there will be any genuine reform of the system during the 1990s.

11

Education Policy: Market Forces or Market Failure?

MALCOLM McVICAR and LYNTON ROBINS

Educational Reforms at School Level

The educational system in England and Wales has been transformed
since 1980. The changes include: the restructuring – twice – of the
public examination system; the introduction of the national curriculum, with phased testing; the privatisation of the schools inspectorate;
the extensive revision of teacher education with the performance of
existing teachers now being regularly appraised; the publication of
school examination and test results in the form of 'league tables'; and
the reduction in the role of local education authorities through the
implementation of local management of schools (LMS) and the
enhanced role of school governors, the opportunity for schools to
'opt out' from local control, and the creation of new non-LEA
controlled City Technology Colleges (CTCs). Impressive as these
measures are in terms of the breadth and depth of changes propa-
gated, they tell only part of the story.

Policy unfolded also against the background of:

- the centralisation of education policy decision-making
- an intensifying resource problem, and
- growing public unease about poor standards

Firstly, there has been continuity between Thatcher-led and Major-led
governments in terms of restricting the number of participants in 'the
education debate' to the advantage of the political Right and White-

hall. The old partnership of consensus government – the so-called 'secret garden' of education decision-making – which was wrecked in the 1980s has not been repaired in the 1990s. Teachers, local authorities and the HMI remain largely excluded from the policy process, with even the most politically moderate teacher organisations having been driven into supporting direct action in the absence of consultation by government.

Secondly, education spending has been a principal casualty in the financial struggle between central and local government with Conservative local councillors frequently in disagreement with their Minister at the DFE. As a result of cutbacks stemming from rate-capping, some schools in the hardest hit authorities had to confront drastic options by 1993 and were forced into reducing teaching staff by 10 per cent in larger schools and by 25 per cent in smaller schools with pupils moving on to a part-time education of a four-and-a-half day week. Consistent with the funding crisis faced in many schools, the National Confederation of Parent Teacher Associations reported that many local parent organisations were no longer raising money for 'luxuries' as they did in the past, but were now involved in raising money for the essential part of school budgets used to pay for 'textbooks, for building work . . . even, in some cases to pay teachers' (*Guardian*, 26 May 1992). At the international level, the resources crisis was revealed in an Organisation for Economic Co-operation and Development (OECD) 24 nation study which showed that in 1988 the UK spent less of its GDP on education than any other member and as a consequence the UK had one of the highest teacher/pupil ratios, was one of the poorest providers of nursery education, and had one of the lowest proportions of young people going on to full-time tertiary education.

Finally, despite much rhetoric about the need to improve standards by wrestling education from the control of 'trendy' educationalists and the need for greater parental involvement in schools, the rising standards which many had been prepared into anticipating have not materialised. Indeed, more official and semi-official reports commented on the continued existence of poor and/or declining standards in a variety of subjects than the occasional report which registered some improvement. Much publicity was given to Sir Claus Moser's observation that 'hundreds of thousands of British children have received educational experiences not worthy of a civilised nation' which seemed to crystallise how many parents were thinking. Public confidence in the education system in Britain was lower than in any other EC member or Scandinavian country. Gallup reported that only 37 per cent of Britons sampled expressed faith in their education system whilst over 70 per cent of Danes, West Germans, Swiss and Finns said that they had faith in their respective systems (*Guardian*, 12 Feb. 1991).

The Legislation

There is considerable disagreement amongst commentators on both the internal coherence within specific pieces of legislation as well as the relationship between successive Acts. On the one hand, some have recognised a market-based logic behind the legislative programme of the Thatcher and Major governments. Education, they argued, was seen by the government as being in the hands of 'producer' interests – teachers and LEAs – who fashioned the service to suit their purposes, which were primarily concerned with social engineering. In contrast, the 'consumers' – parents and employers – who wanted higher standards from schools wielded too little power to have any influence. The implementation of a market-led system in education with 'some diversity of product, information about the scope of choice and the quality of performance, as well as the opportunity to choose' (Ranson, 1990) would enable customers to drive up quality. Successive legislation was recognised by some as motivated consistently by the market rationale. Others disagreed, and whilst they conceded that many reforms were inspired by the political Right they felt that the reforms produced little operational coherence. One commentator argued that education policy veered all over the place 'like a mouse on Speed' whilst others speculated that policy resulted from 'bright ideas' which crossed the table at a Friday night dinner party and landed on the Minister's desk the following Monday.

The 1980 Education Act

The Act introduced the Assisted Places Scheme which was designed to allow a relatively small number of parents on modest incomes to send their children to private schools. This measure was consistent with a policy of increasing parental choice, although its critics saw it simply as a way of subsidising the private sector from the public purse. The Act also gave parents using state sector schools greater choice over which

206 Education Policy

school their children would attend through obliging each LEA to 'make arrangements for parents to prioritise the schools they wanted their children to attend and has a duty to comply with these preferences unless it would prejudice the provision of effective education' (McVicar, 1990).

The 1986 Education Act

The 1944 Education Act required all state schools to have a body of governors, on which parents could be represented although it was not mandatory for them to be so. In fact it was possible for a single governing body to govern many different schools. For example, between 1965–9 a quarter of English and Welsh LEAs had only one governing body for all their schools. The 1986 Act brought radical change and provided for an increased number of parent governors on schools' governing bodies which, with other changes, reduced the number of local authority governors to a minority position. This was accomplished by changing the composition of governing bodies; in schools of over 600 pupils governor representation increased from two to five, with LEA representation being decreased, and a co-opted membership which usually represented the local business community. The Act provided for the secret postal ballot of all eligible parents for the election of parent governors. To be eligible, a parent must have a child attending the school at the time of the election. The period of office is four years, but a parent governor can continue to serve if his or her child leaves before the term ends.

The 1988 Education Reform Act

The 1986 Act enlarged the responsibility of school governors and the 1988 Act built further on this through the introduction of Local Management of Schools (LMS). The central purpose of LMS, with greater parental and community involvement, was to ensure that individual schools were managed effectively and responsive to 'customer' needs. The Act also specified that a national curriculum be taught to pupils until they reached the age of sixteen. A core curriculum would include English, maths and science, together with seven foundation subjects covering history, geography, technology, music, art, physical education and a foreign language. Religious education would also be taught as well as certain cross-curricular themes such as citizenship.

The Act also introduced the national testing of pupils at four key stages of 7, 11, 14 and 16 years old. The introduction of testing has been highly contentious and in the summer of 1993 the main teacher unions boycotted the test for 14 year olds, criticising them for their lack of integrity and the hurried way in which they were introduced. Although committed formally to keeping the tests the Government conceded a review which has subsequently modified the testing programme.

In line with increasing parental choice, the Act enhanced previous provisions for open enrolment:

> The open enrolment provisions of the Education Reform Act require LEAs to abandon the planned admission levels (PALs) of Section 15 of the 1980 Education Act. . . . Effectively, the role of LEAs in planning the size and number of schools in an area will be replaced by a system in which this is determined through the 'market' of parental choice. (Clough *et al.*, 1989)

The Act abolished the Inner London Education Authority (ILEA) and weakened the position of local authorities further by creating 'grant maintained schools' financed directly by the DFE. Parents of eligible schools can vote on 'opting out', but, once having opted out, future parents would not be able to vote on 'opting back'. Some feared that grant-maintained schools would be encouraged to develop as grammar schools and thus re-introduce pupil selection. The Government responded that grant-maintained schools would not normally be allowed to change character within five years of opting-out. Others saw grant-maintained status being applied for by LEA-controlled grammar schools threatened with comprehensivisation. It would, then, in these circumstances, defend selection rather than introduce it.

Choice and Diversity

The 1992 White Paper, *Choice and Diversity: a New Framework for Schools*, formed the basis of the Education Bill. The proposals continued to promote the market themes established under the Thatcher governments, with the opting-out process being streamlined and the LEA role being reduced further. From the DFE's point of view, far fewer schools than anticipated had decided to opt out to achieve grant maintained status. In fact, by 1993 only 315 schools out of a total of 25,000 had opted out. The White Paper and the Bill contained proposals to make it easier for schools to opt out, and created two new Funding Agencies for Schools – one for England and one for Wales – through which grant maintained schools would in future receive their funding. The legislation also contained proposals for the identification and treatment of 'failing schools' – poorly performing schools would be taken over by education 'hit squads' who will attempt to identify and remedy problems and thus raise standards. Since 'failing schools' are likely to be under LEA control, it is assumed that solutions to raised standards will invariably include moving them to grant maintained status. Through these arrangements, it has been argued, the Education Bill continues the attack on local authorities' power begun in 1980 and developed in 1986 and 1988.

Commentary

Substantial literature now exists which examines numerous aspects of Conservative education policy. Here two points are explored briefly; firstly, what impact has recent legislation had on the day-to-day running of schools and, secondly, how effective has the introduction of market forces been in raising quality. There is little doubt that the combined effect of the major Acts has resulted in real changes in school leadership, with an administrative culture in which decision-making was tied in with the authority at county level replaced by a managerial culture in which decisions are made locally. Schools have taken on a number of business functions, such as marketing, contract management and budgeting, which in larger schools are performed by formal bureaucracies. In smaller schools these functions are performed by headteachers, who alone carry the burden of what they see as additional, frequently unnecessary, paperwork (see *Guardian*, 7 Sept. 1993).

Classroom teachers have experienced numerous changes, particularly resulting from the introduction of the national curriculum and testing. Many complained that the national curriculum was too extensive, that testing was over-bureaucratic and over-complex, and that results published as league tables of schools would be misleading. It has been calculated that a teacher with a class of 35 pupils was expected to make eight thousand assessment judgements during a year; a situation in which testing would assume as great an importance as teaching in terms of classroom priorities. Arguments voiced by the teaching unions as well as by parental representation were taken into account by the Dearing Review of the national curriculum and its assessment. A more streamlined curriculum is promised and, in line with the Review, the DFE has scrapped league tables for results of tests administered to 7 and 14-year-olds.

Finally, there is the question of whether the creation of an educational marketplace will drive up standards in schools as they compete one with another. From the outset many commentators were intrigued by the seeming contradiction between creating a free market in education based on the existence of a state-imposed national curriculum. They felt that a free market should imply that schools would be free to offer their curriculum 'product' in competition with other schools' 'products'. If a true market exists in education, parents would be free to exercise choice and select the curriculum product which most satisfied their needs. In fact choice is very restricted. A limited number of City Technology Colleges exist, some fifteen only by 1993, and *Choice and Diversity* makes reference to the possibility of diluted and restricted subject specialisation additional to the national curriculum. But this does not represent authentic choice for parents. The only real market choice, for the few, is to avoid the national curriculum altogether by paying for their children to attend private schools where the political control of the national curriculum does not apply. But, placing these doubts on one side, the question remains whether increased competition for pupils will drive up the quality of education in terms of improved academic standards (Robins, 1993).

It has been argued that education and other public services cannot be compared with manufactured consumer goods and that arguments about the efficacy of the market are not appropriate, especially 'where the consumer is part of the production process' since:

> many services in the public sector have the characteristic that it is difficult for either producer or consumer to judge quality, and perhaps even whether the service has been produced at all. The nature of what is intended to be produced . . . is necessarily imprecise because it is about the generalities of life not the particulars and because results may only become apparent in the very long term! (Walsh, 1991)

This point is proving pertinent with respect to education since an increasing number of school managements have embraced the concepts and prescriptions of the quality movement. Indeed, some have set up internal quality assurance procedures and are seeking BS 5750, together with the explicit quality commitment of 'meeting customer requirements' (*Guardian*, 1 Dec. 1992). But as Walsh has argued the concept of quality in the public services is problematic, and this has been reflected in some preliminary measurements of what customers required schools to deliver. In piloting a quality audit questionnaire to pupils, the priority of the 'need for more understanding by teachers' and 'curricular issues' came 8th and 13th respectively in a list of 18 items (Macbeath, 1993). Of greater priority was the condition of the school, complaints about the toilets, and requests for a longer lunch period. Another study culled 25 factors 'which can make a school more attractive than its neighbours' from discussions with over a thousand head-teachers, governors, LEA representatives and parents (Dennison, 1989). Again, as with pupils' responses, quality issues are frequently far removed from concern about academic standards. Although the criteria were not prioritised in any way, they revealed that quality judgements concerning a school may be based as much on the attractiveness of school buildings, the convenient location of the school, or the convenience of school hours for working parents as on the quality of teaching or examination results. The market, it seems, will work in ways which drive schools into providing quality in the 'peripherals' of school life rather than in the curriculum issues which have been at the centre of the 'great debate'.

Finally, because some schools will be better supported and receive more resources than others, competition is likely to result in reinforcing the existence of first, second and even third class schools. The poorest section of the community will have no choice but to use local schools and '. . . if the consumers' knowledge of quality is difficult to articulate and use in relation with the producer then it may not serve to enhance their power' (Walsh, 1991). Wragg speculated, then, that the education market will operate in a way which will

> leave a sector of the population, the least well-off and most needy, in cheap, cheerless, third-class schools run by clapped-out and impoverished authorities, following a people's basic curriculum, set and tested by the Government. There will be no money for anything beyond it. (*Observer*, 17 May 1992)

This remains to be seen, but it seems likely that at least one unintended consequence of the market-led drive for quality will end in the creation of slum schools.

Post-16 Education Policy in Britain

Post-16 education policy must be regarded as an integral part of overall education policy and as such is, of course, influenced by Government's overall macro-economic and social policy objectives. Just like school education, post-16 education has been affected by the Government's economic priorities of reducing the role of the state, reducing the level of direct taxation, the privatisation of public services and the introduction of private sector management techniques into public sector organisations. These influences have been very significant.

Post-16 education policy in Britain needs to be divided into further education, roughly covering the ages of 16 to 19 and non-advanced education for adults, and higher education, including roughly all advanced education after the age of 18. There are some common trends and policies within these two sectors but there are also some substantial differences which need to be treated differently.

Higher Education

Higher education policy in the United Kingdom since the early 1980s has been a curious mixture of a few long term policy objectives together with a large number of contradictory short term policies. British higher education in 1994 is very different to British higher education in 1984, although whether it is exactly where the successive Governments wanted to be by the end of that decade is another matter. Thus we can see a mixture of incrementalism and long-term strategic planning resulting in what taken together has clearly been a very significant policy shift.

Higher education in the United Kingdom in 1984 consisted of two distinct sectors:

- the university sector comprising 50 autonomous organisations governed by charter and financed directly by a Government quango;
- the public sector; 30 polytechnics and approximately 50 other higher education colleges mainly under the ownership and control of local education authorities but increasingly financed from a central Government quango through local education authorities.

By the late 1980s the public sector had actually outgrown the university sector and there had been clearly a significant expansion of both sectors during the 1980s. Within each sector there were very substantial differences between the type of institution and the work that they did. The institutions varied in size, financial resources, the range of disciplines offered and their status. There were also very significant differences in funding between the two sectors. The universities had traditionally been funded for research as well as for teaching whereas the public sector had not been funded for research.

Underlying the mixture of pragmatic incrementalism and ideological planning which has characterised higher education policy have been a number of themes which have been fairly consistent, and which were identified earlier in the schools' sector:

- the reduction in the scale of public expenditure as a percentage of the total expenditure on higher education;
- reduction in local authority powers and the eventual removal, to begin with, of higher education and then further education totally from local government;
- breaking the tripartite relationship between teacher unions, LEAs and institutions;
- strengthening management with the introduction of 'new managerialism' and centralisation of power and authority.

Each of the themes identified above will now be addressed separately. Few commentators would challenge the argument that the last fourteen years have seen a change in the balance of power between central and local government, with the power and authority of the latter being eroded gradually. Nowhere is this erosion more obvious than in the field of education policy and it was first seen in the field of higher eduction policy. In the late 1970s there were two sectors of higher education in the United Kingdom: the universities and the public sector, which consisted of a mixture of local authority funded colleges, and with a number of directly funded institutions. This was a complex and diverse sector which central government had always found it very difficult to control especially in regard to funding where there was a tradition of demand led financing.

Soon after its election in 1979 the Conservative Government set about bringing this diversified sector under a greater degree of central co-ordination. To begin with it needed the co-operation of the local authorities and the voluntary organisations which had a stake in some colleges and so it formed an advisory board, the National Advisory

Board, with representatives of those organisations giving advice to the Secretary of State on higher education policy. Although the colleges were still owned by local authorities and other bodies, the financing was channelled through this central advisory board which gradually increased its powers significantly during the early 1980s. At the same time, the Government introduced much tighter controls over course approvals and reduced the fee levels paid on the Government's behalf by local education authorities to dissuade institutions from expanding. The emphasis was very much on limiting the growth in higher education with some significant cuts in spending as a way of curtailing public expenditure within the overall macro-economic policy.

Paralleling this greater control and centralisation in the public sector, the Government required the University Grants Committee (UGC) to carry out a series of budgetary reductions in its sector leading to the threat of closure of a small number of universities. This was avoided but only by draconian cuts being concentrated on a select number of institutions. What was also evidenced in the early 1980s was the Government's use of the public sector as an agent for change in the university sector. This is something to which we will return later.

Government education policy until the late 1980s could reasonably be characterised as incrementalist but the Education Reform Act 1988 was far from being an incrementalist measure. This Act represented a very significant set of co-ordinated, planned policies for the then DES. The Act abolished the UGC and replaced it with a new quango, the Universities Funding Council (UFC). The Government had been dissatisfied with the UGC's ability to control the sector. The Government had also decided to remove the public sector from local authority control and create free standing corporate organisations. Under the 1988 Act, 30 polytechnics and 50 other colleges of higher education became independent of their LEAs and were formed into autonomous higher education corporations (HECs). They were to be financed directly from a new national body, the Polytechnics and Colleges Funding Council (PCFC). They were to be bodies corporate, that is independent, legal organisations in their own right. In many ways the PCFC paralleled and was based on the old UGC/UFC.

Clearly, the achievement of corporate status led to a very significant change in the management responsibility in the new PCFC sector colleges. The degree of autonomy enjoyed by polytechnics and other colleges previously had varied but even the most autonomous had relied heavily on the LEA for legal advice, estates, finance and personnel support. The move to a totally independent organisation meant that the full range of managerial responsibilities rested with the new boards of governors and their management teams.

Cuts in Funding

In 1979 the Government was elected with a clear mandate to reduce the scale of public expenditure. As this related to higher education the scope was both to limit the growth in the sector and to shift the balance between state funding and private funding. The Government changed the funding methodology during the 1980s with the aim of reducing the average unit of public sector funding and increasing private and commercial inputs to education. As the 1980s developed and Government policy moved towards the expansion of higher education, the emphasis shifted. Government policy changed to the expansion of higher education, without a commensurate increase in funding. This led inevitably to a lowering of the unit of resource per student. Between 1987 and 1991 the unit of resource in higher education fell by 17 per cent in real terms. College management had to achieve increases in productivity and supplement state income from commercial and other activities. These activities included recruiting more overseas students, running full-cost recovery courses, providing consultancy and selling specialist services on the commercial market. A number of the colleges formed limited companies to undertake commercial activities and, in order to protect the charitable status of the parent institution, covenanted profits back to it.

One of the aspects of 'improving productivity' was to contract-out a number of services previously provided by directly-employed staff. Thus, many colleges have contracted out, via competitive tender, caretaking, cleaning, catering and security. The most important development in competitive tendering, however, related to student numbers.

In 1989 both the UFC and the PCFC were meant to introduce a system whereby colleges, in return for having a high percentage of their funding protected from one year to the other, competed for the balance of their activities and new students with other institutions. This meant that colleges were competing for part of their core business. This system worked well in the PCFC sector and did indeed result in a lowering of the unit of resource. However, in the UFC sector the universities effectively operated a cartel which prevented the unit of resource being driven downwards. This is one of the reasons for the abolition of the UFC in 1992.

Student Loans and Finances

The reductions in funding were also directed at student support. The Government introduced significant changes to the system of student finance in 1990. The maintenance grants awarded on a means tested basis to students on mandatory courses (i.e. those approved by the Government) were frozen in cash terms which clearly meant a reduction in real terms and instead students had access to a Government quango, the Student Loans Company, which would make available loans to students in each year of their course of study with low interest rates repayable when they were at work and their incomes had gone beyond a certain threshold level. After initial resistance, the evidence was in 1993 that students were beginning to use these loans quite significantly. Encouraging them to do so was the withdrawal of social security benefits in terms of housing, unemployment, and income support from students in 1990. Students are no longer able to claim a whole range of welfare benefits which they had access to previously. Government, in response to evident student need, introduced a very limited hardship scheme, administered through colleges without any clear national guidelines on how this money was to be distributed.

The New Managerialism

The former public sector had a much stronger tradition of senior academic staff moving into explicitly management positions than did the university sector. The local authority background and the imperatives of the different financing systems in the former PCFC sector meant that institutions required a clearly defined and targeted management function. This new 'managerialism' has been found in a number of public services during the 1980s (for a further discussion of this see Farnham and Horton, 1993). The differences in the emphasis given to explicit management roles in the two sectors reflects in part on the different funding regimes which the two sectors have enjoyed.

The creation in the 1992 Act of a unified university sector has brought together two component parts with very different management styles and management ethos. It will be interesting to see which of the two cultures changes the most over the next decade. One interesting development relates to the erosion of the professional monopoly of senior posts. Until the late 1980s it was most exceptional for a senior post in a university or college to be taken by someone from the private sector. In the early 1990s there have been a number of senior posts where people have been appointed from outside the education service.

The new managerialism has had a particular impact on industrial relations in higher education. The emphasis on the use of private sector management techniques has led to the introduction of a number of initiatives which have been fiercely resisted by the professional associations and trade unions. The introduction of staff appraisal, for example, which is an extremely sensitive issue, was achieved in the ex-public sector during 1992 on the explicit understanding that it was not linked to remuneration systems. The separate introduction of a limited scheme of performance related pay in 1992/3 met with very considerable resistance from the trade unions.

Erosion of the Binary Line

In the Further and Higher Education Act 1992 the Government achieved a policy development which many thought would never occur. The universities and the public sector were brought together into one unified sector. PCFC and UFC were brought together into three funding councils, the Higher Education Funding Councils for England, Wales and Scotland. In many ways this has been the most radical development in higher education policy since the Second World War.

The creation of an integrated system is not, of course, achieved overnight. The institutions forming this new whole have different cultures, different management styles and structures, different funding regimes and, in many ways, different missions. Research has always been very well founded in the universities whereas few of the public sector organisations had established themselves at anything like the same level. The public sector had, on the other hand, been much closer to the market, more responsive to the needs of new groups of students, especially those in part-time education and was generally thought to be more responsive to changes in demand. The polytechnics in particular had often been criticised by the older universities as being the stalking horses for Government policy and their inclusion in the new sector was seen very much as (to mix metaphors) the bringing of Trojan horses into the university camp. It was felt – not least by some in the

Government – that this new sector would very much create a number of tensions which would force the older universities to change.

The Government also used the 1992 Act to remove responsibility for science policy away from the Department for Education and Science into the new Office of Science and Technology, part of the Cabinet Office. This led to the DES changing its name to the Department for Education and losing a significant part of its role. The Research Council now came under the OST and in early 1992 a major review was underway into the future of research funding.

Further Education

Just as the 1988 Education Reform Act removed the polytechnics and other colleges from LEA control, so the Further and Higher Eduction Act 1992 removed most further education from local government. In many ways this is a radical extension of the higher education policy which has far-reaching implications for the development of education in the UK. On 1 April 1993, approximately 400 separate colleges left LEA control and became free-standing corporations with the same range of legal rights and responsibilities which the polytechnics had gained on becoming corporate in 1989.

In parallel to the creation of PCFC, the Government established a new quango to act as an intermediary body between it and the colleges, known as the Further Education Funding Council and the Chief Executive of the PCFC, William Stubbs, became the new Chief Executive of FEFC.

There are many similar developments from the old polytechnic sector paralleled in the new FE sector, such as the creation of Colleges Employers Forum, like the Polytechnic and Colleges Forum, and the use of a range of funding mechanisms similar to those used in the former public sector. Rather than funding on the basis of enrolment numbers alone, new arrangements link funding to outcome. Since a massive 25 per cent expansion in numbers is anticipated over the next three years, colleges are in the position of having to recruit more strongly in order to maintain their current levels of funding. However, funding is now also based on additional performance and exit indicators such as student retention rates and examination results. This new competitive environment in Further Education will bring in changes similar to those experienced in the higher education sector, including changes in management style, a revised balance of power between management and unions, and the centralisation of power through financial control.

This new post-16 sector was considerably more diverse than the former public sector of higher education. The pattern of post-16 education varied both within and between local education authorities. Typically any single LEA might have 16–19 education provided in an 11–18 or 13–18 school, thus as a 'sixth-form', alongside further education colleges catering solely for post-16 education and sometimes even with specialist sixth-form colleges, which were providers of post-16 education but to a very different philosophy to most further education colleges.

The imposition of a market-led system on to this newly-formed sector, which contained two main categories of institution which had traditionally functioned with differently balanced course provision and operated within distinct cultures, posed problems at ground level. For example, locally established agreements on course provision between neighbouring colleges have frequently been abandoned in the wider competition for students. Where past local collaboration provided one viable minority course in an area, the new order has resulted in course duplication and a spreading of student numbers too thinly to make any course viable. Sixth form colleges, which are seen as being vulnerable because of their small size and elitist recruitment (Clarke, 1993) have been pushed into providing courses for adults. Anxiety has also been expressed that sixth-form colleges are poorly equipped to provide lower-level skills-based courses and that in offering them they risk their enviable reputation for academic excellence.

There has also been a considerable expansion of higher education institutions 'franchising' parts of their courses to FE post-16 colleges. It is worth noting that many of those FE colleges which run franchised courses for income generation are experiencing cultural dissonance. Tutors are teaching undergraduates, but not within the culture of higher education. Resource constraints within colleges have resulted in excessive teaching loads, minimalist remission for preparation to teach at degree level, together with staff timetables which embrace courses at levels far removed one from another in intellectual terms.

Clearly the role of local government in education has been significantly diminished both in the 1989 and the 1992 Acts. The developments in school education which to some extent is following on that of post-16 higher education may well lead to the end of local authority involvement in education altogether.

Conclusion

Looking back over Government policy since 1979 it is possible to see a mixture of long-term, ideologically based commitments to certain objectives and short term incrementalism where there is no clear policy priority evidenced. Although much of the policy development since 1979 has been incrementalist, short-term, apparently lacking in strategy, if you were to put a description of the situation in 1979 alongside the description of the educational system in 1993 the differences would be tremendous.

The role of local education authorities has been transformed and is probably on track for ending within the next few years apart from residual special services. There has been a centralisation of power over schools, further and higher education, which would have been regarded as un-achievable in 1979. This power extends not just to the level of financing, the unit of resource, and the level of student finance but also to the National Curriculum and the method of assessment. There is a degree of *dirigisme* in Government policy more reflective of the old fashioned French system than of the UK in 1979. The influence of the American Right on the development of educational policy by the British 'New Right' has been considerable and should be the subject of further detailed study. In particular, the increased emphasis on testing and assessment in the UK has been directly imported from the USA, where it is now established orthodoxy.

The influence of the business community on the educational world is much greater now than it was in 1979. Business interests are directly represented on school, colleges and university governing boards, with a requirement that they should actually be in a majority for the new universities and the post-16 institutions. There are a whole variety of initiatives designed to build links between business and commerce and education, such as the Business Education Partnership, the introduction of National Vocational Qualifications and so on.

The growth of 'new managerialism' has been a significant feature of public sector higher education, further education and increasingly in the schools. Whether this trend will continue throughout the 1990s is open to challenge yet at the moment it is clear that this has affected significantly the balance of power between trade unions and employers and the power of management within the educational system. The teaching trade unions, whether at school or higher education level, are much weaker now than they were in 1979.

At the same time, by 1993 the Government had committed itself to an expansion of further education, was midway through a very significant expansion of higher education and had broadened the base of parental involvement in school education quite significantly. It is not necessarily the case that these developments will lead in the direction the Government wished or anticipated. It may well be, for example, that increased parental power will work against the Government wishes as was shown in 1993 in the reaction against tests for 14 year olds, where there was an alliance between Parent Teacher Associations, school governing bodies and the teaching unions against the Secretary of State's plans. Education is firmly on the political agenda in the early 1990s. It promises to be an agenda of change and even turmoil.

12

'A Poisoned Chalice?' Personal Social Services Policy

NEIL EVANS

Introduction

This chapter will focus on those aspects of welfare known as the personal social services for:

- elderly people;
- children and their families;
- people with mental and physical disabilities;
- those with alcohol and drug problems;
- people with mental health needs.

Increasingly such services will be provided not just by local authority Social Services Departments (SSDs) but by a plethora of organisations, private, voluntary and not-for-profit. The discussion will centre on the implications of two major new pieces of legislation:

- The National Health Service and Community Care Act (1990).
- The Children Act (1989).

For SSDs the responsibilities placed upon them by this legislation embodied both the challenges and opportunities which characterised their fluctuating fortunes in the 1980s. Successive governments since 1979 have both extended the remit of SSDs and created mechanisms for greater accountability and stricter control. Social workers were accused of contributing to a disintegration of the family as the bastion of morality in society and to the inexorable increase in public spending. Even the most churlish of Ministers though was unable to blame SSDs for the reality of demographic changes including an increase in those aged over 80 from 0.7 million in 1951 to 2.1 million in 1990 or for the burgeoning increase in expenditure on private residential and nursing home care. Perhaps reluctantly the government accepted the conclusion of the Barclay Committee in 1982 that

> There are many things being done by social workers which it would be to the detriment of chiefs to have left undone and if social workers did not do them then many of them would not be done. (Barclay, 1982)

and the view of Sir Roy Griffiths that

> Major restructuring can be disruptive and time-consuming and before it is contemplated it has to be shown that existing authorities are incapable of delivering. (Griffiths, 1988, p. iv)

Local Authority Social Services Departments while surviving threats to their very existence were to be subject to a number of significant changes. They should become:

- Purchasers rather than primarily providers of services;
- More exposed to competition in a *mixed economy of care*;
- More clearly accountable to *consumers* offering needs-led services and working in partnership with parents and children;
- Subject to greater *central control* both financially and through increased inspection and guidance from the Department of Health and the Audit Commission.

For social workers concerns about the quality of the emotional and psychological experiences of their clients would appear to be overtaken by the demands of service planning, multi-agency collaboration and financial accountability.

Community Care

The consensus around the virtues of community care which developed from the mid-1950s was based in part on reservations about the quality of care in large-scale institutions and in part on growing evidence of the preference for domiciliary or locally based provision on the part of users of services. Such a consensus was largely restricted to the rhetoric of community care rather than a reflection of agreement on strategic measures to develop alternatives to institutional care. In fact, the inertia built into the budgeting systems of the NHS and local authorities proved a major obstacle to significant change in the 1960s and 1970s. It has been the ideological commitment of the Thatcher and Major governments to 'rolling-back' the state through the targeting and rationing of services which has underpinned the potentially radical recasting of community care policy through the 1980s and early 1990s.

The process of 'trans-institutionalisation' in the 1970s and early 1980s, involved the development of smaller-scale institutions or care in the community still provided by health or local authorities. The first Thatcher government sought to assert the primacy of the family as the provider of care *by* the community. At the same time, as a consequence in part of the diminution of local authority responsibilities, central government support for private provision of residential and nursing home care through income support (then called supplementary benefit) payments rose from £10 million in 1979 to over £1 billion in 1989. It was the Audit Commission Report *Making a Reality of Community Care* in 1986 which drew attention to this 'perverse incentive' to place people in residential care which directly conflicted with the policy of care by the community set out in 1981.

Community based health and social care agencies would clearly experience less call for their services if social security funded private residential care expanded to meet the growing demand from an ageing population. The Commission urged that:

> a rationalisation of funding policies must be undertaken so that present policy conflicts are resolved . . . a more rational organisational structure must be established . . . [and] . . . the organisational structure of the different agencies need to be aligned and greater managerial authority delegated to the local level. (pp. 3–4)

The notion of the mixed economy of welfare was firmly supported with the Commission emphasising the role of local managers in control of budgets and with freedom to purchase services from 'whichever public or private agency seems appropriate'. The Commission recommended that a 'high level review of the current situation be set in train [and] . . . the one option that is not tolerable is to do nothing about present financial organisational and staffing arrangements'. The Department of Social Security (DSS) which in the short term applied limits to the weekly fees to be paid to private home owners was unable to contain the demand for a benefit which was not cash-limited. Eligibility was determined by a means test rather than an assessment of the *need* for residential care. The government moved with some speed to appoint Roy Griffiths in 1986 to produce recommendations for the future of community care.

The Griffiths Report 1988

The choice of Sir Roy Griffiths reflected a pervasive characteristic of the Thatcher government's approach to policy-making in the personal social services, as in the public sector more generally. Out went Royal Commissions and large Committees of Inquiry reflecting a broad range of relevant (or, it is argued, vested) interests. Rejected were the processes of undertaking research or seeking formal evidence. Favoured was the model of an individual or small group charged with formulating specific recommendations within the context of firmly established, if not always explicit, parameters. In this case Griffiths based his review on the 1986 report of the Audit Commission discussed above, and the report of the House of Commons social services Committee on *Community Care with special reference to adult mentally ill and mentally handicapped people.*

Griffiths in March 1988 summed up the sense of confusion and lack of direction in community care policies in two telling phrases: the first referred to a feeling that:

> the Israelites faced with the requirement to make bricks without straw had a comparatively routine and possible task [and a sense that] community care is a poor relation, everybody's distant relative but no-body's baby. (p. iv)

The Report reaffirmed a shift in focus for Social Services, who should act

> as the designers, organisers and purchasers of non-health care services, and not primarily as direct providers, making maximum possible use of voluntary and private sector bodies to widen consumer choice, stimulate innovation and encourage efficiency. (p. 1)

They should ensure that the 'needs of individuals within the specified groups are identified, packages of care are devised and services co-ordinated and where appropriate a specific care manager assigned'. While Griffiths held back from a specific recommendation that they become the 'lead' authorities responsible for planning and implementing community care policies this indeed was the inevitable consequence of his proposals, unpalatable though this was to a government content to strip local authorities of functions rather than add to them. For Griffiths the proposals for a Minister clearly and publicly identified as responsible for community care and social services funded by a ring-fenced specific grant followed naturally from his belief that policy should be matched by resources.

It is widely assumed that the deafening ministerial silence which greeted the low-key publication of the Griffiths report on the day after Chancellor Nigel Lawson's Budget of 1988 reflected reluctance to endorse the pivotal role accorded to local authorities by Griffiths. It was not until November 1989 that the government committed itself to specific proposals, which appeared in the 1989 White Paper *Caring for People*.

Caring for People: Community Care in the Next Decade and Beyond

The White Paper formed the basis for the relevant part of the National Health Service and Community Care Act 1990 (NHSCC Act) which was implemented in phases between April 1991 and April 1993. It follows closely the Griffiths proposals and has as its core feature the re-direction of the DSS budget for private institutional care to SSDs for the provision of support in the home or in residential care following an assessment of need as well as of means. The White Paper (p. 5) sets out the following key objectives:

- To promote the development of domiciliary, day and respite services to enable people to live in their own home wherever feasible and sensible;
- To ensure that service planners and providers make practical support for carers a high priority;
- To make proper assessment of need and good care management the cornerstone of high quality care;
- To promote the development of a flourishing independent sector alongside good quality public services;
- To clarify the responsibilities of agencies and so make it easier to hold them to account for their performance;

- To secure better value for taxpayers' money by introducing a new funding structure for social care.

These objectives are to be achieved through the process of 'care management' which should include (DOH/DSS, 1989):

- identification of people in need;
- assessment of care needs;
- planning and securing the delivery of care;
- monitoring the quality of care provided;
- review of client needs.

The government deferred the full implementation of the new Act until April 1993 claiming that local authorities were not ready in 1991 to take on their new responsibilities. It is widely assumed that the real reason for delay was the uncertainty about the financial implications of the changes at a time when the new Prime Minister, John Major, was intent on disentangling the government from the poll tax. Nevertheless some important developments did take place between 1991 and 1993 including the production of annual Community Care Plans for each Social Services Department, the publication of complaints procedures and the establishment of 'arm's-length' inspection arrangements for local authority residential establishments. Finally, by April 1993 SSDs were required to publish their priorities and criteria of 'need' which would underpin the assessment for community care services.

The lengthy period between the passage of the NHSCC Act through Parliament and its implementation fully in April 1993 has allowed the Department of Health to provide an unprecedented level of advice and guidance to local authorities. The latter have been unsure as to whether their role as lead agencies will in fact be a 'poisoned chalice' with blame heaped upon them when inadequate resources fail to permit the raised expectations of services users to be met. The Secretary of State, Virginia Bottomley, was in no doubt about what community care means to the current government, 'it is about the services and support which will enable people affected by age or disability to live as independently as possible.'

The aim is to support people in their own homes or in 'homely surroundings whenever this can be done'. Nor was she in any doubt as to where responsibility for the success or otherwise of the policy should lie: 'If implementation is to be effective, there must be close working links between all agencies – social services departments, NHS bodies, housing authorities and associations, voluntary organisations and private service providers. These working links must take full account of the views and needs of those being cared for and their carers.' The challenge for social work is clear as resources 'are inevitably limited by what the taxpayer can afford', thus organisational processes will need to change and 'new skills, attitudes and relationships at both managerial and professional levels' (*Foreword to Community Care in the Next Decade and Beyond: Policy Guidance*, 1990) will need to be developed. Failures in the implementation of the Community Care legislation will be laid squarely at the door of local authorities.

The Department of Health Policy Guidance emphasises the centrality of three activities:

● Community care planning.
● Care management and assessment.
● Commissioning and purchasing.

The publication of a Community Care Plan is a statutory responsibility of local authorities as is the requirement to consult as a part of the process of preparing the plan. The DoH views the planning exercise as crucial to encouraging

> health and local authorities as they move towards the role of 'enabler' rather than main provider, of all care services. To do this effectively major providers of care services, service users, and their carers, all need to be involved during the planning process.

The DoH ideal is a joint plan produced by Social Services Departments with the local health authority thereby emphasising the seamless service available in the community. Unfortunately, it is unlikely that the annual planning cycle will be sensitive enough to overcome a major limitation of the White Paper and the subsequent Act in failing to differentiate clearly between social care and health care needs.

Services for people with disabilities and older people have been bedevilled by boundary disputes between SSDs and health authorities and exhortations by the DOH to develop a seamless service are no substitute for clarity of policy. For many years the focus of the conflict over responsibilities has been the fate of people discharged from long-stay institutions into the community. In the 1990s the community care developments have trailed two or three years behind the major changes in the NHS, particularly the establishment of Trusts and GP fundholders typifying the split between purchaser and provider (see Chapter 9). The knock-on effects of changes in one service can be exemplified by the impact on agencies in the community of the hospital discharge policies which have significantly reduced the length of stay in acute hospitals.

A low priority accorded to health care needs of people with disabilities by health commissions and uncertainty over the responsibility for drug and alcohol services are further examples of the limitations of planning between Social Services, Health and Housing authorities and the DSS in resolving critical resource issues.

In addition to collaborating with other statutory agencies SSDs are expected to collate evidence of the care needs of the local population. Thus care management and assessment procedures should be designed both to meet individual care needs and to inform the strategic planning process. The year 1993/4 was the first year in which local authorities were to have received budgets for expenditure previously the responsibility of the DSS. The £539 million allocated to community care was said by the DoH to represent 135 per cent of what the DSS would have been expected to pay for new residents in private care. The aims of targeting those in greatest need and of achieving better value for money by designing packages of care as alternatives to residential provision are dependent on the process of assessment and care management. This is claimed by the DoH to be based on a needs-led approach which has two key aspects:

- a progressive separation of the tasks of assessment from those of service provision in order to focus on needs, where possible having the tasks carried out by different staff;
- a shift of influence from those providing to those purchasing services.

Care management will aim to (ibid., *Forward to Community Care in the Next Decade: Policy Guidance*, 1990, p. 23):

- respond flexibly and sensitively to the needs of users and their carers;
- allow a range of options;
- intervene no more than necessary to foster independence;
- prevent deterioration;
- concentrate on those with the greatest needs.

To meet these aims the process of care management will involve an assessment of the needs of service users and their carers. Much of the literature from both DoH and Social Services emphasises the need for a cultural shift in favour of the empowerment of service users through participation in the process of articulating their needs rather than relying on social workers to determine which services will be provided from the available range. To support such a shift in the direction of needs-led services, SSDs have shown no lack of initiative or ambition. For example, Dorset in their draft 1993/94 Community Care Plan undertake to develop services which are: accessible, acceptable, integrated; informative; enabling; confidential; flexible; efficient; high quality; consistent; participative and non-judgemental albeit 'within the limits of resource available' (ibid., p. 3).

At the very least Social Services have markedly improved the quality of information available about services, established the first steps towards clarifying eligibility criteria, set in place complaints procedures and in some cases provided service users with copies of completed assessments and accompanying care plans. The extent to which such changes can be considered a radical move in the direction of consumer choice will be discussed later.

The Department of Health is quite clear in its policy guidance about the need to separate *purchasing* or commissioning of services from their *provision*:

> Care managers should in effect act as brokers for services across the statutory and independent sectors. They should not, therefore, be involved in direct service delivery, nor should they normally carry managerial responsibility for the services they arrange. This removes any possible conflict of interest. Care managers should be able to assume some or all of the responsibility for purchasing services necessary to implement a care plan. (DoH, 1991, p. 24)

As yet it is unclear how many departments have devolved budgets to care managers. While in early care management schemes such budget holding appeared to be a pre-condition for individually designed packages of care, this has been undermined with the award of block contracts to private and voluntary care providers as April 1993 approached. The rhetoric of needs-led services with personalised packages of care is challenged by the DoH's commitment to developing a mixed economy of care.

> The development of an environment where a number of high quality providers can compete to offer a choice of service provision is important. This will enable Social Services Departments to negotiate for services on favourable financial terms and create pressure for maximum efficiency and effectiveness in the provision of services; ensure a wide range of choice for service users and reduce the scope for monopoly abuse such as the restriction of supply. (DoH, 1991, p. 34)

The private sector has been largely confined to residential care and has had some success in seeking protection from threats to its income from SSDs actively encouraging community based alternatives.

The Secretary of State has instructed local authorities to use 85 per cent of their community care budgets to purchase services in the non-statutory sectors. While she no doubt assumes that market opportunities will lead the private sector to develop domiciliary care services what is apparent is that, at least initially, the restriction on how Social Services can spend their budgets will serve to bolster and sustain residential care. Nor is it certain that the financial muscle of these departments as purchasers of services will allow them through the tendering procedures to establish 'non-commercial' specifications in contracts. While the qualifications and experience of staff can be taken into account this does not extend to terms and conditions of employment, for example, commitment to equal opportunities and anti-discrimination policies.

A rather different problem could confront voluntary organisations if their need to meet the competitive demands of a new market-led environment compromises an independent role *vis-à-vis* the local authority. The economic recession of the early 1990s subjected many voluntary organisations to severe financial pressures and thus the temptation to bid for community care contracts will be powerful. Whether their independence and pressure group activity influencing statutory agency policies can be sustained in a quasi-commercial environment is open to question.

Community Care – Contemporary Policy Agenda

The NHS and Community Care Act (1990) embodies the government's concern to achieve value for money by extending consumer choice through the mixed economy of welfare to facilitate user or needs-led service provision. It is on these criteria that their community care policy will be judged.

Whatever the rhetoric underpinning the NHS and Community Care Act the single most significant government aim has been to curtail the burgeoning bill for residential and community care in the face of increasing demand from an ageing population. The notion of a 'demographic time-bomb' has had a powerful impact on Conservative sensibilities. Economy, efficiency and effectiveness are to be sought in the family and the community rather than in institutions and residential care. While local authorities are beneficiaries of the re-direction of DSS income support funds the responsibility for future shortcomings in services will surely be laid at their door by Ministers.

How far SSDs can redefine their task to that of purchasers or commissioners of services maintaining a regulatory role in relation to a diverse range of providers time will tell. Sustaining the necessary system of financial management, the information base required and the complex planning process when the initial start-up funds provided by central government are exhausted will test the commitment of departments. This, at a time when the very existence of many shire county SSDs will be threatened by local government re-organisation in the mid-1990s. For some social workers the role of care manager in developing innovative responses to the needs of services users is a stimulating challenge, for others the separation of purchaser and provider functions has few attractions. The spectre of the purchasing role being removed from Social Services perhaps to GP fund-holders remains real in the eyes of the more pessimistic social workers.

The government's emphasis on the mixed economy of welfare can be argued merely to reflect what has always been the reality of personal social services. Informal care and the private sector have traditionally played a critical role with state services providing a less than tempting safety net. How far will consumer choice be extended with an increasingly diverse range of providers of services responding to market opportunities? In fact, the most dependent members of the community who are likely to be identified as those in greatest need are not well-equipped to exercise consumer sovereignty, shop around and generate significant demand in traditional market terms for new services. The power of the private residential home owners lobby and the SSDs predilection for block contracts suggest only limited scope for individual consumers to impact on the range of services available. For many users of services and their carers the success of the NHS and Community Care Act will be judged on the basis of the degree to which services are genuinely needs led. The empowerment of users implies a radical shift in the relationship between them and care managers.

While the process of assessment may be cast in needs-led terms there remains the reality of cash-limited budgets. The caveat that needs will be met within the 'available resources' suggests that the assessment process will be centrally concerned with rationing those resources. In fact, assessment itself is to be rationed. A screening or preassessment process will determine who will have a full assessment, the latter being a precondition of obtaining a comprehensive package of care. Nor, of course, will the identification of need generate a service. A further test of means will determine whether community care funds will be available to purchase the required services. The experience of state-menting of children with special needs established in the 1981 Education Act does not offer any cause for optimism. Local Education Authorities have demonstrated an almost infinite capacity for prevarication to avoid statements of need which would then commit them to providing appropriate education.

The signs are that Social Services are becoming equally entangled in what is seen as a legal minefield if assessments generate statements of need which they are unable to meet. Central government is unlikely to dissuade local authorities from their traditional path of caution which might well involve avoiding specifying needs when the necessary resources are not immediately available. In fact, the abrupt abolition of the Independent Living Fund (ILF) and the restriction of its successor to those under retirement age has significantly reduced the scope for many disabled people to tailor services to their own needs. Support from community care funds can only be provided by way of services and not cash.

The advantage of the ILF was that as a cash benefit the recipient was able to take direct control of the process of designing a package of care. Far from permitting this level of empowerment for those receiving Community Care support the government has reduced the amount of financial support for disabled people to a top-up of community care services identified and provided by care managers. In fact, Nicholas Scott, Minister for the Disabled, made clear that if support for a disabled person in the community would require expenditure above a certain level, £500 a week at 1992 prices, then residential care would be necessary regardless of the person's preference!

The sensitivities of the government have been evident in the reaction to a public outcry concerning the discharge or 'dumping' of patients

from psychiatric hospitals. Families and carers have criticised the level
of support available in the community. The media have highlighted a
concern amongst the public at large about the risk presented by some
discharged patients. The Health Secretary, Virginia Bottomley, in
August 1993 announced an intention to introduce supervised discharge arrangements which will allow doctors and social workers
greater powers to control patients in the community. The proposals
fall short of permitting forced medication but will place restrictions on
where the individual lives and allow a key worker the right of access to
the patient. A refusal to take medication could lead to a recall to
hospital after a review of the case.

Child Care and the Children Act 1989

The high priority accorded to child care work by Social Services
Departments reflected the evidence in the 1980s and no less in the
1990s of a level of child abuse, particularly child sexual abuse,
dramatically higher than had been previously thought. While the right
sought a reaffirmation of traditional family values the Conservative
administrations since 1979 have struggled to provide a response to the
increasingly evident but uncomfortable fact that the home might be an
extremely dangerous place for some family members.

Child care policy is embroiled with the complex task of resolving
questions around the nature of the state's responsibility towards
children and conflict surrounding notions of parents rights and
responsibilities. The 1970s saw the identification of the 'welfare of
the child' as the most important consideration in situations of
conflicting interests among family members. Unfortunately the 1980s
have not produced a resolution of the lack of certainty about how best
the welfare of children be protected and promoted. Social workers have
felt attacked, both for efforts to shore up families and when separating
children from parents if this has appeared to be the appropriate option.
Committees of Inquiry have not provided consistent answers.

In 1985 at the end of a 300-page report the Committee of Inquiry
into the death of Jasmine Beckford concluded that 'society should
sanction, in 'high risk' cases, the removal of such children for an
appreciable time'. Unfortunately the Committee offered little guidance
in the identification of 'high-risk' stating 'we do not define 'high-risk',
mainly because we think that it is not susceptible of definition'.

234 'A Poisoned Chalice?'

Nevertheless the unequivocal message to social workers was to be more decisive and ready to contemplate permanent removal of children from parents. By 1988 the Butler-Sloss Report into 'an unprecedented rise in the diagnosis of child sexual abuse during the months of May and June 1987' in Cleveland concluded that:

> Social Services, whilst putting the needs of the child first, must respect the rights of the parents; they also must work if possible with the parents for the benefit of the children. These parents themselves are often in need of help. Inevitably a degree of conflict develops between these objectives. (p. 11)

While the abuse of children is not a new phenomenon contemporary media and public concern has thrust it on to the political agenda over the past twenty years in a quite unprecedented fashion. The use of Inquiries to investigate the circumstances of child abuse 'scandals' has no parallel in the public sector. Generally the concerns have been around the untimely deaths of children, Colwell to Beckford, but most recently, in Cleveland, Rochdale and the Orkneys, the challenge has been to what is alleged to be misuse of Social Services and police powers to intervene in family life to remove children.

In July 1988 the team led by Lord Justice Butler-Schloss produced a Report of the Inquiry into Child Abuse in Cleveland 1987 for the Secretary of State for Social Services. The increase in the diagnosis of child sexual abuse and consequent removal of children to the care of the local authority sparked an intense media and parliamentary furore during 1987. The Inquiry revealed the antithesis of interagency collaboration with the two paediatricians lined-up with the SSD Child Abuse Consultant against the police and the police surgeon. At issue was the reliability of the anal dilation test as an indicator of child sexual abuse.

The Inquiry Team recommended changes in both *management* and *interagency co-operation*:

- senior managers in SSDs need to ensure that they have efficient systems available to allow accurate monitoring of service activity which will alert them to problems that need to be resolved;
- staff engaged in social work practice in the field of child abuse and child sexual abuse need structured arrangements for their professional supervision and personal support. The work is stressful and it is important that their personal needs are not overlooked;

- no single agency – Health, Social Services, Police or voluntary organisation has the pre-eminent responsibility in the assessment of child abuse generally and child sexual abuse specifically. Each agency has a prime responsibility for a particular aspect of the problem. Neither childrens' nor parents' needs and rights can be adequately met or protected unless agencies agree a framework for their inter-action. (pp. 14–15)

While reaffirming the primacy of the needs of children Butler-Schloss reached a rather different conclusion from Blom-Cooper emphasising as she did the need to 'avoid the necessity of removing a child from home'. Families should be supported during investigations, kept informed in writing and advised of their rights of appeal and complaint.

The systems for interagency and multidisciplinary collaboration in the identification of, and intervention in, cases of child abuse set in place gradually since the mid-1970s appeared to have failed. Child care policy was under virtually continuous review during the 1980s. The 1984 Report to the Select Committee for Social Services led to an interdepartmental working party which published a consultative document *Review of Child Care Law* in September 1985. A White Paper *The Law on Child Care and Family Services* (Cmnd 62) appeared in January 1987 and formed the basis for the Children Act of 1989, implemented in October 1991.

The government established a number of important principles in the White Paper:

- While the state may assist parents the 'prime responsibility for the upbringing of children rests with parents'.
- 'Services to families in need should be arranged in a voluntary partnership with parents'. As far as possible children in care should remain in contact with their parents and return home as soon as feasible.
- Only a court should authorise the transfer of a parent's legal rights to the local authority. This should only happen if a child has been harmed or is at risk of being harmed, and 'a court order is the best method of safeguarding the child's interests'.
- The period of removal of a child from parents in an emergency, prior to a full court hearing, should be reduced and be open to challenge by parents.

Whilst the government sought to rationalise the more than twenty routes into local authority care the eventual provisions of the 1989 Act fell short of establishing a family court system. While ensuring greater uniformity of practice amongst the different courts which might be concerned with arrangements for the care of children, the government has yet to grasp the nettle of legal vested interests which would be required to set up a single form of family court.

The Children's Act (1989), its authors would claim, contains elements of both greater protection for children and a further clarification of the rights, or at least responsibilities of parents. While the child's welfare should be the paramount consideration in court proceedings the presumption is that this can, in all but the most exceptional circumstances, be secured within the family. Even in those situations which require a child to be 'looked-after' by the local authority parents should be involved in the decision-making and planning for the future. Parental responsibility must be encouraged by active partnership with social workers. An example of the attempt to meet children's needs while not riding roughshod over parental rights is found in the replacement of the 28 day Place of Safety Order which previously could have been used to remove a child with little opportunity for parents to oppose such action before the Courts. The new Emergency Protection Order (EPO) is for a maximum of eight days with a possible extension for a further seven days and allows the right of challenge by parents after 72 hours. The Court may also make directions in respect of parental contact with the child. But responding to previous criticisms of the difficulty of securing access to children thought to be at risk and obtaining a medical examination the Children's Act has introduced a Child Assessment Order lasting for seven days which does not involve the removal of the child from home. The crucial test of the success of the Act will be the degree to which the claimed 'even-handedness' actually does enable a partnership between parents and the local authority to develop. Where it is feared that a child is at risk from a parent the degree to which social workers and the courts can protect the one without alienating the other must be open to doubt.

The Government claims tentative but tangible evidence of the Act's success in its first year of operation. In the Preface to the first report to Parliament on the working of the Act, the Secretary of State, Virginia Bottomley claims:

- Although the trends have not stabilised, in the first year almost 3000 or broadly 50 per cent fewer emergency orders were made giving authority for the removal of a child from home. The reduction in these orders suggests that local authorities are being more discriminating than previously and are using the power of emergency intervention more appropriately.
- There has been a substantial fall in the number of children entering compulsory care. Some 1600 were subject to a care order under the Children Act in the first year compared with nearly four times as many under similar orders previously. This is a strong indication that the culture of a working partnership with parents is becoming a reality in the vast majority of authorities.
- Some 5000 or 10 per cent fewer children were being 'looked after' by local authorities at the end of March compared with a year before. This was what the Act intended. In general, the best place for children to grow up is in their own homes with their own families. This aim of the Act is being achieved with authorities working together with families to provide help to keep the family together.

A closer examination of the statistics contained in the Report suggests a more cautious conclusion than that of the Minister. While in the first quarter of the Act's operation, i.e., October–December 1991, approximately 700 applications for Care Orders were made, by the final quarter of the first year this figure had risen to over 1000. Applications for Supervision Orders and emergency protection orders also showed a marked increase during 1992 though the rate of increase slowed later in the year. It is probable that the complexity of the new legislation led to caution in the early months of its implementation. No doubt the spirit of partnership engendered a renewed commitment on the part of social workers to try to resolve family difficulties without recourse to the law.

The awareness that Courts would endeavour to deal with applications as far as possible without making an Order will also have influenced Social Services when considering initiating proceedings. Only time will reveal whether the increasing number of applications for Care Orders reflects a deferring of court action as social workers seek to find alternatives, not always successfully. The Department of Health is convinced that the much reduced figure for children entering care compared with the period prior to October 1991 and the Children Act's implementation can not be explained solely by 'time lag and start-up' effects of the new legislation but reflects a radical shift in the direction of partnership between parents and social workers.

For those who would reserve judgement the question of the adequacy of the resource allocation required to provide support services in the community remains. The Act extends Social Services responsibilities in a number of areas, for example, Section 17 confers a duty to safeguard and promote the interests of children 'in need'. In addition, to children at risk of abuse, those with disabilities and young people leaving care up to the age of 21 are identified as priorities for services. Ahead of the Act the Association of Metropolitan Authorities claimed that the costs of implementation would be more than two and a half times the DoH's estimates. In its first review of the working of the Act (Cohen, 1992) the Association of County Councils (ACC) is optimistic and upbeat concluding that while

> the Government may have legislated too enthusiastically, and have issued too much guidance and not enough money but nevertheless there is real hope that the world will become a better place for vulnerable children and young people (and) the rarefied heights of policy are being scaled by the practitioners who normally frequent the valleys of child care concerns.

While it would be churlish to interpret the ACC's review, which is entitled 'A new deal for children', as a part of their campaign to preserve counties in the face of impending local government re-organisation (see Chapter 2) there is a sense in which Social Services Departments are challenging public apathy or outright hostility to their efforts in the child care field. It is galling in the extreme for hard-pressed social workers when media coverage of the Children Act has focused on a handful of cases in which children have sought a 'divorce' from parents or to force a parent to resume contact with them. The innovative services developed in recent years to support families have rarely been of interest to a media intent on attacking social workers for adherence to an 'ideology of political correctness'. Whether it be in the apparent failure to control the delinquency of young children, the recidivism of the of the 'joy-rider' or in the decisions to refuse certain couples as adopters social workers continue to be ridiculed in some sections of the press.

Overview and Future Trends

For Social Services Departments the early 1990s have seen the implementation of two major pieces of personal social services legislation, the Children Act 1989 and the Community Care Act 1990 discussed in this chapter. The challenges for the late 1990s are becoming clear:

• the Government's review of public expenditure in an effort to reduce budget deficits, with a particular emphasis on containing social welfare expenditure, will place resources under continuing threat. Within a European context of demographic change, pensions, social security and health care policies are likely to place increasing demands on individuals and families to meet their needs rather than look to the state. The impact on SSDs is likely to be profound as the residualisation of welfare isolates those unable to provide through either the market or family and informal supports.

• the image of the homeless, lonely ex-hospital patient unwanted by an uncaring community is a powerful one. It underpins the tension between central and local government, over the responsibility for community care 'failures'.

• the developing split between purchasing and providing functions calls for a radical re-appraisal of the role and training of social workers. For many wedded to notions of counselling, therapeutic intervention or, indeed, action to challenge social inequalities the tasks of case management, purchasing packages of care, tendering, contracting and contract compliance will be anathema.

• the tensions between the diverging understandings of the concept of user-led services will become increasingly evident. For some empowerment and the development of advocacy services implies a more significant user role in articulating their demands for more, or better provision. For others the development of consumerism reflects a need to control the expansionist aspirations of professionals. The raised expectations of users of services provided within the Community Care and Children Acts are likely to fall foul of the need on the part of SSDs to ration entitlement and 'target those in greatest need'.

• the oft-repeated Government espousal of the virtues of and necessity for, interagency planning and collaboration has been rewarded with some notable examples of co-operation between health and social care providers in recent years. The challenge remains to prevent such achievements fading in the face of the competition between provider units engendered by the quasi-market mechanisms that are developing.

• the implementation of the Community Care Act is revealing a number of conflicts which remain to be resolved. While the privatisation of services will allow opportunities for robust entrepreneurs, health and social care authorities have yet to develop codes of practice which will contain the danger of conflicts of interest amongst those commissioning services who might have a financial interest in the subsequent contracts. While the market mechanisms of competition for business will be a powerful and not necessarily healthy discipline on provider units it is not clear where accountability lies for commissioner or purchasers.

There is some evidence that the latter's financial muscle may be misused in an aggressive assertion of power. While it might be expected that commissioners will be called to account for the sensitivity of their assessments of need and the quality of their planning, in fact, the vulnerability of many users of personal social services limits their opportunity to offer a forceful and consistent oversight of the activities of those charged with purchasing relevant services.

As a traditional public service ethic, for all its faults, becomes eroded it is critical that new mechanisms for ensuring the protection of vulnerable young, elderly and disabled people are set in place. While the efficient, effective and economical provision of services might be the major goal of government, public sentiment is likely to be susceptible to financial scandals and any evidence of the abuse of those most at risk in the community. Local government in its 1970s heyday might yet be viewed nostalgically as a bastion of endangered, or even lost, standards of financial and ethical probity as we move into the twenty-first century.

13

Social Security Policy under the Conservatives

MICHAEL HILL

Introduction

In the examination of social security policy since 1979 there is a need to highlight four themes.

The first, and much the most important of these, is the fact that a government committed to cutting public expenditure has had to cope with the fact that not only is social security the largest public expenditure programme but it is also one whose growth it is particularly difficult to curb. The factors influencing growth – an ageing population and economic decline – would have been likely to present problems to a government of any ideological persuasion. Whilst in some respects the Conservatives approached the case for cutting social security benefits with some enthusiasm, they had to face dilemmas relating to the extent to which others of their policies pushed social security costs up whilst political considerations made some of the more obvious ways of cutting expenditure difficult.

The second theme concerns the approach adopted to cutting income maintenance expenditure, the attack upon 'universal' benefits and therefore particularly upon the Beveridge design for social security. Targeting was the watchword for much Conservative social security policy, encouraging private provision and continuing the process that was steadily moving means-tested benefits to the centre of the state system. Again going down this policy road was not simple in practice. It posed problems about disincentive effects, affecting choices between work and benefits, which governments continue to struggle to solve.

The third theme to be explored concerns the extent to which Conservative social security policy since 1979 must be placed in the context of Conservative acceptance, indeed often encouragement, of an increasingly unequal society. This orientation had implications for the levels of benefits. It also had implications within the benefit system for specifically stigmatised groups – particularly the unemployed and the heads of single parent families – upon whom the government was prepared to bestow additional disadvantages.

The final theme fits less well with the other three, but nevertheless must not be disregarded. This concerns the extent to which the social security system was affected by the processes of institutional change in this period. After an initial hesitation the government recognised social security as a natural candidate for the process of 'agency' creation, developed by the 'next steps' initiative. Yet even before that social security was affected by a muddled and rather contradictory series of moves on the boundaries between the responsibilities of central and local government, which the author has elsewhere described as 'the delegation of implementation problems' (Hill, 1989; Fimister and Hill, 1993). In this context it is important not to be led by all the subsequent rhetoric to forget how much the government's community care agenda was driven by a social security problem they initially created for themselves.

In this chapter these themes will be considered in turn. In each section it will be shown how important they were for policy between 1979 and 1993, and how important they remain today. Their relevance for future developments in social security policy will be followed through into a final section which discusses this.

Before moving to the four themes, however, it is necessary to start with a brief section which comments on the system inherited by the Conservatives in 1979.

Social Security in 1979

The model for social security established in the late 1940s, after the Beveridge report, presumed that the main planks of the system would be contributory insurance benefits – for retirement, widowhood, sickness and unemployment – supported by Family Allowances. Means-tested benefits were viewed as ingredients of a 'safety net' system for those not covered by insurance benefits, and were expected to become little needed. By the 1970s it was very clear that the latter aspiration was not being realised. There were a number of reasons for this – the setting and maintenance of the insurance benefit rates at low levels so that supplementation was often required, the increase in single parent families, the rise in unemployment and the tendency for governments to meet emergent problems of high costs for low income people (rents, rates, etc.) by new means-tested benefits. A particularly significant development here was the response of Edward Heath's Conservative government to evidence of increased poverty amongst the working poor of reintroducing the subsidy of low wages, through Family Income Supplement.

Labour Governments' responses to these issues had been ambivalent. On the one hand they had sought to strengthen the Beveridge design by adding earnings related provisions to supplement insurance benefits and by improving Family Allowances (renamed Child Benefit). On the other hand they were aware of the need to maintain the levels of means-tested benefits in order to prevent extreme poverty and they had contributed to the process of elaborating new kinds of benefits. Significantly the 1974–9 Labour Government did not really reverse the shift, started by Heath, of rent support for low income people away from general subsidy to assistance through means-tested benefits (Malpass, 1990).

It is important to note that at the end of its period of rule the Labour Government was engaged in a search for ways to improve, and strengthen rights to, means-tested benefits. A leading participant in that activity emphasized acceptance of the centrality of means-testing as the new political reality (Donnison, 1979). He was opposed by others on the Left who still urged a 'back to Beveridge' or 'new Beveridge' strategy (Lister, 1975, 1986). While the argument was still going on Mrs Thatcher won power and set social security development on a course far different from that envisaged by Donnison (see his observations on this in Donnison, 1982).

Social Security Expenditure 1979–93

Since the Thatcher government came to power committed to cutting public expenditure it was inevitable that they should have given attention to social security expenditure, forming as it does nearly a third of all public expenditure. But it is not merely the size of the social security budget which is relevant, but also its rate of growth. Despite sustained efforts to cut social security provisions the Thatcher and Major governments found that social security expenditure continued to rise at a rate well in excess of the growth of any other element in public expenditure. We therefore find the paradox that, over the period 1979 to 1993, a considerable number of cuts were made to the social security system whilst at the same time public expenditure on social security grew rapidly.

There are two major sources of the growth of this expenditure. One of these was a steady increase in the numbers of people over pension age. The other was growth in the numbers of people with very low incomes in need of social security supplementation. Of key importance here was the growth in the numbers of unemployed people. Unemployment rose substantially in the early years of the Thatcher era, fell slightly in the late 1980s but then rose again and remains very high at the time of writing. But in addition amongst those in work there was throughout this period a growth in the numbers with very low earnings levels, and therefore able to claim means-tested benefits. Conservative governments continued the policy of shifting the subsidy of the housing of low income people from assistance through the housing budget (the subsidy of council housing), or through control over the levels of private rents, to subsidy through the social security system (rebates for individuals).

Despite the impact of the demographic trend, of unemployment and of the transfer of housing subsidy costs to social security, the growth rate of social security expenditure was lower in the 1980s than in the last period of Labour rule (see Hills ed., 1990). What we can deduce from this is that the Thatcher governments made strenuous efforts to curb social security costs. The following measures can be identified:

- Changes to the uprating rules – in the 1970s the rule determining inflation-proofing for the levels of many benefits was that they should go up with either earnings or prices, whichever was higher. The Conservatives changed the general rules to take only prices into account and on some occasions deliberately refused to uprate some benefits at all.
- Cuts to insurance benefits – involving some direct cuts to benefits but principally: abolition of earnings-related supplements to short-term benefits; replacement of sickness benefit by statutory sick

pay; tightening of qualifying rules for unemployment benefit; abolition of maternity and death grants.

- Cutting of means-tested benefits by 'simplification'; the steepening of the rates at which they taper off as individual incomes rise; the abolition of entitlements to special additional grants.

- Efforts to prevent certain groups from getting entitlements at all – most youngsters aged under 18; most full-time students; married female labour market participants; prematurely retired people with private pensions.

- The operation of more rigorous controls to prevent claims from unemployed people allegedly not 'actively seeking work'; to increase contributions from 'responsible' males to unsupported mothers; to prevent fraudulent claims.

We thus see an array of changes to social security occurring in the period 1979–93 which combined a concern to cut costs with two other features of Conservative policy which were identified in the introduction: the shift away from social insurance and the concentration of the main impact of change upon certain underprivileged groups.

The Attack on Universalism

The list above identifies the shift of much of the responsibility for sickness and maternity benefits on to employers and the abolition of earnings-related short term benefits as key aspects of the move away from universalistic social insurance benefits. There was also a rather more complex move on pensions.

Norman Fowler initiated, when Secretary of State in the early 1980s, a review of social security policy. One aspect of that review was an examination of the State Earnings Pension Scheme (SERPS). The report expressed the view that this scheme would impose excessive burdens on future generations. Fowler's initial idea was to replace the latter altogether by a funded scheme, but then he drew back when he recognised what heavy short-term costs the government would impose upon itself inasmuch as it would lose the use of contributions to fund current benefits. In the end, instead he weakened the benefits guaranteed under SERPS to the detriment of shorter-term contributors such as married women, relaxed the conditions for alternative private schemes and adopted measures to encourage new kinds of private 'personal pensions'. When all the records of this decision-making process are available, it will be interesting to investigate why the government were so concerned about pensions costs which would not fall on the Exchequer until far into the future, to the extent that it was initially prepared to reduce current income. It may well be found that a desire to benefit the private pensions industry really lay at the root of this measure.

The other side of this attack on social insurance was a set of changes to means-tested benefits, premised upon the reasonable proposition that if they were to be regarded as central to income maintenance policy some rationalisation was appropriate. This took the government into a range of complex issues where claims to be concerned about the incomes of the poorest, concerns about rights to benefits and concerns to simplify benefit structures were likely to come into conflict.

The incoming Thatcher Government took on board the case for the reform of the Supplementary Benefit System as set out in the review report which had been presented to the Labour Government (DHSS, 1978). It enacted these changes in the Social Security Act 1980. This involved some, fairly marginal, simplification of the rules relating to entitlement to Supplementary Benefit, together with extensive codification of the discretionary powers. New rules relating to additional payments to the basic benefits were more restrictive, with grants for clothing replacement largely eliminated. The initial effect of this change was a marked reduction in single payments to Supplementary Benefit claimants. It looked, for a year or so, as if the new system had succeeded in reducing both the costs of these additional payments and the extensive demands made upon the administration by individual applications for help. This short-term saving for the government proved to be illusory, claimants and their advisers subsequently learnt how to extract help from the system, using the structure of rules clarifying entitlement; the demand for single payments rose sharply.

This experience was important, influencing the government's decision in the middle of the 1980s to undertake a further review of the system. That review, the Fowler review (HMSO, 1985), brought forward a very much more radical restructuring of the Supplementary Benefit system. The new scheme, enacted in the 1986 Act, renamed Supplementary Benefit 'Income Support'. It introduced a structure which discriminated very much less elaborately between different categories of claimants, replacing specific additions to individuals' weekly benefits by a uniform structure of premiums, taking into account, for example, whether individuals were disabled or pensioners or the heads of one parent families. The 1986 Act also abolished entitlements to single payments, except in the special cases of help for maternity needs and funerals (though in this case the benefits were limited and replaced the universal National Insurance related maternity and death grants). The system of entitlement to single payments was replaced by a discretionary cash-limited Social Fund, providing most of its help (70 per cent) through loans reclaimable from weekly benefits.

The 1980 changes may perhaps, with the benefit of hindsight, be described as a victory for welfare rights. Whilst it did involve the elimination of some kinds of discretionary payments it did enshrine in regulations rights to many others. In contrast, the 1986 Act can therefore be seen as a backlash against that victory, with rights to additional single payments largely eliminated. The success of welfare rights 'take up' campaigns in exploiting the loopholes in the 1980 Act may well have contributed to this subsequent backlash.

The 1986 Social Security Act also replaced Family Income Supplement by Family Credit, and in so doing developed for this benefit a means-test rather more compatible with that used for Income Support and for Housing Benefit. In other words, it created a situation in which the working poor could expect to get a benefit which, if they had children, would sustain them at an income above the Income Support level. In this way the government tried to tackle what it described as the 'unemployment trap' under which it is possible for individuals to be deterred from taking work by the fact that their income situation will be worse than if they remain on benefit. Unresolved problems about this 'trap' remain however: notably because of the ways the various systems deal with (or fail to deal with) mortgage costs and child care costs.

The story of means-tested housing support in the 1980s is one of a hasty legislative decision (in the Social Security and Housing Act 1982), followed by an attempt to make social security savings by cutting housing benefit in 1983. These events led on to the urgent need for second thoughts, with these being embodied in the 1986 Act. The first Act brought together some aspects of the support for the housing costs of Supplementary Benefit claimants with the local authority administered rent and rate rebate schemes and rent allowance scheme. Its aim was to eliminate the anomalies about the existence of the various means-tested housing support schemes operating side by side. In practice some of the of the anomalies of the previous system were eliminated, but new ones were created (Hill, 1984).

Once Housing Benefit was established not only did it face administrative problems, it also proved to be very costly in both administrative and benefit terms. The growth in benefit costs was largely attributable to government housing policies, involving pressure upon local authorities to increase rents. Since large proportions of local authority tenants were entitled to Housing Benefit the effects of these rent increases was to increase sharply the cost of the Housing Benefit scheme.

When, in 1983, the Secretary of State for Health and Social Security came under pressure from the Treasury to make economies he found it convenient to make most of these in cuts in the value of the Housing Benefit scheme. Cuts were achieved by steepening the rate at which benefit tapered off as individual incomes rose.

However, this taper steepening intensified another problem, the problem of the 'poverty trap'. The poverty trap is the name given to the phenomenon by which individuals find that as their earned incomes rise they lose benefit income, at rates above the highest income tax rates, because of reductions in means-tested benefits. By the middle 1980s the combination of separate means-tested rules for different benefits had the effect of making the poverty trap a serious problem. In some circumstances individuals found that an increase of a pound in earned income led, after tax and benefit losses, to a reduction in disposable income. The recognition of the problem of the poverty trap made it urgent to establish a system in which the rules operating for the different systems of means-tested benefit were compatible with each other. The 1986 Act did this. But as the government refused, at the same time, to reduce the rates at which benefit entitlement tapered off they merely made the poverty trap effect less erratic. The net effect was to increase rather than diminish the problem.

At the centre of the reforms to social security associated with Norman Fowler, the 1986 Social Security Act, was the development of a structure with three benefits – Income Support, Family Credit and Housing Benefit – all based upon broadly similar principles. Both Family Credit and Housing Benefit take income after tax and National Insurance deductions into account, rather than gross income as had been the case in the past. This was thus a modest move towards an

integrated tax and benefit system, as envisaged by advocates of
negative income tax (see, for example, Minford, 1984).

Social Security and Inequality: Stigmatised Groups

The attack on levels of social security benefits obviously needs to be
seen in the context of a government stance on inequality in which the
achievement of tax cuts, particularly at higher levels, was a key
objective. By contrast at the other end of the income distribution the
Conservatives attacked trade unions' efforts to protect wage levels and
eliminated statutory measures to prevent low pay rates (see Chapter 6).
They repeatedly warned the nation about the dangers of workers
pricing themselves out of jobs. This approach to income distribution
meant that their own policies were likely to increase the problem of the
'unemployment trap' unless they also attacked benefit levels.

The main elements in the attack upon benefit levels have already
been cited. What needs further emphasis here are three points. First,
there was a particularly strong attack upon benefits for the unemployed. Second, there was a deliberate weakening of benefit provisions
for young workers. Under 18s were more or less taken out of the
system altogether and offered support only through training schemes,
Income Support rates for single people aged between 18 and 25 were
reduced under the 1986 Act so that they had insufficient to maintain
independent homes. The limited range of ways in which students had
been able to get some benefit support were largely eliminated. Third,
provisions for single parent families were weakened in ways aimed to
force parents to consider low paid part-time work.

In looking at the government's benefit cutting strategies overall one
can detect a tendency to evade making direct attacks upon the incomes
of pensioners and the chronically sick despite the fact that these were
the benefits for which demand was growing strongly. As far as child
benefit was concerned the government wobbled uncertainly, initially
making cuts but then apparently taking note of well organised
campaigns to protect this form of support. Clearly whilst the Conservative ideologues disliked the universalist aspect of this benefit some
of them also saw how it might facilitate the acceptance of low paid
work by parents and (by contrast with Family Credit) did not
contribute to the poverty trap problem.

Another contradiction in Conservative policy concerns the insurance contribution. In a strategy to weaken insurance one might have expected that the contribution would be questioned. It does contribute to the poverty trap, and there is a significant entry threshold effect. The centralised recording and maintenance of contribution records is an administratively expensive activity, yet one that is increasingly irrelevant for the benefit system. Yet far from contributions disappearing during the long period of Conservative rule they have been increased. This is because the government commitment to the cutting of income tax has had to be offset by other forms of tax. The government persists in trying to maintain the illusion that insurance contributions, even if but weakly linked to benefit entitlements, are not tax.

Finally in this section two aspects of recent social security policy need mentioning, both of which have distinctive parts to play in the Conservatives' selective strategy. First, as far as benefits for disabled people are concerned there has been, with effect from 1992, a measure of rationalisation with some marginal improvements to the support available with high levels of disability in the establishment of the Disability Living Allowance, and a shift from support solely based upon assistance with mobility to more general help to those amongst the disabled able to work (Disability Working Allowance). This latter measure may also be seen as an aspect of Conservative efforts to increase the acceptability of low paid work.

The second area of policy change concerns the treatment of single parent families. Here we see a much more ideologically charged policy intervention, clearly inspired by moral messages from across the Atlantic (Murray, 1984). It has been argued that benefit policies and housing policies actively encourage single parenthood and family breakdown. The main legislative response to this belief has been the Child Support Act of 1991. This takes a provision which has always been a characteristic of the administration of means-tested benefits, the liability of absent fathers for the support of their children, and generalises it to require (a) the operation of a routinised formula to determine levels of support, (b) enforce liability for the support of a 'first' family as a responsibility which largely overrides any obligations to a subsequent family, and (c) sets out to use a social security inspired formula as an universal one to apply throughout matrimonial and child support settlements regardless of whether or not one of the parties is dependent upon benefits. Thus a political commitment has been translated in a comparatively mechanical way into a device to try to save public money.

This new system is expected to have a range of effects. The lone unmarried mother who applies for benefit is going to be required to disclose information about the father of her child or suffer a severe benefit penalty, unless she can satisfy the Child Support Agency that harm or undue distress would be caused for her if the man were contacted. As suggested above, subsequent families will be disadvantaged by the new policies, and often driven into poverty. But the system seems also likely to undermine a recent development in matrimonial law which one might have expected the 'moral majority' to support, which seeks to secure flexible arrangements between estranged parents so that children can move freely between them. Now there will be the imposition of a rigid maintenance formula based upon assumptions of clear cut long-term care arrangements. The new legislation will also upset many recent agreements between parents, in particular the 'clean break' divorce in which one party secures her home in return for the other having little or no maintenance obligations.

Institutional Change in Social Security

In this section there is a need to focus on two issues: the creation of Agencies and the areas of social security policy where there have been developments in central/local relations. The Department of Social Security has been transformed into little more than a small headquarters organisation with policy making responsibility for a network of Agencies – amongst which the Benefits Agency, the Contributions Agency and the Child Support Agency are the big three.

This transformation of the social security policy delivery system need not necessarily be seen as a part of Conservative privatisation strategy. After all some very 'statist' governmental systems operate largely through Agencies – the striking case of this is Sweden. However, Agencies are able to gradually change the contracts of service of their staff and they are engaging in what is called 'market testing', the exploration of ways to privatise or set up quasi-market systems. It may be that in due course, for example, insurance companies, or consortia of current management staff, will be allowed to tender for the delivery of parts of the social security service to the public.

An accompaniment of the development of the Agencies has been a series of developments in the streamlining of benefit calculation and delivery, the organisation and furnishing of local offices, public relations and public information. Many of these have been very positive developments in a system hitherto notorious for unpleasant offices, curt treatment of claimants, the losing of case-papers and so on. However, rationalisation is often reducing the number of contact points for the public, and many of those left are being turned into little more that points where staff have to communicate electronically with real decision makers elsewhere. In the end what really matters is whether or not benefits are available to meet needs – there is a danger of it becoming a case of 'nice office, polite staff, beautiful goldfish tank, pity about the benefits!'

Turning now to the part played by local government in social security it is important to note that whilst the period 1979 to 1993 has seen reductions to the role of local government in other areas (see Chapter 2) in social security it has seen an increase. The major source of that increase has been described above, the development of the Housing Benefit system. This has facilitated the routinisation of Income Support calculation by shifting many of the awkward issues about rent commitments and household composition to local government (see Hill, 1989; Fimister and Hill, 1993).

Another consequence of this shift is that it has been the Housing Benefit system which has had to cope with the rebate implications of the various twists and turns of local taxation policy over this period.

The other source of increase in local government involvement in what is now *de facto* rather than *de jure* social security policy lies in the area of community care. Here a crucial source of change was a political decision taken early in the Thatcher years which rebounded on the government.

Before 1980 the Department of Health and Social Security kept a tight limit on the extent to which they would meet the charges incurred by low income people in private residential care. Then the rules were relaxed, greatly increasing the extent to which the system would meet higher charges. There was a dramatic growth of private sector homes. So the Conservative Secretary of State was placed in a dilemma between his commitment to the development of the private sector and his concern to keep income maintenance expenditure under control. In 1983, in an effort to achieve this, he imposed national limits.

In 1986 a report by the Audit Commission on 'community care' talked of the 'perverse effects of social security policies' in this area of care. It pointed out that anyone entitled to means-tested benefit 'who chose to live in a residential home was entitled to allowances' up to the limit imposed by the benefit rules, regardless of the strength of their case for such comprehensive care.

The Audit Commission team noted the extent to which private homes are unevenly distributed geographically. The consequence of this was, they said, that 'while central government attempts to achieve equitable distribution of public funds across the country, through the use of complex formulae within the National Health Service and local government, the effects can be largely offset by Supplementary Benefit payments for board and lodging' (Audit Commission, 1986, p. 3).

After the Audit Commission report on community care, the government commissioned Sir Roy Griffiths to make recommendations on community care policies as a whole. He recommended (HMSO, 1989) that there should be a system under which local authority social services departments decided on social, not income, grounds that care was necessary and then had a responsibility to ensure individuals got that care, either from the public or private sector. If the individuals were unable to pay the care costs from the standard benefits or from other income it would then be the responsibility of the local authority to provide a subsidy. The government broadly accepted Sir Roy Griffiths' proposals, enacting them in the National Health Service and Community Care Act of 1990. This means that since April 1993 new entrants to private and voluntary sector residential homes have to prove to local authorities that they have a need for such care before they can get public support at levels comparable to those provided hitherto automatically by the social security system. Local authorities have become the rationers of most of the care costs of such individuals, responsible for paying them with the help of a transitional input from the social security budget.

There are other aspects to the community care reform (see Chapter 12) but it must not be forgotten that an important part of the rationale for that reform has been a government need to solve a social security cost control problem. Taken together the Housing Benefits development and community care can, therefore, be seen as the delegation of some parts of the social security system where routinisation is difficult or impossible, a process of shifting implementation problems to local authorities (Fimister and Hill, 1993).

Where is the Social Security System Going?

In the period 1979 to 1993 we have seen the erosion of national insurance so that it can no longer be regarded as at the centre of the British social security system. That erosion has been most significant for short-term benefits, less so for the support of the elderly and the long-term sick. As the means-tested benefits system has moved centre stage it has been changed in ways which facilitate the routinised delivery of benefits – simplification for benefit delivery purposes if not necessarily simplification from the recipient's perspective. The process of change in the latter system has also involved the erosion of some forms of support. In 1979 it could be said, whatever its complexities, the British system of income maintenance probably offered more comprehensive coverage of the population than any other system. That is no longer the case as far as benefits for young people are concerned. It is also probably also not now the case for many single parents.

This chapter has examined the wide variety of ways the social security system has been raided. Yet its cost continues to grow, placing social security ministers – whether they like it or not – in increasing political difficulties in finding new ways to cut the scheme to satisfy the Treasury. That has inevitably brought the spotlight upon the remaining pieces of the national insurance system. It must be acknowledged that, in a system with an elaborate structure of means-tested benefits, cuts to insurance benefits will not affect the very poor. Indeed, some of the victims of such cuts will have substantial private resources. The cuts will, however, disadvantage those just a little bit above the state determined 'poverty line', shifting new groups down on to it.

Debate on this topic is, at the time of writing, focusing upon invalidity benefit. This is the insurance benefit which long-term sick people receive if they have been labour market participants. It is not means-tested and once secured it continues so long as the sickness continues. Numbers of recipients of this benefit have increased recently, a phenomenon which John Major has seen as implicit evidence of benefit abuse. But there is a number of explanations for this growth. First, there is a need to take into account the ageing of the population. Second, there is a need to bear in mind the impact of job shortages – bearing particularly heavily on people towards the end of their working life and upon people with health problems or disabilities. Third, we have a benefits system which treats unemployed people much less well than sick people. Insurance benefits for the unemployed are set at lower rates than invalidity benefits, their receipt is rigorously policed and they 'exhaust' after a year. Any good benefits adviser will point out to unemployed people with health problems that the sickness/invalidity support system offers a better deal. What is more the government's own employment service staff have given similar advice; shifting people from the unemployment register to the sick list has been seen as making a contribution to reducing the politically important unemployment rate! It is interesting to note that the same phenomenon of raised numbers of sickness benefit claims and political attempts to do something about that 'problem' were observed in the high unemployment of the inter-war period (Whiteside, 1988).

However, as suggested above, invalidity benefit could be cut or even withdrawn with the support of those with very low incomes amongst this group of people shifted on to means-tested benefits. It would produce some savings for the Treasury. Once that were done it may be predicted that the cutters' attention would shift, indeed it would almost inevitably have to shift, to the politically much more dangerous area where big expenditure savings could be made. This is an attack upon the flat rate 'Beveridge' pensions.

As governments worry about the cost of pensions two options are canvassed. One of these is to raise the pension age. Here particular attention is paid to the fact that the official age for women is 60 while it is 65 for men. Raising the former is regularly canvassed and naturally produces vociferous protests. However, the central problem is that changing the pension age will not in itself create jobs. Reducing the numbers of pensioners increases the numbers of the unemployed. Inasmuch as governments worry less about the latter this perhaps reduces their political problems – but it does not solve the real dependency ratio problem.

The other solution is more privatisation, combined perhaps with taking Beveridge pension rights away from those already well covered by private schemes. There are obviously savings to be made here without hurting individuals. The author is one of many middle class people who expects, when he retires, that the insurance pension will contribute something less than 10 per cent of his income. But there are three problems about this remedy. First, it would totally undermine the rationale for the insurance contribution. We have been told, since the 1940s, that we have an expectation of benefits in return for our contributions. It has been shown above how these expectations have been eroded, but the expectation of a pension is by far the most general and universal of these expectations. Second, private schemes are only as strong as the economy which supports them. If that economy is in di.ficulty what responsibility does the government have to under-write private schemes? This problem has been highlighted by evidence that Robert Maxwell had been systematically raiding his employees' pension scheme. An official committee is currently looking into ways of providing private pension scheme contributors with better statutory protection.

The other problem about privatisation is rooted in a widely held economic fallacy. It is believed that whilst public pension schemes are potential burdens on future employees private schemes, which have to be funded, are not. But saving in a private pension scheme is not a process of putting money away in bank vaults, it is the accumulation of claims on future productive enterprise. Money is invested, and as pension consumption demands grow it has to be disinvested. In either the public or the private case the future working population has to pay – the only difference is that in the first case they have to pay through taxes and in the second by contributions to profits.

The point in both these arguments is that the crucial problem for Britain, and societies like her, is the ratio between dependent and non-dependent populations. The exchange between them can be structured in a variety of ways some of which may be more politically acceptable than others, but the fundamental problem cannot be evaded short of disregarding the needs of the dependants

So how can we expect social security policy to evolve in the future? The Conservatives seek ways to achieve savings yet cannot easily find them. They have largely destroyed social insurance but would find it politically difficult to complete the process. Their commitment to low rates of income tax makes moves that would render it quite apparent that national insurance is just an income tax with another name – politically dangerous. A rash prediction will be risked here that we will not see substantial social security changes under Major's first administration.

But what if we try to look beyond that? If the Conservatives were to be re-elected for a fifth term there will certainly be ideologues who will urge the completion of the destruction of social insurance.

If Labour were to be elected it will face a greater conflict than ever before between its traditional adherence to the Beveridge model and a recognition that in the short run, and with the limited resources its

Treasury ministers would be likely to provide for social security reform, that the simplest way to attack the problems of poverty which it will inherit would be by strengthening the means-tested benefits. Social security cost pressures are particularly threatening to any electoral pledges not to increase taxation. That statement of the obvious is also part of the present Conservative dilemma.

People with universalist commitments are inevitably looking for ways of strengthening the benefit system which neither simply try to reimpose a version of the Beveridge scheme nor take the present harsh means-testing system for granted. Support for this position comes from the clear evidence that the Conservatives have failed to solve the key problems about the relationship between earnings and benefits – the poverty trap and the unemployment trap. In the search for new ideas the 'basic income' idea has an appeal – involving extending state guaranteed incomes (like child benefit) to adults and clawing back earnings through taxation (see Walter, 1988; Parker, 1989). Yet, as Parker acknowledges a shift to such a scheme involves a sequence of elaborate legislative changes. It is perhaps a feasible option for some future centrist coalition, secure in power for a long period under some form of proportional representation.

Otherwise the agenda is likely to be one of improving, and really simplifying, means-tests, acknowledging that if the poverty trap is to be ameliorated then tapers must extend a long way up the income distribution. If this is the approach adopted there is an important secondary issue to be confronted. The thrust of change over the past 15 years has been towards a system which can be routinised and operated with a minimum of contact between officials and claimants. In the 1960s and 1970s there was some argument as to whether it was better to have a social assistance scheme in which entitlements were specified as clear 'rights', or whether it was desirable to have an element of discretion which allowed for 'creative' responses to exceptional situations (Titmuss, 1971). The 1986 Act was claimed to deal with this tension by a combination of a routinised Income Support scheme and the discretionary Social Fund. Yet the latter's loans system and cash limits undermine its responsiveness. Ironically, moreover, the thrust towards an impersonal system with a minimum of personal contact applies even here. There are still unresolved issues about the right way to balance a simple straightforward rights based means-tested benefit system with provisions that enable effective responses to be made to exceptional situations.

Whilst it may seem inappropriate to end this section and this chapter on a small issue it is in fact the case that unless we move into a political climate in which the reality of the growth of the 'dependent population' is adequately confronted, which means confronting the tax implications of the income exchanges necessary, then the politics of social security will tend to become very much the politics of minor adjustments to the system.

14

British Policy in Northern Ireland: Between Activism and Consolidation

ARTHUR AUGHEY

Introduction

There is reasonable agreement amongst historians and political scientists about the defining characteristics of government policy in Northern Ireland since 1969. In his *The Irish Question and British Politics* D. G. Boyce has argued that the recent eruption of the Ulster crisis in British politics 'was not what it had been between 1886 and 1922, an essential part of the education of a whole generation of British politicians' (Boyce, 1988, p. 10). According to Boyce, what had been central to British party politics at the turn of this century was, by the late 1960s, entirely peripheral to it. Neither the modern Labour Party, though heir to many of the prescriptions of the old Liberal Party, nor the modern Conservative Party, despite its direct lineage from the historic Unionist Party, had any wish to implicate themselves in the supposed alien controversies of Northern Ireland politics. The crisis of the second half of the century 'was to be kept firmly within the neutral zone defined by "bipartisanship": there would be no taking sides in this new phase of the Irish Question' (pp. 11–12). The policy implications of this tacit understanding between the major parties of government have been continuity and consistency.

The substance of this historical interpretation is subscribed to by the political scientist M.J. Cunningham in his excellent study of British strategy in Northern Ireland since 1969. Summarizing the political experience of the last 20 years, Cunningham has proposed that 'British policy is best understood as having both a strategic continuity and the capacity for tactical adjustment; a focus on the latter can blind one to the importance of the former'. He concluded:

> three points are worthy of emphasis. Firstly, sufficient inter-party accord has characterised Irish policy to allow one to talk of bipartisanship. Secondly, strains are more evident in security than constitutional policy as the differing party emphases on 'law and order' surface. Thirdly, caution must be exercised in any assessment to separate the rhetoric of opposition from more thorough-going divergences in the policy prescriptions of the parties. (Cunningham, 1991, pp. 248–9)

Cunningham's assessment is that these 'thorough-going divergences' are of less importance than the 'inter-party accord'. Of course, such effective bipartisanship is not necessarily unusual in British policy. There often does exist a front-bench consensus on a number of matters and it is most common on those issues which involve considerations of foreign policy outwith the immediate claims of domestic politics. It is here that considerations of *raison d'état* tend to take precedence over partisanship. If one accepts the historical reasoning of Boyce and integrates it with the political analysis of Cunningham, then it is possible to interpret Northern Ireland as having many of the characteristics of an external rather than an internal policy issue. A rather stark hypothesis but one which does express a certain truth.

To propose this view of British policy is not to deny the continuing reality of the Union of Great Britain and Northern Ireland. Indeed, the material importance of that Union has become ever clearer since direct rule from Westminster was reluctantly imposed in 1972. It is a reality defined in substantial transfers of resources to meet the welfare needs of citizens in Northern Ireland; to meet their needs for security; and to meet their needs for economic development. The sums are large. It has been estimated in a recent survey that Northern Ireland's present 'subvention' from the general Exchequer is £2500 billion per annum. That amounts to £1600 per adult; £6400 per family of four. There is absolutely no possibility of the Irish Republic sustaining such a level of public expenditure under any conceivable plan of Irish unity or even joint authority (Cadogan Group, 1992, p. 31). It is also a reality embodied in common institutions, rights and obligations. The proposition merely highlights what both Boyce and Cunningham have detected: namely, a widespread perception by policy-makers, which reflects an even wider-spread popular attitude in Great Britain, that Northern Ireland is different. This difference demands, therefore, different (constitutional) policy prescriptions from those which might apply elsewhere within the United Kingdom. This is accepted because Northern Ireland's concerns are taken to be beyond the experience and sometimes beyond the sympathy of opinion in Great Britain.

Attaching to Northern Ireland policy is the de-stabilising conditionality of its place within the state. As Cunningham has intimated, such a disposition on the part of politicians and officials in particular has been conducive to two apparently contradictory positions. On the one hand, it has been conducive to quite radical constitutional initiatives, the formula for which was established shortly after direct rule by the first secretary of state for Northern Ireland, William Whitelaw. This formula was to be substantially modified in November 1985 with the signing of the Anglo-Irish Agreement. One could call this the active mode. On the other hand, it has been equally conducive to a policy of constitutional stabilisation and the management of irreconcilable political differences. This could be called the consolidating mode. The reason for the practical compatibility of these opposite dispositions is that Northern Ireland policy, if not treated with indifference by the generality of MPs at Westminster, is subject to the dictates of conventional political wisdom. That is a convenient state of affairs for policy-makers to operate within since it is they who tend to determine what actually is conventional wisdom. Short of an abject surrender to terrorism, acute international embarrassment or the outright expulsion of Unionists from the UK, there is significant room for manoeuvre (activism) or non-manoeuvre (consolidation) on the part of the British government. The continuities within this flexible framework have been twofold. The first has been that Northern Ireland's problems ought, as far as possible, to be abstracted from the prevailing procedures of British parliamentary practice. Direct rule was designed to be temporary and no attempt has been made so far to reform it. The second has been that stability can only be achieved by accommodating in a balanced institutional form the right of the Unionist majority to remain part of the UK and the aspiration of the Nationalist minority to become part of a united Irish state (Aughey, 1989, pp. 33–40).

Conservative Policy, 1979–85

These two policy dispositions, the active and the consolidating, are to be found across the parliamentary spectrum. They are reflected in Conservative attitudes which, as the journalist John Whale perceptively remarked on the occasion of Thatcher's election victory in May 1979, were a bit like Old Testament theology. 'You find a strong threat of authoritarian changelessness, yet there is always a nevertheless. Both immobilists and advocates of change can find signs for their comfort.' British policy orthodoxy, he suggested, has been that Northern Ireland must stay part of the UK because a majority want it that way. Conservatives have never questioned this even in the days when Whitelaw 'was exploring the idea that the problem also had an Irish dimension'. Beyond that, however, the Conservatives have been pragmatic:

> Nevertheless, that very pragmatism allows the advocates of change to hope; because it also means that once a system is shown to be no longer workable, the Tories waste as little time as possible in going on reworking it. The Heath government changed its mind about many things besides Northern Ireland; and it would be no real surprise if the Thatcher government did the same. (Whale, 1979)

And the Thatcher government did do the same. The policy of the Conservative government in the 1980s changed from the consolidating to the activist mode and confounded the expectations of Ulster Unionist politicians. Their belief was that the new Conservative government would move towards regularising the peculiar, unresponsive parliamentary procedures of direct rule (the British dimension) and away from institutionalising any formal relationship with the government of the Irish Republic (the Irish dimension). The Conservative manifesto of 1979, with its stress upon local government reform, appeared to confirm those expectations. As it turned out, the Conservative government was to pursue a course of action quite the reverse of that proposed in opposition. The developments which culminated in the Anglo-Irish Agreement of November 1985 had been set in train as early as 8 December 1980 when the British and Irish Prime Ministers met in the first Anglo-Irish summit in Dublin. The institutional arrangement established in its wake, the Anglo-Irish Council, was held by Thatcher not to involve any significant constitutional departure. As she put it in the House of Commons in 1982, no commitment existed on the part of the British government to consult with Dublin about Northern Ireland. That was purely a matter of domestic politics, a position she reaffirmed in 1984 (Wilson, 1989, p. 187). Subsequent events and revelations show that the Prime Minister was accurate in her definition of the status quo but inaccurate in her suggestion as to the direction of government policy. Her Cabinet Secretary, Sir Robert Armstrong, was committed to giving Dublin such a consultative role and equally implicated in ensuring the effective institutionalisation of that role. Thatcher appears to have had two main purposes in her consultations with the Irish government. The first was to explore whatever avenues were necessary to defeat IRA terrorism and the second was to isolate the IRA's political wing, Sinn Fein. There can be no doubt that the Prime Minister supported the Union and thought that the commitments by both governments in the Anglo-Irish Agreement would stabilise it. But by putting her name to the Agreement, Thatcher committed the British government to a new departure in Anglo-Irish relations the destination of which she herself could not determine.

The Anglo-Irish Agreement

The avowed strategic purpose of the Agreement was to encourage an attitudinal change in the cultures of Unionism and Nationalism in Northern Ireland and to foster the conditions for compromise such that their opposing identities and purposes could be accommodated within a balanced set of political institutions. The Agreement had reversed the priority of previous initiatives by establishing a functioning 'Irish dimension' before attempting to establish some form of power-sharing devolution within Northern Ireland. It set up an Anglo-Irish Conference, the function of which is to provide the Irish government with a consultative role in the internal affairs of Northern Ireland and which allows it to make recommendations for appointment to public bodies responsible for the administration of policy. This Conference is serviced by a Secretariat, stationed in Belfast, composed of both British and Irish civil servants, the duties of which are to oversee and to monitor the progress of Conference decisions. It also helps to draw up the agenda for Conference meetings. The Agreement acknowledges the right of the Irish government to 'put forward views and proposals on matters relating to Northern Ireland' and stresses that 'determined efforts' will be made by the British government to resolve any differences between itself and Dublin on these proposals. The provision for joint chairmanship indicates the equality of the two states though the British government does not accept that any of its sovereignty over Northern Ireland has been ceded. On 'the modalities of bringing about devolution in Northern Ireland' and on proposals 'for major legislation and on major policy issues' the Irish government is recognised to have a major role to play. That role is not only to ensure equality of recognition for the Nationalist 'ethos' but also to act as a representative of the Nationalist community. In short, within the Conference and within the activities of the Secretariat, the task of the Irish participants is to advance the policy interests and concerns of the SDLP. The text of the Agreement is written in a bland style which actually conceals the significance of what the Conservative government had openly conceded: that the UK cannot determine adequately the welfare of a proportion of its own citizens. The expected quid pro quo has been Irish co-operation in the eradication of Republican terrorism by security and judicial means; and its willingness to underwrite the main lines of British policy in the North. The purpose in this regard is not just for domestic legitimacy. It is also to legitimise British policy in Northern Ireland on a world stage.

The principle of balance has been given here a new strategic meaning and the intellectual origins of that meaning lie not in the prescriptions of British policy-makers but in the persuasive logic of the New Ireland Forum Report which was published on 2 May 1984. The stated purpose of that report, drawn up by the main constitutional Nationalist parties in Ireland, was to provide the basis for 'lasting peace and stability' in a 'new Ireland' and to suggest 'possible new structures and processes through which this objective might be achieved'. The three possible structures for this new Ireland proposed – joint authority, federal Ireland, Irish unity – were, of course, famously rejected by Thatcher at the Chequers summit meeting with the then Prime Minister of Eire Garret FitzGerald in November 1984. But as FitzGerald's memoirs recount, the Forum Report's analysis of the problem was, if not the text, then always the sub-text of the secret deliberations between British and Irish officials and politicians in the preparation of the Agreement itself. That analysis proposed that Catholic support for Sinn Fein could only be diminished and a new impetus imparted to political dialogue in Northern Ireland when the 'alienation' of the Nationalist tradition was addressed by according it equal respect with that of the Unionist. In particular, this meant recognising that the government of the Irish Republic should play a guarantor role for the Nationalist tradition in policy formulation in Northern Ireland. It was the Northern Ireland Office which was sceptical of that proposition and its possible consequences for inter-communal stability. Thatcher was also sceptical of it. But it was the Cabinet Office and the Foreign Office which made most of the running in these deliberations and their officials found the argument persuasive. Thus, the preamble to the Agreement proclaims 'the need for continuing efforts to reconcile and to acknowledge the rights of the two major traditions that exist in Ireland', a phrase which could have been lifted directly from the Forum Report. Article 1, which claims to define the status of Northern Ireland, makes this plain. Both governments affirm 'that any change in the status of Northern Ireland would only come about with the consent of the majority of the people of Northern Ireland' and both recognize that for the moment that such a majority does not exist. But it does make provision that when such a majority shall exist both governments 'will introduce and support in their respective Parliaments' legislation to give effect to a united Ireland'. The symmetry implied in that formulation is equality of recognition for Unionist and Nationalist 'traditions'; and it corresponds neatly with the new symmetry of state involvement implied in the Conference and the Secretariat. Indeed, it was that symmetry which guaranteed the widespread support for the Agreement in British and Irish public life as well as in Europe and the United States. However, even within its own terms of reference, the Agreement raised as many problems as those which it appeared to address. Of these problems, two are worthy of mention simply because they confronted British policy-makers with a new dilemma in the years following the Agreement's signing.

Firstly, not only the Agreement but all British policy statements on Northern Ireland have stressed the essential principle of democratic consent. However, the Agreement itself was an infringement of that same principle. Unionists were neither involved in nor consulted about its structure or content. The justification for this which is most often cited – that there was no point consulting the Unionists for they would not have consented anyway – simply confirms its undemocratic status (in Unionist eyes at least). Even if, after the fact, Unionist leaders might have come to see some merit in the status guarantee of Article 1 of the Agreement (which they did not) it would have been impossible for them to convince their electorate of its worth. For the Agreement did not involve the Irish government making any commitment to revise or to revoke Articles 2 and 3 of its Constitution, Articles which express a territorial claim to Northern Ireland. And subsequent events were to confirm Unionist suspicions of the insubstantiality of the Republic's assurances. In March 1990 the Irish Supreme Court ruled, in an action taken by two Ulster Unionists to test Article 1 of the Agreement, that Articles 2 and 3 of the Irish Constitution impose 'a constitutional imperative' to expedite the 'reintegration of the national territory' (Maginnis, 1990). This was one of the reasons, but not the only reason, why these Articles were to play such a central role in Unionist strategy in the Talks process which began in January 1990. Not only did the British government appear to miscalculate the extent of Unionist hostility to the Agreement, it did not appear to understand the nature of that hostility. Unionists did not at all perceive a new structural symmetry in Anglo-Irish relations. They simply perceived a new asymmetry which seemed to provide for the privileged empower-ment of the Nationalist aspiration to unity at the expense of the democratic right of the Unionist electorate to remain fully part of the UK. And this only encouraged suspicion of political initiatives rather than helping to defuse that suspicion. It heightened Unionist fears of London's willingness to consider dramatic changes in Northern Ireland's constitutional status. This was exactly the reverse of what British supporters of the Agreement claimed to intend.

Secondly, if the British government had failed to calculate the response of Unionists it had also misunderstood the dynamics of the nationalism of the SDLP. If the Anglo-Irish Conference was to be the stick to move the Unionists towards a more accommodating position then the carrot was the invitation of Article 4 and the enticement of Article 2(b). Together both provisions suggested that if Unionists were to accept devolved government within the framework of the Agreement which would secure 'widespread acceptance throughout the commu-nity' (i.e., some form of power-sharing) then the scope of the Anglo-Irish Conference would be subsequently reduced. This did not entice the Unionists; but neither did it correspond to the direction of SDLP policy. The assumption that the SDLP would settle for power-sharing devolution (albeit within a modified Agreement) as an alternative to a more ambitious pan-Irish project is a dubious one. In Article 5.8 of the Forum Report constitutional Nationalist parties in general, but the SDLP in particular, wanted Unionist agreement and consent to 'structures of Irish unity'. It was essential that Unionists 'negotiate their role in any arrangements which would embody Irish unity'.

Crucially, it would be for the 'British and Irish governments to create the framework and atmosphere within which such negotiations could take place'. For the SDLP, the Agreement was a first step towards that framework and that atmosphere. This was made quite clear in the discussions in 1988 between the leader of the SDLP, John Hume, and the leader of Sinn Fein, Gerry Adams. In those talks Hume tried to convince Adams that there was no longer any need for the 'armed struggle' because the Agreement was tantamount to providing what Sinn Fein had always demanded: a declaration of intent by the British to withdraw from Ireland. For Hume, the British government was now 'neutral' on the Union and an IRA ceasefire would help to transform that neutrality into active encouragement of a 'new Ireland'. The British government was poised to become a 'persuader' in Anglo-Irish relations, 'persuading' Unionists that the game was up and that they had better come to terms with the reality of the logic of Irish unity. Hume failed to convince Adams on this but it was a task to which he was to return in 1993. He did reveal, though, the intended direction of SDLP policy. It no longer had, in that felicitous phrase, 'any ideological commitment to devolution' (Aughey, 1992, p. 266). Indeed, going over the old ground of seeking an 'internal compromise' now seemed a retrogressive step to Nationalists. The Agreement was in place; Unionists were isolated; the SDLP had indirect influence on policy through Dublin's role in the Conference; the Secretariat provided it with a privileged access to authority. The new form of direct rule which the Agreement had brought – direct rule with a 'green tinge' – served the purposes of Nationalism much better than that imaginable under devolved government (Brew and Patterson, 1987, p. 45). So the devolutionary centrepiece of the Agreement seemed just as unobtainable as ever for British policy-makers. First, because of heightened Unionist fears and secondly, because of heightened Nationalist expectations. The structural ingenuity of the Agreement still had to confront those unintended consequences of its own making.

Experience of the Agreement

The Agreement had been fashioned by a small group of senior officials from Dublin and London who had reported in strict confidence to their respective Prime Ministers and departmental heads. FitzGerald's memoirs are an invaluable source of information on the way in which that mixture of abstract rationalism and political calculation, which constitutes the provisions of the Agreement, could become the centre-piece of British policy (FitzGerald, 1991, chs. 15, 16, and 17). Other memoirs are equally important. The response to the British govern-ment's Northern Ireland policy of such a senior figure in the Cabinet as the Chancellor, Nigel Lawson, is very instructive and merits quoting at length.

> The Agreement . . . had been negotiated in total secrecy, largely by the Cabinet Secretary, Robert Armstrong. Not without cause, Margaret clearly regarded the Cabinet as far too leaky to be taken into her confidence. Geoffrey [Howe], as Foreign Secretary, was of course fully in the picture, as were Tom King, who had been appointed Northern Ireland Secretary in the reshuffle two months earlier, and his predecessor, Douglas Hurd. But with the possible exception of Michael Heseltine, then still Defence Secretary, the rest of us, so far as I am aware, knew nothing of it until it was presented to us for our approval, almost as a fait accompli. (Lawson, 1992, p. 669)

That the Agreement, which represented such a profound re-ordering of the priorities of Conservative policy, should have been decided upon in this manner reveals much about the workings of the Cabinet system and the prevailing attitude of senior politicians to Northern Ireland affairs. As Lawson recounts, he had 'considerable doubts about its wisdom' and 'indicated as much in Cabinet'. But he 'did not go so far as to oppose it'. Nor, he reports, did anyone else. Nevertheless, it is difficult to follow Lawson's logic even though one is compelled to accept his prescience.

He argues that the failure of previous grand initiatives had made him sceptical of optimistic rationalism (activism) in Irish affairs. 'I had no doubt', he goes on, 'that the Anglo-Irish Agreement would be a political liability, in the sense that the resulting alienation of the Unionist majority would far outweigh any accretion of support from the Republican minority, and I could not imagine any objective observer would believe otherwise' (ibid., p. 670). The implication of this, for good or ill, is that if the Cabinet had been better informed, and a more objective and sceptical political intelligence had been brought to bear on the discussions, then the Agreement would not have been signed. The question, for Lawson, was whether the domestic 'political' cost would be outweighed by the 'military' benefits that might come from greater security co-operation with the Republic. He was sceptical at the time 'and the subsequent black comedy of attempts to persuade the Irish courts to extradite suspected terrorists did not make me any less sceptical'. A soundly based political scepticism one would imagine. Yet it is hard to understand Lawson's conclusion that he 'was not sufficiently confident of where the balance of advantage lay to oppose the Agreement'. It seems quite obvious where he believed the balance of advantage to lie. Unless, that is, senior Cabinet ministers were relatively indifferent as to where the balance lay (which is what Lawson's memoirs intimate).

Lawson's view that the alienation of Unionists would be the main result of the Agreement was echoed later in Thatcher's plaintive cry to FitzGerald: 'You've got the glory and I've got the problems' (FitzGerald, p. 570). She was clearly dismayed by their reaction and also by the resignation from his post at the Treasury of her close personal friend, Ian Gow. Her instinct in this case (according to FitzGerald) was to do something to placate Unionist outrage but the Irish government resisted this. Nevertheless, the Prime Minister promised, after discussion with James Molyneaux and Ian Paisley, the leaders of the Ulster Unionist and Democratic Unionist Parties, to operate the Agreement 'sensitively' (Aughey, 1989, p. 91). And that meant evading the implementation of some of the more contentious objectives secretly arrived at in the discussions of 1984–5, notably on reform of the security and judicial system. The Nationalist response to this was to accuse the British of bad faith. But such confusions were implicit in the very structure of the Agreement. For instance, under its provisions, the Irish government has become the partisan of the Nationalist interest. But insofar as the British government remains the sovereign authority in Northern Ireland it cannot play that role for the Unionists. Correctly and logically, it cannot be both sovereign and partisan. The Nationalist understanding of the Agreement, of course, has always been that the British government should be neither a Unionist partisan nor committed to the Union. That is a significant difference. And this enables one to grasp the contradictory reception by Unionists and Nationalists of statements by British Cabinet ministers.

For instance, when Tom King gave his opinion in Brussels on 3 December 1985 that 'Northern Ireland, which is our fervent wish, remains part of the United Kingdom' he faced a storm of criticism from Irish politicians and had to make an apology in the House of Commons. Northern Secretaries should not say such things, it was implied, because they could only give succour to a Unionism which was in terminal decline. Their task should be to 'persuade' Ulster Unionists, as John Hume demanded, to accept the necessity of their destiny in a new Ireland. When he became Secretary of State in 1989, Peter Brooke seemed to confirm this Nationalist perspective when he proclaimed that the British government had no selfish or strategic interest in Northern Ireland. For Unionists, on the other hand, these were the words of a colonial administrator and not the words of a British minister responsible for the good governance of a part of the United Kingdom.

The Agreement has brought the British government some relief from international (mainly American) pressure to 'do something' about the Ulster crisis. It has also achieved its objective of stabilising the SDLP vote and weakening the political position of Sinn Fein – though, as FitzGerald's memoirs show, even the Irish government, which made such an issue of this, recognised that the support for Sinn Fein had peaked already in 1985 (p. 529). There has been increased co-operation between the Royal Ulster Constabulary and army and the security forces in the Irish Republic, though clearly not enough to satisfy British expectations. Indeed, by the end of the 1980s British government attitudes to the Agreement seemed to have changed somewhat. The British affection for the Hume–FitzGerald analysis and for the representatives of the Dublin government seemed to have cooled. British ministers and their advisers now appeared more concerned to promote measures of consolidation (which means attempting to get the Unionists 'on board') rather than pursuing a more active policy (which means advancing the aims of Nationalists).

For instance, in an interview with the *Irish Times* on 27 September 1991, Peter Brooke denied that the Agreement was about compelling Unionists into ever closer co-operation with the Irish Republic. He was also dismissive of proposals to develop the scope of the Agreement. 'The Anglo-Irish Agreement will overturn itself', he argued, 'if it tries to carry more weight than it is at any time capable of carrying.' He was also prepared to consider the possibility of pursuing some aspects of 'Mr. Molyneaux's agenda', namely reforming the procedures of direct rule and providing for greater scrutiny of Northern Ireland business at Westminster. At a speech to the Conservative Party Conference in October 1991, Brooke stated that treating Northern Ireland differently from the rest of Great Britain was 'a policy which as far as possible we seek to avoid'. Such comments, of course, do not imply that no value attaches any longer to the Agreement. It merely states that the government now seemed more sceptical about the practical possibilities of Anglo-Irish co-operation. Seven years is a very long time in Irish politics and dealing intimately with Dublin has been an education in itself.

Further suggestion of this change was provided in a speech delivered by Douglas Hurd, the Foreign Secretary, to a Conservative Political Centre meeting at the same Conservative Party Conference. He had this to say about current British expectations:

> Many may believe that the debate about Northern Ireland is still about partition and the border. Indeed some of the statements from Northern Ireland politicians may still feed that idea. . . . The debate has moved on. There is a stronger sense of realism. The discussion now focuses not on the border or the unification of Ireland, but on how Northern Ireland can run its affairs within the United Kingdom, taking account of the identities and wishes of both the majority and the minority communities.

The Republic had a role to play in ensuring the necessary atmosphere to achieve the return of stability in Northern Ireland. But, Hurd made plain, it could not be seen 'as a rival for sovereignty' (Hurd, 1991). Of course, there were contingent and circumstantial factors embedded in these comments. The most important of these was the uncertainty of the outcome of the forthcoming General Election and the consequent need for Conservative leaders to cast wide their net for possible support (in this case, towards the Unionists). There was also the partisan consideration of how best to deal with Nationalist politics in Scotland. In playing the Unionist card in Scotland, as the new Prime Minister John Major was to do in Glasgow on 22 February 1992, it was difficult for the Conservatives not to be more upbeat about the Union of Great Britain and Northern Ireland. However, the political moral seemed clear enough. The key word in the policy vocabulary of the Conservative government, especially after the General Election of April 1992, is realism. And realism can be taken as the guiding light of the recent – chastened – deliberations about political arrangements to replace or amend those of the Agreement. These became a possibility once Brooke admitted the possibility of finding (in the words of the Unionist Manifesto of 1987) 'a replacement of and an alternative to' the Agreement. His attempt to achieve this goal in the summer of 1991 was a shambles and an embarrassment. Greater progress was made in 1992 by Brooke's successor, Sir Patrick Mayhew, though without ultimate success. The conceptual contours of this latest episode of the Conservative government's attempt to square the circle of the

Ulster crisis need to be considered in the light of what was to take place at the end of 1993.

Talking Realistically about Northern Ireland

The government's position in the Talks 'process' was to argue that it had no 'hidden agenda'. In the three strand negotiations – about, respectively, structures of governance within Northern Ireland; institutions of co-operation between Northern Ireland and the Irish Republic; and relationships between the British government and the Irish government – the Conservatives hoped that some mutually acceptable arrangements would emerge from the discussions. This was always a fond hope. The experience of the last 25 years provided little ground for optimism. And the comprehensive formula of the Talks that 'nothing is agreed until everything is agreed' was far too ambitious. In the stakes of all or nothing politicians were more likely to settle for nothing.

The SDLP and the Irish government wanted to promote a settlement that was substantially Irish and only residually British. But they were determined not to lose the advantages of the Agreement. Certainly, there was never any willingness on their part to consider trading the Agreement for power-sharing in Northern Ireland, even power-sharing with an Irish 'dimension'. The SDLP does not want to be involved in an 'internal settlement' which would implicate itself in governing what it deems to be a failed political entity. On this point it was supported throughout by the Irish government. The Unionists, on the other hand, wanted an arrangement that was substantially British and only residually Irish. They wanted to confirm Northern Ireland's statehood as a part of the United Kingdom and to remove the involvement of the Republic in the internal affairs of Northern Ireland. Their purpose has been to regain ground they feel has been lost since 1985. In principle, the Unionists were willing to advance an internal settlement based on some form of responsibility sharing with 'external' linkages to the Republic because that was one means to recover some influence in the governance of Northern Ireland. Yet even the Unionists were reluctant to push too hard for a new British–Irish Agreement for fear of arriving at a settlement even less congenial than the existing one.

When the current round of Talks came to an end in November 1992 the British government was again presiding over a policy stalemate. It was committed to the Talks process and anxious to see it resumed. Nevertheless, political events since November appeared to make a successful outcome even less likely. The experience of the Talks and the apparent impossibility of devising a set of devolved arrangements to satisfy the conflicting purposes of Unionists and Nationalists intimated two possible and alternative courses of policy development. The first course would be to construct an Anglo-Irish Agreement 'mark two'. Its logic would be the same as the first. Because 'something should be done' about the Northern Ireland problem and because the local parties appear unable to agree then it is the responsibility of the two sovereign governments to take the initiative. And because it is not in their power to compel agreement on devolved power-sharing then the only course is to develop intergovernmental co-operation leading to joint sovereignty. The second alternative would be to seek a less ambitious form of devolution and to reform the procedures of direct rule. This would allow for the expansion of local government powers in Northern Ireland while providing for greater scrutiny of Northern Ireland business in the House of Commons. In particular, the conduct of the Anglo-Irish Conference and Secretariat could be monitored by a Commons select committee. This would represent, in substance, a return to the Conservative manifesto of 1979 and a downplaying of the Agreement. In both cases, the traditional core of public policy – a devolved parliamentary assembly – would have to be shelved indefinitely. The first course would favour the purposes of the SDLP. The second course would favour the purposes of the Ulster Unionist Party but not those of Ian Paisley's Democratic Unionists. Debate about the future of Northern Ireland since November 1992 has flowed between these two poles of analysis.

The SDLP, the Irish Foreign Minister, Dick Spring, and Labour's spokesman on Northern Ireland, Kevin McNamara, have advanced the idea of joint sovereignty/joint authority. Their separate arguments form part of a definite strategy to encourage the Conservative government along an activist path congenial to the aim of Irish unity. During the Talks the SDLP submitted to Strand One a position paper which proposed an executive commission which would be composed of six members, three elected within Northern Ireland and one nominated by the European Community, the British government and the Irish government respectively. This is an idea that has been around for quite some time in Nationalist politics. Stripped of its European gloss the SDLP was advocating an institution of joint authority. Early in 1993 the leader of the party, John Hume, started a new series of meetings with the leader of Sinn Fein, Gerry Adams, the purpose of which has been to resolve the differences in analysis made plain in the first series of Hume–Adams talks in 1988. The new discussions show a clear impatience on the part of the SDLP leader. He shares the feeling of many of his colleagues that Irish unity is only a matter of time and that the British government should not prolong the agony but force Unionists to face up to the prospect of its departure. A commitment to joint sovereignty would be an interim measure smoothing the way for the British to leave and for Ireland to unite. It is the next (assumed) logical step in Anglo-Irish relations. Hume has been trying to convince Adams that joint sovereignty is an attainable objective; that it is worth the cessation of the IRA's campaign; that it is a necessary stage on the way to unity; and that by subscribing to it Sinn Fein can be brought in from the political wilderness to be a participant in the main Talks process.

In the Summer of 1993 the Irish Foreign Minister, Dick Spring, advanced his own ideas about the future of Anglo-Irish relations. Speaking to the Anglo-Irish inter-parliamentary body in Cork on 30 June, Spring argued that there was no immediate prospect of reaching an agreement between Unionist and Nationalist in Northern Ireland. Since that was the case he proposed that the Agreement be expanded by the two governments 'to avoid any danger of a political vacuum' (*Irish Times*, 1 July 1993). In the *Guardian* of 8 July Spring fleshed out what he meant. His proposal was very close to that of the SDLP's submission to Strand One. And like the SDLP he believed that a new arrangement entered into by the two governments should be put to a referendum in both parts of Ireland. These political speculations by one of the leaders of the Republic's coalition government came shortly after the leaking of a Labour Party background paper (*Options for a Labour Government*), which seemed to show a willingness on the part of McNamara, if Labour had been elected in April 1992, to consider joint sovereignty as an option.

The response of Prime Minister Major to the leak of the Labour document was an interesting indication of prevailing thinking in the Conservative government. Speaking in the House of Commons he argued that the 'policy, if it is the policy of the Labour Party, is a recipe for disaster'. He also called for the resignation of McNamara (*Belfast News Letter*, 30 June 1993). Indeed, Conservative statements since the ending of the Talks suggested that active policy commitments like joint sovereignty were definitely off the agenda. The government seemed to be looking instead to consolidate and to stabilise the situation in Northern Ireland. For instance, in his Liverpool speech of 23 April 1993, Sir Patrick Mayhew explicitly ruled out joint sovereignty. And in an earlier interview with Frank Millar of the *Irish Times*, Mayhew distanced himself from the ambitious proposals of the SDLP. He appeared to limit the government's purpose to a modification of the existing Agreement in order to make it acceptable to the Unionists. He stated that:

> the Nationalists gained a very good deal at Hillsborough. I think they would gain very much more, as would everybody in Ireland, North and South, if Unionist hostility to the Anglo-Irish Agreement were assuaged by it being substituted with another agreement that could carry their support. (*Irish Times*, 6 April 1993)

The tone of Mayhew's extensive interview was appropriately conservative.

Indeed, a confusion of purpose and a significant disagreement between the Irish and British governments opened up with the rumours of a 'deal' between the Ulster Unionist Party and the Conservatives over the crucial Maastricht vote of 22 July 1993. If it was a deal no one is calling it such. The Prime Minister's response to claims that the government had bought Unionist support was that: 'Nothing was asked for, nothing was offered and nothing given.' However, in the aftermath of the vote on Labour's amendment on the Social Chapter, the Ulster Unionist Party put out a statement announcing that the people of Northern Ireland 'now look to the Government to restore accountable democracy to Northern Ireland' (*Belfast Telegraph*, 23 July 1993). The Conservative government's precarious majority in the House of Commons makes them more amenable to the persuasion of Molyneaux that accountable democracy means a consolidation of direct rule from Westminster and a reform of local government in Northern Ireland (where power-sharing has had some success). Of course, the very notion of any concession to Unionists has severely annoyed Irish Nationalists. But the idea of regularising the procedures for Northern Ireland business in the House of Commons has been supported by the impeccably impartial Standing Advisory Committee on Human Rights in Northern Ireland (SACHR). Concern for responsible and responsive government at Westminster is not just a Unionist issue. How was a workable compromise to be reached between these two positions, a position of constitutional activism advocated by Nationalists and a position of constitutional consolidation advocated by Unionists?

The Downing Street Declaration

The Downing Street Declaration on 15 December 1993 represents, in a way, an attempt by the British and Irish Prime Ministers to pull together the threads of those divergent possibilities in a manner which does not outrage either Unionist or Nationalist or provoke even greater destabilisation. The Declaration itself is complex and convoluted – as one would expect of a document designed to provide something for everyone. Indeed, it is a ragbag of propositions invoking previously made assurances and statements. It includes aspects of the Anglo-Irish Agreement; extracts from speeches by Secretaries of State for Northern Ireland; phrases from leaders of the Ulster Unionist Party and the SDLP. Significantly, it also includes the language of the President of Sinn Fein, Gerry Adams. For, as the text makes plain in paragraph 1, the purpose is to provide 'the starting point of a peace process designed to culminate in a political settlement'. Decoded, that means proposals to get the IRA to stop its military campaign. The 'peace declaration' is intended to appeal to the 'men of violence'.

The reason why is plain enough. The Agreement did not undermine the IRA campaign, and the fears which its provisions aroused led to a new and dramatic upsurge in Protestant paramilitary violence. The yearly death rate from the Troubles had fallen steadily throughout the 1980s until the signing of the Agreement in November 1985. The toll for that year was 54 compared with 101 in 1981 (the year of the Hunger Strikes) and 476 in 1972 (the worst year of all for deaths). Each year since 1985 has experienced a higher death rate. And in 1992 Loyalist paramilitaries were responsible for more deaths than the IRA. This was the first time that this had happened since the Troubles began. In 1985 Loyalist paramilitary groups were effectively dormant. Only three deaths in that year were attributed to them. In 1989 they claimed over twenty killings. In 1991 this had doubled to 42. And this trend has been maintained into 1993. Indeed all measures of violence – armed robberies, intimidations, explosions, shootings, fire-bombings – have been sustained at a higher level than in 1985. This has frustrated British politicians some of whom appear to lay part of the blame at the door of the Irish government. For instance, Ken Hind, a former Parliamentary Private Secretary to Peter Brooke, annoyed Irish representatives at a meeting of the Anglo-Irish parliamentary body in December 1991 by reminding them that political violence was now five times higher in Northern Ireland than it was at the time of signing of the Agreement (*Irish Times*, 16 December 1991). Whatever the reasons, getting the IRA to stop its campaign without encouraging the Loyalist paramilitaries to step up theirs was an attractive prize for London and Dublin.

The tortuous circumstances of the emergence of the Declaration need not detain us. Nor is it necessary to delve into the murky details of contacts (many of which have not been revealed) that British officials had with Sinn Fein – and which their Ministers denied – throughout 1993. The Declaration tells its own story. Unlike the Anglo-Irish Agreement, the purpose of the Downing Street Declaration is openly to entice Sinn Fein into political negotiations (paragraphs 10 and 11) rather than to explicitly marginalise them as in 1985. This was what – as far as we can tell – the secret discussions between the government and Sinn Fein were about. It was a policy which paralleled other forms of political rehabilitation including John Hume's joint statements with Gerry Adams and the President of the Republic's famous shaking of the Sinn Fein President's hand. These developments had created a momentum for peace which Sinn Fein believed it could exploit to the advantage of IRA objectives. Sinn Fein, with the encouragement of Hume, tried to bounce the British government into radical constitutional change on its own terms. Whether the British government was prepared to pay the IRA's price in full was answered in the Declaration. It did not. It did not admit the 'value' of Irish unity. It did not commit itself to 'persuading' Unionists into a united Ireland. It did not set out a specified time for withdrawal.

The second thing that strikes one about the Declaration is its origin. The initiative was an Irish government one and an initial document was submitted to the British government as early as June 1992, that is while the inter-party Talks in Belfast were taking place. At no time did the British government itself make public its own view about the governance of Northern Ireland. It has continued to remain neutral on *arrangements of rule* if not on the existence of the Union itself. This, in theory, is a most curious attitude for a sovereign government to take. Yet it is not so curious in the post-1985 conditions in Northern Ireland. The statement by John Major and Albert Reynolds simply confirms a trend towards the joint responsibility of the two governments for policy in Northern Ireland. It accentuates the 'joint authority' intimations of the Anglo-Irish Agreement (even though the Declaration itself does not enhance the powers of the Irish government nor admit joint authority).

The third point is the extent to which the language of the British government has changed. The political balance sought is still that between the democratic right of the Unionists in Northern Ireland to remain within the United Kingdom and the aspiration of Nationalists to Irish unity. But the manner in which it is expressed has changed. The language is much 'greener'. In paragraph 2, 'Northern Ireland's statutory constitutional guarantee' is reaffirmed and the Irish government acknowledges it. But it is paragraph 4 which sets out the British position most clearly. It is only in one line of that labyrinthine formulation that the 'democratic wish of the greater number of people of Northern Ireland' gets a direct mention and even then in the context of possible support for a 'sovereign united Ireland'. The rest of the paragraph reads like a checklist of contemporary Nationalist phraseology. The statement by both Brooke and Mayhew that the British government has no 'selfish strategic or economic interest in Northern Ireland' is repeated as in the phrase of the former Irish Prime Minister, Charles Haughey, 'the totality of relationships'. It repeats the Forum/Agreement language about 'the rights and identities of both traditions in Ireland' (Unionists speak of 'two states') and commits the British government to 'encourage, facilitate and enable' agreement between those traditions. Further, it acknowledges that such agreement 'as of right' may be a united Ireland.

The next sentence is both the most striking *and* the most heavily qualified. It states:

> The British Government agree that it is for the people of the island of Ireland alone, by agreement between the two parts respectively, to exercise their right of self-determination on the basis of consent, freely and concurrently given, North and South, to bring about a united Ireland, if that is their wish.

As if to confirm that Irish self-determination is to be exercised by a single people, the paragraph concludes by referring to the 'people of Britain' and 'the people of Ireland' as if they were entirely distinct and already constituting separate entities. That is the sort of definitional politics which Unionist politicians find most threatening for they understand themselves to be British people as well as a people in Ireland. This is all the more curious given the clear Unionist rhetoric of John Major at his party conference in October 1993. But what of the substance of the British position? Has it changed as significantly as the language used to describe it?

The simple answer would appear to be: not quite. One might argue that it merely tells us what everyone already knew. Namely, that Northern Ireland's position within the United Kingdom is conditional on a majority of Northern Ireland voters continuing to support that position. And that no British government would prevent the two parts of Ireland agreeing to unity if that is what voters on both sides of the border want. The right of the people of Ireland to self-determination is effectively *partitioned*, North and South. And while the Irish government no where in the statement acknowledges Northern Ireland to be a part of the United Kingdom, it too accepts that position. This is not an Anglo-Irish Agreement mark two but mark one again in greener language. Yet once spoken, such words are irretrievable. The 'Britishness' of Northern Ireland is that bit more contingent and its 'Irishness' that bit more definite.

Will it bring the rewards of 'peace' in Northern Ireland? It seems unlikely that the IRA can halt its campaign or its political spokesmen in Sinn Fein can renounce support for violence on the strength of the Declaration alone. Unlikely, though not out of the question. However, one calculation of the government may have been to hoist the IRA by its own petard of peace. For the IRA to reject the Declaration may be just as damaging as to accept it given the momentum for 'peace' which it had encouraged. And so the focus shifts back to the constitutional parties. Does the Declaration make it more or less likely to achieve a political compromise? It is impossible to say. For the problem in Northern Ireland has not changed with the agreement of the two Prime Ministers. At the moment only the Democratic Unionists have denounced the statement in its entirety. For the moment the Ulster Unionists have been kept on board and kept sweet with the appointment of a new House of Commons Select Committee for Northern Ireland. The SDLP cannot be seen to reject an agreed document with the Irish government (even if it is not what Hume wanted). The Alliance Party is supportive. The British government's objective (paragraphs 2 and 9) remains to get the three stranded Talks going again and hope for the best.

Conclusion

The consistent element of Conservative Northern Ireland policy since 1979 has been to 'balance' the right of Unionists to remain part of the United Kingdom and the aspiration of Nationalists to have a unified Irish state. In that policy it has shown continuity with its predecessors, Labour and Conservative. The character of that 'balance', though, has changed over the last 15 years. The early years saw the government pursuing a course which stressed the priority of accommodation between the parties within Northern Ireland as a precondition of any 'Irish dimension'. The Anglo-Irish Agreement shifted the priority to an intergovernmental balance as the precondition for an internal compromise. Power-sharing was to be a function of an Irish dimension – the Intergovernmental Conference – and not vice versa. The alienation thereby of the Unionists and their non-cooperation with the Agreement encouraged an attempt to modify the arrangements of 1985 in the inter-party Talks which began in 1991. The purpose was to get Unionist acceptance of a new set of balanced institutions which would include a strong British–Irish dimension. Yet, as we have shown, Nationalists were now looking for something more. They were looking to move the debate beyond what Unionists were prepared to concede.

The events of the last year were the consequence of these heightened Nationalist expectations based on assumptions about the Anglo-Irish Agreement and its consequences for the British commitment to the constitutional status of Northern Ireland. The common position of Hume of the SDLP and Adams of Sinn Fein was that Britain should move from being 'neutral' on the Union to being a 'persuader' of the Unionists to accept the value and legitimacy, the inevitability, of Irish unity and British disengagement. The Downing Street Declaration represents an attempt by the government to confront those expectations. In particular, it has been about trying to bring Sinn Fein into the inter-party Talks. And that has meant the British government re-expressing its constitutional commitment to Northern Ireland in a way which might entice the IRA to lay down its arms. This is a very delicate and dangerous balancing act. The 'guarantee' to Unionists is now hedged about with all sorts of Nationalist rhetoric such as 'self-determination', 'the totality of relationships', 'the people of the island of Ireland' and so on. Yet the government knows full well that to concede too much to terrorist demands would signal a green light for ever greater violence from loyalists. Hence the importance, along with the Irish government, of emphasising the need for 'consent', the 'democratic wish of the greater number of the people of Northern Ireland' and so on.

For the 'peace initiative' of 15 December to work, as paragraph 1 makes clear, it is imperative to move towards a 'political settlement'. It remains difficult to see what the contours of that settlement will be. For if the Downing Street Declaration is a case of squaring the circle in terms of carefully crafted verbal compromises it is by no means certain that the British government can translate that into squaring the circle of political ambitions in Northern Ireland. The real work is yet to be done. And it remains to be seen how the British government can balance the Unionist aim to consolidate the Union and the Nationalist aim to encourage an active policy of constitutional change.

15

Foreign and Defence Policy under the Conservatives

FERGUS CARR

Introduction

The aim of this chapter is to outline and assess the changing role of Britain in international affairs as it has emerged post-1979. It will examine the central features of policy since 1979 and set them against the transformation of the international system in the same period. It will then review the key issues in contemporary foreign and defence policy.

Foreign and Defence Policy: The Post-War Pattern

The Conservative Government of 1979 inherited a complex legacy in foreign and defence policy. Britain's external role had been shaped by a number of forces. In 1945 Britain had an empire that stretched from Africa to Asia and a consequent global defence strategy. Britain was also a victorious power that sat in the first rank of diplomatic forums. By 1973 Britain had become a middle-ranking power whose defence policy was largely concentrated on Europe. Defence commitments had been cut and the armed forces reduced through a series of 'reviews'. Successive British governments had found it difficult to reconcile a global role with sustained poor economic growth and balance-of-payments problems.

By 1979 Europe had become the central focus of British trade and defence policy. European primacy had emerged through the loss of the global role. In some perceptions Europe would always mark the end of a process and not the beginning. At the same time Europe was more than the EC, it was NATO and the link to the USA. The 'special relationship' sat alongside the EC sphere of policy and offered Britain a wider role. It fell to Margaret Thatcher to reconcile the development of Britain's Community interests with the 'special relationship'.

The New Cold War

Thatcher's tenure as Prime Minister spanned the era of the new Cold War. Her arrival in office coincided with the demise of superpower *détente*. *Détente* had been characterised by a reduction in Cold War tensions and the movement from confrontation to co-operation. The strategic arms race was placed within the framework of arms control, the Strategic Arms Limitation Talks (SALT), which institutionalised the nuclear balance of power. The decline of *détente* was caused by several factors not least a perceived challenge to America's interests in the Third World (see Halliday, 1989). From the fall of Saigon to the invasion of Afghanistan the Soviet Union was seen as increasingly threatening international order. In Europe concern grew over the 'decoupling' of American strategic forces from NATO. SALT was seen to neutralise nuclear strategic forces and grant greater significance to regional forces. In this context Soviet theatre nuclear and conventional forces in Europe became a pressing issue for NATO leaders. The Carter administration did respond but was defeated at the polls by Ronald Reagan.

Reagan denounced *détente* as a 'one way street which the Soviet Union has used to pursue its own aims' and began a programme of substantive expansion in nuclear and conventional forces. Ideology returned to prominence in East–West relations. Progress towards arms control faltered over theatre nuclear forces and the 'Star Wars' or Strategic Defense Initiative (SDI). Moscow cemented the move into Cold War with its inflexible policies and intolerance of internal dissent. In eastern Europe Poland became the barometer of international tension as martial law was declared in 1981 and Solidarity banned in 1982. Nuclear weapons became a central element of public debate as Cruise and Pershing II missiles were deployed in NATO countries.

British policy replicated policy in the original Cold War, with support for the United States as the key element.

Thatcher, Reagan and Bush

Thatcher and Reagan developed a distinctive relationship. Thatcher found a 'striking similarity between Britain's and American's aims and policies'. The two leaders shared a common ideological viewpoint with respect to both foreign and domestic policy.

The Anglo-American partnership was cemented with nuclear weapons. In 1980 it was announced that Polaris would be replaced with another American missile, the Trident (C4). When the United States decided to develop the more powerful (D5) version Britain's purchase was revised accordingly. The costs of the programme had risen to over £9 billion by 1990. The government maintained its commitment despite cost and the criticism that Britain did not need a superpower deterrent. The Thatcherite commitment to nuclear deterrence was, however, beyond question and with it the commitment to the United States. The twin commitment was further demonstrated with the deployment of American Cruise missiles in Britain from 1983. This deployment came at a time of increasing domestic sensitivity to nuclear weapons. The deployment of Cruise soon became a test of alliance loyalty as European governments faced mounting domestic criticism. Thatcher was resolute in the defence of Cruise and sought to prevent other European governments wavering in their commitment.

British support for the United States went beyond alliance policy for Europe. In 1981 Thatcher supported American plans for a Rapid Deployment Force (RDF) and offered British forces for inclusion. London supported Washington over its Lebanon policy in 1982 and its strategy for the Persian Gulf. In the Westland affair of 1986 Thatcher favoured America over Europe. When American aircraft bombed targets in Libya Britain stood apart from its EC partners in support of the action. In 1988 London was once again isolated in its defence of America following the shooting down of an Iranian airliner.

The Anglo-American relationship was not as close after the departure of Ronald Reagan. Thatcher and Bush retained a harmonious relationship but the international system was changing and with it America's needs. East–West relations were turning to a new *détente* under the prompting of the Soviet leader Mikhail Gorbachev. In 1987 a treaty was signed eliminating intermediate-range missiles such as

Cruise and thereby ending a major cause of tension in Europe. Of greater significance were the east European revolutions of 1989. The regimes fell because they had proven incapable of resolving their countries economic crises, because they had failed to secure political legitimacy and because Gorbachev would not support them. Poland set the pace with Solidarity securing victory in elections in June 1989.

In May 1989 the 'iron curtain' between Hungary and Austria was taken down enabling East German refugees to reach the west. The East German government failed to contain its people's aspirations and in November 1989 the Berlin wall was opened. In March 1990 free elections led to reunification of East and West Germany. The emergence of one German state in October 1990 transformed European politics and American interests. It was Germany that was of critical importance to the new Europe and not Britain.

Defence Policy 1979–90

The central commitment of British defence policy in 1979 was NATO. Defence roles in NATO accounted for over 95 per cent of the defence budget. Britain alone of the European members of the alliance contributed to all three levels of NATO strategy, strategic nuclear, theatre nuclear, and conventional. Four main defence roles were exercised by Britain within the alliance. First, the nuclear role consisting of the strategic deterrent (Polaris to Trident) and theatre nuclear forces comprising aircraft, short-range missiles and aircraft. Secondly, the direct defence of the United Kingdom including land, sea, and air forces. Thirdly the defence of the European mainland of which the British Army of the Rhine (BAOR) and RAF Germany were the main elements. Finally the maritime role, safeguarding the Eastern Atlantic and Channel areas and contributing to forward defence in the Norwegian Sea.

In 1979 the Conservatives made defence the 'first charge on our national resources'. Thatcher's government accepted NATO's call for a 3 per cent annual increase in real terms in defence expenditure. The result was that by 1985–6 the defence budget had grown to be one fifth larger in real terms than in 1979. The significance of this expansion should be underlined by the context of the 1980s recession and the overall government policy of cutting public expenditure. Apart from the United States, Britain spent more on defence in absolute and per capita terms than any other NATO member. Nevertheless even this level of funding could not continue to improve weapon systems and maintain defence roles. John Nott was charged with conducting a review of policy which was presented in 1981.

Nott's defence review 'The Way Forward' retained all four defence roles. The continental commitment was retained but BAOR reduced to three in theatre divisions. The commitments to strategic deterrence and the direct defence of the UK were also maintained. It fell to the maritime role to bear the brunt of the cuts. The surface fleet was to reduce from 59 destroyers and frigates to 50. A new and cheaper frigate the type 23 would replace the proposed type 22. The carrier, the *Ark Royal* would be completed but only two of the three ships in this class would be kept. The older carrier *Hermes*, the assault ships *Intrepid* and *Fearless* and the Falklands patrol vessel, Endurance would be phased out. The Royal Naval Base and dockyard at Chatham would close and Portsmouth would be subject to 'a very sharp reduction'.

The Falklands war of 1982 posed a direct challenge to the government's defence policy. The vital role of the Navy was acknowledged in a modification to the Nott review. The government decided to retain all three carriers, *Ark Royal*, *Invincible* and *Illustrious*. The assault ships and the *Endurance* were also given a reprieve. A surface fleet of 55 destroyers and frigates was also to be maintained.

The Falklands war therefore exacerbated an already stretched defence budget. As the government could not contemplate either cutting a defence role in NATO or a non-NATO commitment economies had to be found elsewhere. The stress was placed upon efficiency savings and 'management'. However, as the proportion of GDP allocated to defence fell from 1985–6 and commitments were not cut a 'funding gap' developed (see Greenwood, 1991). The defence White Paper of 1988 noted that with the ending of real growth in the defence budget 'difficult choices have to be made between priorities in our forward plans'. It was not though until 1990 that a defence review began, the 'Options for Change' programme. 'Options for Change' was presented by the Secretary of State, Tom King, as the process of restructuring British forces to meet the changing security environment of the new European order. The commitment to Trident was to be maintained and a sub-strategic force of dual capable Tornado aircraft.

Forces were to be allocated to the direct defence of the UK and to the Falklands, Cyprus, Gibraltar, Belize and until 1997 Hong Kong. Force deployments for the BAOR were to be halved and RAF

Germany reduced from four bases to two. The surface fleet would retain the three carriers but frigate and destroyers numbers would be cut to 40. An overall reduction of regular manpower of 18 per cent was also to be implemented.

In November 1990 British force reductions were complemented by the Conventional Armed Forces in Europe Treaty (CFE). CFE was applicable from the Atlantic to the Urals. NATO and the Warsaw Pact agreed to limit each alliance to 20,000 battle tanks, 30,000 armoured combat vehicles, 20,000 artillery pieces and 6800 combat aircraft. No single state was to possess more than one third of the combined total. The treaty ended NATO's inferiority in key conventional offensive forces and provided for verification procedures.

The CFE Treaty was concluded at the Conference on Security and Cooperation in Europe (CSCE) Paris summit. The summit declared the Cold War over and issued a Charter for the New Europe. The Charter established new political structures to support CSCE including a secretariat in Prague, an office for free elections in Warsaw and a conflict prevention centre in Vienna. The summit also endorsed a number of Confidence and Security Building Measures (CSBMs) which included provision for the exchange of military information. The Paris summit was Thatcher's last as Prime Minister. The Summit fell in the midst of a Conservative leadership challenge triggered by policy differences with regard to the EC (see Chapter 4).

Britain and the New World Order

Thatcher's legacy to her successor Mr Major was of orthodoxy and continuity in foreign and defence policy. Defence policy remained wedded to nuclear deterrence, NATO, and the Anglo-American special relationship. European policy had been firmly placed within the 'old consensus', conditioned by Altanticism and concern for sovereignty. The policies of the 1980s were distinguished by the relative lack of change and the restatement of older values. The challenge for Mr Major is to adapt British policy to meet a world that has changed. The new world order that emerged between 1989 and 1991 may not reflect President Bush's vision of a just society but it is real enough. The central features of change are the collapse of communism in Europe, the end of the Warsaw Pact, the unification of Germany and the collapse of the Soviet Union. Change has been both profound and dramatic. The collapse of communism in eastern Europe was followed by the assertion of separatism and nationalism in the Soviet Union. The ill-fated Soviet coup of August 1991 accelerated the processes of change it was trying to arrest. In December 1991 the USSR ceased to exist and with it Gorbachev's position. The successor organisation the Commonwealth of Independent States (CIS) proved equally unsuccessful in resisting the forces of separatism.

The new order presents new challenges and problems for British foreign and defence policy. The post-Cold War era challenges the 'givens' of post war policy; the Soviet threat, deterrent strategy, Atlanticism, and opens up the possibility of new roles for the EC and United Nations. In Europe the new environment can be seen to make possible political union and a defence role for the EC. For the United Nations the end of the Cold War holds out the possibility of an active and interventionist role. At the same time the collapse of communism has introduced new security challenges in Europe from intercommunal violence in the former Yugoslavia to the rivalries of the Soviet successor states. This is coupled to the economic crises confronting the eastern States. British policy has had to respond to these challenges in addition to elements of continuity from the old agenda.

Britain, NATO and European Security

Britain has remained wedded to NATO and its strategy for the new European order. In July 1990 NATO's North Atlantic Council London Declaration set the parameters for future Alliance policy. The London Declaration recognised that Europe had entered a new era and that NATO had to adapt. In particular the political role of the Alliance was to be enhanced and a new relationship sought with former adversaries. The primary vehicle for this is the North Atlantic Co-operation Council (NACC) founded in 1991. The NACC membership spans NATO, and Central and Eastern Europe including the successor states to the Soviet Union.

Whilst NATO has seen itself as an agent of change it has also seen its 'essential purpose' as unchanged. The Alliance has accepted that a new security architecture of interlocking institutions has emerged in Europe. The North Atlantic Council perceives the roles of the Western European Union (WEU), CSCE, NATO and EC as complementary but believes the Alliance has a particular function. The Rome meeting of the North Atlantic Council in 1991 adopted a new Strategic Concept which outlined four security tasks fundamental to NATO's rationale:

1. 'To provide one of the indispensable foundations for a stable security environment in Europe . . .'
2. 'To serve, as provided for in Article IV of the North Atlantic Treaty, as a transatlantic forum for Allied consultations on any issues that affect their vital interests . . .'
3. 'To deter and defend against any threat of aggression against the territory of any NATO member state.'
4. 'To preserve the strategic balance within Europe.'

The transatlantic basis of the Alliance has also been underlined by North Atlantic Council declarations. At the Athens meeting in June 1993 it was found that the 'substantial presence of United States armed forces in Europe and the continuing political and military commitment and active engagement in European security of both the United States and Canada will remain indispensable'.

NATO provides an important element of continuity for Britain's defence policy. The Alliance provides a framework for the maintenance of transatlantic relations and security in a period of rapid change. The collapse of the prevailing order in Europe has given way to a series of security concerns. The former Soviet nuclear arsenal has become the effective property of four states, Russia, Belarus, Kazakhstan and the Ukraine. Whilst they have signed the Strategic Arms Reduction Talks (START) Treaty, the Ukraine has yet to ratify the agreement. This reflects Ukrainian desires for greater support from the United States and security guarantees against Russia. Russia has laid claim to Sevastopol and the Black Sea fleet. Territorial instability, separatism and ethnic tensions are also challenging the successor states including the Russian Federation. NATO has consequently recognised that the 'predominant threat' it faced in the past has given way to 'multifaceted' and 'multidirectional' risks. Risks are seen as arising from the problems of the post-communist era in Europe or from wider concerns including the proliferation of weapons of mass destruction and international terrorism. The Strategic Concept plans for contingencies in 'peace, crisis and war'. A new stress is placed upon preventive diplomacy and crisis management. Strategic nuclear deterrence is to be retained but overall force levels including sub-strategic nuclear and convential forces cut. In order to meet the new needs of the Alliance mobility and flexibility of forces have been stressed. Britain is to play a leading role in this respect taking command and providing the core of NATO's new rapid reaction forces.

Defence Policy: 'Defending our Future'

British defence policy has been reviewed in light of NATO's new Strategic Concept. The 1993 White Paper, 'Defending our Future' (Cmnd 2270) commits Britain to three defence roles. The first is 'the protection of the UK and dependent territories', the second 'to insure against any major external threat to the UK and our Allies, and the third, 'the promotion of the UK's wider security interest through the maintenance of international peace and stability'. The White Paper further sought to encapsulate the 'options for change' programme.

The Secretary of State for Defence, Malcolm Rifkind stressed the White Paper was a response to the end of the Soviet threat and the need for more flexible capabilities. The Navy was selected to bear the brunt of cuts which were rationalised by the decline of threat in the North Atlantic. Four new submarines in the Upholder class are to be sold or moth-balled, the surface fleet is to be cut to 35 frigates and destroyers, mine countermeasures vessels cut by nine and naval manpower to 52,500. The army which had suffered the major cuts under 'options' is being reduced from 156,000 to 116,000 regular soldiers. The RAF is to lose a Tornado air defence squadron and Tornado F3 fighter numbers will be cut to 100. Critics of the White Paper either believed it had gone too far in cutting forces or had failed to be radical enough in redefining Britain's defence role. The defence roles identified are very broad in scope and require forces in excess of those planned. The White Paper seeks to demonstrate that the same forces will undertake several different tasks and fulfil the roles. The 'over stretch' of resources relative to potential commitments therefore remains. The White Paper also continues to endorse a 'traditional' pattern of commitments, from strategic nuclear weapons, to NATO while adding a new stress on peacekeeping.

'Defending our Future' argues that the 'old distinction between "in" and "out of area" is no longer relevant'. Britain is seen as needing a flexible response to meet a variety of risks in Europe and beyond. Mobility is to be afforded through the procurement of a new helicopter carrier for the Navy, replacements for the assault ships and new helicopters for the Army and RAF. The White Paper echoes NATO's strategy and describes strategic nuclear forces as the 'ultimate guarantee of our security'. The Secretary of State did not, however, expand on how Britain would deal with President Clinton's moratorium on nuclear testing. The costs of defence were anticipated to reduce over the next three years from 3.9 per cent of GDP to 3.2 per cent. The reduction would still, however, leave British expenditure above average for NATO members.

Defence, Trade and Iraq

In November 1992 John Major announced that Lord Justice Scott would conduct a judicial inquiry into Britain's trade with Iraq. The announcement followed the collapse of an Old Bailey trial of three former executives of Matrix-Churchill, a machine tool company. The executives had been charged with breaking export regulations covering trade with Iraq. The trial ended after the testimony of Alan Clark, former Minister of Trade, 1986–9. It had become clear that ministers had known of Matrix-Churchill's exports and their potential for use in Iraqi munitions production. Four ministers; Tristan Garel-Jones, Kenneth Clarke, Michael Heseltine and Malcolm Rifkind tried to stop the disclosure of documentary evidence by signing Public Interest Immunity Certificates. The judge overruled the ministers and released documents which 'told an astonishing story of how government ministers had evidence dating from 1987 that Matrix-Churchill had been exporting its machine tools to Iraqi munitions factories' (Sweeney, 1993, p. 15). Matrix-Churchill machine tools have subsequently been found in Iraqi nuclear facilities by United Nations inspectors.

The Matrix-Churchill case came on top of the 'super-gun affair'. In April 1990 customs officers in Teeside seized steel cylinders bound for Iraq. The claim that the cylinders could form a super-gun was denied by Iraq but after the Gulf war confirmed. Evidence linked the artillery expert Gerald Bull, Iraq and a number of companies in the production of component parts of the hugh artillery piece. Export licences had been granted for the cylinders despite it was revealed warnings to the government by Conservative MP Sir Hilary Miller.

British trade with Iraq was 'governed' by guidelines revealed to the House of Commons in 1985 by Sir Geoffrey Howe. The guidelines were set during the Iraq–Iran war and were:

1. 'We should maintain our consistent refusal to supply any lethal equipment to either side.'
2. 'Subject to that overriding consideration, we should attempt to fulfil existing contracts and obligations.'
3. 'We should not, in future, approve orders for any defence equipment which, in our view, would significantly enhance the capability of either side to prolong or exacerbate the conflict.'
4. 'In line with this policy, we should continue to scrutinize rigorously all applications for expert licences for the supply of defence equipment to Iran and Iraq.'

The spirit of the guidelines is quite clear but the terminology lacks precision. The definition of 'lethal', 'prolong', or 'exacerbate' is by no means self-evident (see Pythian and Little, 1993). Between 1980 and 1990 trade credits granted to Iraq amounted to £3517 million. Iraq had become a valuable export market and machine tools and other equipment did not directly violate the wording of the guidelines. In 1988 when a ceasefire between Iraq and Iran was concluded the guidelines were secretly revised to read for note (3); 'We should not in future approve orders for any defence equipment which, in our view, would be of direct and significant assistance to either country in the conduct of offensive operations in breach of the ceasefire.' This weakened the restrictions upon exports to Iraq and enabled an enhanced trade.

The consequences of British trade policy with Iraq was literally 'arming the enemy'. In this, Britain was far from alone (see Timmerman, 1992). Whatever the outcome of the Scott Inquiry the episode demonstrates the defence implications of trade and the necessity of more rigorous non-proliferation strategies.

Britain, the EC, Foreign and Defence Policy

John Major inherited a Conservative Party divided over European union. British policy toward Maastricht and the difficulties of ratification are discussed in Chapter 4. The following concerns the foreign and defence aspects of Maastricht.

In 1990 Chancellor Kohl and President Mitterrand called for European Political Union (EPU) with a common foreign and security policy. Franco-German proposals identified the WEU as the body to provide a security policy for the new union. The WEU's origins lie in the Brussels Treaty of 1948 between the UK, France and the Benelux countries. The Brussels Treaty formed the European alliance which preceded NATO. At Maastricht the EC members envisaged the implementation of a common foreign and security policy (CFSP) including the eventual framing of a common defence policy. The WEU is to 'elaborate and implement decisions and actions of the union which have defence implications'.

Maastricht largely confirmed existing practice with regard to foreign policy co-ordination. In accord with British interests foreign policy was not made part of the Community decision making procedure. CFSP stands alongside the Community as a 'Third Pillar' of European union. The 'Third Pillar' reflects intergovernmentalism and makes the European Council responsible for setting the guidelines and principles of CFSP. The Council of Ministers is to take decisions in accord with the guidelines and when 'it deems necessary, the Council shall define a common position'. The Council can further define those matters on which a decision is to be taken by a qualified majority. Once joint action is to be adopted national policies must conform to the common EC position. There is no imperative, however, to adopt a common position nor is there a commitment to a single foreign policy (see Lodge, 1993, p. 244). Britain also negotiated an opt out clause that when circumstances change and in cases of 'imperative need' members can take 'necessary measures'.

The inclusion of security and defence objectives within Maastricht challenged Britain's Atlanticist orientation. The Foreign Secretary, Douglas Hurd, did not 'see any point, and some danger indeed, in duplicating what NATO does'. The British objective was to subsume the WEU within NATO. The means was to accept the revitalisation of the WEU but as the European pillar of NATO. Technically Maastricht and NATO's Rome Declaration are complementary. Maastricht states that union policy will 'respect the obligations of certain member states under the North Atlantic Treaty and be compatible with the common security and defence policy established within that framework'. The Rome Declaration envisaged the 'reinforcement of the role of the WEU both as the defence component of the process of European unification and as a means of strengthening the European pillar of the alliance'. In practice the development of the WEU leaves open the question of its future role and relationship to NATO. In May 1992 France and Germany announced the formation of a 35,000 strong Euro-corps.

The Euro-corps gave real substance to the WEU and enhanced British concerns. In December 1992, however, NATO reached agreement with France and Germany that in the event of an emergency in Europe the corps would be placed under NATO command. This agreement brought Paris a little closer to NATO and eased fears of competition with the Alliance. It has been the tragedy in the former Republic of Yugoslavia though that has most blunted the security aspirations of the EC.

Britain and the United Nations

In January 1992 John Major chaired a special summit of the United Nations Security Council. The meeting recognised the importance of the United Nations to the new world order. The Prime Minister captured the rationale of the summit when he declared that it was 'a time of great hope in international affairs but also of uncertainty and potential instability'.

The end of the Cold War offered a new role for the Security Council. Freed from the immobilism of Cold War vetoes the United Nations now had the capacity to intervene in disputes. The Gulf war had seemed to confirm the birth of a new era. The Security Council had agreed to resolutions which condemned the Iraqi invasion of Kuwait, called for a withdrawal, imposed sanctions and finally authorised 'all necessary means'. Britain made a significant commitment of forces to the Gulf campaign of some 35,000 troops, 300 tanks, 69 combat aircraft and a range of naval forces. Britain's support for the American-led coalition revived the special relationship. The conditions and correlation of interests involved in the Gulf crisis are, however, unlikely to be replicated. The mutual dependence of the United States and United Nations and the interests of coalition partners from Saudi Arabia to Britain produced an unusual momentum for the world body. In addition the motives of Security Council members such as the Soviet Union and China led to support for the United States. These factors together with the unambiguous nature of Iraqi aggression and the significance of oil made it unlikely that the Gulf campaign would serve as a precedent for the future (see Matthews, 1993). Indeed, despite the scale of the Gulf operation a durable peace has yet to be found. After the war Saddam Hussein survived a Shia uprising in the south and a Kurdish uprising in the North of Iraq. The Iraqi leader began a violent repression of these communities which led to the Kurds fleeing to the borderlands with Turkey and Iran. The UN responded with resolution 688 demanding an end to repression and John Major initiated the idea of 'safehavens' for the Kurds in northern Iraq. From August 1992 Britain joined France, America and Russia and imposed a 'no fly zone' over southern Iraq. The allies have clashed with Iraq over the zone and the imposition of ceasefire resolutions concerning the destruction of non-conventional weapon facilities. A wider peace involving the Palestinians has proven equally difficult to attain though in late August 1993 hopeful signs of an accord between the PLO and Israel were emerging.

It has been peacekeeping that has been the central contribution of the UN to the new era. In 1992 peacekeeping operations cost 3 billion dollars, four times the previous highest figure. Since 1988 the UN has created as many peacekeeping operations as it did in the previous four decades. The special summit called upon the new Secretary-General Boutros Boutros Ghali, to make recommendations as to how the UN could better contribute to order in the new era. Ghali's report, 'An Agenda for Peace', outlined the complexity of contemporary intra-state rather than inter-state conflicts. The Secretary-General recommended an incremental approach to peacekeeping. He urged the adoption of preventive diplomacy, to stop disputes escalating; peacemaking, to diplomatically resolve disputes; peacekeeping, to deploy a UN presence in the field and finally 'peacebuilding' to prevent a relapse into conflict. Whilst there are no agreed definitions of peacekeeping the implications of Ghali's recommendations would be a substantive increase in commitments to the United Nations. In 1993 the House of Commons Foreign Affairs Committee explored the implications of an expanded UN role for UK policy. The Committee reviewed the resource needs of preventive diplomacy, the enforcement elements of peacemaking and the long-term costs of peacebuilding.

In an address to the United Nations in September 1992 Douglas Hurd warned that 'we risk loading the United Nations with too heavy a burden of, in effect, intervention and partial administration'. The Foreign Secretary believed the costs would be too great to bear. His warning proved accurate as the UN entered a major financial crisis in August 1993. Britain is one of the few states to meet its obligations on schedule. The USA and the Russian Federation for example, owed a total of $848 million toward the regular budget and $1195 million toward peacekeeping (*Guardian*, 4 August 1993). Britain has rejected proposals for a standing UN army and changes to the permanent membership of the Security Council. The Foreign Secretary has further made clear a preference for preventive diplomacy rather peacekeeping or peacemaking. The collapse of Yugoslavia, however, reveals the difficulties confronting all three.

The Collapse of Yugoslavia

In 1974 Yugoslavia adopted a new constitution which created a virtual confederation of the country's six constituent republics. The system survived Tito's death but not the collapse of Communism. In 1990 multiparty elections brought separatists to power in Slovenia and Croatia. In Croatia a Serbian minority sought autonomy and in February 1991 declared its own autonomous region of Krajina. The drift to civil war began in the spring of 1991. Slovenian defence forces successfully resisted the national army (JNA). In Croatia the Serbian minority turned to the predominantly Serbian JNA and police for armed support. The EC warned that military action would lead to sanctions and began a diplomatic initiative. The EC sought to play the role of moderator. The problem was that the protagonists had little common ground and little desire to find some. In attempting to accommodate all the parties the EC satisfied none. In September 1991 the EC launched a peace conference at the Hague chaired by Lord Carrington. The EC proposed a confederal solution, a free association of sovereign States. Bosnia, Croatia, Macedonia and Slovenia accepted the plan; Serbia rejected it. Croatia and Slovenia received recognition from Germany in December 1991 and from the EC in January 1992. Greece demanded that Macedonia change its name and renounce all claims on the Greek province of the same name before recognition would be granted. In Bosnia, the most ethnically complex of the republics, the Serb minority looked to membership of a 'Greater Serbia' rather than accept majority Muslim rule. Bosnian independence was declared on 3 March 1993 and was followed by violence between Serbs, Muslims and Croats.

The problem for the EC was that as mediation failed a larger role beckoned. Intervention on the ground in the form of a large peace-keeping force was the logical step in seeking to stabilise relations between the communities. From the outset Britain urged caution and opposed French proposals for a WEU 'interposition' role in Croatia. Douglas Hurd has argued that the only thing which would have guaranteed peace with justice would have been an expeditionary force but that would have created 'a new Northern Ireland . . . and no government has at any time seriously proposed that'. As war engulfed Bosnia as well as Croatia the likelihood of an EC/WEU intervention declined. Britain was hesitant to commit forces to a conflict without foreseeable end and for which no clear mandate existed. It fell to the United Nations to deploy a protection force (UNPROFOR) in April 1992.

In the summer of 1992 the situation in Bosnia deteriorated. Escalating violence combined with 'ethnic cleansing' created the worst refugee crisis in Europe since the Second World War. Some 10,000 people fled their homes each day in Bosnia. Pressure grew on the international community to act. Douglas Hurd toured the region and the British government, the holders of the EC Presidency, called an international conference in August. The London conference condemned the violence but failed to halt the civil war. Lord Carrington resigned and was replaced by Cyrus Vance and Lord Owen.

Despite the failure of the London conference the international community remained reliant upon sanctions and humanitarian aid. NATO and the WEU sought in air and sea operations to monitor UN sanctions imposed on Serbia and Montenegro. Britain co-sponsored Security Council resolution 770 which authorised 'all means necessary' to ensure the delivery of humanitarian aid and provided 1800 soldiers for the protection of aid convoys in Bosnia. Sanctions were toughened when the Bosnia Serbs rejected the Vance–Owen peace plan in January 1993. NATO also began the enforcement of a 'no fly zone' over Bosnia. Britain and other EC members rejected, however, American proposals for air strikes against Serbian positions or lifting the arms embargo to allow Muslims free access to arms supplies. The tentative response to the plight of the Bosnian Muslims was in stark contrast to the American cruise missile strike on Baghdad in June. As criticism of the United States mounted and Sarejevo was imperilled President Clinton called for the use of NATO air power in August 1993. NATO agreed to use air strikes but in terms of a strict proportionate response. Britain remained opposed to the idea of strategic bombardments of Serb positions.

Lord Owen has succinctly concluded that 'rightly or wrongly the world's political leaders have decided they do not wish to be combatants'. Unfortunately this has been the choice not whether they wish to support peacekeeping in the traditional sense. Intra-state conflict erodes the impartiality of the peacekeepers making them part of the political situation rather than apart from it.

Britain and the Politics of Transition

South Africa and Hong Kong

The Gulf crises, the collapse of the Soviet Union and the disintegration of Yugoslavia have dominated the international agenda. The process of transition in South Africa has been 'marginalised' by this agenda but nevertheless affected by it. The collapse of Soviet influence in Southern Africa has encouraged Pretoria to pursue constitutional reform with the African National Congress (ANC). In 1990 Nelson Mandela leader of the ANC was released from detention, the ban on the ANC lifted and in 1991 negotiations began on the development of democratic institutions. The Conference for a Democratic South Africa (CODE-SA) was established involving a number of political organisations including the National Party (NP) and the ANC. Nelson Mandela's commitment to a negotiated settlement enabled President de Klerk to take the reform process further despite opposition from a number of 'constituencies' (see Hamill, 1993). Britain has supported the reform process and the pursuit of an internal settlement based upon multiparty consensus. The reform process has narrowed the gap between Britain and other Commonwealth members. Although John Major was isolated at the Harare Commonwealth summit in 1991 when advocating an immediate lifting of sanctions, agreement was reached on a 'programmed' removal in relation to process in the reform progress. South Africa's isolation in international sport was, however, immediately ended and in 1992 the EC lifted further sanctions following de Klerk's referendum victory which endorsed the reform process.

The transition process has been placed in jeopardy by political violence between the ANC and Buthelezi's Inkatha movement. The scale of the violence and the failure of the state security forces to control it led to a breakdown of relations between the ANC and the government. In 1993, however, agreement was reached on a target date, 27 April 1994, for a general election, by universal suffrage, to create a constituent assembly charged with the introduction of a new constitution. The assembly will be presided over by a government of national unity based on power-sharing principles. External involvement in the electoral process is likely with regard to monitoring and observation but Britain and other actors will undoubtedly resist a greater commitment in the face of political violence. The threat of civil war remains with Buthelezi's boycott of the negotiations and opposition to the 'liberation election'.

Unlike the South African case, Britain has direct responsibility for the transition process in Hong Kong. In 1997 British leases will expire and the colony will become part of the Peoples' Republic of China (PRC). Negotiations between Britain and China led to the Joint Declaration of 1984 which granted the PRC control from 1 July 1997 and made Hong Kong a Special Administrative Region (SAR). It was agreed that Hong Kong would have a high degree of autonomy except in foreign affairs and defence. The formula was for 'one country, two systems' in which China held sovereignty but Hong Kong could retain its own political, economic and social system.

The brutal repression of the pro-democracy movement in Tiananmen Square in June 1989 shattered the confidence inspired by the Joint Declaration. The events revealed just how far Beijing was from acceptance of democratic change. In Hong Kong Tiananmen produced demands for greater autonomy after 1997 and democratisation in the transition process. The colony has not enjoyed an elected government but a Governor who works through an executive council and legislative council. The Governor appoints ten of the fourteen member Executive Council which acts like a cabinet. In 1985 24 of the 57 strong Legislative Council were elected but not by universal franchise. Half were elected by electoral colleges and half by 'functional constituencies' such as 'finance' or 'medical'. Beijing has sought the retention of this executive-dominated system through the transition process. The Basic Law, China's new constitution for Hong Kong, approved in 1990 by the National Peoples Congress envisaged a Chief Executive of the SAR who would succeed the current governor and a legislature in which the majority of the seats would not be directly elected until 2012 (see Rafferty, 1991). In the first legislature of the SAR only 20 out of the intended 60 seats would be directly elected.

In order to answer local demands for greater democracy Britain increased the number of directly elected seats in the Legislative Council to 20 in 1991. The 1991 elections were won by liberal political parties which in turn have pressed for further democratisation turning the Legislative Council into an 'adversarial legislature' (see Lam, 1993). This is the context in which Beijing viewed the political reforms proposed by Governor Chris Patten in October 1992. The reforms which included broadening the franchise in the functional constituencies would have enhanced the level of democratisation before the 1995 elections. Beijing denounced the reforms and threatened to proclaim its own electoral rules which would be implemented in 1997. In April 1993 talks between Britain and China on the reform process in Hong Kong resumed after London accepted that they would be bilateral without formal representation from the colony. The objective for Britain is to maintain political and economic confidence in Hong Kong whilst working with China. The problem is that Britain has little choice in the matter and balancing Britain's interests with both Hong Kong and China will become more difficult as 1997 approaches.

Conclusions

British foreign and defence policy in the new world order has shown strong elements of continuity with the past. Defence policy remains committed to strategic nuclear forces, NATO and the Anglo-American relationship. Atlanticism has continued to condition policy toward Europe and the international system. These elements have mitigated against the emergence of a 'European identity' or a radical restructuring of defence policy. Britain's foreign policy has recognised the changed nature of the international system but is equally a response to the new disorder within it. The scale and form of international problems have reinforced the tendency to conservatism in foreign policy. The uncertain nature of the new international order has made fundamental change unattractive to decision makers.

16

Conclusion: An Overview of Developments

The focus of this book has been on the contemporary agenda for public policy, and the development of that agenda in the Thatcher and post-Thatcher Conservative administrations. We have seen the uneven and often contradictory ways in which the ideologies and strategies of the New Right have influenced policy in particular areas. Radical policy agendas have emerged in the different policy areas at varying points over the four Conservative governments since 1979; for example, trade union reform was very much a feature of the first two Thatcher administrations, whereas radical change in educational policy only began to appear on the policy agenda late in the second Thatcher Government. Reaching general conclusions over the nature and impact of public policy under the Conservatives is therefore at best a risk-laden enterprise – it is always a question of *which* particular area of policy. Nevertheless, in this concluding chapter we shall attempt to pull together the various strands of policy reform and reach some overall judgements on the status of public policy in Britain.

From Thatcher to Post-Thatcher Conservatism

A first conclusion would have to be that any radical head of steam built up on policy reform under Thatcher has not abated under post-Thatcher administrations. Clearly, presentational aspects of the policy agenda may have shifted from the confrontational to the more conciliatory. Furthermore, Major's early references to the pursuit of the 'classless society' and the Citizen's Charter seemed a deliberate attempt to demarcate his politics from those of his predecessor. However, two points need to be stressed. On the one hand, the *policy* agenda which has emerged since Thatcher's departure has not, in the main, involved a retraction from New Right principles. Indeed it could be argued that to an extent, at least in certain areas of policy, New Right philosophy has been more aggressively pursued since 1990 than before. The opting out of secondary schools (see Chapter 11), the creation of Hospital Trusts (see Chapter 9), and the expansion of the voluntary and private sectors in the provision of social care (see Chapter 12), have all been as much if not more a feature of post-Thatcher policy as under Thatcher. The Major Government's posturing on income support, particularly in areas such as support for single-parents (see Chapter 13), had indicated that New Right radicalism was very much alive. The November 1993 Budget involved a package of reforms to limit invalidity benefit, sick pay, and unemployment benefit, reforms very much in line with those advocated by bodies such as the Adam Smith Institute. The *Independent* went so far as to talk of 'the gradual dismantling of the Welfare State, which began on Budget Day'. It could even be argued that the advancement of New Right policy has been more successful under the cover of the politics of the 'classless' society, than under the more explicit right-wing rhetoric of Thatcher (see Chapter 3).

On the other hand, further evidence that continuity of the Thatcher agenda has been the order of the day has come from the Major Government's own political rhetoric. As was made clear in Chapter 3, the political problems created for Major by a small Parliamentary majority, and growing dissent over Europe from those right-wing sectors of the Tory Party whose support the Prime Minister needed, had forced even the *presentation* of policy on to a right-wing footing. Nowhere was this more apparent than at the 1993 Conservative Party Conference. In a thinly veiled attempt to win over the rank-and-file of the Party, and through them the anti-Europe, pro-Thatcher wing of the Party, minister after minister presented to the Conference speeches of right-wing populist rhetoric. The Home Secretary's stance on law and order was reminiscent of the attacks on a 'lawless Britain' in the run-up to the 1979 General Election – announcing new custodial sentences for young offenders, more prison building, and so on (see Chapter 8). To this was coupled frequent reference to the 'problem' of lone parents, with allusions to forthcoming changes in single-parent benefits and the removal of housing 'privileges' for single-parent families.

The overall framework for these policies and the rhetoric surrounding them, as was discussed in Chapter 1, was what the Prime Minister called getting 'back to basics'. In his speech to the 1993 Conservative Conference he said:

> We are going to lead Britain back to the values of common sense. It is time to get back to basics; to self-discipline and respect for the law; to consideration for others; to accepting responsibility for yourself and your family.

Michael Portillo, as Chief Secretary to the Treasury, elaborated further on the 'back-to-basics' message:

> It is time to return to traditional values . . . Conservatives do make value judgements. For us, there is a difference between right and wrong. We prize the individual who strives to make the most of his or her talents, who demonstrates a sense of duty to family and community, who esteems himself and his country.

The 1993 Conference launched a campaign which was pursued in the months following that played on New Right, and particularly neo-conservative, notions: individual responsibility; family values; respect for authority and nationhood; self-sufficiency, and so on. Margaret Thatcher gave her endorsement of the approach soon after the Conference in an interview with David Frost. It seemed that not only the policies in question but also the rhetoric surrounding them was acceptable to the pro- Thatcher wing of the party. In early 1994, however, the whole campaign, which had shown signs of success in winning grass roots and wider public support, became embroiled in controversy and dissent when a number of Conservative MPs, including a junior minister and a parliamentary private secretary, were forced to resign – Tim Yeo for fathering two children to single-parents, Alan Duncan after press disclosures over the questionable purchase of a council house, and David Ashby over his wife's claims about his personal involvement with another man (*Sunday Times*, 9 Jan, 1994). In response to these events, ministers and other party members presented contradictory versions of what 'back to basics' really meant, the most contentious issue being whether it involved questions of individual morality (ibid.). What was clear in all of this was that the right-wing of the party saw in the campaign central elements of its own philosophy, as Thatcher's endorsement seemed to indicate. However, her own account of the Cecil Parkinson–Sarah Keays affair (Thatcher, 1993, pp. 310–11) hardly seems to square with the high-minded moralising tone adopted by many in the Conservative Party during the Winter of 1993–4. Indeed, Thatcher noted 'Thankfully, this [the affair and the child born 'out of wedlock'] did not mean the end of Cecil's political career.' (Thatcher, 1993, p. 311), sentiments rather similar to those expressed by John Major when Tim Yeo resigned.

The back-to-basics campaign, therefore, whatever its motive forces in political terms, demonstrated that continuity between the Thatcher and post-Thatcher governments applied both to the policy agenda and to certain features of the political rhetoric within which they were packaged. In policy terms it would seem to have most relevance for social provision and social policy – although the issues raised are not in every case within the remit of government. In education, back-to-basics addressed things bordering on nostalgia: 'orderly classrooms, clear timetables, regular tests, home-work, team sport and uniforms' (*Guardian*, 11 Jan. 1994). Its relevance to social security, as indicated above, applies primarily to single-parenthood, and in particular to making men who are 'absent fathers' take some financial responsibility for their off-spring (see the discussion on the Child Support Agency in Chapter 13). In the field of social services back-to-basics seems mainly targeted at social workers, as purveyors of various 'isms' and 'ologies' rather than 'common sense'. Similarly, in criminal justice back-to-basics involves an attack on social scientific 'theory' of the causes of crime and an insistence that 'prison works' and that the duty of the police is simply to 'catch criminals' (ibid. – see Chapter 8). Running deep throughout the campaign has been a rejection of 'progressivism' and a reassertion of populist notions of 'right' and 'wrong'.

If as we have argued, the evidence therefore points to a great deal of continuity between the Thatcher and post-Thatcher policy agenda, we now need to develop at greater length what such continuity has meant in terms of policy outcomes. What have been the major consequences of the Conservative agenda for public policy?

In the preceding chapters discussion of individual areas of policy has revealed a number of common threads of public policy under the Conservatives. Together they constitute an effective *restructuring of the state* in Britain's economic and social affairs.

A Restructuring of the State?

As we have seen earlier (see Chapter 1), a cornerstone of New Right philosophy is the 'minimal' or 'limited' state – the state is seen as having a limited and specific role in relation to civil society. At its most radical, this view holds that outside of defence and the guarantee of the 'rule of law', the state should not intervene in the lives of its citizens. A central belief amongst those on the New Right is that in post-war Western societies the state has grown well in excess of its essential and necessary role. Above all, state provision of and intervention in 'welfare' matters was identified as the primary distortion of the proper role of the state. When Margaret Thatcher took office in 1979, there was much talk of the 'dismantling of the welfare state', amongst both advocates and adversaries, talk which has continued, as we have seen, in the post-Thatcher era.

The conclusion which presents itself after consideration of each of the major areas of public policy, is that it is more accurate to refer to a *restructuring* of the role of the state rather than a fundamental 'dismantling' of the state (McCarthy, ed. 1989). In Chapter 1 we defined this restructuring as involving above all the shift from that of 'provider' to that of 'facilitator/enabler'. Rather than act as the main player in the provision of services, the state has become increasingly an agent which facilitates the provision of services by other bodies. As was made clear in Chapter 3, this has involved at one and the same time the processes of centralisation, decentralisation and fragmentation of government at central and sub-central levels. Central government has on the one hand accumulated powers over the disposal of services, such as education and health, yet on the other has devolved the actual allocation of services to 'provider units'. This has involved in most cases the by-passing or reduction in the role of the local authorities, and an enhancement of voluntary, private, and non-elected agencies in the provision of services. In this way, the shape and scope of the state in British society has undergone a substantial amount of change since 1979.

There are a number of overlapping mechanisms through which this restructuring has taken place, from the shift from public to private provision, to the internal reshaping of the public sector itself. We shall outline them in turn and illustrate the role they have played in specific areas of policy.

Privatisation

A full discussion of the Conservatives approach to privatisation was given in Chapters 2 and 5, with particular emphasis on the privatisation of the 'public utilities'. This, of course, has been the most marked example of the redrawing of the boundaries between the public and the private sectors. However, as was made clear in that discussion, 'privatisation' takes a variety of forms, from the sale of public assets on the open market to 'contracting out' of certain aspects of a service – such as catering and laundry services within hospitals. In many areas of public policy, Conservative governments have proceeded by stealth, releasing particular areas of a service to the private sector on a piecemeal basis.

Privatisation on this basis has featured in virtually every area of public policy, as previous chapters have made clear. In some cases this has involved moving beyond the contracting out of support services, such as cleaning and catering (where privatisation has become almost universal), to the privatisation of the central service itself. For example, in the law and order area private contractors now undertake many key tasks of the penal system, such as the management of remand centres and secure units, prison escort duties and so on. The privatisation of certain policing functions, such as police escorts of large vehicles on motorways, may well follow suit (see Chapter 8). Another notable example of this trend has been the development of 'community care', where private caring agencies and companies have taken caring responsibilities from local authority social service departments (see Chapter 12). The role of the local authorities has become increasingly one of 'enabler' of care provision actually delivered by outside agencies, either private or voluntary. The shift from public to private provision has also been very much evident in the field of housing, where a variety of government measures have limited the construction of public sector housing and encouraged the expansion of owner occupation and private housing (see Chapter 10).

Privatisation has been closely associated with strategies of 'compulsory competitive tendering' (CCT) and 'market testing'. As was made clear in Chapter 2, local government reforms have required local authorities to put a range of services out to tender. A range of bodies, private companies or associations of former employees, are allowed to compete for contracts with specific price commitments. CCT has been applied to both 'blue-collar' services such as refuse collection and 'white-collar' activities such as computing services. Underpinning these developments has been a belief that private sector and market disciplines will be introduced into the public sector, with consequent improvements in efficiency and effectiveness. According to this view, not only would CCT help reduce the overall cost to the public purse of providing a particular service, it will force the agencies concerned to ask hard questions about whether certain aspects of a service are necessary at all. The process is also linked, less explicitly, with weakening the powers of the local authority trade unions (see Chapter 6) and professional associations, such as social workers (Chapter 12), teachers (Chapter 11) and prison officers (Chapter 8).

Separation of Purchaser/Provider and Internal Markets

Where it has not been possible to privatise public sector provision, the Conservatives have sought to achieve similar results in increased efficiency and cost-reduction (and the weakening of the bargaining position of public sector employees) by introducing the 'disciplines of the market' into the administration and management of public services themselves. This has involved breaking down agencies into those branches which provide a service and those which can be identified as a purchaser of services. The rationale for this development is that it should pressurise suppliers of services to do so at the most economical price, and that it prevents suppliers rather than users defining 'users' needs'. 'Consumer power' will take the place of 'producer power'. It is closely linked to the concept of 'internal markets' whereby suppliers compete with one another – ideally on cost and quality – to provide the service required. This is designed to produce what Le Grand and Bartlett (1993) have termed 'quasi-markets'.

Nowhere is this more apparent than in health service reform. As discussed in Chapter 9, hospitals have been enticed to form individual 'trusts' which compete with one another for health contracts from the purchasing units, the district health authorities. Furthermore, general practitioners have been allowed to become 'budget holders' who, as purchasers of hospital services, can 'shop around' for the health care they seek on behalf of their patients. Thus where the separation of purchaser and provider cannot (at least not yet) come about by privatising the supplier – as in 'community care' – it can come about by dividing the public sector into competing agencies.

Private Sector Styles of Management

Another, related, strategy for introducing market disciplines within the public sector has been to reform management structures and styles, often referred to as the 'new managerialism' (see Chapter 3, and Farnham and Horton, 1993). In general, it has been associated with the concept of the 'right to manage', strengthening the powers of managers relative to that of employees (see Chapter 6). Governments have used a combination of financial pressures and, where necessary, legislation (as with the police discipline code – see Chapter 8), to create environments in which public sector managers are placed under pressure to operate according to private sector models of management.

A number of mechanisms have been employed to achieve this goal. Public sector organisations have been encouraged to form 'cost centres' within their organisations – consistent with the 'internal markets' system – and managers of those centres have had to operate with fixed income allocated from the centre. Managers have had to operate within strict financial frameworks which have encouraged them to cut costs on the one hand, and seek forms of income generation to supplement their budget on the other. For example, police training schools have in many areas become cost centres within police forces. Force training officers have been given fixed income within which all costs incurred in training must be covered. In a number of cases training managers have decided to rent out their properties to outside bodies for conferences and the like in order to increase their total budget. Such developments, within the police service and in other public sector organisations, have been given impetus by the Audit Commission, which has been highly instrumental in introducing private sector philosophy into public organisations.

More generally, public bodies have been forced or encouraged to bring into decision-making positions people with experience in the private sector, either to key management positions (for example, the creation of 'general management' within the health service, which in many cases led to the recruitment of former private sector managers – see Chapter 9) or to sit on newly constituted boards of governors (such as schools boards of governors – see Chapter 11). The rationale for such measures has been that they will facilitate the spread of 'best practice' from the private sector throughout the public sector, in terms of improved efficiency and effectiveness. Business plans, quality control, financial management, performance measurement, internal audit, and other features of management strategy have as a consequence become a common feature of public sector management, whatever their practical benefits in service delivery (for a critique see Farnham and Horton, 1993). There is no doubting, however, the extent to which a management culture of 'value-for-money' has permeated the public sector since 1979.

More recently the *Citizen's Charter* has been closely associated with many of the developments outlined in the previous paragraphs; the background and implications of the Charter were discussed in Chapter 3. It has involved the attempt to strengthen 'consumer power' in relation to public services in the absence of genuine consumer choice. Consumers can be given a statement of the standards of service they can expect from any particular public organisation. As previous chapters (for detailed discussions of individual charters see Chapters 8 and 9) make clear, the Charter movement has been implemented in a range of policy areas. As well as aiming to improve the responsiveness of service providers to 'consumers' there has also been an increasing emphasis upon improving public sector management and 'reinventing government', i.e. raising fundamental questions about what government should do, which holds the potential for a further redrawing of the boundaries between public and private.

Public Expenditure

Throughout the period since 1979 there has been constant pressure to restrict the growth of public expenditure, although the extent to which successive Conservative administrations have been successful in their aims is open to question. However, more recently, as the PSBR has moved from a negative amount in the years 1987–90 to a projected £50 billion for 1993–4, pressure has increased to restrain the growth of public expenditure (see Chapter 5 for more detail). Even though part of the increase can be seen as cyclical, i.e. the result of a long and deep recession, renewed pressure has emerged for public expenditure to be reduced. The projected Public Expenditure Control Totals contained in the Autumn 1993 budget for the financial year 1993–4 is £244.7 bn whilst that for 1994–5 is £251.3 bn; according to the Government's own calculations the 1994-95 figure entails a 1.4 per cent cut in public expenditure in real terms. At the same time the PSBR is projected to fall from the £50 bn projected in 1993–4 to £21.0 bn by 1995–6. However, this is based upon the assumption that the economy will grow by around 2.5 per cent in 1994 and perhaps by even more in succeeding years. Should these rates of growth fail to materialise then the pressures for further real cuts in public expenditure, particularly on the welfare state, will become enormous, especially given the hostile attitudes expressed by certain right-wing members of the Cabinet who are opposed to state intervention, and the associated public expenditure, on principle. Michael Portillo, as Chief Secretary to the Treasury, summed up this view in the following terms, 'The government should . . . only take money from taxpayers to spend on things that governments can provide' (Portillo, 1993, p. 6). Thus current levels of public expenditure in general, and on the welfare state in particular, are viewed as both undesirable and unsustainable (for a rather different view on the welfare state see Hills, 1993).

It is quite likely, therefore, that the Government will find itself facing a series of difficult choices over public expenditure in the run up to a general election. The last time it faced such choices in the run up to the 1992 election, according to Nigel Lawson (1992, p. 1015), there was '. . . a worrying discretionary relaxation of public spending control . . .' as government sought to 'buy' votes. At the very least the Major government was in part the author of its own subsequent discomfiture over public expenditure. There is every likelihood that it will employ the same tactics in the run up to the next general election. Thus it seems likely that public expenditure will remain at the centre of political and policy debate for the rest of the decade.

Conclusion

In the last instance it is, of course, difficult to draw any definitive conclusions about recent developments let alone future developments. However, the individual policy-based chapters in this book have documented changes, often of a radical nature, across a range of policy areas. Moreover, most have suggested that more change is likely in the future; in part this will be the result of continuing attempts to redraw the boundaries between public and private sectors, i.e. an ideologically inspired series of attempts to restructure the state. At the same time change will also emerge from the Government's ever more pressing need to control public expenditure. As a result the search for new ways to provide and finance services will be stepped up and it is likely that further attempts will be made to persuade the 'well-heeled' members of society to opt-out of state provision, leaving behind only the poorest and most vulnerable members of society. In such a situation government, once rid of those with a 'voice', may well find it easier to push through more radical cuts in state provision. However, such views are the subject of speculation and we must await the outcomes of developments before any authoritative judgements can be reached.

Guide to Further Reading

Chapter 2

Greenwood and Wilson (1989) provides the most useful general survey of the structure of government in Britain. Hennessy (1989) and Stoker (1991) offer respectively excellent accounts of central government and local government. Hogwood (1987) and Jordan and Richardson (1987) provide good overviews of policy-making in British government.

Chapter 3

Perhaps the best overview of central government is provided in Hennessy (1989) while James (1992) provides a thorough and readable discussion of the prime minister's role and the cabinet. Stoker (1991) and Rhodes (1988) offer comprehensive overviews of government beyond Whitehall. J. Richardson (ed.), *Policy Styles in Western Europe* (London: Allen & Unwin, 1982) provides a valuable, if dated, comparative approach to policy styles. On the constitutional front Mount (1992) contributes an interesting discussion. Pollitt (1990) is the best, and most comprehensive, discussion of managerialism.

Chapter 4

Urwin (1991) offers a general historical overview of the development of the European Community; whereas George (1990) provides a historical account of relations between Britain and the European Community. George (1991) and Pinder (1991) give useful general accounts of how the European Community works. Nugent (1991) provides an excellent account of the institutions and policy-making processes of the European Community. Lodge (1993) offers a comprehensive review of policy developments in the European Community, including the Maastricht Treaty. Keohane and Hoffmann (1991) gives a useful account of the integration process in the European Community exploring the tensions between autonomy and interdependence of member states.

Chapter 5

The economics of the Thatcher years are now rather well documented: good single sources include Mitchie (1992), Smith (1992) and Johnson (1991). A shorter review is presented by Dunn and Smith in Savage and Robins (eds) (1990). Green (1989) provides a challenging alternative view of the economics and politics of Thatcher's economic strategy. Privatisation and supply-side policies are covered in a very wide range of sources: a general review of the main issues and literature is given by Marsh (1991), whilst Parker (1991) is a useful short analysis. More substantial sources include Richardson (1990), Veljanovski (1989) and Vickers and Yarrow (1988).

A detailed but digestible review of post-Thatcher economic policy in so far as it affects British industry is given by Eltis (1993), whilst Gowland (1993) examines the future for British macroeconomic policy after leaving the ERM. Anon. (1993) is a succinct summary of the government's policy position in 1993. Given the key role of the objective of controlling inflation, the article on 'how low is low enough inflation?' in *The Economist* (7 Nov. 1992) is pertinent.

Chapter 6

For up-to-date details of and debates about the government's training and enterprise schemes see the Unemployment Unit's 'Bulletins' and 'Briefings', and the Department of Employment *Gazette*. For a coverage of recent developments in public policy on employment relations refer to Farnham (1993b, Ch. 7).

Chapter 7

For anyone not familiar with the scientific aspects of environmental issues, Goudie (1990) and Simmons (1989) are suitable introductions. There are now many books on environmental ideas and ideologies – Pepper (1984) is a good starting point. The debates surrounding the application of these ideas to politics are covered by Dobson (1990), Atkinson (1991) and Eckersley (1992). Some of the difficulties raised by science–environment policy relations are discussed by Ravetz (1990)

Chapter 8

An excellent overview of developments in British policing and policing policy is provided in Reiner (1992). An interesting radical analysis of law and order policy and the political right can be found in Brake and Hale (1992). For a study of developments in criminal justice and law and order policy across a range of areas see Stockdale and Casale (eds) (1992).

Chapter 9

A useful semi-annual series reviewing the 'progress' of the NHS reforms is published in the *British Medical Journal*. A detailed perusal of the original policy documents (DoH, 1991, DoH, 1992) is essential for anyone seeking an understanding of the patient's charter or the health of the nation debate.

Chapter 10

Birchall (ed.) (1992) is an excellent collection of articles which will serve as a very good starting point for any one interested in housing in the 1990s. The Inquiry into British Housing (1991) is essential reading for anyone interested in housing issues as is the bi-monthly journal *Roof*. On housing associations Cope (1990) and Page (1993) are excellent starting points; Burrows and Walentowicz (1992) is a good starting point for anyone interested in homelessness.

Chapter 11

The key issues raised by recent changes in education, most notably the Education Reform Act, 1988, are well covered in Bash and Coulby (1989) and Flude and Hammer (1990). An useful overview of the changes introduced since 1979 may be found in Education Group II (1991).

Chapter 12

For a wide-ranging collection of essays on the theme of community care the reader edited by Barnet *et al.* (1993) is a useful starting point. In particular, the chapter by Alan Walker (pp. 204–26) provides a robust critique of contemporary policy. Of official publications the Griffiths Report (1988) remains the most readable and provides a rationale for the current legislative framework within which community care services are developing. The issues raised by Inquiries into high-profile child abuse cases between 1980 and 1989 are explored in the Department of Health publication *Child Abuse* (HMSO, 1991). The Children Act Report 1992 (HMSO, Cmnd 2144, 1993) and the discussion of the implementation of the Act by Cohen (1993) are the first major reviews of the impact of this new statutory framework for child care services.

Chapter 13

The continual adjustment of social security policy over the years since 1979 has rendered many excellent discussions of the subject out of date. A recently published book with a rather wider brief, Pete Alcock's *Understanding Poverty* (1993) review many of the key issues, as does the present author's rather older book (Hill, 1990) which he will update in due course. Parker's book (Parker, 1989) advocating basic income provides a good discussion of the many problems about social security in its earlier chapters.

An important way to keep abreast of social security policy issues is to consult regularly the journal *Benefits* and two publications which emanate from the Child Poverty Action Group, *Poverty* and the *Welfare Rights Bulletin*. The latter organisation also produces annually a series of practical guides on social security policy.

Chapter 14

The most comprehensive and detailed examination of British government policy in the 1980s is Cunningham (1991). There is a reasonable survey of specific problems confronting policy-makers in Connolly and Loughlin (eds) (1990). A more sophisticated analysis of the complexities of British strategies in the first half of the 1980s is to be found in

Brew and Patterson (1985), although they failed to foresee the signing of the Anglo-Irish Agreement. For the Unionist reaction to that Agreement see Aughey (1989); and for a survey of the attitudes of policy-makers and politicians see O'Malley (1990). There have been passing references to Northern Ireland in most of the recent political autobiographies. The most serious and by far the most important insights are to be found in the memoirs of the two signatories of the Anglo-Irish Agreement, namely Thatcher (1993) and FitzGerald (1991). The most trenchant commentary is to be found in Lawson (1992)

Chapter 15

Byrd (1991) provides a good overview of defence policy from Thatcher to Major. Lodge (1993) includes a section on external perspectives. Matthews (1993) reviews the Gulf War from a number of perspectives. Rafferty (1991) offers a useful history of Hong Kong down to 1990. Sweeney (1993) and Timmerman (1992) provide accounts of the arming of Iraq. The journal *World Today* is a valuable source of contemporary information on international affairs.

Bibliography

Ainley, P. (1993) 'The Legacy of the Manpower Services Commission', in Taylor-Gooby, P. and Lawson, R. (eds) *Markets and Managers: New Issues in the Delivery of Welfare* (Buckingham: Open University Press).

Alcock, P. (1993) *Understanding Poverty* (London: Macmillan).

AMA (Association of Metropolitan Authorities) (1979) *Policies for Improvement* (London: AMA).

Anon. (1992) 'How Low is Low Enough Inflation?', *The Economist*, 7 Nov, pp. 21–4.

Anon. (1993) 'Monetary Policy', *Economic Briefing*, 5, August (London: HM Treasury).

Atkinson, A. (1991) *Principles of Political Ecology* (London: Belhaven).

Atkinson, R. and Durden, P. (1990) 'Housing Policy in the Thatcher Years', in Savage, S. and Robins, L. (eds) *Public Policy under Thatcher* (London: Macmillan).

Audit Commission (1986) *Making a Reality of Community Care* (London: HMSO).

Audit Commission (1989) *Housing the Homeless: The Local Authority Role* (London: HMSO).

Audit Commission (1992) *Community Care: Managing the Cascade of Change* (London: HMSO).

Aughey, A. (1989) *Under Siege: Ulster Unionism and the Anglo-Irish Agreement* (Belfast: Blackstaff Press; London: Hurst).

Aughey, A. (1992) 'Northern Ireland: A Putting Together of Parts', in Jones, B. and Robins, L. (eds), *Two Decades in British Politics* (Manchester University Press).

Bagehot, W. (1963) *The English Constitution* (Glasgow: Fontana).

Barclay, G. and Turner, D. (1991) *Information and the Criminal Justice System* Home Office Research Bulletin No. 31 (London: HMSO).

Barclay, P. (1982) *Social Workers: Their Role and Task – Report of a Working Party* (London: Bedford Square Press).

Barnet, J. *et al.* (eds) (1993) *Community Care: A Reader* (London: Macmillan).

Bartlett, A. (1990) 'TECs – Will They Succeed?', *Regional Studies*, vol. 24, pp. 77–9.

Bash, L. and Coulby, D. (1989) *The Education Reform Act: Competition and Control* (London: Cassell).

Benn, T. (1980) 'The Case for a Constitutional Premiership', *Parliamentary Affairs*, vol. 33, pp. 7–22.

Bennett, R. J. (1990) 'Vocational Education and Training', *Regional Studies*, vol. 24 (1) pp. 65–82.

Benyon, J. and Bourne, C. (eds) (1986) *The Police: Powers, Procedures and Proprieties* (London: Pergamon).

Berlin, I. (1990) *Four Essays on Liberty* (Oxford: Oxford University Press).

317

Beveridge, W. (1942) *Social Insurance and Allied Services*, Cmnd 6404 (London: HMSO).

Birchall, J. (ed.) (1992) *Housing Policy in the 1990s* (London: Routledge).

Blake, R. (1985) *The Conservative Party from Peel to Thatcher* (London: Fontana).

Blom-Cooper, L. (1985) *Report of the Committee of Inquiry into the Death of Jasmine Beckford* (London: Borough of Brent).

Blowers, A. (1987) 'Transition or Transformation? Environmental Policy under Thatcher', *Public Administration*, 65, pp. 277–94.

Boehmer-Christiansen, S. (1989) 'The Role of Science in the International Regulation of Pollution', in Andersen, W. and Ostreny, W. (eds) *International Resource Management: The Role of Science and Politics* (London: Belhaven).

Bogdanor, V. (1983) 'The Meaning of Mrs Thatcher's Victory', *Encounter*, vol. 60/61, September, pp. 14–19.

Bottomley, K. and Pease, K. (1986) *Crime and Punishment: Interpreting the Data* (Milton Keynes: Open University Press).

Bottoms, A. (1980) 'An Introduction to "The Coming Crisis" ', in Bottoms, A. and Preston, R. (eds) *The Coming Penal Crisis: A Criminological and Theological Exploration* (Edinburgh: Scottish Academic Press).

Boyce, D. G. (1988) *The Irish Question and British Politics* (London: Macmillan).

Boyson, R. (1978) *Center Forward* (London: Temple Smith).

Bradbeer, J. (1990) 'Environmental Policy' in Savage, S. P. and Robins, L. (eds) (1990).

Brake, M. and Hale, C. (1992) *Public Order and Private Lives* (London: Routledge).

Bramley, G. *et al.* (eds) (1989) *Homelessness and the London Housing Market* (Bristol: University of Bristol, School of Advanced Urban Studies).

Brandon, D. *et al.* (1980) 'The Survivors: a Study of Homeless Young Newcomers to London and the Responses to Them', cited in Liddiard, M. (1992).

Brew P. and Patterson, H. (1985) *The British State and the Ulster Crisis* (London: Verso).

Brew, P. and Patterson, H. (1987) 'The New Stalemate: Unionism and the Anglo-Irish Agreement', in Teague, P. (ed.), *Beyond the Rhetoric* (London: Lawrence and Wishart).

Brittan, S. (1975) 'The Economic Contradictions of Democracy', *British Journal of Political Science*, vol. 5, pp. 129–59.

Brooke, R. (1989) *Managing the Enabling Authority* (London: Longman).

Buchanan, J. (ed.) (1978) *The Economics of Politics* (London: IEA).

Buchanan, J. and Tullock, G. (1965) *The Calculus of Consent* (Ann Arbor: Michigan).

Bulpitt, J. (1986) 'The Discipline of the New Democracy', *Political Studies*, vol. XXXIV, pp. 19–39.

Burnham, J. and Jones, G. (1993) 'Advising Margaret Thatcher: the Prime Minister's Office and the Cabinet Office Compared', *Political Studies*, vol. XLI, pp. 299–314.

Burrows, L. and Walentowicz, L. (1992) *Homes Cost Less than Homelessness* (London: Shelter).

Butler-Schloss, L. (1988) *Report of the Inquiry into Child Abuse in Cleveland, 1987* (London: HMSO).

Byrd, J. (ed.) (1991) *British Defence Policy: Thatcher and Beyond* (Hemel Hempstead: Philip Allan).

Cabinet Office (1992a) *Questions of Procedure for Ministers* (London: Cabinet Office).

Cabinet Office (1992b) *Ministerial Committees of the Cabinet: Membership and Terms of Reference* (London, Cabinet Office).

Cadogan Group (1992) *Northern Limits* (Belfast: Cadogan Group).

Cavadino, M. and Dignan, J. (1992) *The Penal System: An Introduction* (London: Sage).

Christie, N. (1993) *Crime Control as Industry* (London: Routledge).

Clarke, H. (1993) in *FE Now*, no. 2 September 1993.

Clarke, J. and Newman, J. (1994) 'Managing to Survive? Dilemmas of Changing Organizational Forms in the Public Sector', in Deakin, N. and Page, R. (eds), *The Costs of Welfare* (Aldershot: Avebury).

Clarke, M. and Stewart, J. (1992) 'Empowerment: A Theme for the 1990s', *Local Government Studies*, vol. 18, no. 2, pp. 18–26.

Clough, N., Lee, V., Menter, I., Trodd, T., and Whitty, G. (1989) 'Restructuring the Education System?', in Bash, L. and Coulby, D. (eds), *The Education Reform Act: Competition and Control* (London: Cassell).

Cmnd 1599 (1991) *The Citizen's Charter* (London: HMSO).

Cmnd 1730 (1991) *Competing for Quality* (London: HMSO).

Cmnd 2101 (1992) *The Citizen's Charter. First Report: 1992* (London: HMSO).

Cmnd 2290 (1993) *Open Government*, Cmnd 2290 (London, HMSO).

Cochrane, A. (1991) 'The Changing State of Local Government: Restructuring for the 1990s', *Public Administration*, vol. 69, pp. 281–302.

Cockerell, M., Hennessy, P. and Walker, D. (1985) *Sources Close to the Prime Minister* (London: Macmillan).

Cohen, N., Judd, J., Jones, J. and Clement, B. (1993) 'What Happened to Democracy?', *Independent on Sunday*, 28 Mar, 1993.

Cohen, P. (1992) *A New Deal for Children?* (London: Association of County Councils).

Coleman, D. (1992) 'The 1987 Housing Policy: an Enduring Reform?' in Birchall, J. (ed.) (1992).

Commission for Racial Equality (1988) *Homelessness and Discrimination* (London: CRE).

Committee on the Civil Service (1968) *Report*, vol. 1, Cmnd 3638 (London: HMSO).

Connolly, M. and Loughlin, S. (eds) (1990) *Public Policy in Northern Ireland* (Belfast: Policy Research Institute).

Cope, H. (1990) *Housing Associations: Policy and Practice* (London: Macmillan).

Cowling, M. (1990) 'The Sources of the New Right', *Encounter*, vol. LXXXV, pp. 3–13.

Cowling, M. (ed.) (1978) *Conservative Essays* (London: Cassell).

Crook, A. (1992) 'Private Rented Housing and the Impact of Deregulation', in Birchall, J. (ed.) (1992).

Crossman, R. (1963) 'Introduction', in Bagehot, W., *The English Constitution* (Glasgow: Fontana).

Crouch, C. (1979) *The Politics of Industrial Relations* (London: Fontana).

Cunningham, M. (1991) *British Government Policy in Northern Ireland 1969–89: Its Nature and Execution* (Manchester: Manchester University Press).

Cutler, T. (1992) 'Vocational Training and British Economic Performance: a Further Instalment of the "British Labour Problem?" ', *Work, Employment and Society*, vol. 6, pp. 161–83.

Daniel, W. and Millward, N. (1983) *Workplace Industrial Relations in Britain* (London: Heinemann).

Dean, H. and Taylor-Gooby, P. (1992) *Dependency Culture* (Hemel Hempstead: Harvester/Wheatsheaf).

Dennison, B. (1989) 'The Competitive Edge – Attracting More Pupils', *School Organisation*, vol. 9, no. 2, pp. 179–86.

Department of Employment (1983) *Democracy in Trade Unions* (London: HMSO).

Department of Employment (1988) *Employment for the 1990s* Cmnd 540 (London: HMSO).

Departments of Health and for Wales (DoH) (1993) *Children Act Report 1992*, Cmnd 2144 (London: HMSO).

DHSS (1972) *National Health Service Reorganization: England* (London: HMSO).

DHSS (1978) *Social Assistance* (London: DHSS).

DHSS (1979) *Consultative Paper: Patients First* (London: DHSS).

DHSS (1981) *Growing Older* (London: HMSO).

DHSS (1983) *NHS Management Inquiry Report* (London: DHSS).

DHSS (1985) *Review of Child Care Law: Consultative Document* (London: HMSO).

DHSS (1987) *Promoting Better Health – The Government's Programme for Improving Primary Health Care* (London: HMSO).

DHSS (1988) *Public Health in England* (London: HMSO).

DHSS (1989) *The Law on Child Care and Family Services* (London: HMSO).

Dobson, A. (1990) *Green Political Thought* (London: HarperCollins).

DoH (1989a) *Working for Patients* (London: HMSO).

DoH (1989b) *Children Act* (London: HMSO).

DoH (1990) *Community Care in the Next Decade and Beyond: Policy Guidance* (London: HMSO).

DoH (1991a) *The Patient's Charter* (London: HMSO).

DoH (1991b) *Child Abuse: a Study of Inquiry Reports 1980–1989* (London: HMSO).

DoH (1991c) *Care Management and Assessment: a Practitioners' Guide* (London: HMSO).

DoH (1992) *The Health of the Nation* (London: HMSO).

DoH/DHSS (1989) *Caring for People: Community Care in the Next Decade and Beyond* (London: HMSO).

Doling, J., Karn, V. and Stafford, B. (1985) 'How Far Can Privatisation Go', *National Westminister Bank Quarterly Review*, August, pp. 42–52.

Donnison, D. (1979) 'Social Policy since Titmuss', *Journal of Social Policy*, vol. 8 (2).

Donnison, D. (1982) *The Politics of Poverty* (Oxford: Martin Robertson).

Donnison, D. (1993) *Homeless Young People in Scotland: The Role of the Social Work Services* (Edinburgh: Scottish Office).

Dorset Social Services Department (1993) *Dorset's Community Care Plan – Draft* (Dorset: Social Services Department).

Dowding, K. (1993) 'Government at the Centre', in Dunleavy, P., Gamble, A., Holliday, I. and Peele, G. (eds), *Developments in British Politics 4* (London: Macmillan).

Dunleavy, P. (1990) 'Government at the Centre', in Dunleavy, P., Gamble, A., Holliday, I. and Peele G (eds) *Developments in British Politics 3* (London, Macmillan).

Dunleavy, P. and Rhodes, R. (1990) 'Core Executive Studies in Britain', *Public Administration*, vol. 68, pp. 3–28.

Dunn, M. and Smith, S. (1990) 'Economic Policy and Privatisation', in Savage, S. and Robins, L. (eds) (1990).

Dunn, R. *et al.* (1987) 'The Geography of Council House Sales in England – 1979–85', *Urban Studies*, vol. 24, pp. 47–59.

Eckersley, R. (1992) *Environmentalism and Political Theory* (London: UCL Press).

Eckstein, H. (1958) *English Health Service* (Cambridge: Harvard University Press).

Education Group II (1991) *Education Limited: Schooling, Training and the New Right in England since 1979* (London: Unwin Hyman).

Eltis, W. (1993) 'How Macroeconomic Policy can Best Assist UK Industry', *Economics and Business Education*, vol 1.1(2), pp. 60–8.

Ermisch, J. (1990) *Fewer Babies, Longer Lives* (cited in Greve, J. 1990).

Farnham, D. (1990) 'Trade Union Policy 1979–89: Restriction or Reform?', in Savage, S. and Robins, L. (eds) (1990).

Farnham, D. (1993a) 'Human Resources Management in the Public Sector: Leading or Following the Private Sector?', *Public Policy and Administration*, Special Edition, Spring.

Farnham, D. (1993b) *Employee Relations* (London: Institute of Personnel Management).

Farnham, D. and Horton, S. (eds) (1993) *Managing the New Public Services* (London: Macmillan).

Fimister, G. and Hill, M. (1993) 'Delegating Implementation Problems: Social Security, Housing and Community Care in Britain', in Hill, M. (ed.) *New Agendas in the Study of the Policy Process* (Hemel Hempstead: Harvester-Wheatsheaf).

Finegold, D. and Sockice, D. (1988) 'The Failure of Training in Britain: Analysis and Prescription', *Oxford Review of Economic Policy*, vol. 4, no. 3, pp. 21–53.

Finn, D. (1987) *Training without Jobs: New Deals and Broken Promises* (London: Macmillan).

FitzGerald, G. (1991) *All in a Life* (London: Macmillan).

Flude, M. and Hammer, M. (eds) (1990) *The Education Reform Act, 1988. Its Origins and Implications* (London: Falmer Press).

Flynn, A. *et al.* (1990) 'Taking the Next Steps: the Changing Management of Government', *Parliamentary Affairs*, vol. 43, pp. 159–78.

Foley, M. (1993) *The Rise of the British Presidency* (Manchester: Manchester University Press).

Forrest, R. and Murie, A. (1983) 'Residualisation and Council Housing', *Journal of Social Policy*, vol. 12, pp. 453–68.

Forrest, R. and Murie, A. (1986) 'Marginalization and Subsidized Individualism', *International Journal of Urban and Regional Research*, vol. 10, pp. 46–65.

Fox-Harding, L. (1991) *Perspectives in Child Care Policy* (London: Longman).

Friedman, M. (1962) *Capitalism and Freedom* (with the assistance of Rose Friedman) (Chicago: University of Chicago Press).

Fry, G. (1987) 'The Thatcher Government, the Financial Management Initiative, and the New Civil Service', *Public Administration*, vol. 66, pp. 1–20.

George, S. (1990) *An Awkward Partner* (Oxford: Oxford University Press).

George, S. (1991) *Politics and Policy in the European Community* (Oxford: Oxford University Press).

Glennerster, H., Owens, P. and Matsaganis, M. (1992) *A Foothold for Fundholding* (London: King's Fund).

Goudie, A. (1990) *The Human Impact on the Natural Environment*, 3rd edn (Oxford: Blackwell).

Gowland, D. (1993) 'UK Macroeconomic Policy after the ERM', *Economics and Business Education*, vol. 1.1(1), pp. 18–21.

Grant, W. (1993) *The Politics of Economic Policy* (Hemel Hempstead: Harvester-Wheatsheaf).

Green, D. (1982) *The Welfare State: For Rich or for Poor* (London: IEA).

Green, D. (1987) *The New Right* (Brighton: Wheatsheaf).

Green, D. (1992) 'Liberty, Poverty and the Underclass', in Smith, D. (ed.) *Understanding the Underclass* (London: Policy Studies Institute).

Green, F. (ed) (1989) *The Restructuring of the UK Economy* (Brighton: Wheatsheaf).

Green, P. (1990) *The Enemy Without* (Milton Keynes: Open University Press).

Greenwood, D. (1991) 'Expenditure and Management' in Byrd, P. (ed.), *British Defence Policy: Thatcher and Beyond* (Hemel Hempstead: Philip Allan).

Greenwood, J. and Wilson, D. (1989) *Public Administration in Britain Today* (London: Unwin Hyman).

Greve, J. (1990) *Homelessness in Britain* (York: Joseph Rowntree Foundation).

Griffiths Report (1988) *Community Care: Agenda for Action* (London: HMSO).

Hailsham, Lord (1976) 'Elective Dictatorship', *The Listener*, 21 Oct. 1976, pp. 496–500.

Hall, S. (1983) 'The Great Moving Right Show', in Hall, S. and Jacques, M. (eds) *The Politics of Thatcherism* (London: Lawrence and Wishart).

Halliday, F. (1989) *The Making of the Second Cold War* (London: Hutchinson).

Ham, C. (1991) 'Revisiting the Internal Market', *British Medical Journal*, vol. 302, pp. 251–2.

Ham, C. (1992) 'What Future for the Regions', *British Medical Journal*, vol. 305, pp. 130–1.

Hambleton, R. (1992) 'Decentralisation and Democracy in UK Local Government', *Public Money and Management*, July–Sept., pp. 9–20.

Hamill, J. (1993) 'South Africa: from Codesa to Leipzig?', *World Today*, vol. 49, pp. 12–16.

Hardin, G. (1968) 'The Tragedy of the Commons', *Science*, vol. 162 pp. 1243–8.

Harris, R. (1988) *Beyond the Welfare State* (London: IEA).

Harris, R. (1990) *Good and Faithful Servant* (London: Faber and Faber).

Harrison, J. (1992) *Housing Associations after the 1988 Housing Act* (Bristol: University of Bristol, School for Advanced Urban Studies).

Hayek, F. (1944) *The Road to Serfdom* (London: Routledge & Kegan Paul).

Hayek, F. (1960) *The Constitution of Liberty* (London: Routledge & Kegan Paul).

Healey, D. (1989) *The Time of My Life* (London: Penguin).

Heclo, H. and Wildavsky, A. (1981) *The Private Government of Public Money* (London: Macmillan).

Hennessy, P. (1986a) 'Helicopter Crashes into Cabinet: Prime Minister and Constitution Hurt', *Journal of Law and Society*, vol. 13, pp. 423–32.

Hennessy, P. (1986b) *Cabinet* (Oxford: Blackwell).

Hennessy, P. (1987) 'The Prime Minister, the Cabinet and the Thatcher Personality', in Biddiss, R. and Minogue, K. (eds), *Thatcherism* (London: Macmillan).

Hennessy, P. (1989) *Whitehall* (London: Secker and Warburg).

Hill, M. (1984), 'The Implementation of Housing Benefit', *Journal of Social Policy*, vol. 3, pp. 297–320.

Hill, M. (1989) 'Income Maintenance and Local Government: Implementing Central Control?', *Critical Social Policy*, 25, pp. 18–36.

Hill, M. (1990) *Social Security Policy in Britain* (Cheltenham: Edward Elgar).

Hills, J. (1993) *The Future of the Welfare State* (York: Joseph Rowntree Foundation).

Hills, J. (ed.) (1990) *The State of Welfare* (Oxford: Clarendon Press).

HMSO (1985) *Reform of Social Security: Programme for Action*, Cmnd 9691, London: HMSO).

HMSO (1989) *Caring for People: Community Care in the Next Decade and Beyond*, Cmnd 849 (London: HMSO).

HMSO (1993) *Social Trends 23* (London: HMSO).

HMSO (1994) *Home Office Research and Statistics Department: Research Findings No.2* (London: HMSO).

Hogwood, B. (1987) *From Crisis to Complacency?* (Oxford: Oxford University Press).

Housing and Construction Statistics, 1981–1992 (1992) *Housing and Construction Statistics, 1981–1991* (London: HMSO).

Hudson, B. (1987) *Justice Through Punishment* (London: Macmillan).

Hudson, B. (1993) *Penal Policy and Social Justice* (London: Macmillan).

Huhne, C. (1993) 'Public Sector Must Change its Culture', *The Independent on Sunday*, 6 June 1993, p. 9.

Hurd, D. (1991) *Conservatism in the Nineties* (London: Conservative Political Centre).

Inquiry into British Housing (1985) *Inquiry into British Housing* (York: Joseph Rowntree Foundation).

Inquiry into British Housing (1991) *Inquiry into British Housing. Second Report* (York: Joseph Rowntree Foundation).

James, S. (1992) *British Cabinet Government* (London: Routledge).

Jenkins, K., Caines, K. and Jackson, A. (1988) *Improving Management in Government: The Next Steps* (London: HMSO).

Johnson, C. (1991) *The Economy under Mrs Thatcher 1979–1990* (London: Penguin Books).

Johnson, N. (1990) *Reconstructing the Welfare State* (Hemel Hempstead: Harvester-Wheatsheaf).

Jones, G. (1985) 'The Prime Minister's Aides', in King, A. (ed.), *The British Prime Minister* (London: Macmillan).

Jones, G. (1989) 'A Revolution in Whitehall? Changes in British Central Government since 1979', *West European Politics*, vol. 12, pp. 238–61.

Jones, G. (1990) 'Mrs Thatcher and the Power of the PM', *Contemporary Record*, vol. 3(4), pp. 2–6.

Jordan, A. and Richardson, J. (1987) *British Politics and the Policy Process*, (London: Allen and Unwin).

Judge, D. (1993) *The Parliamentary State* (London: Sage).

Karn, V. *et al.* (1985) *Home Ownership in the Inner City* (Aldershot: Gower).

Kavanagh, D. (1990) *Thatcherism and British Politics* (Oxford: Oxford University Press).

Kearns, J. (1991) 'Active Citizenship and Urban Governance', *Transactions of the Institute of British Geographers*, vol. 17, pp. 20–34.

Keegan, W. (1984) *Mrs Thatcher's Economic Experiment* (London: Penguin).

Kellner, P. and Crowther-Hunt, Lord (1980) *The Civil Servants* (London: Macdonald).

Kemp, P. (1990) 'Next Steps for the British Civil Service', *Governance*, vol. 3, pp. 186–96.

Kemp, P. (1992) 'Housing', in Marsh, D. and Rhodes, R. (eds) (1992) *Implementing Thatcherite Policies* (Buckingham: Open University).

Kendall, I. and Moon, G. (1990) 'Health Policy', in Savage, S. and Robins, L. (eds) (1990).

Kennet, P. (ed.) (1992) *New Approaches to Homelessness* (Bristol: Bristol University, School of Advanced Urban Studies).

Keohane, R. and Hoffmann, S. (eds) (1991) *The New European Community* (Boulder, Co: Westview Press).

Killeen, D. (1988) *Estranged: Homeless 16 and 17 Year Olds and the Social Security Act 1988* (London: Shelter).

King, A. (1975) 'Overload: Problems of Government in the 1970s', *Political Studies*, vol. XXIII, pp. 162–96.

King, A. (1988) 'Margaret Thatcher as a Political Leader', in Skidelsy, R. (ed.), *Thatcherism* (London: Chatto and Windus).

King, A. (1993) 'Cabinet Co-ordination or Prime Ministerial Dominance?', in Budge, I. and McKay, D. (eds), *The Developing British Political System* (Harlow: Longman).

King, A. (ed.) (1985) *The British Prime Minister* (London: Macmillan).

King, D. (1987) *The New Right* (London: Macmillan).

King's Fund (1992) *London Health Care 2010* (London: King's Fund).

Kirchner, E. (1992) *Decision-Making in the European Community* (Manchester: Manchester University Press).

Lam, J. (1993) 'Hong Kong's Divergent Tensions', *World Today*, vol. 49, pp. 176–9.

Langstaff, J. (1992) 'Housing Associations: a Move to Centre Stage', in Birchall, J. (ed.) (1992).

Lansley, S. *et al.* (1989) *Councils in Conflict* (London: Macmillan).

Lawson, N. (1992) *The View from No. 11* (London: Corgi).

Le Grand, J. and Bartlett, W. (eds) (1993) *Quasi-Markets and Social Policy* (London: Macmillan).

Lee, D. (1991) 'Poor Work and Poor Institutions: Training and the Youth Labour Market', in Brown, P. and Scase, R. (eds), *Poor Work: Disadvantage and the Division of Labour* (Milton Keynes: Open University Press).

Leishman, F. and Savage, S. (1993a) 'The Police Service', in Farnham, D. and Horton, S. (eds), *Managing the New Public Services* (London: Macmillan).

Leishman, F. and Savage, S. (1993b) 'Officers or Managers? Direct Entry into British Police Management', *International Journal of Public Sector Management*, vol. 6, no. 5, pp. 4–11.

Lenman, B. (1992) *The Eclipse of Parliament* (London: Edward Arnold).

Liddiard, M. (1992) *Explaining Youth Homelessness: Issues and Approaches*, in Kennet, P. (ed.) (1992).

Lister, R. (1975) *Social Security: The Case for Reform*, Poverty Pamphlet 22 (London: CPAG).

Lister, R. (1986) 'Burying Beveridge', *Poverty*, 62 (also published as a pamphlet with the same title by CPAG).

Lodge, J. (ed.) (1993) *The European Community and the Challenge of the Future* (London: Pinter).

London Housing Forum (1988) *Speaking Out: Report of the London Housing Enquiry* (London: London Housing Forum).

London Housing Unit (1989) *Just Homes – the Equal Opportunity Implications of the Housing Act 1988* (London: London Housing Unit).

Lord Chancellor's Department (1993) *Mortgage Possession Statistics – Fourth Quarter 1993* (London: Lord Chancellor's Department).

Lowe, P. and Flynn, A. (1989) 'Environmental Politics and Policy in the 1980s', in Mohan, J. (ed.) *The Political Geography of Contemporary Britain* (London: Macmillan).

Ludlow, P. (1991) 'The European Commission', in Keohane, R. and Hoffmann, S. (eds), *The New European Community* (Boulder, Co: Westview Press).

Lupton, C. (1989) 'The Politics of ET', *Talking Politics*, vol. 1 (2), pp. 17–19.

Macbeath, J. (1993) 'Supporting School Development', *Local Government Policy Making*, vol. 19, no. 5, pp. 40–8.

Madgwick, P. (1991) *British Government: The Central Executive Territory* (Hemel Hempstead: Philip Allan).

Maginnis, K. (1990) *McGimpsey & McGimpsey v. Ireland* (Dungannon: Tyrone).

Major, J. (1992a) 'Public Services on the Move: The Citizen's Charter', text of a speech to *The Economist* Conference on the Streamlining of the Public Sector and Newly Privatised Industries, 27 Jan 1992 (Prime Minister's Office).

Major, J. (1992b) Text of a speech given by the Prime Minister at *Service for the Citizen* Conference, 3 Dec 1992 (Prime Minister's Office).

Major, J. (1993) *Conservatism in the 1990s: Our Common Purpose* (London: Carlton Club Political Committee/Conservative Political Centre).

Malpass, P. (1990) *Reshaping Housing Policy* (London: Routledge).

Malpass, P. (1992) 'Housing Policy and the Disabling of Local Authorities', in Birchall, J. (ed.) (1992).

Marsh, D. (1991) 'Privatisation under Mrs Thatcher: a Review of the Literature', *Public Administration*, vol. 69, pp. 459–80.

Marsh, D. and Rhodes, R. (1989) *Implementing Thatcherism*, University of Essex Department of Government, Essex Papers in Politics and Government, No. 62.

Marsh, D. and Rhodes, R. (1992a) 'The Implementation Gap: Explaining Policy Change and Continuity', in Marsh, D. and Rhodes, R. (eds), *Implementing Thatcherite Policies* (Buckingham: Open University Press).

Marsh, D. and Rhodes, R. (eds) (1992b) *Policy Networks in British Government* (Oxford: Clarendon Press).

Mather, G. (1991) 'Government by Contract', in Vibert, F. (ed.), *Britain's Constitutional Future* (London: IEA).

Matthews, K. (1993) *The Gulf Conflict and International Relations* (London: Routledge).

McCarthy, M. (ed.) (1989) *The New Politics of Welfare* (London: Macmillan).

McCormick, J. (1991) *British Politics and the Environment* (London: Earthscan).

McGhie, J. and Lewis, P. (1993) 'Tories put Friends in High Places', *Observer*, 4 July 1993, p. 11.

McVicar, M. (1990) 'Education Policy: Education as a Business?', in Savage, S. and Robins, L. (eds) (1990).

Meager, N. (1991) 'TECs: A Revolution in Training and Enterprise, or Old Wine in New Bottles?', *Local Economy*, vol. 6(1), pp.4–20.

Middlemas, K. (1991) *Power, Competition and the State, vol. 3 The End of the Post-War Era: Britain since 1974* (London: Macmillan).

Millward, N. and Stevens, M. (1986) *British Workplace Industrial Relations 1980–1984* (Aldershot: Gower).

Millward, N. *et al.* (1992) *Workplace Industrial Relations in Transition* (Aldershot: Dartmouth).

Minford, P. (1984) 'State Expenditure: a Study in Waste', *Economic Affairs*, April–June.

Minford, P. *et al.* (1987) *The Housing Morass* (London: IEA).

Mitchie, J. (ed.) (1992) *The Economic Legacy 1979–1992* (London: Academic Press).

Moore, J. (1987) *The Welfare State: The Way Ahead* (London: Conservative Political Centre).

Morton, J. (1988) *The Criminal Justice Acts 1987 and 1988* (London: Macmillan).

Mount, F. (1982) *The Subversive Family* (London: Counterpoint).

Mount, F. (1992) *The British Constitution Now* (London: Heinemann).

MSC (1977) *Training for Skills* (London: Manpower Services Commission).

MSC (1983) *Towards an Adult Training Strategy* (London: Manpower Services Commission).

Murray, C. (1984) *Losing Ground* (New York: Basic Books).

Nash, M. (1992) 'Dangerousness Revisited', *International Journal of the Sociology of Law*, vol. 20 (4), pp. 337–49.

National Consumer Council (1989) *In the Absence of Competition* (London: HMSO).

NEDO (1986) *Changing Work Patterns* (London: National Economic Development Office).

NHSME (1991) *Integrating Primary and Secondary Health Care* (London: NHSME).

NHSME (1992) *Local Voices* (London: NHSME).

Nugent, N. (1991) *The Government and Politics of the European Community* (London: Macmillan).

Nugent, N. (1992) 'The Deepening and Widening of the European Community: Recent Evolution, Maastricht, and Beyond', *Journal of Common Market Studies*, vol. 30, pp. 311–28.

O'Malley, P. (1990) *Northern Ireland: Questions of Nuance* (Belfast: Blackstaff Press).

O'Riordan, T. (1981) 'Environmentalism and Education', *Journal of Geography in Higher Education*, vol. 5 pp. 3–18.

O'Riordan, T. (1991) 'Stability and Transformation in Environmental Government', *Political Quarterly*, vol. 62, pp. 167–85.

Ostreng, W. (eds), *International Resource Management: The Role of Science and Politics* (London: Belhaven).

Page, D. (1993) *Building for Communities: A Study of New Housing Association Estates* (York: Joseph Rowntree Foundation).

Parker, D. (1991) 'Privatisation Ten Years On: A Critical Analysis of its Rationale and Results', *Economics*, 1991, pp. 154–63.

Parker, H. (1989) *Instead of the Dole* (London: Routledge).

Peck, J. (1991) 'Letting the Market Decide (with Public Money): Training and Enterprise Councils and the Future of the Labour Market Programmes', *Critical Social Policy*, vol. 11(1), pp.4–17.

Pepper, D. (1984) *The Roots of Modern Environmentalism* (London: Croom Helm).

Peters, B. (1992) 'Bureaucratic Politics and the Institutions of the European Community' in Sbragia, A. (ed.), *Euro-Politics* (Washington, DC: The Brookings Institution).

Pinder, J. (1991) *European Community* (Oxford: Oxford University Press).

Pirie, M. (1991) *The Citizen's Charter* (London: ASI).

Pirie, M. (1993) 'More Thatcherite than Thatcher', *Spectator*, 10 April, pp. 14–16.

Pollitt, C. (1990) *Managerialism and the Public Sector* (London: Blackwell).

Ponting, C. (1990) *Secrecy in Britain* (Oxford: Blackwell).

Portillo, M. (1993) *Ethics and Public Finance* Lecture to the 'Church at Work in London', 15 Sept. 1993.

Prime Minister (1991) *The Citizen's Charter*, Cmnd 1599 (London: HMSO).

Pythian, M. and Little, W. (1993) 'Parliament and Arms Sales: Lessons of the Matrix Churchill Affair', *Parliamentary Affairs*, vol. 46, pp. 293–308.

Rafferty, K. (1991) *City on the Rocks: Hong Kong's Uncertain Future* (London: Penguin).

Randall, G. (1988) *No Way Home* (London: SHAC).

Ranelagh, J. (1991) *Thatcher's People* (London: HarperCollins).

Ranson, S. (1990) 'From 1944 to 1988: Education, Citizenship and Democracy', in Flude, M. and Hammer, M. (eds), *The Education Reform Act 1988: Its Origins and Implications* (London: Falmer Press).

Ravetz, A. (1990) *The Merger of Knowledge with Power* (London: Mansell).

Raynsford, N. (1989) 'Housing' in McCarthy, M. (ed.) (1989).

Reiner, R. (1992) *The Politics of the Police* (Brighton: Harvester-Wheatsheaf).

Rhodes, R. (1988) *Beyond Westminster and Whitehall* (London: Allen and Unwin).

Richardson, J. (ed.) (1990) *Privatisation and Deregulation in Canada and Britain* (Aldershot: Dartmouth).

Richardson, J. and Jordan, A. (1985) *Governing under Pressure* (Oxford: Blackwell).

Riddell, P. (1993) *The Thatcher Government* (Oxford: Martin Robertson).

Ridley, N. (1988) *The Local Right* (London: Centre for Policy Studies).

Ridley, N. (1989) 'Controlling a Natural Monopoly', *Financial Times*, 6 Nov. 1989.

Robins, L. (1993) *Quality and Choice in the British Education System*, Paper delivered to IASIA, Toluca.

Ryan, M. (1983) *The Politics of Penal Reform* (London: Longman).

Savage, S. and Robins, L. (eds) (1990) *Public Policy under Thatcher* (London: Macmillan).

Scarman, Lord (1981) *The Scarman Report: The Brixton Disorders*, Cmnd 8427 (London: HMSO).

Schwarz, M. and Thompson, M. (1990) *Divided We Stand: Redefining Politics, Technology and Social Choice* (Hemel Hempstead: Harvester-Wheatsheaf).

Scraton, P. (1985) *The State of the Police* (London: Pluto).

Scruton, R. (1980) *The Meaning of Convertism* (London: Penguin).

Seldon, A. (1981) *Wither the Welfare State* (London: IEA).

Shaw, S. (1992) 'Prisons', in Stockdale, E. and Casale, S. (eds), *Criminal Justice under Stress* (London: Blackstone Press).

Sheldrake, J. and Vickerstaff, S. (1987) *The History of Industrial Training in Great Britain* (Aldershot: Avebury).

Simmons, I. G. (1989) *Changing the Face of the Earth* (Oxford: Blackwell).

Smallwood, D. (1992) 'Building Societies: Builders or Financiers?', in Birchall, J. (ed.) (1992).

Smith, D. (1992). *From Boom to Bust: Trial and Error in British Economic Policy* (London: Penguin Books).

Social Services Committee (1992) *Fifth Report: Resourcing the National Health Service: The Government's White Paper: Working for Patients* (London: HMSO).

Spinelli, A. (1972) 'The Growth of the European Movement since the Second World War', in Hodges, M. (ed.), *European Integration* (Harmondsworth: Penguin).

Steel, D. and Heald, D. (1982) 'Privatising Public Enterprise: an Analysis of the Government's Case', *Political Quarterly*, vol. 53(3), pp. 333–49.

Steel, D. and Heald, D. (eds) (1984) *Privatising Public Enterprise* (London: RIPA).

Stewart, J. (1992) 'The Rebuilding of Public Accountability', in Stewart, J., Lewis, N. and Longley, D. (eds), *Accountability to the Public* (London: European Policy Forum).

Stewart, J. and Walsh, K. (1992) 'Change in the Management of Public Services', *Public Administration*, vol. 70, pp. 499–518.

Stockdale, E. and Casale, S. (eds) (1992) *Criminal Justice under Stress* (London: Blackstone Press).

Stoker, G. (1991) *The Politics of Local Government*, 2nd edn (London: Macmillan).

Streeck, W. (1989) 'Skills and the Limits of Neo-Liberalism: the Enterprise of the Future as a Place of Learning', *Work, Employment and Society*, vol. 3 (1), pp. 89–104.

Sweeney, J. (1993) *Trading with the Enemy* (London: Pan).

Thatcher, M. (1993) *The Downing Street Years* (London: HarperCollins).

Thompson, G. (1986) *The Conservatives' Economic Policy* (London: Croom Helm).

Thornton, R. (1990) *The New Homeless: the Crisis of Youth Homelessness and the Response of the Local Housing Authorities* (London: Centrepoint).

Timmerman, K. (1992) *The Death Lobby* (London: Bantam Books).

Timmins, N. and Cash, W. (1988) *Crisis and Cure: Guide to the NHS Debate* (London: Newspaper Publishing).

Titmuss, R. (1971) 'Welfare Rights, Law and Discretion', *Political Quarterly*, vol. 42.

Tivey, L. (1982) 'Nationalized Industries as Organized Interests', *Public Administration*, vol. 60, pp. 42–5.

Tomlinson, B. (1992) *Report of an Inquiry into London's Health Service, Medical Education and Research* (London: HMSO).

Townsend, P., Davidson, N. and Whitehead, M. (1992) *Inequalities in Health* (London: Penguin).

Training Agency (1989) *Training and Enterprise Councils: A Prospectus for the 1990s* (Sheffield: Training Agency).

Travers, T. (1989) 'Community Charge and other Financial Changes', in Stewart, J. and Stoker, G. (eds), *The Future of Local Government* (London: Macmillan).

Urwin, D. (1991) *The Community of Europe* (Harlow: Longman).

Veljanovski, C. (1990) 'The Political Economy of Regulation' in Dunleavy, P., Gamble, A. and Peele, G. (eds) *Developments in British Politics 3* (London: Macmillan).

Veljanovski, C. (1991) 'The Regulation Game', in Veljanovski, C. (ed.), *Regulators and the Market* (London: Institute of Economic Affairs).

Veljanovski, C. (ed.) (1988) *Privatisation and Competition: A Market Perspective* (London: Institute of Economic Affairs).

Waldegrave, W. (1992) 'A Revolution in Whitehall', Speech to the Institute of Directors, 20 July 1992 (London: Cabinet Office).

Waldegrave, W. (1993a) *Public Service and the Future* (London: Conservative Political Centre).

Waldegrave, W. (1993b) Speech to the Institute of Directors Annual Convention (London: Cabinet Office).

Wallace, C. and Chandler, J. (1989) 'Some Alternatives in Youth Training: Franchise Corporatist Models', unpublished paper, Polytechnic of South Wales.

Wallace, H. (1983) 'Negotiation, Conflict, and Compromise: The Elusive Pursuit of Common Policies', in Wallace, H., Wallace, W. and Webb, C. (eds) *Policy-Making in the European Community* (Chichester: Wiley).

Walsh, K. (1991) 'Quality and Public Services', *Public Administration*, vol. 69, pp. 503–14.

Walter, J. (1988) *Basic Income: Escape from the Poverty Trap* (London: Marion Boyars).

Wass, D. (1984) *Government and the Governed* (London: Routledge & Kegan Paul).

Watkins, A. (1991) *A Conservative Coup: The Fall of Margaret Thatcher* (London: Duckworth).

Watson, E. (1988) 'Vulnerable Groups and Homelessness', in Bramley, G. *et al.* (eds) (1991).

Wessels, W. (1991) 'The EC Council: the Community's Decision-making Center' in Keohane, R. and Hoffmann, S. (eds), *The New European Community* (Boulder, Co: Westview Press).

Whale, J. (1979) 'The Tories and Northern Ireland', *Magill*, vol. 2, no. 8, May 1979.

Whiteside, N. (1988) 'Unemployment and Health: An Historical Perspective', *Journal of Social Policy*, vol. 17, pp. 177–94.

WHO (1981) *Global Strategy for Health for All by the Year 2000* (Geneva: WHO).

Wilson, T. (1989) *Ulster: Conflict and Consent* (Oxford: Blackwell).

Worsthorne, P. (1988) 'Too Much Freedom', in Cowling, M. (1978).

Young, H. and Sloman, A. (1982) *No, Minister* (London: BBC).

Young, S. (1987) 'The Nature of Privatisation in Britain, 1979–1985', *West European Politics*, vol. 9, pp. 235–52.

Index

1133 25966